NIHILISM
BEFORE
NIETZSCHE

NIHILISM
—*BEFORE*—
NIETZSCHE

Michael Allen Gillespie

THE UNIVERSITY OF CHICAGO PRESS
Chicago and London

The University of Chicago Press, Chicago 60637
The University of Chicago Press, Ltd., London
© 1995 by The University of Chicago
All rights reserved. Published 1995
Paperback edition 1996
Printed in the United States of America

04 03 02 01 00 99 98 97 96   2 3 4 5

ISBN: 0-226-29347-5 (cloth)
ISBN: 0-226-29348-3 (paperback)

Library of Congress Cataloging-in-Publication Data

Gillespie, Michael Allen.
Nihilism before Nietzsche / Michael Allen Gillespie.
p. cm.
Includes bibliographical references and index.
1. Nihilism (Philosophy) 2. Nietzsche, Friedrich Wilhelm,
1844-1900. 3. Descartes, René, 1596-1650. I. Title.
B828.3.G55 1994
149'.8—dc0   94-12205
                                                      CIP

⊛ The paper used in this publication meets the minimum
requirements of the American National Standard for
Information Sciences—Permanence of Paper for Printed
Library Materials, ANSI Z39.48—1984.

Contents

Preface

It is customary in a preface for an author to explain how a book came to be and how it is related to the world in which it appears. A preface thus attempts to give the reader some idea of the intellectual terrain the book traverses by directing his or her thoughts to the questions that shape that terrain. The question that determines the topography of this book is the question of nihilism. What is nihilism? Where did it come from? What is its meaning?

Such questions are never easy to answer but they are rendered particularly difficult in this case by the ambiguity of the concept of nihilism. The concept of nihilism has taken on a number of various and often contradictory meanings largely because it has been used as an ideological bludgeon to denigrate nearly every intellectual or political movement that someone or other has found objectionable. It is not my purpose to enter into these ideological debates. If the owl of Minerva takes wing at dusk, it often does so to escape the cacophony of name-calling that characterizes the speech of a benighted humanity. I do not want to call names but to investigate the origins of these names and try to determine how they attained their power. To this end, I examine the genealogy or intellectual pedigree of nihilism. In particular, I am interested in the development of the concept of nihilism in the period before it was given its determinative definition by Nietzsche. As will soon become evident, I believe that Nietzsche misunderstood nihilism and that this misunderstanding has misled nearly all succeeding thought about nihilism.

In this book, I seek to show that nihilism is not the consequence of the death of God and the diminution of man as Nietzsche claimed, but the result of a new concept of divine omnipotence and a corresponding concept of human power that arise in the late Middle Ages and come increasingly to characterize modern thought. This claim should not be taken to mean that I believe all modern thought is nihilism. Much of modern thought, including liberalism, humanism, and neo-Aristotelianism, for example, clearly follows a different path. In fact, I do not even want to claim that the strain of modern thought which I do investigate had to end in nihilism. At any number of points, thought might have moved in a different direction. However, the fact that much of modern thought has followed this path gives it a specific momentum and trajectory and thus a certain energy and force that must be reckoned with.

I also do not want to give the impression that this study is a comprehensive history of the development of this concept. It would be a mammoth undertaking to describe the development of nihilism in all of its particulars. I focus instead on what I take to be the crucial turning points in this development. I thus examine the thought of only a relatively small number of thinkers. Nor do I seek to give an exhaustive interpretation of any of these thinkers. Instead, I focus on those moments of their thought that are important for the development of the concept of nihilism. This focus may give the impression that I do not believe these thinkers have anything positive to offer, but this is certainly not the case. The modern world is not bankrupt, and much that is of value is the consequence of the work and thought of the very thinkers whose other ideas I find so problematic. My project aims not at condemning particular thinkers but at identifying those core elements in the thought of each that helped to produce nihilism so that we can more clearly come to understand what nihilism is. There is thus much positive that goes unremarked.

I also do not want the reader to suppose that I believe ideas to be omnipotent. In fact, the purpose of this study is in large measure to dispute just such a notion. The world exercises an enormous force upon us. Natural necessity, chance and contingency, subconscious passions and drives, the structure of economic and political life, and many other factors determine us in ways we do not understand and cannot ultimately control. At our best and most courageous, we confront the questions this world poses and in our own limited ways seek to answer them. This quest, however, is not without its dangers. Questions disrupt and unsettle our lives and we are often all too ready to accept partial truths and gross simplifications to escape from their perplexity. The tragedies of our own century have taught us, however, that it is better to suffer the anxiety that questions engender than to give overhasty answers to them. With these difficulties and dangers in mind, we must still attempt to give at least tentative answers to the perplexing questions that punctuate our existence.

In closing this preface, I would like to thank all those individuals and institutions who have made the completion of this project possible. My thanks are especially due to the National Endowment for the Humanities and the Duke University Research Council for their financial support, and to my research assistants Paul Ellenbogen, Thomas Heilke, Murray Jardine, John Robertson, David Strom, Electra Thomas, and Steve Wild. I would also like to thank all the many friends and colleagues who have read portions of the manuscript and offered me their criticism and advice. Finally, my deepest thanks to my wife, Nancy Henley, to whom this book is dedicated. It was conceived in the same moment as the love that has sustained me in its completion.

Introduction

Near the end of the nineteenth century Nietzsche proclaimed, "Nihilism stands at the door," and asked, "Whence comes this uncanniest of all guests?" (*NL,* KGW VIII 1:123).[1] He believed that he had discovered the answer to this question in the fact that "God is dead." With few exceptions, we who live in Nietzsche's shadow have come to accept this interpretation of nihilism as definitive. But does this answer come to the essence of nihilism and grasp its true significance? It is the purpose of this book to argue that it does not, that nihilism has a different origin and meaning than Nietzsche imagines.

Nihilism, according to Nietzsche, is the consequence of the fact that God and all eternal truths and standards become unbelievable. The highest values devalue themselves. The pursuit of the truth reveals that there is no unequivocal truth. Understanding nihilism thus depends upon understanding the death of God. Nietzsche argues that God died because man became too weak to sustain him, too weak to create and recreate the God or truth necessary to maintain belief in the prevailing order. In his metaphorical language, God died out of pity for man, out of pity for man's weakness and frailty. "Two thousand years," Nietzsche remarks, "and no new god" (*AC,* KGW VI 3:183). In contradistinction to the profusion of divinities that streamed forth in the ancient world, this impotence betokens the precipitous decline of human creative capacities, a fundamental weakening of the will. This decline, which began with Socrates and Christianity, is the long drawn-out death of God that only now is becoming apparent. Its consequences are ominous:

> How much must collapse now that this faith has been undermined because it was built on this faith, propped up by it, grown into it; for example the whole of our European morality. This plenitude and sequence of breakdown, destruction, ruin, and cataclysm that is now impending—who could guess enough of it today to be compelled to

play the teacher and advance proclaimer of this monstrous logic of terror, the prophet of a gloom and eclipse of the sun whose like has probably never yet occurred on earth.(*FW*, KGW V 2:255)

The death of God, according to Nietzsche, leads to a world in which everything is permitted. The great wars and totalitarian experiments of our century have borne an all too faithful witness to Nietzsche's prescience and we have consequently come to accept his explanation of the origin and meaning of nihilism as correct.

We have responded more ambivalently to his proposed solution. If nihilism is the consequence of the diminution of man, what is needed to overcome nihilism is the magnification of man. Man in other words must become overman. This solution was widely discredited by its association with Nazism, but even divorced from the image of the Aryan superman, it still offends our democratic sensibilities. However, the appeal of Nietzsche's solution in the face of modern society is powerful, and many democratic thinkers have tried to reconcile his idea of the overman with a more egalitarian and communitarian ideal of an overhumanity. Other thinkers substitute the idea of difference for Nietzsche's idea of hierarchy, transforming his notion of a vertical order of rank into a horizontal disorder of otherness. Still others have tried to interpret the overman as one who is constantly overcoming the shackles placed upon him by nature, or language, or other human beings, thus turning the teaching of the overman into a doctrine of liberation. There are clearly grounds for reading Nietzsche in these ways, but it is not clear that such readings can so easily be separated from Nietzsche's inegalitarianism and the "monstrous logic of terror" he predicts. Even these efforts to discover a more democratic Nietzsche, however, do not ultimately question his notion of the origin and meaning of nihilism. When it comes to our understanding of nihilism, we are almost all Nietzscheans.

To understand why Nietzsche's notion of nihilism is insufficient, we must investigate the origins of nihilism. In what follows, we will see that Nietzsche's definition of nihilism is actually a reversal of the concept as it was originally understood, and that his solution to nihilism is in fact only a deeper entanglement in the problem of nihilism. Contrary to Nietzsche's account, nihilism is not the result of the death of God but the consequence of the birth or rebirth of a different kind of God, an omnipotent God of will who calls into question all of reason and nature and thus overturns all eternal standards of truth and justice, and good and evil. This idea of God came to predominance in the fourteenth century and shattered the medieval synthesis of philosophy and theology, catapulting man into a new way of thinking and being, a *via moderna* essentially at odds with the *via antiqua*. This new way was in turn the foundation for modernity as the realm of human self-assertion. Nihilism thus has its roots in the very foundations of modernity although it only came about as the result of a series of subsequent transformations of this beginning. This book is an investigation of these transformations, of the strange twists and turns of human thinking that led to nihilism. It is the story of the way in which the late-medieval conception of an omnipotent God inspired and informed a new conception of man and nature that gave precedence to will over reason and freedom over necessity and order. It begins with Descartes' notion of thinking as willing, passes through Fichte's notion of the absolute I, and culminates in the explicit nihilism of the nineteenth century. It is the story of nihilism before Nietzsche.

The first section of the book attempts to locate the origin and trace the development of the notion of absolute will. It focuses on the rise of the modern world out of the crisis of late medieval Christianity. Chapter 1 argues that the nominalist idea of an omnipotent God is the source of this notion of an absolute will, and that it is this notion that lies behind Descartes' project for the conquest of nature. Scholasticism rested on the assumption that God and the cosmos are essentially rational. Nominalism argued that it contradicts God's divinity to assume that he is subordinate to nature or reason. The intention of this critique was to reaffirm the importance of scripture, but its effect was to sever reason and revelation. It thus liberated natural science from the constraints of religion and opened the door for empiricism, but it also established an omnipotent divine will unrestrained by any rational notion of the good. The nominalist revolution thus fostered a growing doubt about the ground of science and morality in a cosmos ruled by a willful, transrational God. The rise of natural science is consequently concomitant with the rise of universal doubt. To secure himself and his science, man must build ramparts against divine caprice or malevolence. The first to raise up such ramparts was Descartes.

Chapter 2 is a consideration of the foundations of Descartes' bastion of reason. Descartes dreamed of a universal science that would enable man to master nature, but such a science was called into question by the radical skepticism engendered by the possibility of an omnipotent God. Descartes believed he had found a ground for human knowledge that was invulnerable to all deception in his principle *ego cogito ergo sum*. This principle is the basis for human freedom and the mastery of nature. Man knows that he is and knows that he is as a thing that thinks. To think, for Descartes, however, is ultimately to will. His fundamental principle is thus a self-confirming act of the will, made possible by the fact that this will, like that of God, is infinite. Man thus has the capacity to assert himself even against God. Man, however, does not have God's perfect knowledge and is therefore not omnipotent. In the first instance, man is thus free only within the circle of his self-thinking. Outside this bastion of reason, the chaos set loose by the possibility of a malicious God still reigns. Descartes' universal science, which is meant to master this chaos, thus depends upon a demonstration that God is not malicious and does not deceive us.

Descartes' God is not a deceiver because he is perfect and he is perfect in Descartes' view because he is infinite. Human beings, by contrast, are limited, needy, and therefore self-interested beings who deceive their fellows to secure their own interests. As infinite, God does not distinguish himself from others and as a result does not recognize interests of his own that are different from those of his creation. Therefore, he cannot deceive us and as a result is irrelevant for science. The Cartesian method thus can make man master of nature. The transrational God of nominalism thus becomes the guarantor of reason and science. There are indications, however, that this harmony is artificial and unstable. Descartes' God has lost his independence and become a mere representation within human thinking. At the same time, the human will is conceived as infinite, and human freedom is posited as potentially absolute.

The second part of the book is a consideration of the way in which this notion of an absolute will became explicit in the thought of German idealism and Romanticism. While this potentiality was latent in the thought of Descartes, it was counterbalanced by the rational element in his thought. Moreover, it was almost entirely obscured by his rationalist followers and his empiricist opponents.

Empiricism also has its origins in the nominalist revolution, but in contrast to Descartes and rationalism generally, it concludes that God is basically irrelevant for the study of nature and the conduct of human life. It is thus possible to understand the natural world on the basis of experience alone. Man is an object in motion endowed with a limited, natural reason which can grasp the universal causal connections that govern all things. If God exists, he is not a transcendent and omnipotent being who intervenes in nature but the guarantor of nature's laws. Empiricism in this sense solves the problem of an arbitrary and willful God, through a denial of divine freedom and omnipotence or through a denial of divine existence.

Empiricism, however, comes to the skeptical conclusion in Hume's thought that causality is merely a habit of perception that is not grounded in any intrinsic property of objects. This conclusion renders a definitive natural science impossible and consequently opens empiricism up to the same kind of insecurity engendered by the idea of divine omnipotence. Empiricism also fails to give a satisfying explanation of the idea of human freedom as freedom *from* nature that becomes increasingly predominant in modernity. Descartes laid the groundwork for such a radical notion of human freedom, but he did not develop it explicitly. This task was accomplished by Rousseau.

Rousseau came to see freedom as the capacity of the will to transcend and transform nature. He accords to man the same type of freedom that Christianity attributed to God. Man, too, can begin a chain of causality without the necessity of a prior natural cause. The rationality of this freedom, however, seems to consist in little more than abstract generality, and in practice this generality seems to be merely a momentary determination of the will. Thus, with Rousseau and Hume the caprice that both rationalism and empiricism sought to exclude reappears in the innermost citadel of modern reason as the foremost principle of the human heart.

Chapter 3 is a consideration of the way in which the latent potentialities of Descartes' notion of the infinite human will are realized in Fichte's reworking of Kant's notion of practical reason. For Kant, the fundamental philosophical problem is the antinomy of freedom and natural causality. He argues that the idea of natural causality is insufficient without freedom but that the idea of freedom seems to contradict the idea of natural causality. Freedom and nature thus seem to be mutually necessary and mutually contradictory. Kant's answer to this problem is transcendental idealism. The antinomy arises in Kant's view, not because the world is itself antinomious but because finite human reason tries to transcend its own limits and obtain knowledge of the infinite. The solution to the antinomy is thus the recognition of the inherent limits of human understanding and the recognition of two separate but possibly isomorphic realms of reason, a phenomenal realm governed by laws of nature and a noumenal realm governed by the moral law of freedom, that is, a realm of pure

reason and a realm of practical reason. These two realms in Kant's
view reflect the two different sides of consciousness and are held
together by the transcendental unity of consciousness itself. However, the exact character of this unity in Kant's thought remains dark.

One of the first to try to find his way through this darkness was
Fichte. In contradistinction to Kant, who had tried to balance the
claims of nature and freedom, Fichte believed that he could establish
a comprehensive system on the basis of practical reason or freedom
alone. This was the goal of his *Science of Knowledge*. For Fichte, the
I is all. However, his I is not the empirical I of individual human
beings but the absolute I of the general will or practical reason. This
I is perfectly autonomous, positing itself as an empirical I, as the
realm of subjectivity, and limiting or negating itself in establishing the
not-I, the objective or phenomenal realm of nature.

The I is thus alienated from itself. The empirical I knows itself to
be absolute but because of the constraints placed upon it by the not-
I (i.e., the phenomenal world), it is unable to realize its own essence.
The I thus seeks reconciliation first by interposing an order of concepts between the finite and the infinite. This path of theoretical reason fails, however, because these concepts are finite and thus essentially at odds with the I's infinite essence.

The path of practical reason is more successful. If the not-I cannot
be reconciled with the I, the not-I must be abolished and absolute
freedom established. To accomplish this, Fichte tries to demonstrate
that the phenomenal world is only an expression of the will of the
absolute I that manifests itself in and through our emotions,
instincts, and drives. This absolute will appears in us as a striving for
the infinite. In striving for the infinite, however, the empirical I eventually comes to the end of its strength. At this point it seems to experience an external object, but in fact it experiences only its own weakness. The I itself is thus the source of the objective world. This
recognition that the not-I is only a moment of the I, however, does
not produce reconciliation and perfect freedom. As finite, the I is
eternally unable to attain the infinite and be fully free. The highest
state that it can attain is thus longing, which is the basis for its endless progress toward its goal.

In the political realm this notion of the will leads Fichte to advocate a totalitarianism of freedom. Most individuals are enchained by
natural desire and must be forced to be free. In his early thought, he
argues that this can be achieved under the hegemony of scholars.
Later, the people becomes the repository of the inner will to free-

dom. Fichte's political imperative is in fact an extension of the categorical imperative to political life. The individual can never become perfectly free and infinitely powerful, but he can participate in both as a moment of the absolute I which is manifest in the feelings and emotions of the people.

Nominalism emphasized the supremacy of divine will. Modernity in a variety of ways sought to construct a bulwark against the chaos that this will entailed. Descartes' conception of the self-certainty of consciousness and empiricism's notion of an infinite natural causality helped to constrain the power and scope of divine caprice. Fichte's absolute I, however, embodies and empowers it. Like the nominalist God, this I has creative capacities that transcend natural reason. Indeed, it replaces God as the transrational source of nature and natural law. The traditional God of Christianity in this sense becomes superfluous.

It was for this reason that Jacobi characterized Fichte's philosophy and idealism in general as *nihilism*. For Jacobi, idealism recognized no truth beyond consciousness and, therefore, lacked any objective standard against which to measure itself. It thus dissolved everything into subjectivity. Jacobi consequently locates the source of nihilism not in the diminution of the will but in its magnification, in the doctrine of an absolute human will and freedom.

Chapter 4 is a consideration of the development of this notion of absolute will and the concomitant notion of nihilism in German Romanticism and idealism. The intellectual debt of the early German Romantics to Fichte was widely recognized and led Jacobi's admirer Jean Paul to characterize them as "poetic nihilists." These poetic nihilists find not God or nature but only a dark demonic force behind the phenomena, a force that reason cannot comprehend and that man can grasp only through his feelings. As in Fichte, the feelings are merely the expression of this absolute force or will in the individual. Access to this demonic will, however, can be attained only by shattering the constraints that customs impose upon us. Such knowledge thus arises only out of immorality and crime. Ludwig Tieck's William Lovell is archetypal and Lovell's voyage of discovery leads him to the heart of this demonic darkness. It is a voyage into sensuality and crime that is justified as a necessity of self-knowledge and the knowledge of the demonic force that rules the world. He is not a villain but a courageous and tragic hero. Tieck thus justifies the bestial as the way to the divine.

Even the greatest opponents of this Romantic nihilism, Goethe and Hegel, could not ultimately free themselves from its spell. Goethe's *Faust* was intended as a critique of these demonic heros but ends up almost affirming them. Faust too is a demonic seducer and a murderer. Goethe, however, is unwilling to condemn him because he believes that the demonic is only a moment of the divine. His evil in the end is justified as a means to higher goodness. Hegel's attempt to restrain philosophic nihilism follows a similar path and comes to a similar conclusion. He attempts to provide a solution to the essential nihilism of Fichte's thought by turning negation against negation. He too begins with the Kantian antinomy but he resolves it not by universalizing practical reason or will, but by focusing on the necessity present in the contradiction itself. The demonic will of Romanticism becomes for Hegel the cunning of reason. Like Goethe, he thus turns the demonic to the service of the divine. The actions of demonic, world-historical individuals are excused and even exalted as the means to the production of the rational state in which the civil servant serves as the agent of reason and the guiding force in human life.

Even the loose fetters with which Goethe and Hegel attempted to bind the demonic, however, were unbearable to their successors. The Romantics turned away from Faust to Byronic heros such as Manfred who like Lovell and Faust seek forbidden knowledge and in their search violate the most sacred laws. In contradistinction to the early Romantics, however, these heros do not repent but glorify their crimes. The Left Hegelians similarly turned away from Hegel's speculative synthesis of the rational and the actual, but retained the Fichtean principle of dialectical development that Hegel sought to overcome. They saw this dialectical development, however, not in isolated individuals but in actual societies. In this way, the essential element of infinite and unrelenting self-assertion and negation that characterized the Fichtean I becomes the concrete historical will of classes and parties that aim at revolution.

These revolutionaries became known in Germany as nihilists. In part, this was the result of the conjunction of Left Hegelianism and the critics of Romanticism, the so-called Young Germany movement. Karl Gutzkow, for example, distinguishes two types of revolutionaries in his novella, *The Nihilists:* those who are essentially egoistical and those who work in the service of the greater good of humanity. He rejects the former as Romantic and reactionary but praises the latter as effective reformers. Even Gutzkow's good nihilists, however, remain within the broader horizon of Romanticism, for they are motivated not by moral principle but by their feelings. Where feelings rule, however, the possibility that violent or perverse passions will predominate cannot be excluded.

The third section of the book is a consideration of the development of explicit nihilism in Russia and Germany in the latter half of the nineteenth century as a moral and political doctrine. Chapter 5 examines the development of nihilism in Russian thought and literature. In Russia as in Germany, nihilism arose out of Left Hegelianism and in reaction to Romanticism. While this movement turned to materialism and populism, its essential characteristic was its attempt to establish a superhumanity that could fulfill the Cartesian dream of a universal mastery of nature. The nihilists were convinced of the ultimate omnipotence of the human will. They went much further than their German contemporaries who believed that the dialectical structure of reality placed insuperable limits on the human will. These Russians believed that instantaneous change was possible if only enough men of integrity willed it. They called such "new men" the intelligentsia.

Bazarov, the protagonist of Turgenev's *Fathers and Sons,* is the preeminent literary example of such a new man. Nihilism, for him, is the rejection of all authority and especially the authority of the human heart. This rejection of Romanticism notwithstanding, he is still a Romantic on the model of Faust or Manfred who measures the world in terms of his own titanic ego, who asserts the negative force of absolute freedom in the form of the absolute criticism of all reality, and who discovers in the end that this entails his own negation as well. His death, however, is justified as conducive to further life. Like his mentors, Goethe and Hegel, Turgenev thus attempts to demonstrate that the negative force of freedom is subordinate to a higher order of nature.

Many nihilist revolutionaries were outraged by Bazarov, whom they saw as a caricature of their movement. Nikolai Chernyshevsky's *What Is to Be Done?* was written to present a more favorable picture of the nihilists. Other nihilists such as Dmitri Pisarev, however, saw Bazarov as the hard and merciless type of revolutionary they had to have if they were to win. While Chernyshevsky's vision was more appealing to the nihilists themselves, Turgenev and Pisarev's vision of the nihilist was ultimately triumphant, because it was really the only viable model for challenging the autocracy. This vision of the nihilist became the model for terrorists such as Nechaev and later Bolshevik revolutionaries such as Lenin, Trotsky, and Stalin. The notion of absolute freedom that had its origin in the nominalist notion of God thus came to a monstrous crescendo in Stalin's terror.

Chapters 6 and 7 examine the transformation of the demonic element of Romanticism into what Nietzsche called the Dionysian. Nietzsche argues that his thought on the most fundamental level is Dionysian and thus thoroughly antimetaphysical. Heidegger rejected this claim but did not seriously investigate the Dionysian in Nietzsche's thought. Relying on the Dionysian, postmodernist interpreters suggest that Nietzsche is in fact a fundamentally postmodern, deconstructionist thinker. I try to show that even Nietzsche's concept of the Dionysian remains tied to the metaphysical tradition in ways that he himself does not understand.

This fact is particularly important for evaluating Nietzsche's concept of nihilism because he develops and understands it within the opposition of Dionysus and the Crucified. His interpretation of nihilism is a complete reversal of the earlier usage of the concept. Previously, nihilism was understood as the consequence of the hubristic magnification of man. In Nietzsche's view, it is the consequence of the democratic diminution of man. On the basis of this new understanding, Nietzsche argues that the solution to nihilism is a turn to the superhuman, that is, a turn to exactly that notion that previously was conceived to be the essence of nihilism.

Chapter 6 examines the way in which Schopenhauer's concept of absolute will forms the basis for Nietzsche's transformation of the demonic into the Dionysian. Schopenhauer was a student of Fichte and was deeply indebted to him. His essential notion of the will to life is decisively informed by Fichte's notion of the absolute I. However, like the Romantics, he interprets it as a demonic will underlying the phenomena. This Romantic element in Schopenhauer's thought leads him to a darker view of the character and meaning of this will. The essentially positive striving for reconciliation and freedom that characterized Fichte's I becomes in Schopenhauer the delusive force of the demonic will to life that enslaves us in a hopeless and continual war of all against all. Schopenhauer sees only two possible solutions. We can mirror the world and the will as artists or we can become ascetics. Both paths, however, are possible only for the genius who is chosen by an incomprehensible act of the will. The rest of humanity is doomed to participate in the cycle of crime and suffering.

Nietzsche saw this Schopenhauerian will as the will to nothingness and identified it with the diminution of man. Indeed, he believed that it constituted the essence of the bourgeois society he despised. Nietzsche, however, does not simply reject this will. Instead, he argues that Schopenhauer has misunderstood it, has assumed that the weakest form of the will is the will itself. For Nietzsche, the crucial choice is between Dionysus and the Crucified. The Crucified is the weak form of the will that in general seeks preservation and pleasure and in the extreme practices asceticism. It produces only banality and despair and is the source of nihilism. The Dionysian is the will in its strength as the will to power, the will not to mere self-preservation but to self-overcoming. It thus ends not in resignation but in affirmation, in a great yes to life with all its tragic suffering.

Chapter 7 examines Nietzsche's notion of the Dionysian and tries to show how it is the basis for his project of cultural renewal. Nietzsche's hopes for cultural renewal were bound up in his early thought with Wagner's project for the spiritual regeneration of Germany. In *The Birth of Tragedy*, he attempted to show that such a cultural transformation had been achieved by the Greeks and that it could consequently be brought about again in Germany. The crucial element in such a transformation was Dionysus. Dionysus for Nietzsche is the God of reconciliation who unifies all of the disparate phenomena. This reconciliation, however, is not rational but musical. In contrast to Hegel's absolute knowledge, which is the basis for a permanent reconciliation, Nietzsche's Dionysian wisdom is fleeting, a momentary harmony of forces that remain eternally apart. This reconciliation thus ends not in permanent peace or the rational state but in tragedy. Through tragedy, however, we attain a greatness that elevates us above our suffering.

Nietzsche's opposition of Dionysus and the Crucified is overdrawn. In fact, his notion of the Dionysian is derived from the notion of the Christian God in ways Nietzsche does not altogether understand, in large part because he does not recognize his conceptual debt to the earlier Romantic idea of the Dionysian and the idealist conceptions of the will. The Dionysian will to power is thus in fact a further development of the idea of absolute will that first appeared in the nominalist notion of God and became a world-historical force with Fichte's notion of the absolute I. This means that God is not as dead for Nietzsche as he believes; only the rational element in God is dead, the element that was grafted onto the Christian God to temper his omnipotence. Nietzsche's Dionysus, to speak in Nietzsche's own metaphorical language, is thus not an alternative to the Christian God but only his final and in a sense greatest modern mask.

The account of the origin of nihilism presented in this book, as even this brief synopsis makes clear, is in part a retelling of the story of modernity, and it is thus important to distinguish it from several similar accounts. Perhaps the best known of these is that of Martin Heidegger. Heidegger too sees nihilism as the result of the rise of will in modern thought. His notion of will, however, differs from the one employed here. For Heidegger, the modern notion of will can be understood only within the framework of the revelation of Being as subjectivity and thus in terms of Cartesian metaphysics. I argue that Cartesian metaphysics can be understood only as a response to and secularization of the earlier notion of an omnipotent divine will. Heidegger either does not recognize or does not admit the connection of the two notions of will. He certainly has a vested interest in distinguishing them from one another, because his own notion of Being, which he holds up as a solution to the problem of nihilism that is the product of the modern philosophy of will, draws heavily on the earlier notion of an omnipotent divine will. Being in his thought is an omnipotent power beyond nature and beyond reason, akin to the *deus absconditus* of nominalism.[2] Because Heidegger misconstrues the nature of the will, he does not understand its real meaning for nihilism.

My argument also resembles the argument presented by Hans Blumenberg in *The Legitimacy of the Modern Age*.[3] I agree with Blumenberg's general thesis that modernity developed in response to the intractable questions that arose out of late medieval thought, but I argue, contrary to Blumenberg, that the modern notion of will, or what Blumenberg calls self-assertion, is not a new construct that reoccupies an intellectual position that skepticism opened up, but the secularization of the idea of divine omnipotence. My argument in this respect is thus more akin to the secularization thesis of Karl Löwith and Amos Funkenstein. I also disagree fundamentally with Blumenberg's attempt to ground the legitimacy of modernity on self-assertion or will. Focusing on its role up to the Enlightenment, Blumenberg fails to see that this notion is also at the heart of the later intellectual developments that lead to nihilism. He thus does not understand the way in which self-assertion also delegitimates modernity.

Bernard Yack discusses these later developments with great care and insight, focusing particularly on Marx and Nietzsche, in *The Longing for Total Revolution*.[4] Yack too rejects the secularization thesis. He believes that the ideals that Nietzsche and Marx represent are thoroughly modern manifestations of a longing for the lost golden age of antiquity. It is this longing, in his view, that leads them to such extremes in their efforts to reconstitute this lost age. For Yack, there is thus a kind of teleological necessity in modern radical thought. I do not want to dispute this basic point, which I believe to be correct, but I do want to argue that the "essence" of nihilism and modern radicalism generally lies not so much in the longing for a substantive goal but in the repeated rejection of all attained goals as limitations on human freedom. I thus emphasize the essentially negative and destructive character of modern radicalism. Yack points to the longing for a perfected way of life; I try to show through an analysis of this longing itself why it can never be satisfied with any finite solution and therefore necessarily rejects every goal that it itself establishes; why, in other words, modern radical thought, whether in Nietzsche or the Russian nihilists, necessarily worships a dark god of negation.

This focus on the negative, however, is not intended as a condemnation of modernity. In fact, I want to argue that Nietzsche's account of the origin and nature of nihilism has led us wrongly to devalue the modern world, especially in implicating liberalism in nihilism. In his view, liberalism is the final triumph of slave morality and destroys the last remnants of the old hierarchical order. It thus produces the banal last man, and it is the last man whose weakness finally destroys God. Liberalism, for Nietzsche, thus plays an important role in the nihilistic destruction of traditional values.

My argument suggests that this view is fallacious. Nihilism is not the result of liberalism but of a strain of modern thought that is largely at odds with liberalism, which sees man not as a limited and imperfect being who "muddles through," but as a superhuman being who can create the world anew through the application of his infinite will. While liberalism may end in relativism, it rejects such Promethean visions; and while it may in some instances produce banality and boredom, it does not produce a politics of terror and destruction. Indeed, despite the fact that liberalism has in many respects embraced relativism, it has shown great resilience in the face of terroristic regimes.

Nihilism arises in the context of a new revelation of the world as the product not of reason but of will. The argument presented here suggests that the solution to nihilism thus lies not in the assertion of the will but in a step back from willing. Understanding how such a step back from willing can be achieved, however, requires a more fundamental encounter with the question of the origin and nature of the notion of will. The solution to nihilism thus can arise only out of a deeper understanding of the collapse of the scholastic synthesis that gave rise to the nominalist notion of will. Only in this way can we adequately understand the character of modernity and of nihilism.

Chapter One

DESCARTES AND THE DECEIVER GOD

INTRODUCTION:
SCIENCE AND THE PATH OF DOUBT

Ego cogito ergo sum is engraved over one of the great gateways to modernity, and we who have passed through this gateway have come under its spell. Indeed we have been transformed by it, for this principle has helped give a new meaning to what it is to be a human being and thus helped establish a whole new range of political, ethical, and philosophical possibilities. Insofar as modernity rests upon this principle, man is no longer understood as a rational animal or as a child of God. These conceptions of what it is to be a human being have not been lost or forgotten, but they have been gradually displaced. They thus no longer define the cultural world in which we live. We moderns have instead increasingly come to understand ourselves as subjects opposed to a hostile world that must be conquered and subordinated to our will.

It would be a mistake, however, to assume that modernity is nothing other than subjectivity. Modernity is an aggregation of various elements, and we misunderstand the fruitful ambiguity of our tradition if we do not recognize this fact. Humanism, empiricism, and liberalism, for example, cannot be adequately understood merely as forms of subjectivity. This said, it also cannot be denied that subjectivity and its imperatives increasingly find a place everywhere.

To understand ourselves and our world, it seems we must come to terms with the principle of subjectivity, *ego cogito ergo sum*. But how can we understand it, if we do not understand the question to which it is an answer? Every statement or proposition is the answer to a stated or unstated question and the meaning of any proposition can consequently be determined only in light of the question that it answers. The question propels us and guides us in a particular direction toward a particular sort of answer. *Ego cogito ergo sum* is the principle of Descartes and the question it answers is the question that propelled his thought. To understand this principle and the modern notion of subjectivity we thus must come to terms with Descartes.

Descartes was born in 1596 into a world torn by the religious wars of the Reformation. Coming from a wealthy family, he was given an outstanding education at the newly founded Jesuit school, La Flèche. He was such an extraordinary student that his teachers granted him the liberty to read and study whatever he wished. He mastered much of the traditional scholastic literature and studied some of the occult sciences as well. His real passion, however, was mathematics. After leaving La Flèche, he studied law and embarked upon a military career. However, he never saw action and actually devoted most of his time to the study of mathematics and the sciences. It was during this time, in 1619, that Descartes was struck by the idea that changed his life, the idea of a universal science based upon mathematics. The idea for this science he apparently drew from Francis Bacon, but the idea that it should take a mathematical form was his own. According to his own fragmentary and perhaps fictional account of the origin of this idea in his *Olympica,* it came to him in a dream. Whatever its origin, Descartes was not slow to appreciate its enormous significance. He believed that such a science might make it possible to completely transform human life, to give man the mastery over nature that Bacon had sought and thus guarantee him the security and prosperity that he had hitherto lacked.

Descartes recognized that this project would be an enormous task and concluded that he would have to make comprehensive intellectual and practical preparations to undertake it. He thus did not begin work on it in earnest until 1628. The first fruits of his labor were his fragmentary *Rules for the Direction of the Mind* and *The World or Treatise on Light* which he suppressed when he learned of Galileo's condemnation. In 1636, he published the *Discourse on the Method for Rightly Conducting One's Reason and for Seeking Truth in the Sciences* and three scientific treatises that were meant to serve as examples of this method. In response to questions about part 4 of the *Discourse,* which sketched his metaphysical speculations, Descartes published his *Meditations on First Philosophy* in 1641. He answered the criticism that this work aroused in 1644 with his *Principles of Philosophy.* This work was followed in 1649 by his *Passions of the Soul,* which laid out the framework for his moral philosophy. Shortly thereafter, during a visit to Sweden, Descartes contracted pneumonia and died in early February 1650.

Descartes' work was widely read in educated circles in his own lifetime and was extremely controversial not only because of its philosophical, mathematical, and scientific innovations, but also because of its problematic treatment of religion. Its immediate and unequivocal impact upon Arnauld and Malebranche is undeniable, as is its important influence on Leibniz and Spinoza. The importance of his thought, however, was not broadly recognized until the 1660s and 1670s, when it was adopted as part of the standard curriculum of many European universities. The profound impact that Descartes' thought had on succeeding generations has justly led to his reputation as the father of modern philosophy.

Descartes' fundamental principle can be understood only in the context of his great attempt to establish a universal science. In Rule 2 of the *Rules* he describes what such a science must be and do:

> All knowledge is certain and evident cognition. Someone who has doubts about many things is no wiser than one who has never given them a thought; indeed, he appears less wise if he has formed a false opinion about any of them. Hence it is better never to study at all than to occupy ourselves with objects which are so difficult that we are unable to distinguish what is true from what is false, and are forced to take the doubtful as certain; for in such matters the risk of diminishing our knowledge is greater than our hope of increasing it. So, in accordance with this Rule, we reject all such merely probable cognition and resolve to believe only what is perfectly known and incapable of being doubted. (AT 10:362; CSM 1:10–11)[1]

This was the problem that Descartes set out to solve—how to overcome all doubts and attain knowledge that was not merely probable but certain. In the *Rules* and his other early works, Descartes tried to found this certainty upon the immediacy of intuition, the "indubitable conception of a clear and attentive mind" that "proceeds solely from the light of reason alone" (AT, 10:368; CSM, 1:14). Descartes came to see, however, that intuition in itself was not a sufficient basis for the certainty that his science demanded. Nature could not be mastered without an investigation of that which transcends nature. As a result, he was forced to undertake a metaphysical investigation that cast aside all received opinions and followed a path of radical doubt in search of a certain foundation. This search led to the discovery of his fundamental principle.

This principle was first set forth in the *Discourse,* which was intended to introduce the public to the new method of Descartes' science. It is written in autobiographical style and presents this new method as an integral part of a new kind of human being, represented by Descartes himself. Like his predecessor Montaigne, Descartes thus presents himself as a model for emulation. But unlike Montaigne, who advocated self-sufficiency and acceptance of fate in the face of a fundamentally incomprehensible world, Descartes lays out a plan for mastering himself and the world. Thus, Descartes' project is motivated not by a longing for serenity, transfiguration, or sanctification but by a desire for security and prosperity.[2]

After an account of his education (part 1), his method (part 2), and his provisional code of morality (part 3), Descartes describes his first meditations on the foundations of philosophy (part 4). He expresses his doubts about the propriety of describing these meditations, since they are so metaphysical and out of the ordinary that they may not be to everyone's liking. Still, he feels himself constrained to speak "in some measure" of the firm foundation he has discovered for his new science. He tells the reader that while it is sometimes necessary in matters of conduct to follow the most uncertain principles as if they were indubitable, in the pursuit of truth it is necessary to reject as absolutely false anything about which there is the least doubt. He thus determines "never to accept anything as true if I did not have evident knowledge of its truth, . . . to include nothing more in my judgments than what presented itself to my mind so clearly and so distinctly that I had no occasion to doubt it" (AT, 6:18; CSM, 1:120).

Like his *Rules for the Direction of the Mind,* Descartes' first meditations begin with the problem of doubt and follow the path of doubt in search of certainty. Because the senses deceive us, he rejects the truth of all sensation; because men make mistakes in even simple geometric reasoning, he rejects all geometric demonstrations, and because we often have the same thoughts in dreams as awake, he decides to treat everything that previously entered his mind as nothing but a dream. Having followed this path to its skeptical conclusion, however, he remarks that when he tried to think everything false he noticed that "it was necessary that I, who was thinking this, was something. And observing that this truth *'I think, therefore I am'* was so firm and sure that all the most extravagant suppositions of the skeptics were incapable of shaking it, I decided that I could accept it without scruple as the first principle of the philosophy I was seeking" (AT, 6:32; CSM, 1:127).

The account of this discovery in the *Meditations* is more extensive. The *Discourse* was written in French and intended for the general public. Following the provisional code of morality outlined in part 3 of the *Discourse,* Descartes thus avoids raising questions that might upset religious beliefs or morals, speaking of his metaphysical reflections only "in some measure" so that feeble spirits would not use them to cause trouble (AT, 6:31; CSM, 1:126).[3] He apparently has in mind here "those meddlesome and restless characters, who, called neither by birth nor fortune to the management of public affairs, are yet forever thinking up some new reform," and he remarks that he would not have published the *Discourse* if there were the slightest thing in it to aid such folly (AT, 6:15; CSM, 1:118).

The *Meditations,* by contrast, are written in Latin and intended for a more learned and ostensibly more prudent audience. Even this enterprise is not without its dangers, however, for the ideas may spread to the less learned. Still, the risk must be taken in Descartes' opinion, for nothing firm can be established in philosophy without following this path. Although fire and knives "cannot safely be handled by careless people or children, no one thinks that this is a reason for doing without them altogether" (AT, 7:247; CSM, 2:172).

Like the *Discourse,* the *Meditations* are written in an autobiographical style and are in one sense simply an expansion of part 4 of the *Discourse.* The first paragraph of the First Meditation emphasizes this connection, summarizing parts 1–3 of the *Discourse.* At least on the surface, the *Meditations* seem to be a more explicit discussion of the fundamental doubts that first motivated Descartes' thought. Beneath these surface similarities, however, there are a number of differences that call into question the continuity of the two works. The debate about the relationship between the *Discourse* and the *Meditations* reflects the deeper debate about the character of Descartes' thought as a whole. One school of thought sees Descartes as a scientist who was preeminently concerned with physics and who saw metaphysics and theology as impediments that had to be circumvented if reason was ever to triumph in the world. In this reading, the *Discourse* and Descartes' mathematical and scientific works are characterized as his true teaching, and the *Meditations* and his other theological and metaphysical writings either a smoke screen to conceal his true intentions from the scholastic authorities who had condemned Galileo, or an exceptionally clever way of destroying scholasticism from within and thus preparing the ground for the ultimate triumph of his science.[4] The other leading school sees Descartes as the great defender of religion in the face of skepticism. In this reading, Descartes is no simple apostle of the new science. Indeed, his doubts are a genuine reaction to the decline of faith in his time, and his

thought is an attempt to reconstitute a metaphysical-theological synthesis. For these scholars, Descartes represents the rejection of
Renaissance skepticism and a reawakening of genuine religious life.[5]
From this perspective, *Meditations* are the summit of Descartes'
thought.

There is considerable support for both interpretations. Descartes
clearly tries to provide a secure metaphysical basis for his new science.
Galileo, in his view, failed because he lacked a metaphysics to back up
his science.[6] Descartes also clearly recognizes the theological concerns of his contemporaries and the Church. He was shocked by the
condemnation of Galileo and subsequently withdrew his scientific
work *The World* from publication, because of its similarities to
Galileo's work. It is not clear, however, that he withdrew it from fear
of persecution. He remarks in the *Discourse* that he had not seen anything objectionable in Galileo and as a result thought he might be
mistaken about the innocuous nature of his own work (AT, 6:60;
CSM, 1:142). Even if he feared revolutionary change, however, he
may still have favored gradual and peaceful reform under the leadership of science.

His attempt to construct a metaphysical foundation for physics,
however, cannot simply be explained by his desire to placate his
potential enemies. His original project was clearly the development
of a new science, but by the time of the dreams recounted in the
Olympica, he had also become concerned with metaphysical questions. Science and metaphysics are not necessarily incompatible. In
fact, science needs metaphysics, for it is threatened not only by
scholasticism but also and more ominously by skepticism, and must
displace both if it is to succeed.

Descartes begins the *Meditations* by proclaiming his desire to
secure some lasting result in the sciences by making a clean sweep of
his opinions and constructing his knowledge anew from the very
foundations. It is important to note that this decision itself is already
motivated by the doubt that many of his youthful opinions are true.
He concludes that in order to attain the truth he must withhold his
assent from what is not plainly certain and indubitable, that he must
treat everything that can be doubted as if it were false. As in the *Discourse*, it is the application of Rule 2 (quoted above) that sets
Descartes on the path of doubt.

In contradistinction to his treatment in the *Discourse,* however, his
account of this voyage of doubt here takes the form of a dialogue
with himself.[7] He begins, as he did in the *Discourse,* with a rejection

of the senses because they sometimes deceive us. He responds here, however, that the senses do not usually deceive us and in fact often give us indubitable evidence. Sense-deception alone is thus an insufficient ground for skepticism.

He next suggests that the source of universal doubt is madness, for madmen are sometimes deceived even about those things that are closest to them, such as their own bodies. On this basis all sense-data may be doubted. This doubt is more profound because more incorrigible. Sense-deception occurs at the limits of our perception, when things are either very small or very distant. Madness is deception about what is closest to us and is due not to a limitation of our capacities but to a biological dysfunction that disjoins the imagination from the senses. Descartes, however, concludes that he cannot be mad, because madness, as he understands it, is the inability to distinguish reasonable and unreasonable judgments.[8] Doubting, however, presupposes a capacity to make such distinctions. Because Descartes doubts, he cannot be mad.

While actual madness may be rare, Descartes recognizes that dreaming is a kind of madness that afflicts all human beings.[9] What we experience may be illusory because it is all only a dream. Dreaming is a more profound source of doubt because it represents a universal, if only episodic, disjunction of imagination and reality. Descartes concludes, however, that even if this is the case, the things we experience within dreams are images of something, and these original things must be real. The imagination necessarily draws its images from reality even if it puts them together in unreal ways in dreams. Dreaming and, by the same argument, madness therefore cannot be the source of truly universal or hyperbolic doubt.[10]

While dreaming may not lead to total skepticism, it does pose real problems for Cartesian science. Physics, astronomy, and medicine in Descartes' view consider only composite objects. They may employ mathematics to describe their objects, but they take as their starting points the particular composite objects that the imagination portrays. Although dreams call into question all composite things, they leave untouched the simplest things which imagination arranges and rearranges in dreams. As a result, while dreams may undermine science generally, they do not call mathematics into question, since mathematics treats only these simple things and is indifferent to whether composite things exist.[11]

The most profound source of doubt in Descartes' view is the idea of an omnipotent God:

> Firmly rooted in my mind is the long-standing opinion that there is an
> omnipotent God who makes me the kind of creature that I am. How
> do I know that he has not brought it about that there is no earth, no
> sky, no extended thing, no shape, no size, no place, while at the same
> time insuring that all these things appear to me to exist just as they do
> now? What is more, since I sometimes believe that others go astray in
> cases where they think they have the most perfect knowledge, may I
> not similarly go wrong every time I add two and three, or count the
> sides of a square, or in some even simpler matter, if that is imaginable?
> (AT, 7:21; CSM, 2:14)

In the *Discourse,* human errors or imperfections were recognized as
a source of doubt about mathematical demonstrations. Here again
errors or imperfections resurface as a source of such doubt. In the
Discourse, however, Descartes suggested that a strict application of
the method would obviate such errors since they seemed only to be
the result of momentary human weakness. In the *Meditations,*
Descartes considers the possibility that such errors are unavoidable
and incorrigible.

The source of this doubt is the possibility that an omnipotent God
has either created the world in such a way that it is necessarily misunderstood by man or created man in such a way that he necessarily
misunderstands the world. God, in other words, may have arranged
matters so that even the most clear and distinct judgments about the
simplest things always go astray.[12] It is this possibility of an omnipotent God that decisively calls into question the entire enterprise of
Cartesian science, including mathematics.[13]

The profundity of the doubt that the possibility of divine deception evokes should not be minimized. Pascal and Hume, for example, considered it the most severe form of skepticism.[14] Descartes'
previous doubts were actuated by circumstances or conditions that
could be overcome through the consistent application of his method.
Divine deception would be incorrigible. The idea of an omnipotent
God thus seems to lead ineluctably to the conclusion that we may be
continually and hopelessly deceived.

On this basis, some scholars have argued that Descartes is wrong
to characterize this condition as deception, since the concept of
deception assumes that we can discern the difference between illusion and reality.[15] Such an argument assumes that Descartes'
omnipotent God is a consistent deceiver. Descartes is unwilling to
accept this view because it assumes a rational consistency that is
incompatible with divine freedom. A truly omnipotent God can do

anything. If even the possibility of divine inconsistency exists, however, the problem of divine deception for science and mathematics becomes acute.

Descartes considers two possible ways of saving knowledge from the radical doubt that divine deception seems to entail: the path of piety and the path of atheism. Neither, however, is sufficient. If God is supremely good, Descartes argues, "perhaps God would not have allowed me to be deceived in this way" (AT, 7:21; CSM, 2:14). Descartes, however, knows that he is sometimes deceived and, if this is not contrary to God's goodness, then it cannot be contrary to God's goodness that he be always deceived. The path of piety thus fails.[16]

On the surface, the path of atheism seems more promising, but it too is ultimately untenable. If we could know that God does not exist (which we cannot), we would still have to admit that we make mistakes and are therefore imperfect beings. In one way of looking at things, we seem in fact to be worse off if our capacities for sensing and knowing are the result of chance or a continual succession of antecedents than if they are created by God. The doubt of the radical materialist in this sense seems more profound than that engendered by the possibility of a divine deceiver.[17] Such a view brings Descartes much closer to Bacon and Hobbes. Descartes himself, however, does not take this alternative seriously, in large part because it would render mind itself impossible. While it is thus conceivable to the meditator, its possibility is exploded by the recognition of the *res cogitans* in the Second Meditation. Moreover, the argument that atheistic doubt is more profound is true only if the possible sources of doubt are limited in a way that is ultimately unacceptable to Descartes. Chance or fate could never equal the perfection of a beneficent God. The reverse, however, would also seem to be the case, that is, a malicious God would be better able to deceive us. Moreover, such a God would not only have the power to create us imperfectly but also could change the laws of reason and nature to render the true judgments we have already made false. The deceptions of an unthinking nature, by contrast, could be eliminated by the consistent application of Descartes' method.

Descartes concludes that it is necessary to avoid giving credence to opinion altogether, and to this end decides to suppose that there is not a God who is supremely good and the source of truth, but rather an evil genius or malicious demon (*genius malignus*) who is supremely powerful and intelligent, and "who has employed all his energies in order to deceive me" (AT, 7:22; CSM, 2:15).[18] Furthermore, he decides to treat all external things as traps set by this evil genius to ensnare his credulity. He concludes that if he cannot attain truth, he can at least avoid error by not believing anything. If his power does not enable him to penetrate through the divine deception, it does enable him to avoid affirming that illusion is reality. The positive result of the First Meditation is thus the recognition of doubt as a human capacity to avoid errors of judgment, even if those errors are induced by an omnipotent God. Through doubt, man can avoid error but he cannot thereby attain certainty and become master and possessor of nature. This goal requires a further capacity.

Descartes begins the Second Meditation by asserting the necessity of discovering an Archimedean point on which to stand in the pursuit of certainty and power. He finds this point in man himself. Descartes argues that even if he is deceived by some evil genius, he undoubtedly exists. "Let him deceive me as much as he can, he will never bring it about that I am nothing so long as I think that I am something. . . . this proposition *I am, I exist,* is necessarily true whenever it is put forward by me or conceived in my mind" (AT, 7:25; CSM, 2:17). Descartes' Archimedean point is thus the certainty of his own existence.

Some scholars have argued that this so called *sum* argument of the *Meditations* is crucially different from the *cogito* argument of the *Discourse*.[19] Such an interpretation, however, is belied by Descartes' own comments on the two passages in the "Objections and Replies" that were published as an extended appendix to the *Meditations*. In his reply to the second set of objections, Descartes construes the *Meditation* passage in question as "I think, hence I am, or exist" and as "I exist so long as I think" (AT, 7:140, 145; CSM, 2:100, 104; cf. also AT, 7:173–74; CSM, 2:122–23). On the basis of these passages and the absence of any overt statement by Descartes distinguishing the two versions of his fundamental principle, it seems likely that he saw them as equivalent.

The account of the path of doubt and its culmination in the *Principles* is similar to that of the *Meditations,* although it also adopts elements from the argument in the *Discourse*. Descartes adduces sense-deception and dreaming as reasons for doubting sensible things, and human error or imperfection and divine omnipotence as reasons for doubting the demonstrations of mathematics. He likewise points to the human capacity to avoid error that he noted at the end of the First Meditation, although here it is described as a sort of freedom. This line of reasoning leads him to the recognition that "this piece of knowledge—*I think, therefore I am,* is the first and most certain of all to occur to anyone who philosophizes in an orderly way" (AT, 8A:7; CSM, 1:195).

The account in the undated and unpublished *Search after Truth* is much the same. Here Descartes adopts yet another form, presenting his ideas in the context of a dialogue between three idealized characters, Epistemon, Eudoxus, and Polyander. Sense-deception, dreaming, and divine omnipotence are adduced as sources of doubt. Epistemon, who represents the scholastic spirit, is hesitant to follow this path of doubt because it is very dangerous and leads "straight into the ignorance of Socrates or the uncertainty of the Pyrrhonists" (AT, 10:512; CSM, 2:408). Eudoxus, who represents the scientific spirit, admits the great dangers of this path, but points out that lack of courage to face these doubts has prevented science from being established on a firm foundation.

Descartes' solution to such doubt in this work is given yet another formulation. Eudoxus explains to Polyander, who represents ordinary, everyday man, that "you cannot deny that you have such doubts; rather it is certain that you have them, so certain in fact that you cannot doubt your doubting. Therefore it is also true that you who doubt exist; this is so true that you can no longer have any doubts about it" (AT, 10:515; CSM, 2:410).

The basic principle that guarantees certainty thus arises out of doubt. Eudoxus asserts that "it is really from this universal doubt which is like a fixed and unchangeable point, that I have resolved to derive the knowledge of God, of yourself, and of all the world contains" (AT, 10:515; CSM, 2:410). The fundamental principle in the first instance appears not as *ego cogito ergo sum* but as *ego dubito ergo sum.* However, since "doubting [is] thinking in a certain way . . . I exist, and I know that I am, and I know these facts because I doubt, i.e., because I think" (AT, 10:521; CSM, 2:415).

Ego cogito ergo sum is the answer to the radical doubt that arises in the face of the omnipotent God. This conclusion points to a fundamental question that was concealed at the very beginning of modernity. Cartesian rationalism and the modern world present themselves as a new beginning, as enlightenment, but behind this bright dawn of reason stands the dark and mysterious form of the omnipotent God. To come to terms with modernity, we must thus examine this question more fully.

THE OMNIPOTENT GOD

The idea of divine omnipotence may have played some role in the early Judeo-Christian tradition, but there is little evidence that it was widely recognized or accepted until the end of the Middle Ages. God's infinity and incomprehensibility were clear from an early period. Pseudo-Dionysus and the tradition of apophantic theology, for example, argued that God was utterly different from all creatures and consequently could be comprehended only by means of the *via negativa,* that is, through contradiction. The medieval Jewish thinker Maimonides also defended such a "negative way."

The unintelligibility of God, however, is only one element of his omnipotence. More important is his radical freedom. The idea of divine freedom was antagonistic to much of patristic and scholastic thought, which attempted to reconcile Christian theology with classical philosophy and especially with the pagan notion of a rational cosmos. Augustine is something of an exception to this general trend, and Augustinianism in this sense provided the foundation for the later flowering of the idea of a radical omnipotence. This idea was probably first explicitly propounded in the Muslim *Shari'a,* or law, with which nascent scholasticism came into contact through Maimonides. The *Shari'a* denied any necessity to nature and analyzed it as a sequence of discrete atomic events independent of one another.[20]

This notion was sharply at odds with the mainstream of scholasticism, which emphasized the priority of reason within divine omnipotence. The metaphysics of traditional scholasticism is ontologically realist in positing the extramental existence of universals such as species and genera as forms of divine reason known either by divine illumination, as Augustine proclaimed, or through an investigation of nature, God's rational creation. Within such an ontology, nature and logic reflect one another, and one can describe nature by means of a syllogistic logic that expresses the relationships among all universals. Moreover, we can know of God's existence and his nature not merely through revelation but also through a philosophical analysis of creation. Thus, while revealed theology continues to play an important role and conveys certain truths inaccessible to reason, scholasticism generally believes that logic and natural theology are more elevated and profound paths to the truth about earthly matters than scripture. On this basis, it is possible to grasp the fundamental truth about human beings and their earthly duties and obligations. Human beings are governed by a natural law that is known through the observation of nature and the syllogistic deductions that describe the relationship between man, nature, and by analogy God. In this form, scholasticism achieves its most thorough synthesis of Christianity and ancient philosophy.

The influence of pagan philosophy on Christian doctrine, however, had long disturbed many within the Church because it led to a neglect of scripture and turned men's thoughts away from the contemplation of a future world toward a reconciliation with this world. More importantly, it demeaned God, whose power and grace were subordinated to the cosmos and logic of the pagans. This concern with pagan influence was exacerbated by the increasingly important role that Aristotelianism began to play in scholasticism. Aristotelianism had played little role in early Christianity. Many of Aristotle's texts were unknown and his influence was largely confined to logic. The reintroduction of Aristotle to the West, however, led to an expansion of his role within scholasticism. The curriculum at the University of Paris, for example, was reorganized in 1255 to require the study of all of Aristotle's works. This reflected the development of an independent system of philosophy alongside theology and of a new kind of Christian thinker who sought to recover the truth of ancient authors without reconciling it with orthodox Christian belief.[21] This new importance of Aristotelianism aroused considerable concern in its own right, but perhaps even more unsettling was the fact that these new Aristotelian works had been introduced to scholasticism through the Arab scholars Avicenna and Averroës. This connection provoked the suspicion that a heretical Islamic element was being imported into Christian doctrine. These suspicions culminated in the condemnation of Aristotelianism by the Bishop of Paris, Etienne Tempier, first in 1270 and then more sweepingly in 1277, and the condemnation of Aquinas in 1284 by John Peckham, the Franciscan archbishop of Canterbury. Although this condemnation had little immediate impact upon the study of Aristotle and Aquinas, it did provide official support for the critics of this strain of scholasticism.[22]

A minority opposition had long been active within scholasticism. This faction was essentially antirealist and read Aristotle in an antirealist manner. Roscelin and his great student Peter Abelard had called realism into question in the twelfth century by denying the extramental existence of universals. They adopted a position that has generally been characterized as nominalism, since they maintained that universals were mere names *(nomina.)*[23] However, Roscelin and Abelard remained voices crying in a realist wilderness and indeed were attacked by Anselm of Canterbury on theological grounds, since it seemed to him that their notion of universals was an implicit denial of the Trinity. The final philosophical rejection of Aristotelianism and realism has its origin in the work of Henry of Ghent, Duns Scotus, and perhaps more decisively William of Ockham. Their success was the result of the conjunction of antirealism with a more radical understanding of divine omnipotence.

The strain of scholasticism that found its apex in Aquinas generally asserted that, while God was omnipotent, he was also rational; that he had laid down his laws for all time; and that man could thus understand God and his intentions not merely through scripture but perhaps even more profoundly through an analogical investigation of nature.[24] While no one denied God's *potentia absoluta* (absolute power), these scholastics generally thought that he had bound himself to a *potentia ordinata* (ordered power) through his own decision. The possibility that God was not bound in this way but was perfectly free and omnipotent was a terrifying possibility that nearly all medieval thinkers were unwilling to accept.[25] Augustine, for example, asserted that God's holy order rationalized his omnipotence.[26] Albertus Magnus and Aquinas believed that God's *potentia* was inseparable from his *iustitia* and his *sapientia*.[27] Bonaventure rejected the possibility of an unrestrained *potentia absoluta* because it implied disorder within the divine, which he found contradictory.[28] Peter Abelard argued that God is compelled to act according to his essential goodness, justice, and wisdom.[29] Even Duns Scotus, who asserted that *de potentia absoluta* God could do everything that was not contradictory, concluded that even if God did act *inordinata*, it would entail the immediate creation of a new order.[30] God is thus suprarational for Duns Scotus and not irrational. Henry of Ghent more clearly articulated a doctrine of divine freedom and made the will into an autonomous power, but it was only with William of Ockham and the nominalist revolution that the awesome and terrifying consequences of this notion of divine omnipotence began to be fully understood.[31]

WILLIAM OF OCKHAM AND THE NOMINALIST REVOLUTION

William of Ockham was born in England between 1280 and 1285. He entered the Franciscan order at an early age and began his studies at Oxford around 1309. He may have been a student of Duns Scotus but, if not, was certainly well acquainted with his fellow Franciscan's work. Most of his nonpolitical works were completed between 1317 and 1324. In 1324, Ockham was summoned to the papal court in Avignon to defend himself against charges brought by the Oxford Thomist John Lutteral that fifty-six of his propositions were heretical. While there, he apparently came into contact with the great German mystic Meister Eckhart as well as Michael of Caesna, the head of his order, who was involved in a dispute with Pope John XXII over the question of Franciscan poverty. In 1326, fifty-one of Ockham's propositions were declared open to censure although none was finally condemned. More important matters, however, had come to occupy him during his stay in Avignon. Ockham sided with Michael against the pope on the question of poverty, and in the course of his investigation of their dispute came to the conclusion that the pope had contradicted the gospels and was thus not a true pope.

The Poverty Dispute turned upon a decisive theological distinction. The Franciscan order believed that Christ had renounced his kingdom and worldly dominion and that they should imitate him by taking a vow of poverty. Moreover, they believed that this asceticism represented a moral position superior to that of the rest of the Church.[32] Pope John XXII argued that Christ could not have renounced his kingdom because it would contradict what was ordained by God. The Franciscans replied that while God could not do this by his ordained power, he could do so by his absolute power, that is, God was not bound by his past actions or plans.[33] Only if God was recognized as omnipotent in a way that was unacceptable to the predominant strain of scholasticism could the Franciscan position be maintained. The Poverty Dispute in this sense was the concrete form of the debate over the relationship between divine will and reason. In his attempts to refute this position, the pope rejected the distinction between God's ordered and absolute power. Ockham and his fellow Franciscans saw this rejection as a revival of Abelard's heretical position that God is bound to save some from all eternity by his own previous will. They vigorously denied this conclusion, arguing that if God is free and sovereign, he can predestine whomever he chooses.[34] Hence, the pope was a heretic.

Ockham fled from Avignon with Michael in 1328 and was excommunicated. At Pisa, he joined the party of Ludwig of Bavaria, whose election as emperor the pope did not recognize. There he apparently became acquainted with Marsilius of Padua. He spent the next fifteen years defending the emperor's cause but ultimately came to a recon-

ciliation with the new pope, Benedict XII. Shortly thereafter, some-
time between 1346 and 1349, he died, probably from the Black
Death.

Ockham decisively rejects the scholastic attempt to reconcile theology and philosophy. This does not mean, however, that theology
was of little importance to Ockham, as many Anglo-American scholars long believed. Recent scholarship has demonstrated that Ockham's thought is intensely theological, arising from and returning to
the question of God's omnipotent freedom.[35] Omnipotence means
the supremacy of God's *potentia absoluta* over his *potentia ordinata*
and of theology over philosophy. Ockham thus aims not so much at
facilitating a nontheological investigation of nature or language but
at a liberation of theology from the yoke of pagan philosophy. His
theology thus gives his metaphysics its direction and meaning.

Faith alone, in Ockham's view, teaches us that God is all-powerful.
To say that God is all-powerful is to say that he can do everything that
is possible and this includes everything that is not contradictory.[36]
Omnipotence also means that everything is or occurs only as the
result of God's disposing will and that there is no reason for creation
except his will.[37] What is, is only because he wills it. Creation is thus
an act of pure grace that can be understood only through revelation.

Moreover, God in Ockham's view does not need to act through
secondary causes but can act directly. Here he follows Duns Scotus in
opposing the Averroëst doctrine that God is bound by natural causality.[38] Thus God does not simply set the cosmos in motion at creation
and look on as a powerless spectator when the drama he has written
unfolds, but also intervenes in the order of nature whenever he
wishes. Such miracles, however, are not in fact unnatural, since nature
is nothing other than an expression of divine will. Miracles merely
shorten the way of creation. They do, however, call into question the
possibility of a strictly human knowledge that is certain and secure.

God's omnipotence also means that he does not create the world
for man and is not influenced by anything that man does. He is, as
Ockham often repeats, no man's debtor.[39] He thus predestines whom
he will. Ockham rejects the idea that the world was created for man's
benefit. While scholasticism had been gradually edging toward such
a conclusion, Ockham tries to avoid even the appearance that God
reacts to man. Omnipotence means an utterly unconditioned will.
Indeed, while he does not deny that God is a God of love, he does
assert that God's love for man is only a passage back to his love of
himself, that ultimately God's love is only self-love.[40]

If God has not created the world for man and is not even bound by his own creation, then he does not act according to human standards and cannot be comprehended by human reason. There is no immutable law or reason. Every order is simply the result of God's absolute will and can be disrupted or reconstituted at any moment. Indeed, Ockham even maintains that God can change the past if he so desires. He thus not only rejects the attempts of various scholastics, following Avicenna and Averroës, to subordinate God to the laws of nature, but rejects all limitations on divine action except for the law of noncontradiction. This rejection of theological rationalism was the beginning of the end of scholasticism. To understand this Ockhamist revolution in the way of thinking more fully we must look systematically at his transformation of metaphysics.

Divine omnipotence in Ockham's view entails the essential difference of God's being from the being of all created things, including man. There is no univocity of being. God is infinite in the fullest sense and man is incapable of attaining the infinite either extensively or intensively.[41] God is also the only necessary being. The world to its very core is contingent and governed only by the necessity that God momentarily imparts to it.[42] There thus are no universals, no species or genera. There are likewise no intrinsic ends for individuals that arise out of and correspond to the essence of their species. Indeed, there is no difference between essence and existence. Put in another way, the divine ideas are nothing other than the creatures themselves.[43] Everything is therefore radically individual, called into being out of nothing by God either directly or by means of secondary causes. None of the things that are follow necessarily from such secondary or natural causes—God alone is the ultimate ground of the possibility of each and every thing and can maintain any one thing without the rest of reality.[44]

On an ontological level, Ockham's thought represents a complete and unequivocal rejection of realism, since the binding power of categories limits God's power. If realism is taken seriously, it is ultimately impossible for God to annihilate an individual without annihilating the species. God thus cannot create universals without contradicting himself, that is, without limiting himself in a way incompatible with his omnipotence.[45] He is thus bound by his own nature to create only individual things. Divine omnipotence, properly understood, thus entails radical individualism.

On the logical level, Ockham's innovations were no less revolutionary. For scholasticism, ontological realism had gone hand in hand with syllogistic logic. If the basic premise of realism, the extramental existence of universals, is accepted and if these universals are identified with God's thoughts in the neo-Platonic manner of Porphyry, Boethius, and the Arabs, then logic becomes a universal science that explicates the necessary and essential relations of all created things. No real knowledge of scripture is necessary, to grasp the truth of nature. The rejection of realism thus undermines syllogistic logic. If all things are radically individual, then universals are merely names *(nomina)*, verbal tools created by finite human beings for the purpose of dealing with the vast array of radically individual things.[46] Universals in this sense have *only* a logical meaning. Logic thus becomes a logic of names or signs rather than a logic that expresses the real relations among things.

Nominalism is also at odds with the syllogistic science of scholasticism. All logical explanations in Ockham's view are merely human creations that do not reflect divine wisdom. God understands each thing individually as he created it by means of a *cognitio intuitiva* and thus has no need of universals.[47] Human finitude renders men incapable of grasping creation simply as a collection of radically individual beings. A new principle of logical explanation is thus necessary. The principle that Ockham presents is the principal of parsimony, his famous razor. It is important to note that parsimony becomes the chief principle not because of the belief that nature does nothing in vain, as both Aristotle and later thinkers argued, but because nature is radically individual and every universal is thus a distortion of reality. To minimize this distortion it is necessary to minimize the number of universals, hence Ockham's formulation of the principle as the injunction: "Do not multiply universals needlessly."[48]

Divine omnipotence, however, raises a fundamental epistemological problem, since it opens up the possibility of divine deception.[49] This possibility follows directly from the notion of omnipotence because a truly omnipotent God can act directly without employing secondary causes. This means that God can conserve any one thing apart from all other things. Thus, for example, God can maintain the existence of an individual human being without any other supporting causes, that is, without the rest of nature. He can also conserve the impression of an object when the object itself has ceased to exist, and he can foster the impression of an object without the necessary intervention of the object itself. For Ockham, the idea of divine omnipotence thus means that human beings can never be certain that any of the impressions they have correspond to an actual object.

In one sense, it is incorrect to speak of this as deception, since everything ultimately has its origin in God's omnipotent will. That God chooses to act immediately rather than mediately thus only shortens the way of creation. From the perspective of humanity's attempt to comprehend and control the natural world, however, the difference may well be decisive. Ockham believes that God acts in such a manner only rarely, but this does not remove the epistemological problem, for even if he were never to act in such a manner, the mere possibility of his doing so would be sufficient to undermine the certainty of all knowledge.

Confronted with these epistemological problems, Ockham develops a new notion of knowing that rejects the syllogistic science of scholasticism in favor of natural reality. Human knowledge in Ockham's view begins with the intuitive cognition of individual facts. Normally, knowledge of facts is secure because there is no mediation between individual things and human perception. In their intuition of facts, human beings emulate God, who knows everything intuitively. In this sense, there is no knowledge of created things prior to investigation, since their existence is not logically necessary. For Ockham as for Duns Scotus, nothing that depends on God's free decision is philosophically deducible. Each thing is individual, unique, and radically contingent. The criterion of knowledge is thus not the logic of the syllogism and the truth of its premises, but the certainty of the intuition.[50] In this respect, internal facts such as acts of the will are known with greater certainty than sensation. Ockham even cites Augustine's claim that the greatest certainty is the certainty that "I know that I am living."[51]

In this way, Ockham severely circumscribes the realm of human knowledge. Like Duns Scotus, he rejects the notion of divine illumination and thus the possibility of understanding God through an introspective self-examination. He also rejects the whole idea of a syllogistic science of nature. In place of both, he sets the intuition of facts, that is, of made (from *facere*, 'to make') or created things, and establishes the standard of truth as the certainty of these facts. However, knowledge for man cannot simply consist in the intuitive understanding of each individual thing in its individuality. Unlike God, man has need of universals and generalizations. Nonetheless, every multiplication of universals is a step away from actuality. Knowledge itself becomes not an expression of the essence of things as it was for scholasticism but an impression of contingent relationships or similarities between individual existences. There are no species by nature but only individual things that resemble one another and that thus can be signified, that is, represented by a sign.[52] We thus know only by correlations or approximations.

Knowing has a variety of meanings for Ockham. Science in his view means the certain knowledge of true propositions and includes the truths of faith. We also know through evident propositions based on immediate intuitions. Thirdly, we know when we have an evident cognition of a necessary truth that is not factual, for example, the principle of noncontradiction. Finally, we know when we have a cognition of a necessary truth which is deduced from an evident cognition.[53]

Ockham distinguishes between certain and evident truths. The truths of theology, for example, are certain because they rest upon scripture, but they are not evident, that is, there is no evidence for them because they do not depend upon intuitive cognition as the truths of natural science do. Theology is therefore more certain than natural science because it rests upon God's infallible intuition, while natural science depends upon the fallible capacities of men. Moreover, since everything in creation is contingent and deduction is therefore impossible, all knowledge of causal connections is based upon experience. Thus, both theology and natural science require investigation, although the method of investigation in each case is different. Both sciences also differ from logic, which in Ockham's view is a rational but not a real science. All of this is encapsulated in one of the alternative forms of the razor: one should affirm no statement as true or maintain that something exists unless forced to do so by self-evidence, that is, by revelation, experience, or a logical deduction from a revealed truth or a proposition verified by observation.[54]

Ockham replaces syllogism with hypothesis as the basis for the comprehension of God and nature. The rejection of realism and divine illumination undermines all deductive theology and cosmology. Furthermore, the radical contingency of all created things means there can be no sufficient reason for any facts, since God can interrupt any series of natural causes by means of his *potentia absoluta*. Science can generalize upon the basis of what is established by intuition, but there neither is, nor can be, any necessity in the propositions at which science arrives.

Nominalism laid the foundation for a theological revolution. Theology for Ockham is not a deductive or analogical science. The radical difference between God and man means that God and the central beliefs of religion can be known only through revelation. Theology can prove God's existence, infinity, and supremacy but not his singularity, his perception of external things, or his capacity for free creation.[55] Ockham in this sense represents the first step on the road to the insight that faith alone is the basis of salvation.

The effect of the notion of divine omnipotence on cosmology was equally revolutionary. With the rejection of realism and the assertion of radical individuality, beings could no longer be conceived as members of species or genera with a certain nature or potentiality. In Aristotelian terms, the rejection of formal causes was also the rejection of final causes. As a result, only material and efficient causality remained. The relations between the various material beings can be determined only by efficient causality and this causality can be known only by observation. Moreover, since each event is the result of the meeting of two unique entities, no necessary generalizations are possible. Therefore, science at best can be merely hypothetical.

Ockham in this way establishes the foundation for a science that is based on experience and hypothesis, which examines the contingent relationships among extended entities to determine the efficient causes that govern their motion, and which attempts to provide a quantitative rather than a qualitative explanation of phenomena.[56] While Ockham did not actually develop a science on these principles, they remain the indispensable ontological and epistemological presuppositions of Renaissance and early modern science.

Ockham's nominalism had revolutionary consequences as well for man's understanding of himself and his relationships with other men. Following Aristotle, scholasticism generally understood man as a rational animal who occupied the preeminent place in the categorical order of creation and whose end and obligations were determined by the natural law governing this place. Nominalism rejected this view of man. For Ockham, individual human beings have no natural end, and there is no natural law such as Aquinas had imagined to govern human actions. Man like God is free. In this respect, Ockham follows Duns Scotus, who asserted the preeminence of will and the doctrine of liberty in man on the basis of his observation that will can always command acts of understanding while the understanding can never command the will.[57] Ockham, however, goes beyond Scotus in opening up this realm of freedom not merely by rejecting the scholastic notion of final causes, but also by rejecting the application of efficient causality to men.[58] For Ockham, man in principle is thus free from nature itself.

Man is thereby also placed in a problematic position vis-à-vis God, since this assertion of human freedom and independence seems to contradict God's omnipotence. Ockham rejects the fatalism that Duns Scotus had seen in the doctrine of divine omnipotence, because it rests on the fallacious assumption that the past is unalterable. Ockham believes that a truly omnipotent God cannot be subject to time and thus can alter the past to change the present or future.[59] Human choice, however, still seems illusory, since human beings are created beings subject to divine will. Ockham rejects this conclusion, arguing in Augustinian fashion that God gives human beings only general capacities and rules for action. However, this solution is hardly satisfying, and Ockham's failure to provide a convincing answer to this question leaves human freedom crucially exposed to the absolute tyranny of God.

The ontological freedom that Ockham attributes to human beings does not entail moral freedom. The fact that humans can do whatever they please does not mean that they may do so. They are subject to the moral law which God establishes. In fact, their culpability arises out of the fact that they have the freedom to obey or disobey, and are free even from any utilitarian motive, since obedience does not guarantee salvation and disobedience does not necessitate damnation. Humans are obligated to obey divine law not out of fear or hope but out of gratitude to God as the source of their being. The reverse, of course, is not true—God has no moral obligation to human beings and indeed in no sense reacts to them. To assert otherwise would open the door to Pelagianism.

The content of the moral law is also determined by this radical difference between man and God. What it commands is not what God wills but what he wills that we will.[60] Moral law in this sense is radically subordinate to divine choice and completely beyond the capacity of human reason to deduce or explain. It does not correspond to eternal truths that shape God's will and God does not choose it because he realizes that this law is better than any other, but simply because he wills it. God is indifferent to what he chooses and the moral law is good not in itself but only because he wills it. Moreover, there are no limits set upon what God can demand. He can even command that we hate him.[61] Whatever his commandments may be, they are by definition good and binding. God's will alone determines what is good and evil, and he is not even bound by its own previous determinations.

Obedience to God's laws in Ockham's view does not guarantee

salvation. As radically free, God saves whomever he chooses. Indeed, contrary to almost all of his predecessors, Ockham asserts that God can even save those without infused grace, if he so wills. This assertion, not surprisingly, led many to see Ockham as a semi-Pelagian, since it seems to imply that human beings can attain salvation without grace. Ockham would argue in his defense that while a human being might attain salvation without God's grace, he could do so only as a result of God's will and not by any actions of his own. While such an arbitrary divine will seems contrary to justice, nothing in Ockham's view could be further from the truth. God has given all human beings the gift of life and can give the further gift of eternal life to those he chooses. Ockham actually ameliorates the position defended by Aquinas, Henry of Ghent, and Scotus, who all maintain that every fallen being deserves eternal punishment. Ockham insists that no creature is intrinsically worthy of either eternal punishment or eternal life independent of or prior to divine institution.[62]

This moral law is made manifest not by nature or logic but by revelation. Moreover, since everyone is directly and uniquely related to God, there is no definitive or privileged interpretation of revelation. Each is ultimately bound only by his own conscience. As a result, papal authority in matters of faith is nil—indeed, there are no better or worse judges of the moral law and, therefore, no basis for clerical authority of any sort in moral matters.[63]

There is even less occasion for papal authority in political affairs. Each individual is free and unique. The only basis for ethical life is thus free self-determination.[64] Human beings are born free and have the right to choose their own ruler and therefore ostensibly their own form of government.[65] It would be a mistake, however, to see this liberation from the traditional structures of authority that characterized medieval society as the advent of modern liberalism. While nominalism clearly rejects the basic structure of medieval life and thought, it does not establish man as a free being capable of mastering nature and securing himself in the world. Rather it announces the utter insignificance of human beings in comparison to God. Moreover, rather than establish man as lord of nature and his own destiny, it leaves him afloat in a universe utterly dependent upon a capricious divine will.[66] Nominalism points not toward the dawn of a new enlightenment but toward the dark form of an omnipotent and incomprehensible God.

Although Ockham was excommunicated from the Church and his teaching was repeatedly condemned in Paris from 1339 to 1347, his thought soon became ascendent in much of Europe. There was a strong Ockhamist tradition in England under the leadership of Thomas Bradwardine, the archbishop of Canterbury, and later Robert Holcot and Adam Woodham. The Ockhamists were equally strong in Paris under Nicholas of Autrecourt and John of Mirecourt. While there were clear differences among these thinkers, they were united in their rejection of the realism of traditional scholasticism. In fact, the influence of Ockhamism outside Spain, where scholasticism continued to flourish, was so great that by the time of Luther there was, for example, only one university in Germany that was not dominated by the nominalists.

Nominalism sought to tear the rationalistic veil from the face of God. With this violent act, the rational order that Aristotle, the patristic authors, and the scholastics had sought to establish was swept aside and humanity was brought face to face with the all-powerful God. Nominalism presented human beings with a Christianity freed from all pagan influences; but it was also a Christianity in which Christ played only a minor role. The doctrine of the Trinity was maintained but enormously weakened. Indeed, Ockham was able to sustain this doctrine only by contradicting his own theory of universals.[67] Within the Trinity, however, God the creator and destroyer became preeminent, and the redeemer and God of love faded into the background. This God who stepped forth as if newly born beyond reason and justice, beyond love and hope, was a God of infinite power whose dark and incomprehensible form was as much an object of terror as of love and veneration.

The figure of this dark God was itself a profound source of anxiety and concern, but it was the fortuitous conjunction of this new notion of God with the devastation of the Black Death and the papal schism that brought the medieval world to an end. The idea of the nominalist God was originally developed to reassert the primacy of biblical Christianity against the claims of the more extreme rationalizing scholastics. The success of this idea, however, owed a great deal to the circumstances of the times. Such an arbitrary and capricious God became increasingly plausible in a world devastated by plague and internecine political and theological strife. Historical circumstances thus gave a real substance and magnitude to this conception of God. Under such conditions it is thus little wonder that this God was a source of profound anxiety and insecurity in the succeeding centuries.

The intellectual history of this period is replete with attempts to come to terms with this God, to render him less dangerous and less terrifying to human beings. This was already apparent in the nominalist movement of the fourteenth century. On one hand, Thomas Bradwardine and John of Mirecourt reiterated and in some respects even radicalized Ockham's assertion of divine liberty and omnipotence as well as divine indifference. Mirecourt, for example, was condemned in 1347 for his radically Ockhamist assertion that someone totally without love could attain eternal life if God so willed it.[68] Where Ockham had tried to leave room for human freedom, Bradwardine argues that "the divine will is the efficient cause of everything whatsoever."[69] On the other hand, Nicholas of Autrecourt, John Buridan, Nicholas of Oresme, Albert of Saxony, and Marsilius of Inghen turned to a scientific investigation of nature in part because of the destruction of substantial forms but also because nature was conceived as a reflection of the motions of divine will.

Traditional metaphysics had understood God as the highest being. From the perspective of nominalism, however, such a description is untenable, for there is no hierarchy of beings or orders of perfection stretching to and including God. God is not an entity and hence cannot be known even by analogy, as Aquinas had maintained. From the perspective of traditional metaphysics, the nominalist God is thus nothing. Such a conclusion, of course, is not unique to nominalism and indeed was proclaimed much more explicitly by Ockham's contemporary and acquaintance in Avignon, the great German mystic Meister Eckhart. This nothing, however, is nothing only from the perspective of the categorical metaphysics of Aristotle and scholasticism. The God of nominalism is not a substance. His being resides in his omnipotence as the pure will that is the source of all things and of all relationships between things. God is thus not merely to be understood through his actions, as Aquinas had argued; he is his action. He is, in other words, the causality at the heart of *creatio ex nihilo*.[70] Nature in this sense is established as a collection of unique individual entities that are brought into existence and determined in their existence by divine will understood as causality.[71] The investigation of nature carried out within the nominalist movement is thus in part an attempt to gain a measure of security through an investigation of nature as God-infused being, that is, as being infused with divine will as causality. This new idea of the relationship of God and nature played an important role not merely in the nominalist movement but also in Renaissance and early modern science, beginning with Nicholas of Cusa and continuing at least until Leibniz and Newton.[72]

The importance of nominalism for later intellectual movements was profound. Through the predominance of nominalist thinking in England it played an important role in the development of English empiricism, especially for Bacon and Hobbes.[73] It was also important in a less well recognized way for the Reformation, the Counterreformation, and skepticism.

Luther and Calvin were clearly indebted to nominalism, although the extent of this debt is much disputed. Although Luther was not principally a systematic theologian, he declared himself to be an Ockhamist and his theology was deeply indebted to the nominalist Gabriel Biel.[74] Luther's emphasis upon the individual and his direct connection to God, his substitution of scripture for scholastic philosophy, and his denial of clerical hierarchy in favor of conscience as a guide for moral action all owe much to nominalism.[75] He and Calvin raised up God's awesome omnipotence in opposition not merely to scholastic metaphysics but also to Renaissance science and humanism. Illustrative is Calvin's famous remark that the sun rises every day not because of the law of nature but because God wills it, with the obvious corollary that if God does not so will, the sun will not rise.[76]

While the Reformers exalt this omnipotent God, they also seek to make him more accessible to man by turning to scripture and the heart, to feelings, conscience, and the certainty of faith achieved through revelatory experience. The God of the Reformation is less austere and remote than the nominalist God, more Christlike, closer to man, a God of love, still awesome and magnificent but less terrifying than the God of Ockham. Such a God, however, is still fundamentally arbitrary. He predestines men for salvation and damnation solely according to his will and without regard to their deserts. The Reformation thus accepts and proclaims the nominalist doctrine of divine omnipotence but seeks to reduce the terror that this induces by opening up a new way of understanding divine will.

In opposition to the Reformation, the Counterreformation attempted to reestablish the scholastic synthesis of philosophy and theology on a basis that took the nominalist challenge into account. Preeminent in this effort was Francisco Suarez. Suarez criticized the Ockhamist insistence that universals are merely words and that everything is radically individual, proclaiming the necessity of the distinction between essence and existence; but he also insisted that there are as many essences as existences, that is, that there are as many categories as there are individual things. He attacked Ockham and the other nominalists for what he characterized as moral positivism, but he also criticized Aquinas's theory of law for not emphasizing the will as the source of law. His revival of scholasticism was thus very much indebted to and informed by nominalism. His great compendium the *Disputationes Metaphysicae* and Aquinas's *Summa Theologica* continued to serve as secondary sources to Aristotle in the philosophy curriculum of schools run by the Jesuits and others, but the realism that was essential to scholasticism had become unbelievable. While scholasticism flourished in Spain until the seventeenth century, it was regarded in much of the rest of Europe as little more than a set of logical games, leading Erasmus, for example, to characterize it as "higher lunacy."[77]

The Counterreformation found a much surer source of support in skepticism, which clearly owes a great deal to nominalism.[78] The rediscovery of ancient skepticism that occurred in the late fifteenth and early sixteenth centuries with the reintroduction of the work of Sextus Empiricus certainly also played an important role, but this skepticism had long been known to Christianity through Augustine's *Against the Academics,* and most Christians had accepted his assertion that skepticism was overcome by revelation. The nominalist God, however, called into question the very certainty that Augustine's God guaranteed. Nominalism in this sense opened up the gates of faith to the skeptics' attacks by calling into question God's truthfulness. The Reformers' attempt to resurrect this Augustinian notion of divine illumination as the basis for inner certainty of faith and salvation was thus jeopardized from the outset by their conception of divine omnipotence, and they were hard put to defend themselves against the Counterreformation's skeptical arguments. Erasmus, for example, argued in his *On the Freedom of the Will* that the problem of free will was too difficult for humans to understand, and recommended a skeptical suspension of belief and adherence to the traditional views of the Church. Luther responded to this fideistic attack with his famous assertion that the "Holy Ghost is not a skeptic." The skeptical demand for an unquestionable criterion was used with great success by such Counterreformation thinkers as Gentian Herret to undermine the Reformation notion of inner certainty. This skepticism, however, was a sword that cut both ways. The Reformers were quick to learn from their antagonists and were only slightly less successful in using the same demand for a well-founded criterion to undermine the faith in the tradition that Erasmus and others advocated.

Skepticism was further developed as a critique of human knowledge by Montaigne in his "Apology for Raymond Sebond" and by Francisco Sanchez in his *Quod nihil scritur.*[79] Sanchez is particularly important to our discussion since his doctrine strongly influenced Descartes' two great contemporaries, Mersenne and Gassendi. Sanchez was a thoroughgoing nominalist who developed his argument for a mitigated skepticism not through a history of human ignorance and error, as Montaigne and Erasmus had done, but through a critique of Aristotle and scholasticism. He combined the most trenchant strains of both nominalism and skepticism. His arguments and the arguments of Montaigne as well as those of Montaigne's disciples Pierre Charron and Jean-Pierre Camus were extremely influential in Parisian intellectual society of the early seventeenth century, especially among the so-called *libertins* who occupied positions of social and political prominence. At the same time men like François Veron used these arguments against the Calvinists in the great public debates of the period.

DESCARTES AND THE DECEIVER GOD

The influence of nominalism was thus widespread in the early seventeenth century in the development of English empiricism, in the new science of nature, in the theology of the Reformation and Counterreformation, and in the growth of skepticism. However, if nominalism stands behind this revolution in the way of thinking that characterized the fifteenth and sixteenth centuries, it is the foreboding figure of the omnipotent God who stands behind nominalism, calling into question all the efforts of merely human reason to understand the world and denying the possibility of any kind of knowledge that transcends human reason.

It was the idea of such a God that Descartes had to face and that was the source of the question that lies behind his fundamental principle. Descartes' thought can thus be understood at least in part as the attempt to open up a space for man, a realm of freedom invulnerable to the powers of this God. The basis for this realm of human freedom is Descartes' *ego cogito ergo sum.*

Descartes first became acquainted with nominalism and the problem of the omnipotent God in the course of his education at La Flèche. He studied Aristotle and Aquinas in his course on metaphysics, and Suarez and Lessius in moral philosophy.[80] He was well acquainted with the realist position through Aquinas and Suarez and also with the nominalist position, which is extensively portrayed (although not always by name) in Suarez. His acquaintance with scholasticism and nominalism, however, was undoubtedly more extensive than this. Descartes claims to have read every book at La Flèche, including those on alchemy and magic (*Discourse,* AT, 6:5; CSM, 1:113). During this period or somewhat later he apparently read the works of the skeptics (*Discourse,* AT, 6:29; CSM, 1:125; *Replies,* AT, 7:130; CSM, 2:94). He also probably heard the great Counterreformation debater François Veron, who was at La Flèche, although it is unlikely that Descartes was his student as has sometimes been assumed.[81] It has been suggested that there may have been a nominalist strain at La Flèche and that Varon, possibly one of Descartes' teachers, is likely to have taught divine indifference.[82] It is thus fairly clear that Descartes left school with at least a general understanding of nominalism and the intellectual movements of his time that were indebted to nominalism.[83]

It is difficult, however, to determine the extent of Descartes' knowledge of nominalism and scholasticism in general. In his desire to portray his thought as originating *ab ovo,* he goes to considerable lengths to conceal his sources. Scholasticism with its interminable and fruitless debate had done little in Descartes' view to ameliorate human suffering or increase human power and freedom. Scholasticism saw human beings living in a closed universe in which there was no room for human freedom and initiative. While Descartes believed that a clean break with this past was necessary, he recognized that the conceptual universe in which he thought and wrote was fundamentally determined by scholasticism and that he had to use at least some of the language of scholasticism if he wanted to be understood.

Most of Descartes' knowledge of scholasticism clearly came through Suarez, who was probably the source of his knowledge of Augustine, John Scotus Erigena, Anselm, Bonaventure, and much of Aquinas, as well as Ockham and the nominalists Robert Holcot, Marsilius of Inghen, Gabriel Biel, Gerson, Peter d'Ailly, and Andreas of Newcastle.[84] Descartes was probably well acquainted with Duns Scotus from texts at La Flèche and certainly knew the mathematical work of the nominalist Nicholas of Oresme, the scientific works of Nicholas of Cusa, and at least the medical works of Francisco Sanchez.[85] He was also acquainted with many of the arguments about divine omnipotence and indifference from the work of Guillaume Gibieuf's *De libertate Dei et creatura,* but since this work was not published until 1630, it was probably not the original source of his ideas of divine omnipotence or divine deception.[86]

Indeed, the omnipotent God or at least his alter ego, the evil genius, had already made his appearance in Descartes' early, fragmentary work, the *Olympica.* This work purports to be an account of Descartes' three great dreams of 10 November 1619, which were decisive for his "marvelous" idea of a universal science. The fragmentary character of the work and the uncertainty of the text, however, make any interpretation problematic. The chief question that arises in this work is how the evil genius or evil spirit can be reconciled with the goodness and omnipotence of God. The solution to this problem developed in the *Olympica* follows a Stoic path akin to that of Montaigne and Renaissance humanism.

Descartes' idea of a universal science based upon mathematics represents an alternative to this Stoic path. During the nine years after his famous dreams Descartes devoted himself to the study of mathematics and science, especially optics and anatomy. For Descartes, the basis for his new science, laid down in the fragmentary *Rules,* was the certainty of intuition, "the undoubting conception of an unclouded and attentive mind" that "springs from the light of reason alone" (AT, 10:368; CSM, 1:14). Descartes' abandonment of the *Rules* was concomitant with a developing skeptical crisis that overcame him in the period 1628–29. The origin of this crisis is unclear, but Descartes' association with the *libertins* in Paris and the Oratorium circle around Cardinal Bérulle may have played some role in its development. This skeptical crisis led Descartes to abandon his naive reliance on intuition and natural reason as the basis of certainty in favor of a metaphysical solution.[87]

Descartes did not, however, abandon his idea of a universal science but sought to give it a metaphysical foundation. In a letter to Mersenne of 15 April 1630, he makes clear the connection of these metaphysical investigations to his science: "I believe that all those to whom God has given the use of reason are obliged to use it mainly to know Him and to know themselves. That is how I tried to begin my studies, and I would not have been able to find the basis for my physics if I had not looked for it along these lines" (AT, 1:135). He continues in the same letter, describing the importance of divine omnipotence in this metaphysics:

> Do not be afraid to proclaim everywhere that God established these laws in nature just as a sovereign establishes laws in his kingdom. . . .

One will tell you that if God established these truths, He would also be able to change them just as a king changes his laws; to which one should reply that it is possible if His will can change. But I understand these truths as eternal and unvarying in the same way that I judge God. His power is beyond comprehension, and generally we assume ourselves that God can do everything we are capable of understanding but not that He cannot do what we are incapable of understanding, for it would be presumptuous to think that our imagination has as much magnitude as His power. I hope to write all this within the next two weeks in my *Physics.* (AT, 1:135–36)

Descartes expands upon this in a letter to Mersenne of 27 May 1630, where he calls into question the necessity of eternal truths: God's will is eternal but there was no necessity that impelled him to create eternal truths and, therefore, they could be different (AT, 1:151).[88] He argues in a similar and perhaps even stronger manner in the *Replies* that "if anyone attends to the immeasurable greatness of God he will find it manifestly clear that there can be nothing whatsoever which does not depend on him. This applies not just to everything that subsists, but all order, every law, and every reason for anything being true or good" (AT, 7:435; CSM, 2:293–94).

These passages give us some idea of the importance of the divine omnipotence for Descartes. Descartes recognizes the tremendous problem that such a God entails but argues in his early thought that this God's will and the laws that it establishes cannot change because they, like God, are eternal. Such a theological assumption guarantees the truth of clear and distinct ideas that is the basis of his science. Descartes, however, does not explain why he believes God's will to be unvarying nor does he try to prove this claim. Moreover, he himself calls this claim into question with his assertion that God's power is incomprehensible. If we cannot comprehend the extent of God's power, we cannot know that his power and will are as unvarying as Descartes suggests. Thus, this theological solution to the problem of divine omnipotence, which Descartes may have borrowed from Duns Scotus, fails. Indeed, this solution to the problem of divine omnipotence is in many respects equivalent to the path of piety which, as we have seen, Descartes rejects in the *Meditations.* In this respect, it complements his solution to the problem in the *Rules* and perhaps even in the *Olympica,* both of which are more or less equivalent to the path of atheism which he also rejects in the *Meditations.* The failure of Descartes' early attempts to discover a foundation for his science that would secure it from the tyranny of the omnipotent God forces him in a new direction and leads him to construct a bastion against this God and his infinite powers. This is the project of Descartes' metaphysics.

The problem of divine omnipotence was probably unavoidable for Descartes once he had formulated the basic principles of his universal science, for this science rests upon assumptions about the relation of nature and God that are more or less identical to those of nominalism. The rejection of substantial forms, final causes, univocity, and syllogistic logic as well as the affirmation of divine indifference, God's will as efficient causality, symbolic mathematics, and matter as extension are common to both. His science, in this sense, rests upon a nominalistic foundation. Because of his insistence upon certainty and mathematics as the basis of this science, however, he is unable to follow the empiricist path of experience and probability. Because they did not seek to establish an absolutely certain science, Bacon and Hobbes did not have to face the problem of divine deception. For Descartes, by contrast, this problem was unavoidable, for, in Descartes' view, if we do not know certainly, we do not know at all.

Descartes' ultimate solution to this problem is his principle *ego cogito ergo sum*, which establishes a bastion and refuge from this all-powerful God. In this realm, certainty is guaranteed, and science prevails under the hegemony of the free human will. Contrary to what we might assume, this realm is not identical with atheism, for there is room for God himself therein. Within the walls that Descartes establishes, however, this God, like everyone and everything else, is subject to human laws, and thus can act only according to standards of reason established by Descartes' fundamental principle. *Ego cogito ergo sum* establishes a new notion of truth as certainty and a new notion of man as a free, self-positing, self-asserting being. The corollary of Descartes' famous principle, written in somewhat smaller letters upon his gateway and often overlooked by those fleeing before the omnipotent God, is perhaps equally illuminating for the character of modernity: "Abandon all doubt, ye who enter here."

That doubt has not disappeared is an indication that Descartes' bastion was not as secure as he assumed, an indication that the omnipotent God of nominalism found a way to pass through Descartes' magnificent fortifications. The story of this assault and ultimate conquest of the Cartesian citadel is the story of the omnipotent God and the absolute I. It is a story that begins with the Cartesian ego and passes through the thought of Fichte before coming to its ominous conclusion in the nineteenth and twentieth centuries.

Chapter Two

DESCARTES AND THE ORIGIN OF THE ABSOLUTE I

Ego cogito ergo sum is the bulwark that Descartes raises up against the omnipotent God and the radical skepticism that he engenders. It is his bastion for the defense of human reason and freedom. This principle, however, is not merely a bastion or refuge—it is also the Archimedean point upon which Descartes stands in his attempt to move the world, the basis for the universal science with which he seeks to win back the earth for man by dethroning this arbitrary and irrational God and making man the master and possessor of nature. Descartes thus does not merely strive to preserve some small portion of human freedom and reason in the face of the overwhelming onslaught of theological absolutism, but, much more audaciously, to gather together the forces of the human spirit for a massive counterattack that aims at reconquering nature and also, as we shall see, at subjecting this almighty God himself to the rule of reason.

This project rests on a new notion of thinking and being fundamentally at odds with both scholasticism and nominalism. Scholasticism, as we have seen, was based on ontological realism and conceived of thinking in terms of syllogistic logic. The nominalist revolution rejected the extramental existence of universals in favor of a radical individualism, and abandoned syllogistic logic in favor of a logic of signs. The world that this new way of thinking posits is not intrinsically rational but factual, that is, it is made (from the Latin *facere*, 'to make') by naming. Thinking, as nominalism understands it, is a giving and connecting of names. Insofar as all general names are distortions of reality, however, thinking attains only probable or hypothetical knowledge and even this knowledge is rendered problematic by the towering form of nominalism's omnipotent God.

While Descartes draws on both these traditions, he ultimately rejects them and develops a new way of thinking. In his view, neither can defend knowledge against divine omnipotence and radical skepticism. Scholastic logic is merely a form of rhetoric that gives the appearance of verisimilitude to the speech of those who know nothing (*Discourse,* AT, 6:17; CSM, 1:119; *Rules,* AT, 10:379–80, 406; CSM, 1:20, 36–37; *Search,* AT, 10:516; CSM, 2:410–11). Nominalism merely reduces the world to a chaos of matter in motion and imagines knowledge to consist merely in giving names to sensations and connecting these names into statements (*Replies,* AT, 7:182–83; CSM, 2:128). Knowledge and sensation, however, are two different things: knowing is not just uniting names but "the things signified by names" (*Replies,* AT, 7:178; CSM, 2:126). Descartes admires and shares the Baconian desire for a universal science that will explain the causal connections of all things, but he sees great pitfalls in the nominalist path of Bacon and Hobbes. Their reliance upon experience is especially troubling, for while it allows them to draw many probable and useful conclusions, it can never attain the certainty necessary to preserve science and human dignity from the attacks of theological absolutism and radical skepticism.

THINKING AS INTUITION IN DESCARTES' *RULES FOR THE DIRECTION OF THE MIND*

What is necessary in Descartes' view is a universal science such as Bacon had imagined, based, however, not on mere experience but on experience understood and analyzed by a new way of thinking. Descartes' model for this new way of thinking is mathematics. He is able to restructure all other forms of knowledge on the model of mathematics, however, only because he first rethinks mathematics itself.[1] Indeed, mathematics strictly defined is subsumed along with all of the other substantive sciences into this new way of thinking, the *mathesis universalis,* or universal science, with which Descartes hopes to conquer nature and subdue the omnipotent God.

The aim of thinking, as Descartes sees it, is not contemplation but action, and he consequently seeks knowledge of eternal truths not for their own sake but to enable man to understand the world and turn it to his use (*Discourse,* AT, 6:61–63; CSM, 1:142–43). Descartes thus does not seek the most profound knowledge of the highest things but certain and evident knowledge of what is close at hand. He is not concerned with the knowledge of what things ultimately are but with how they are conjoined and affect one another. He believes that this knowledge can be attained only as the result of correct judgment. Hence, he begins his *Rules* with the declaration that "the aim of our studies should be to direct the mind with a view to forming true and sound judgments about whatever comes before it" (AT, 10:359; CSM, 1:9).

Judgment is affirming or denying that something is the case, that two or more things belong together. For example, we judge that body and extension belong together in the assertion "Body is extension." Judgment is thus the basis of all thinking. Judgments, however, often go astray, and we act on the basis of prejudice and opinion. In order to attain the certain and evident knowledge necessary for a universal science, it is thus necessary to understand the source of false judgments and to articulate a method or rule that will help avoid such errors.

The source of error, as Descartes sees it, is our mistaken reliance upon the senses and imagination, neither of which can provide certain knowledge. This reliance leads us to the false conclusion that the truth is to be discovered in the realm of objects. This faith in the senses arises in childhood when the mind is so dependent upon the body and the senses that it comes to accept their testimony as valid. We thus accept the independent existence of objects without question. Even when we become adults and attain a measure of independence from the body and are able to judge matters more truly, we often succumb to prejudices. While we may recognize them as false, we cannot banish them from our minds and they continually return to inform our thinking whenever we cease to hold the proof of their falsity before us. Moreover, the effort required to think without the aid of the senses and the imagination, which is necessary to true judgment, quickly fatigues the mind and throws us back upon our prejudices. Finally, in order to think we must attach our concepts to words, but we thereby lose touch with the reality these words represent and consequently think and speak without truly understanding (*Principles*, AT, 8A:33–38; CSM, 1:217–221).

What is needed in Descartes' view is a method for directing the mind toward certain and evident knowledge. This method is laid out in the *Rules*. The truth about the natural world may be hidden but it is not occult, and occult powers are thus not needed to uncover it.[2] The basis for true knowledge is found in the certainty of intuition, which grasps what is innate and eternal:

> By "intuition" I do not mean the fluctuating testimony of the senses or the deceptive judgment of the imagination as it botches things together, but the conceptions of a clear and attentive mind, which is so easy and distinct that there can be no room for doubt about what we understand. Alternatively, and this comes to the same thing, intu-

ition is the indubitable conception of a clear and attentive mind which proceeds solely from the light of reason. Because it is simpler, it is more certain than deduction . . . Thus everyone can mentally intuit that he exists, that he thinks, that a triangle is bounded by just three lines, a sphere by a single surface, and the like. Perceptions such as these are more numerous than most people realize, disdaining as they do to turn their minds to such simple matters. (AT, 10:368; CSM, 1:14)

With this notion of intuition, Descartes moves beyond both scholasticism and nominalism. Deduction is relegated to a secondary role and experience devalued as a source of error (AT, 10:365–66; CSM, 1:12). The new basis of knowledge is the intuition of those truths made evident by the light of reason alone, by what Descartes calls our natural light. The intuition of these simple things cannot be false because they are directly seen and not the product of judgment (AT, 10:420, 432; CSM, 1:45, 53). Indeed, they are the basis of all judgments and as such cannot be deduced (AT, 10:370; CSM, 1:15).

Since the certainty of intuition depends upon the immediacy of mental vision, the number of axioms available through simple intuition is relatively small. Thus, deduction is necessary as an aid to intuition (AT, 10:368–70, 383; CSM, 1:14–15, 22).[3] Truths which are not immediately evident can be grasped through a series of judgments that are intuitively certain at each step. Deduction thus rests on immediate intuition. Since the mind cannot encompass such a series in a single gaze, however, deduction also depends on memory, which can err. The errors of memory can be minimized in relatively uncomplicated deductions by repeated and ever more rapid repetitions of the proof until the entire series can be grasped in a single intuition. For more extensive proofs, the enumeration of the intuitions at the various steps will minimize error. Intuition in this way is essential to all discursive reasoning.

The system of thought built up in this way constitutes true knowledge. Indeed, in Descartes' view we truly know only the simple things and their intermixture (AT, 10:421–27; CSM, 1:46–49). It is quite difficult, however, to separate these simple things from one another as well as from sensation. Descartes argues that the mind can attain this goal only by turning toward itself and dispensing with all images of the imagination, in this way coming to grasp such simple but unimaginable things as doubt, ignorance, unity and duration (AT, 10:419–20; CSM, 1:44–45). The imagination cannot distinguish between such simple things as body and extension because the differences between them are purely intellectual (AT, 10:444–45; CSM, 1:60).

Such intellectual things are pure because they are not corrupted by the images that derive from sensation and appear in the imagination. This purity, however, leads to a certain problem: purely intellectual things are severed from the actuality they are supposed to inform and explain. This problem arises for Descartes because his notion of intuition is modeled on the neo-Platonic, Augustinian notion of divine illumination. This disjunction was of little concern to Augustine and the neo-Platonists because their goal was knowledge not of this world but of a world to come, and this required not a universal science but a knowledge of God and his will. While such a doctrine may have served Augustine's purposes well, it presents real problems for Descartes, since it sunders the mental and physical worlds. Descartes thus needs a bridge between the realm of eternal truths and the realm of the senses.

In Descartes' early thought, this bridge is the imagination.[4] It is the common ground on which the raw material of sensation and the concepts of the intuition meet to form ideas. Pure concepts such as "manyness" are given a determinant and differentiated form in the imagination in terms of geometric figures and proportions. All conceptual relationships in this way can be understood in terms of plane figures which can be precisely analyzed by a general algebra. In this way, science can organize the eternal truths revealed by the intuition into a rational system which is more than a mere nominalist system of signs, since it grasps what truly is, and yet is fundamentally different from the ontological categories of scholasticism.

While intuition is the basis of Descartes' universal science, the figural representation in the imagination of the truths made available by the intuition is the crucial link between the intellect and the senses that makes this science possible (*Burman*, AT, 5:176–77).[5] The intellect alone knows, but it employs the imagination's powers of representation as an aid to understanding. The intellect in this sense is helped or hindered by imagination, sensation, and memory (AT, 10:398, CSM, 1:32). Ordinarily, external things impress themselves upon the senses and these impressions are transmitted via the common sense to the imagination. Here the form of these impressions is abstracted by the intellect and represented figurally (AT, 10:444–45; CSM, 1:60). The being of external things is grasped on the basis of this representation as extension and the external world is understood as the *res extensa*. As representations, these forms then can be analyzed by application of the figures derived from the intuition. Nature, grasped as *res extensa,* thus can be mathematically described and comprehended.

This conjunction of intuition and sensation in the imagination is the basis for judgment. The impressions of objects, transmitted by the senses, broken down into their constituent parts by the intellect, and represented in the imagination as extension, are compared to the forms made available by the intuition and given determinate form by the imagination. On this basis, the intellect is able to affirm the represented form as necessary or possible or to deny it as an impossibility (AT, 10:420; CSM, 1:45). This determination of possibility is only the beginning of science. Many different orders of connections of things are possible. Once the possible connections are determined, it is necessary to perform experiments to ascertain which connections inform actuality. The basis for judgment and for Descartes' universal science as a whole is thus the certain and evident knowledge made available by intuition and given figural form in the imagination. It becomes the standard against which all experience and all nature is judged.

Judgment goes astray only when we compound elements in the imagination without reference to the intuition. Some of these judgments may accidentally be true, but they are not certain. Descartes does not mean to suggest that we should reject all such speculative judgments, since he recognizes that the pressure of the moment often requires us to act. We must recognize, though, that these judgments are conjectural and give us at best only "moral certainty" (*Principles,* AT, 9B:327; CSM, 1:289–90). The only certain road to truth is self-evident deduction that encompasses all simple natures and the relationships between them. The result is a deductive science that establishes the causal connections of all things.

THINKING AS WILLING IN DESCARTES' LATER THOUGHT

This notion of intuition as the foundation of knowledge is replaced in Descartes' later thought by his fundamental principle, *ego cogito ergo sum.* This was apparently the result of a skeptical crisis engendered by his recognition of the problem posed by the idea of an omnipotent God. While Descartes had been aware in a general way of the idea of divine omnipotence from an early age, he had never really appreciated all of its ramifications, especially for the certainty of mathematics, since he had assumed that the inner light of intuition was a reflection of divine wisdom and therefore certain. He came to see, however, that if God were truly omnipotent, this light might be false and the truths that it revealed merely illusions. It also became clear to him that the mere possibility that such a God exists—and not his actual existence—was sufficient to undermine the certainty of intuition and science.

Descartes' recognition of the need for certainty arose from his experience of the skepticism of his time and his recognition of the inadequacy of the probabilistic arguments to combat it. This skepticism, as we have seen, was itself a by-product of the doctrine of divine omnipotence. Thus, divine omnipotence played an important if indirect role in establishing certainty as the criterion of Cartesian science. Already in the *Rules*, Descartes had expressed real doubts about the truth of sensation, imagination, and memory. His explicit recognition of the possibility of deception by an omnipotent God evoked more profound doubts. None of the modes of thinking he had previously delineated could provide a foundation for truth that is immune to the skepticism that this God engenders. To discover such a *fundamentum absolutum inconcussum veritatis*, Descartes realized he would have to develop a new ground for judgment.

In the *Rules*, Descartes recognized four cognitive capacities: understanding, imagination, sensation, and memory (AT, 10:411; CSM, 1:39).[6] This account is expanded and transformed in his later thought. A thing that thinks *(res cogitans)*, Descartes claims in the Second Meditation, is a thing that doubts, understands, affirms, denies, wills, refuses, imagines, and senses (AT, 7:28; CSM, 2:19). In the Third Meditation, he characterizes himself as a thinking thing who doubts, affirms, denies, knows a few things, is ignorant of many, loves, hates, wills, desires and also imagines and senses (AT, 7:34; CSM, 2:24). Thought for Descartes is everything that we are immediately conscious of and falls into four general categories: will (which includes doubt, affirmation, denial, rejection, love, and hate), understanding, imagination, and sensation (*Replies*, AT, 7:160; CSM, 2:113).[7] In the later *Principles*, he argues that there is an even more comprehensive division of thinking into two modes: (1) perception or the operation of the intellect which includes sensation, imagination, and the conception of things purely intellectual, and (2) action of the will that includes desiring, holding in aversion, affirming, denying, and doubting (AT, 9B:17; CSM 1:204). Finally, in the *Passions* he describes the two categories of thinking which he noted in the *Prin-*

ciples as the two basic functions of the soul, its actions and its passions
(AT, 11:342–49; CSM, 1:335–39).[8] In general, actions are equivalent to the will, and passions to perceptions or forms of understanding. The will includes those actions that terminate in the soul, such
as the love of God and thoughts of nonmaterial objects, and those
that terminate in the body and lead to voluntary motion. The passions or perceptions of the soul include those that have the soul as
their cause (the perceptions of willing, the imagination of things that
do not exist, and the consideration of things solely intellectual, such
as knowledge of God and the soul), and those that have the body as
their cause (such as sensation) (*Burman,* AT 5:154).[9] However, only
those that originate in the body are passions properly speaking, for
those that originate in the soul are both actions and passions or perceptions and, according to Descartes, take their name from the
nobler faculty of actions. Moreover, even those passions that have
their origin in the body depend in part upon the action of the will
that brings them before the understanding, allowing them to be perceived.

This new notion of thinking reworks the account presented in the
Rules in decisive ways. Ordinarily, external objects impress their
forms on the senses which transmit these forms by means of the
nerves to the brain and more specifically to the pineal gland, which
Descartes believed was the primary link between the body and soul.
Sensation in this sense is the lowest part of the mind or soul and exists
only insofar as the mind is conjoined to the body.[10] Still it is the soul
and not the body that senses (*Dioptrics,* AT, 6:109; *Replies,* AT,
7:132–33; CSM, 2:95–96). In the brain, this sense impression causes
an image in the imagination, which Descartes conceives in his later
thought as little more than a "screen" upon which images are projected, the back side of the brain or pineal gland, as it were (*Meditations,* AT, 7:27–28; CSM, 2:18–19).

This process is imperfect, prey to both illusions and delusions.
Illusions which occur at the limits of the physical capacities of our
nerves cause remediable errors. Delusions, by contrast, are the consequence of the disruption of the biological mechanism by which
impressions are transmitted to the brain. Biological processes, which
Descartes calls "animal spirits," can produce changes in the brain that
mimic the senses and give rise in the imagination to images for which
there are no corresponding objects in the world. This is the source of
madness and dreams which render the imagination itself untrustworthy. Thinking thus cannot rely upon sensation and imagination.

Asleep or awake we should be persuaded only by reason (*Discourse,* AT 6:39; CSM, 1:131). Indeed, in Descartes' view we conceive bodies not with the senses or the imagination but only with the intellect; the sensing faculty is passive and useless without the faculty for producing ideas (*Meditations,* AT, 7:79; CSM, 2:55). These ideas are then conjoined in judgments. As in his early thought, judgment remains central for Descartes, but the substantive character of judgment has changed.

For the mature Descartes, judgment is the combination of two different mental capacities, will and understanding. The understanding, which was the primary element in judgment in Descartes' early thought, is passive in the later period, supplanted by the will. The role of the will in judgment, however, can be understood only in the context of its more extensive role in Descartes' later conception of thinking itself.

The will is the active force in perception and directs the understanding toward the images in the imagination. Through will, the understanding becomes active as *percipere* (from *per-,* 'by'; and *capere,* 'to grasp'). Moreover, the will stimulates the brain to form images as an aid to understanding, usurping the previous function of the imagination. Similarly, it displaces the intuition as the agency that summons up the innate ideas and brings them before the understanding (*Replies,* AT, 7:188–89; CSM, 2:132). Thus, while judgment is nominally a combination of will and understanding, Descartes maintains that it is fundamentally a determination of the will (*Comments on a Certain Broadsheet,* AT, 8B:363; CSM, 1:307). On the basis of its judgments, the will then motivates the body either to pursue or to refuse that which judgment has either affirmed or denied. In Descartes' mature works, thinking in all of its forms is thus understood to be crucially bound up with and dependent upon the will.[11]

This emphasis on will is an intrinsic part of Descartes' attempt to find a secure basis for human freedom and reason in the face of the omnipotent God. While his early notion of thinking as intuition and understanding drew heavily on ancient rationalism, his subordination of intuition and understanding to will rests upon the nominalist vision of man as a willing being. In his attempt to construct a bastion against the transrational God of will, Descartes attempts to refound reason upon an inherent human will that is invulnerable to divine deception.

This conjunction of will and thinking is the basis of Descartes' fundamental principle, *ego cogito ergo sum*. As we have seen, this principle is the conclusion of the path of doubt. In our previous consideration of this path, we accepted doubt as self-evident. As a result of our intervening examination, however, it has become clear that doubt has a more specific meaning for Descartes than we previously recognized: it is a form of thinking in general and of will in particular.[12]

As a form of will doubt seems to be unique. In his description of the will in the *Replies, Principles,* and *Passions,* Descartes includes doubt, affirmation, denial, love, hate, desiring, and refusing (AT, 8A:17, 11:342–43, 7:377; CSM, 1:204, 335–36, 2:259). What is clear from even a superficial examination is that with the exception of doubt the forms of will are paired opposites. This is not surprising. Will involves choice; and affirmation and denial, love and hate, and desiring and refusing are the alternatives of choice. In these enumerations, doubt has no opposite. Thus, either doubt does not involve choice in the same way that the other forms of will do or Descartes has concealed the opposite of doubt.

One would expect doubt to be paired with belief or faith. The absence of belief in his account is not difficult to understand. Traditionally, belief begins where knowledge ends, that is, where we can in principle have no proof of truth or falsity. Belief, in other words, is judgment without a foundation. Scholastic science accepted such judgments because they seemed to rest on God, who was the most certain thing of all. The universal science that Descartes sought to establish, however, was a system of well-founded judgments that did not rely upon God and were invulnerable to his potential deception. Faith consequently had no place in Descartes' science.

The Cartesian alternative to faith is certainty. Certainty, though, has much in common with belief or faith, for it is the result of the persuasion of the intellect by an inner or natural light. It persuades us because we cannot believe otherwise. Indeed, this notion of truth as certainty draws upon the neo-Platonic conception of truth which also characterized the Lutheran and Calvinist notion of the certainty of salvation. Descartes thus returns in a roundabout way to Augustine's view that faith is the answer to skepticism, although his new faith is divorced from the divine. Certainty rests not upon a divine guarantee but upon indubitability. What is certain is the indubitable and what is dubitable is the uncertain. There is thus a necessary and inescapable relation between doubt and certainty identical to that between affirmation and negation or desiring and refusing.

Understood in this light, the role of doubt within the will becomes clear. Doubt like all other forms of will has its opposite. This opposite, however, is not simply another form of will narrowly understood. It is rather the certainty that is the essence of understanding. This is already apparent in Descartes' description of thinking in the *Meditations,* where he describes a thinking thing as a thing which doubts, understands, affirms, denies, desires, refuses, and which also imagines and senses (AT, 7:28; CSM, 2:19). In this series, doubt is paired with understanding in a manner similar to that of the other forms of the will. The exact meaning of this connection of doubt and understanding, however, is unclear. On one hand, it seems to indicate the decisive and unique role that doubt plays within the will, since it is the opposite of understanding, another primary mental capacity. On the other hand, it seems to suggest that the understanding itself may be a form of will (*Replies,* AT, 7:144–45; CSM, 2:103). The relationship of doubt and understanding, however, is more complex. While doubt is the opposite of certainty or understanding, it is also the means for attaining understanding, since it sets the standards of certainty. The certain is the indubitable. Doubt for Descartes is not an end in itself as it was for Socrates and Montaigne, but a means to an end that is higher and more useful to man, a universal science that will allow man to secure himself from the ravages of an omnipotent God and become the master and possessor of nature. Insofar as this science pursues theory simply in the service of practice, however, it itself becomes an instrument in the hands of the will that seeks to master and appropriate nature. The will as doubt thus aims not at the aporetic wisdom of Socrates or Montaigne, or the theoretical wisdom of Aristotle and the scholastics, but at the scientific comprehension of the world that seeks the secrets of nature only in order to provide practical benefits to man. Understanding the causal connections between all things, man can interrupt and redirect the motions of nature to his own ends. This knowledge is the Archimedean point that will make it possible for one man, using only his will and bodily power, to move the world. The will as doubt seeks its own negation in science in order to reconstitute itself in a higher and more powerful form for the conquest of the world. Science and understanding in other words become mere tools of the will.

In order to master nature, man must first become master of himself. The initial goal of the will on the path of doubt is thus self-liberation and self-creation. Man, as Descartes understands him, is enchained by illusions that arise from his own finitude or are imposed upon him by an omnipotent deceiver. The will as doubt is able to free

man from these illusions and establish the foundations for true judgment and thus free action. Doubt is not judgment but a decision that
no judgment can be made with certainty, that a question remains that
makes it impossible either to affirm or to deny the case in question.
Doubt thus is the recognition of the absence of an inner light that
reveals the truth as the truth. As such, it is also the decision not to
decide unless there are clear and evident grounds that impel it in one
way or another. In pursuit of certainty, the will as doubt thus rejects
everything that it cannot unequivocally affirm as true, that is, everything which it can in the least doubt.

Of course, there is no guarantee that this path of doubt will lead
to truth, since everything may be dubitable. Descartes, for example,
doubts the laws of mathematics and even the law of contradiction.
This path does guarantee, however, that we will not give our assent
to dubious things. It thus prevents us from being deceived and acting in ways that contradict our best interests (*Principles*, AT, 8A:6;
CSM, 1:194).

The assertion of the will as doubt leads to the rejection of everything we derive from sensation, imagination, and even the understanding (including that which is revealed by the intuition). In this
way, the will demonstrates its superiority to the other cognitive
capacities and asserts its freedom from both God and his creation.[13]
Whether this world is eternal chaos or the product of a beneficent
God or evil genius, the will's capacity to doubt guarantees freedom
from deception. The path of the will as doubt is thus the beginning
of the path of liberation from all arbitrary and irrational authority
(*Principles*, AT, 8A:6–7; CSM, 1:194–95; *Search*, AT, 10:525; CSM,
2:418).

While the will as doubt is able to free itself from all external constraints, the freedom that it attains remains merely negative unless it
can find some ground both for its own existence and for a positive
knowledge of the world that will allow it to assert itself effectively in
the pursuit of its own well-being. Without such a positive self-assertion, the will remains a merely destructive force that purchases freedom at the price of peace and sanity. A purely negative will is independent, but it is also ignorant not merely of the world but of its
own existence. Indeed, as radical doubt the will shatters both the
world and itself into a million pieces, leading Descartes to suppose
that he and the world are nothing (*Meditations*, AT, 7:21–22; CSM
2:14–15). The will's freedom through doubt is the freedom of the
void.

This is the point which Descartes' thought has attained at the beginning of the Second Meditation. He has freed himself from all deception but has also shattered himself and the world. He asserts that he seems to have fallen into very deep water and is unable to set his feet on the bottom, to swim, or to support himself on the surface. This lostness of the will, however, does not lead to paralysis. In the *Discourse,* Descartes suggested that someone in this situation proceed like a man who is lost in a woods by striking off in one direction and persevering until he finds his way out (AT, 6:24; CSM, 1:123). Descartes follows his own advice here, deciding to continue on the path of doubt until he finds something that is indubitable or at least until he knows indubitably that everything is uncertain. As we have seen, it is this path that leads to Descartes' fundamental principle.

The initial difficulty in coming to grips with this principle is its deceptive form. "I think, therefore I am" seems to be the minor premise and conclusion of a syllogism. If this were the case, there would have to be a suppressed major premise, of the form "Everything that thinks is." Such a premise, however, would depend upon knowledge that was prior to the principle itself, and this would mean that the principle was not fundamental. Descartes rejects interpreting the principle as a syllogism (*Replies,* AT, 7:140; CSM, 2:100). While some scholars attempt to construe the principle syllogistically, most generally agree that this cannot be Descartes' intention.[14] Given his rejection of syllogistic logic, it seems unlikely that he would ground his thought on a syllogism.

If we reject the syllogistic interpretation, however, we must find an alternative explanation for the principle. Descartes' assertion that it is based on a simple act of mental vision suggests that it is an intuition (*Replies,* AT, 7:140–41; CSM, 2:100). He asserts, however, that intuitions and the simple things made available by intuition cannot be the basis for truth. Indeed, it was the rejection of intuition that set him on the path of doubt. Moreover, what is truly simple and innate in this principle is not the conjunction of thought and existence but thought and existence in themselves. These simple things are known immediately, but the principle only as a result of reasoning.

Descartes' fundamental principle is not the conclusion of a syllogism or an intuition but a judgment and thus an act of the will. He characterizes it as such in the *Discourse* and the *Principles* (AT, 6:33; 8A:8–9; CSM, 1:127, 196). In the *Meditations,* however, he calls it a necessary conclusion (AT, 7:25; CSM, 2:16–17). He means by this not that it is a logical conclusion, but that it is the conclusion of a judgment, the affirmation of a necessary connection. It is necessary to distinguish here between the proposition that is at the heart of the principle and the recognition and assertion of this proposition *as* the fundamental principle. The truth of the principle resides not in its logical *form* but in the *act* of judgment or will that establishes it as fundamental.[15] The statements "I think, therefore I am," "This proposition: 'I am, I exist,' is necessarily true every time I pronounce it or it is conceived in my mind," and "I doubt, therefore I am" are not logically true but are necessarily true whenever they are asserted by the will. Descartes describes this necessity of the will in the *Principles*: "It cannot be that, when I make this judgment, my mind which is making the judgment, does not exist" (AT, 8A:9; CSM, 2:16–17). In this sense Descartes' fundamental principle is the will's judgment and affirmation of itself as necessary and indubitable; it is, in other words, the will's self-grounding act, its self-creation.[16]

The mechanism of this self-grounding, self-validating act of the will is made somewhat clearer by Descartes in his explanation of the certainty of this and other truths in the *Replies*: "We cannot doubt them unless we think of them; but we cannot think of them without at the same time believing that they are true . . . Hence we cannot doubt them without at the same time believing they are true; that is, we can never doubt them" (AT, 7:145–46; CSM, 2:104; cf. *Principles*, AT, 9B:9–10; CSM, 1:183–84). What becomes apparent in this passage is the crucial role that the will as doubt plays in establishing the truth of these propositions. Doubt, as we have seen, is the means which the will employs to free itself from deception and error by rejecting all that is dubitable or uncertain. It is thus the means by which man frees himself from both God and his creation. As we have seen, however, this is achieved only by a negation of both God and the world that leaves the will in an apparent vacuum. The heart of Descartes' fundamental principle is his discovery that the will cannot doubt or negate itself, that such a negation is in fact a self-affirmation.[17] In this manner, the will constitutes itself as an I that is utterly free and invulnerable to all deception; it is reborn, as it were, out of its own destruction (AT, 7:12; CSM, 2:9). This is the act through which the will constitutes itself as a self and thus as the foundation or subject upon which everything can be established.[18] Indeed, since it arises out of the universal negation of doubt, the subject has no other position than the one it constructs.

The self-confirming or self-validating character of the will's assertion of itself does not rest on the law of noncontradiction or on the peculiar character of first-person assertions, as some have argued, but upon the intrinsic reflexive character of all thinking and all willing.[19] The precise nature of this reflexivity, however, remains obscure as long as we grasp it only in terms of our vague, everyday notions of self-consciousness or subjectivity. We thus must try to determine more carefully what Descartes means by the reflexivity of thinking.

SELF-CONSCIOUSNESS AND THE WILL

While Descartes is often credited with the discovery of self-consciousness, he was not the first to recognize that human beings have a capacity for thinking about their own thinking. Plato asserts in the *First Alcybiades* that the soul has the capacity to contemplate itself, and Aristotle suggests in the *Nichomachean Ethics* that human beings can be conscious of their own perceptions.[20] This ancient notion, however, has little in common with what Descartes means by self-consciousness. Plato and Aristotle argued that man's being is essentially determined by nature or reason and not by the capacity to contemplate one's own thinking. To be self-conscious in the sense that modern continental thought from Descartes to Hegel understands it, however, is to be something in and for oneself, that is, to be free from nature and reason in a way that would have seemed perverse to the ancients.

Self-consciousness assumes the unity of mind and its object, and for the ancients, as Aristotle makes clear, this is possible only for beings that are free of matter, and thus independent and self-sufficient.[21] The only such being, according to Aristotle, is the prime mover, whom he characterizes in the *Metaphysics* as the thinking of thinking.[22] As material beings, humans are not self-sufficient and are determined in large part by objects other than themselves. Human beings thus typically come to know themselves not through introspection but by examining their acts. Only the philosopher who is elevated above matter into a divinity akin to that of the prime mover is capable of pure intuitive introspection.

The modern notion of self-consciousness rejects the notion of man as an essentially natural being and redefines him on the model of the prime mover as fundamentally free and self-sufficient. This transformation owes a great deal to Augustine, although he drew extensively on neo-Platonic thought and Plotinus in particular. Following Aristotle, Plotinus attributes self-consciousness to the highest being, *nous* or mind, but in contradistinction to Aristotle, he asserts that human beings periodically participate in *nous*. To this extent, they are self-conscious in the fullest sense.[23] Augustine adopts this view and attributes self-consciousness to man insofar as he is an image of this God. However, even for Augustine self-consciousness is at best only a secondary capacity of the human soul. Human beings have access to fundamental truths not through reflection but by means of divine illumination.

Whatever its ultimate status in Augustine, this notion of self-consciousness played little role in scholasticism, which accepted the Aristotelian notion that the soul knows itself through its own acts. The modern notion of self-consciousness grows out of a revival of Augustinianism among such Franciscan thinkers as Scotus and Ockham, who argue in Augustinian fashion that knowledge of our psychic experience is unqualifiedly evident and intuitive.[24] Neither Scotus nor Ockham, however, deploys a developed notion of self-consciousness. In fact, neither even conceives of self-consciousness as primary or fundamental.

This tradition lays the groundwork for the modern concept of self-consciousness, but it was only with Descartes that this concept first appeared. Descartes developed the concept in response to a skeptical crisis engendered by his recognition of the problem posed for human knowledge by the idea of divine omnipotence. The problem of skepticism, however, cannot by itself explain Descartes' response, since Augustine's thought was also constructed as an answer to skepticism.[25] To understand the decisive role that Descartes assigns to self-consciousness and human freedom, we must thus examine the differences between Augustine and Descartes.

The problem faced by Augustine and nearly all other thinkers in late antiquity was the problem of the origin of evil. In part, this was the result of the deterioration of social and political life, but it was also due to the inability of ancient philosophy to explain how a rational cosmos could contain evil. This problem was particularly acute for Christianity, for it recognized the existence of evil and offered a remedy to it, but was hard put to explain its origin. In fact, many thinkers, including the young Augustine, discerned what they believed to be a contradiction in the Christian notion of God as creator and redeemer. If a redeemer was necessary, it could only be because of a malicious creation. God in other words must be both infinitely malicious and infinitely beneficent. Manicheanism in this respect offered an attractive alternative: there was not one god but two, an evil god of creation and a good god of salvation. On the surface such a divine dualism appeared preferable to a contradictory monotheism. The defense of Christianity consequently depended upon the demonstration of both divine unity and beneficence. This was made possible by the doctrine of free will, which located the source of evil not in God but in man. For Augustine, the problem of evil thus can be resolved only by the individual reformation of human beings made possible by Christianity.

While this explanation of the origin of evil removes the objection that God is contradictory, it does not make his unity comprehensible. This is achieved by analogy to the reflexivity of the human soul. Since human beings are created in God's image, they can gain some insight into the constitution of divine being by examining their own being. They see in themselves the unity of thinking, willing, and feeling. Both human beings and God in this way are a three in one, a trinity. We can thus understand God by understanding our own thinking. In this way, Augustine uses self-consciousness to defend God.

Descartes' problem was of a completely different nature. Augustine had to reconcile the goodness, justice, and rationality of God with his omnipotence in order to remove the Manichean threat to Christianity. For Descartes, the chief danger is not to God but to man himself, and the chief source of danger is not a Manichean gnosticism that is opposed to God but a skepticism that arises out of divine omnipotence. Descartes thus employs self-consciousness not to defend God but to defend man from God and ultimately to establish a new basis for man, the world, and God himself.[26]

Descartes does not merely give the traditional notion of self-consciousness a new role in his thought but fundamentally transforms it. As we have seen, self-consciousness was understood in both antiquity and the Middle Ages as an act of intuition and thus as a species of contemplation. It was thought to be passive rather than active. Thinking in this sense is a reflection of nature or the eternal forms. In thinking of a triangle, Aristotle tells us in *De anima*, the mind becomes a triangle.[27] Only in Plotinus does *nous* take on a more active character, and there only for the prime mover.[28] This *nous poietes* provides the basis for divine will in Augustine and thus by derivation for the human will as well, although it is never consistently employed in the discussion of human self-consciousness by either Augustine or scholasticism. Thus, while the potentiality for a more active notion of self-consciousness was present for antiquity and scholasticism, neither developed such a notion.[29]

Descartes rejects this traditional notion of self-consciousness as a species of contemplation. It is not one element of thinking but a characteristic of every act of thought. He makes this idea clearer in a letter to Mersenne of July 1641: "I have demonstrated that the soul is nothing other than a thing that thinks; it is therefore impossible that we can ever think of anything without having at the same time the idea of our soul, as of a thing capable of thinking all that we think about" (AT, 3:394; cf. *Principles,* AT, 8A:7; CSM, 1:195). All thinking as thinking is also always self-thinking. All thinking, including even sensation, is thus necessarily reflective.[30] The mind reflects in the first instance not the world or the forms but itself. It is not dependent upon anything beyond itself; it is fundamentally free.

In asserting the reflexivity of all thinking or the universality of self-consciousness in all consciousness, Descartes does not mean that the thinking self is presented alongside what is thought as if it were simply another object. Descartes recognized that such a notion was untenable, since it leads to an infinite regress (*Meditations,* AT, 7:50; CSM, 2:34). We can certainly think of ourselves and our thinking in this way—indeed in many respects this seems to be chiefly what Descartes' predecessors had in mind when they spoke of the thinking of thinking—but this is *not* Descartes' notion of self-consciousness.[31]

In order to understand what Descartes means by self-consciousness, we need to return to his analysis of thinking. For Aristotle, thinking consists in repeating in oneself the actual connections between things in the world. No such immediate connection to the world is possible in Descartes' view, for the world does not present itself to us in its truth and we are not able simply to identify ourselves with it. Rather the raw material of sensation is gathered together and reconstructed by the intellect and represented in the imagination in its essence and truth according to a scheme constructed by intuition or the will. The world thus ceases to be simply available to us through the senses and becomes the *res extensa* that is susceptible to mathematical analysis and technological control. We are able to understand and master nature in this way, however, only because thinking at its very core reflects first itself and only then the world. Thinking is thus poetic in the Greek sense as *poiēsis,* a making that first makes itself and then the world for this self through representation. While this is implicit in Descartes' early notion of imagination, it becomes much clearer in his recognition of the essential role of the will in this representational appropriation and reconstruction of the world.

What does it mean though to say that thinking in the first instance is always a self-thinking, and only then a thinking of objects? The immediate apprehension that characterized thinking for the ancients allowed one to lose oneself in the object. Thinking, as Descartes understands it, can never lose itself in the object, since it stands at one remove from the world, present in each act of thinking and thus in each object. Indeed, it is the object that in a sense is lost in the subject, abstracted from its natural surroundings and established in an artificial realm of the self's devising, re-presented on the screen of the imagination by a self-willing will. All thinking in this sense is poetic, a formative willing of the world. The self that is present in every act of thought is constructed as the subject for whom the representation is, as the spectator or audience for the will's presentation of the world as the *res extensa.*

Insofar as the world is reconstructed by the will as the *res extensa,* it is always necessarily bound up with a *res cogitans*: the world can be recreated as a collection of objects only if these objects are for a subject and rest upon it. The will can recreate the world through representation as the *res extensa* only if it also always recreates itself as that for which the *res extensa* is. The will thus takes possession of the world on the most fundamental level by recreating it so that it is always in its very being *mine.* The self in this sense is not just another object but the essential ground for the whole representational re-creation of the world.

In what sense is Descartes' "poetic" representation of the world in fact a re-creation? Is this activity not poetic in a much more limited sense, that is, does it not produce a mere model of the world that is either a better or worse imitation of reality and that can be judged by comparing it to the real world? Such questions are the product of healthy common sense but rest upon a fundamental misunderstanding not only of Descartes' thought but of the whole revolution in thinking that begins with nominalism and draws its ultimate consequences in our own time. This tradition asserts that there is no "real" world with which this constructed world can be compared; the world is only as it is represented. Such a notion is at odds with both the ancient and medieval notions of world and depends in ways we will have to examine on the idea of divine omnipotence.

THE STRUGGLE FOR MASTERY OF THE WORLD

In a radically nominalist world, human beings are forced by their finitude to employ general concepts to grasp radically individual beings. Such concepts, however, distort reality. These distortions, however, are only part of the problem. Since God creates all beings either directly or by means of secondary causes, he can at any time dispense with secondary causes and act directly on our minds or senses. Thus, it becomes questionable whether actual objects exist. The world is not rational. Indeed, it is not even a relatively tractable chaos of individual beings that we can grasp with fabricated concepts; it is a show or representation of divine will that may or may not correspond to a physical reality. In the face of an omnipotent God, the "real" world dissolves.

Under these conditions, both the philosophic contemplation of the cosmos and the theological deduction of divine will become useless and absurd. The task of thinking in Descartes' view is rather the representation of the world.[32] Such a representation, however, entails a struggle with God for mastery of appearances, a struggle to determine who shall represent and thus possess the world.[33] We always find ourselves amidst representations, within a world of objects that seem to be causally connected to one another in a particular way. As willing beings, we have the capacity to imagine all of the possible causal connections between things and then by means of experiments to determine which are in fact actual. We can then transform these causal connections, according to the image that the will forms in the imagination of a better or more useful order. Such a transformation enables us to conquer and control nature. This reorganization of causality is the technological moment of Descartes' poetic *mathesis universalis*, the fulcrum that rests upon the Archimedean point of his fundamental principle, *cogito ergo sum*. It is thus also the means by which we can win back the world from a capricious God.

On the surface, such a project seems ludicrous: how can man compete with an omnipotent God? Descartes' answer to this question is audacious: man himself in some sense is already omnipotent, is in some sense already God, otherwise the idea of such a struggle would be absurd.[34] Man resembles God in Descartes' view because of his capacity to represent and thereby recreate the world, to make it his own. This capacity, as we have seen, rests upon the reflexivity of thinking and this reflexivity upon the self-willing of the will. It is the will that is man's primary resource and the imperative of that will is to will, that is, to will itself as subject and thus to establish itself as the Archimedean point that makes possible the mastery of nature. The essential nature of the will is thus self-assertion and mastery. Such an essentially divine will to mastery, however, sets man at war with God.

The will, according to Descartes, is the essential characteristic of both God and man (AT, 7:56–57; CSM 2:40). God, as Descartes portrays him, is omnipotent: his will is infinitely powerful and he is radically free. As a result, thinking, willing, and creating are one and the same for him.[35] Moreover, his will is perfectly indifferent and thus bound by no transcendent necessity, law, or reason. Consequently it precedes and is the source of all ideas of goodness and truth (*Replies,* AT, 7:435–44; CSM, 2:293–99).[36] God creates the eternal ideas and might have made them otherwise, that is, might have contravened the law of contradiction or made it false that 2 + 3 = 5.[37] Indeed, his omnipotent will transcends even choice itself, for he creates the very possibilities within which choice occurs.[38]

Descartes recognizes that the supposition of such an omnipotent will means the radical dependence of man, nature, and truth upon God. Being, as Descartes understands it, is created being, a manifestation of God himself in his creative and ordering power. God thus can and does give shape to all things, and they are utterly contingent upon his fundamentally capricious will. This idea of divine will is decisive for Descartes' conception of nature.

Scholasticism understood nature in Aristotelian fashion as governed by material, formal, efficient, and final causes. For Aristotle, the formal and final causes were clearly fundamental.[39] While scholasticism gave efficient causality greater scope, it too gave precedence to formal and final causes. Scholasticism saw God as creator and first mover but interpreted him on the model of Aristotle's craftsman. He created the world according to the eternal forms of reason that comprised his own being. This notion was explicitly defended by Averroës but was also implicit in Aquinas. The nominalist emphasis upon divine omnipotence overturned this conception of natural causality and established divine will and efficient causality as preeminent. God was thus no longer seen as the craftsman who models the world on a rational plan, but as an omnipotent poet whose mystically creative freedom foams forth an endless variety of absolutely individual beings.

Descartes is the inheritor of this conception of nature as the creation of a radically omnipotent will. From the Aristotelian perspective, nature so understood is chaos. Indeed, if we ask the traditional metaphysical question " *What* is nature?" the only possible conclusion is: "Nothing." This "cosmos" is devoid of form and purpose, and the material objects that seem to exist are in fact merely illusions. In such an "uncosmos," the knowledge of God adds little if anything to our knowledge of the world.[40] Whether God does or does not exist, nature operates in much the same way and we must employ the same means to understand it. Descartes suggests as much himself in his *Discourse*. If God created a new world in imaginary space and agitated it diverse ways without any order so that the only result was chaos and left it to act in accordance with the laws which he had established, it would be identical to our own world (AT, 6:43–44; CSM, 1:132–33).[41] Thus, it makes no difference whether there is an omnipotent God or only the laws of nature, for all of the workings of nature can be explained by an analysis of efficient causality. The world in this sense is pure mechanism, not a "what" but a "how."[42] Mastering such a world requires not the acceptance of things as they are, but the representational reconstruction of the world in the imagination as the *res extensa*, for it is only in this manner that it can be mathematically analyzed and controlled.

Man is able to reform the world by virtue of his will. The will in this sense, as Descartes argues in the *Passions*, is the human perfection and the sole basis for human self-esteem (AT, 11:445; CSM, 1:384).[43] Indeed, nothing truly affects man except the free disposition of his will or desire, which is so free by nature that it can never be constrained (*Passions*, AT, 11:359, 445; CSM, 1:343, 384). This will is the source of human freedom and also the ground of human power. It is therefore the source of man's freedom from the omnipotent God and his deceptions, as well as the basis for humanity's conquest of nature.[44]

Despite the profound implications of this Cartesian notion of will for modernity, its origins remain obscure. While there is a certain plausibility to many of the suggested scholastic sources, there is a real problem, since Descartes was already well acquainted with all of them when he wrote the *Rules*, but there is no evidence of this doctrine in that work. Indeed, it is only in the period after 1639 that the notion of will comes to play a prominent role in Descartes' thought, and it is only in the later *Principles* and *Passions* that it becomes preeminent. It thus seems likely that Descartes developed this notion of will as a part of the basic rethinking of the foundations of his thought in response to the skeptical crisis engendered by his recognition of the problem posed by divine omnipotence. Descartes read Guillaume Gibieuf's *De libertate Dei et creatura*, but only after he had already enunciated his doctrine of the divine creation of eternal truths. Thus, it could not have been the source of his idea of divine omnipotence, although it may have played an important role in shaping his later idea of the will. If so, this connection would help to explain the convergence in Descartes' thought of the notions of divine and human freedom.[45]

The human will is able to resist God and reconstruct the natural world because it is the same as the will of God (*Meditations,* AT, 7:57; CSM, 2:40).[46] The pure human will, like that of God, is infinite, indifferent, and perfectly free, not subordinate to reason or any other law or rule.[47] This characterization of the human will as infinite contradicts divine foreordination. Descartes asserts in the *Replies,* however, that while foreordination makes liberty inconceivable, one introspectively experiences the fact that to will and to be free are one and the same (AT, 7:191; CSM, 2:134).[48] The human will thus does not succumb even to the monstrous power of divine omnipotence.

Man in the most immediate sense, however, is not God. While man's will may be equal to God's, his knowledge and power are vastly inferior. God's power is infinite: he creates in a miraculous fashion *ex nihilo* and understands perfectly all things past, present, and future. His will and his knowledge thus coincide. For man, there is a vast disjunction between his will and his power. The will is perfect and incapable of error as long as it does not extend itself beyond its sphere (*Principles,* AT, 8A:21; CSM, 1:207). The limits of this sphere, however, are determined by the extent of his understanding. When the will extends itself beyond these limits, it falls into error because it then judges where it does not know (*Meditations,* AT, 7:56–57; CSM, 2:39; *Replies,* AT, 7:314–15; CSM, 2:218–19).[49]

In the face of this disjunction of understanding and will, Descartes does not opt for a Kantian separation of human activity and knowledge, because he does not believe that the understanding is necessarily limited or that it is fundamentally different from the will. Indeed, the *mathesis universalis* will ultimately give man knowledge and power akin to that of God. The chief obstacle to extending the range of human knowledge and the sphere in which the will can act to secure power lies not in nature or in God but in man's passions (*Burman,* AT, 5:159).[50] We are deceived about the nature of the world because we judge and act solely on the basis of what we imagine or wish to be the case (*Replies,* AT, 7:314; CSM, 2:218). On the surface, our inability to avoid such faulty judgments seems to be an example of divine injustice or divine deception, since God could have created us such that we could not err. According to Descartes, he could have done so, however, only by sacrificing the freedom of the will that is the essence and the glory of our being. It ultimately does not matter whether God actually did create us defectively or not. We have, either by fortune or grace, the capacity to purge ourselves of the errors and deceptions that confuse our understanding, and on that basis to establish an apodictic science. The first step toward such divine knowledge and power, however, is the will's restriction of itself to what it knows with certainty. This self-limitation is the self-assertion of the will as doubt. The primal act of the will is thus its entry onto the path of doubt that establishes thinking for the first time on the firm foundation of *ego cogito ergo sum*.

The will is able to free itself from the errors and deceptions of both God and his creation by means of its own reflexive act. It establishes itself as its own ground and liberates itself from error. On this basis, it can begin the long representational reconstruction of the world. This reflexivity of the will is not only the ground for this great enterprise, it is also the standard of truth for Descartes' apodictic science. The self-reflexive will measures everything else against itself, reconstructs everything in representation on the model of itself, and for all intents and purposes thus becomes God.

The standard of truth which the will employs in judgment is the fundamental principle, *ego cogito ergo sum*. Only what is as clear and distinct as this truth, is valid (*Discourse*, AT, 6:33, CSM, 1:127; *Principles*, AT, 9B:17–18; CSM, 1:204; *Search*, AT, 10:527; CSM, 2:420). Descartes means by this that only those things are true that the will as doubt cannot deny, that is, things that cannot be denied without at the same time being true. Descartes explains this in the *Meditations*: "During these past few days I have been asking whether anything in the world exists and I have realized that from the very fact of my raising this question it follows quite evidently that I exist. I could not but judge that something which I understood so clearly was true; but this was not because I was compelled to judge by any external force, but because a great light in the intellect was followed by a great inclination in the will and thus the spontaneity and freedom of my belief was all the greater in proportion to my lack of indifference" (AT, 7:58–59; CSM, 2:41).

The meaning of certainty for Descartes is far from clear. Some commentators have tried to show that it is nothing other than a secularized version of the certainty of salvation that was so important to Luther and the Reformation.[51] There is some evidence to support such a reading. Descartes asserts in the *Replies* that the passage just cited should prove to all orthodox theologians that he believes that the supernatural light of God is the source of certainty (AT, 7:148; CSM, 2:105). Descartes, however, is probably disingenuous here. In the passage in the *Replies* immediately preceding this one, Descartes distinguishes supernatural illumination from our natural light; and in the passage immediately succeeding the *Meditation* passage in question, he characterizes his judgment about his own existence as a result of his natural light (AT, 7:59–60, 146; CSM, 2:41, 104). His remarks here, as he himself indicates, are meant to convince not philosophers or scientists but only orthodox theologians. Descartes does not deny the possibility of divine illumination. He may even believe that divine revelation supersedes our natural light. In the *Principles,* for example, he asserts that we must trust our natural light as long as nothing contrary to it is revealed by God (AT, 8A:16–17; CSM, 1:203). However, the two are not identical. The natural light arises from the reflexivity of the will that constitutes itself as self-consciousness. The will in this sense can affirm as true only what it cannot doubt, and the only thing that it cannot doubt is itself. Every truth must in this sense be based upon the reflexive certainty of *cogito ergo sum.* Under such strict standards of proof, however, it is difficult to see how one could ever establish a universal science.

TAMING THE OMNIPOTENT GOD

The demonstration of the fundamental principle is a necessary but not sufficient condition for Cartesian science. This science, in fact, depends upon a second principle that guarantees the truth of at least mathematics. As we have seen, Descartes was able to establish the independence of the thinking self on the basis of his fundamental principle. However, to leave this bastion of human freedom and certainty and extend the sway of the human will into the natural world, Descartes has to confront this wild and unpredictable God himself and tame his irrational spirit. In other words, he has to demonstrate that this God is not a deceiver (*Replies,* AT, 7:144; CSM, 2:103). God has to be turned to human use! The universal science that Descartes believes will end skepticism and cure all human ills thus rests in a surprising fashion upon the omnipotent God who was the source of skepticism.

God, Descartes suggests, guarantees the truth of the clear and distinct ideas that are the basis of science, and belief in God is thus necessary for science.[52] Hence an atheist cannot attain certainty (*Replies,* AT, 7:139; CSM, 2:99). Thus, Descartes argues that while Diogenes, Theodorus, Pythagoras, and the skeptics doubted the truth of geometrical demonstrations, "they could not have done so had they known the true nature of God" (*Replies,* AT, 7:384; CSM, 2:263; cf. AT, 7:139; CSM, 2:99).

The key to this transformation of God from evil genius to divine guarantor of truth lies in the peculiar character of Descartes' demonstration of divine perfection in his so-called ontological proof of God's existence. Descartes gives three different but related definitions of God in the *Meditations* and *Replies,* as *idea infiniti* in the Third Meditation, as *ens summe perfectum* in the Fifth Meditation, and as *causa sui* in the First and Fourth Replies.[53] The definition of God as infinite seems to reinforce the possibility that God is a deceiver, since infinity seems to imply incomprehensibility. The definition of God as the most perfect being, however, seems to prove that God is not a deceiver. The final definition goes one step further in subordinating God to reason, that is, to the principle of causality. There is thus an apparent inconsistency in Descartes' definition of God.[54] This apparent inconsistency, however, is overcome by Descartes' new understanding of infinity as the basis of God's perfection.

The demonstration that God is not a deceiver follows from the proof of his perfection. This demonstration rests upon Descartes' fundamental principle. Descartes argues that he finds within himself the idea of perfection and yet knows that this is not intrinsic to his own being because he doubts, that is, because he does not know everything with certainty. The idea of perfection therefore must come from a source beyond him, and this source is God. God, therefore, is perfect.

Descartes was not the first to employ this so-called ontological argument. It had been used by Anselm in his *Monologium* and was repeated by many other scholastics, most notably by Aquinas, who presents it at the beginning of the *Summa* as the fourth way of proving God's existence. Descartes knows the argument in its Thomistic form but transforms it in a nominalistic fashion, interpreting concepts such as possibility, objectivity, simplicity, and infinity in a way characteristic of his own system.[55] For Anselm and Aquinas, the argument rests on the assumption that there are different orders or degrees of reality, and a hierarchy of perfection from accidents to finite beings to infinite beings. Descartes adopts this hierarchy and tries to show how it makes possible a clear understanding of God (*Replies,* AT, 7:165–66; CSM, 2:116–17). This move is contrary to the scholastic intention. Anselm employs the argument not to understand God but to demonstrate how the world participates in divine perfection. The proof of God's existence in his view follows from the fact that we cannot possibly form a concept of God or his essence.[56] For Anselm, God's infinity thus renders him a concealed mystery rather than a clear and evident truth. While Descartes borrows the ontological argument from scholasticism, he radically transforms it for purposes of his own that are very much at odds with its original use.

Descartes' transformation of the idea of God rests upon a new concept of infinity. His second definition of God thus depends on the first and is in fact subordinate to it.[57] An actual infinity for scholasticism was a contradiction in terms. To assert that God was infinite was to assert that he could not be grasped positively, but only negatively in terms of a contradiction. Even Bonaventure, who recognized the differences between the finite and the infinite with great clarity, follows this traditional negative path when defining God.[58] Where Descartes sees God *sub specie infinitatis,* Bonaventure sees him *sub specie divinitatis.*[59] Descartes sees the infinite as something positive and not merely as a negative path. The idea of the infinite is thus not contradictory.[60] More importantly, it is not just a negation of the finite. Descartes' decisive insight is that the finite is the negation or limitation of the infinite.[61]

Descartes adopts as his model not an infinite sequence but an unbounded figure (*Replies,* AT, 7:367–68; CSM, 2:253). What is real is the whole in its complete undifferentiatedness, and every determinate form is always only a limitation and negation of this whole. Therefore, we cannot grasp the idea of God through the amplification of any finite figure, because it is the finitude of this figure that is at odds with God. We can have the idea of God only if we grasp it as a whole at one time (*Replies,* AT, 7:371; CSM, 2:256). Such a geometric example, however, is necessarily an imperfect model for God, since he is truly infinite, having no limitations whatsoever (*Principles,* AT, 8A:15; CSM, 1:202). Descartes, therefore, asserts that other so-called infinite things are merely indefinite. The indefinite resembles the infinite because we do not notice any limits, but it can be truly infinite only if we know with certainty that it can have no limits.[62] God in this sense is infinitely infinite.

Such a description of God is in keeping with the radical definition of divine omnipotence that we saw in the thought of Scotus, Ockham, and the nominalists. The bridge that Descartes builds across the abyss that separates God and man, however, is uniquely his own. Insofar as God is infinitely infinite he certainly cannot be comprehended by a finite being such as man. We can, however, understand

God as clearly and distinctly as a limitless thing can be understood (*Replies,* AT, 7:112; CSM, 2:81).[63] Here Descartes' geometric bridge is one part of the answer. More important, however, is the fact that man is himself infinite, that is, that he has an infinite will.

As Descartes himself indicates, the idea of the divine intellect does not differ from our own except as an infinite number differs from a number of the second or third power (*Replies,* AT, 7:137; CSM, 2:98). This does not mean, however, that we can project from human to divine will.[64] Rather this idea of an infinite divine will is always already innate in us and is established in the same judgment as the fundamental principle (*Replies,* AT, 7:106–7, 123; CSM, 2:77, 88). We establish ourselves by means of doubt, that is, by negation of the real, and thus the knowledge of our own existence includes in it the knowledge of God (*Replies,* AT, 7:111–12, 365; CSM, 2:80, 252).[65]

To understand what Descartes means by this claim, we need to return to our analysis of Descartes' notion of thinking. In the *Rules,* Descartes views thinking primarily as representing. We have seen that this notion of representation is retained in Descartes' later thought but is understood as the result of the will's self-assertion. The will abstracts things from the world, then reconstructs and represents them in the imagination as the *res extensa.* Thinking thus is an establishing of forms and consequently a limiting of the unlimited. The basis for this mode of analysis, which forms the heart of Descartes' science, is his fundamental principle. This principle, as we saw earlier, is the self-grounding act of the will in and through which it establishes itself as the ground or subject of all objects, that is, as the *res cogitans* of the *res extensa.* In its infinity, this human will is identical to that of God. Insofar as it follows the path of doubt and rejects everything as false, it strives to establish itself as the unlimited and therefore as God. It obliterates every concrete form and figure that constrains it. The will's discovery that it cannot deny itself and that it must affirm itself is a demonstration of a limitation of the will and simultaneously the establishment of the I, the *ego* of the *ego cogito ergo sum.* The human will, which is in essence the same as the will of God, thus discovers that it is limited, that it is not God. The discovery of such a limitation, however, is simultaneously the recognition of the necessity of the unlimited, the recognition that the limited, that is, man, only is as the negation of the unlimited, that is, as the negation of God. This truth rests on the same basis as *ego cogito ergo sum.* We cannot doubt it without its being true, that is, we cannot doubt that there is an unlimited, because doubt and the unlimited are identical. We truly know God only in the same act in which we know ourselves or, since thinking in this instance is willing, I will God to be God in the same act that I will myself to be I. In so willing, I establish a realm for myself that is beyond the sway of God. My will is bound by the limit set by my inability to doubt myself. God in this sense cannot be man or any type of finite being because he cannot be bound by these limits. These limits, however, are the source of self-consciousness. God as the infinitely infinite thus cannot be self-conscious, and we can know this with certainty because we can know that God is unlimited.[66] Deception, however, is the consequence of imperfection and no such imperfection is found in God. That is to say, deception requires self-consciousness, which is the basis for distinguishing oneself from others. God, however, is not self-conscious. God thus is no deceiver. If God is no deceiver, then the truths of mathematics cannot be doubted and the only thing that stands in the way of man's perfection is man himself. Through science, man can expand the sphere of his knowledge and his power until it is identical with that of his will, that is, until he becomes master and possessor of nature. While we cannot be indifferent in the course of our struggle with God for the control of nature, our ultimate goal is the establishment of our will as absolute and thus as thoroughly indifferent.

It is important to note that strictly speaking Descartes does not present a proof of the existence of God but a proof of the existence of the infinite. Descartes thus demonstrates that God cannot be the God he was traditionally understood to be, since as infinitely infinite and therefore nonself-conscious he cannot have intentions or a will in the traditional sense. Indeed, he cannot even choose, because he creates the very alternatives that make choice possible. This conclusion points to the underlying meaning of Descartes' proof. It is not meant to demonstrate the existence of God but to show that God is irrelevant for human affairs, to show that even if there is an infinite and omnipotent God, he cannot be a deceiver, a *genius malignus*.[67] If we can know with certainty that there is no *genius malignus*, then we cannot doubt the truths of mathematics. If we cannot doubt mathematics, then *mathesis universalis* depends only upon our capacity to avoid error, and error can be largely avoided by means of the method. We thus can come to know everything actual and possible with certainty; we can produce a perfect universal science and with this science we can master and possess nature. In short, because God cannot be a deceiver, we can become God.[68]

While man at first seemed to be at odds with God in Descartes' view, it becomes apparent that there is no true antagonism. The unpredictable and transrational God of nominalism is revealed as rational and predictable when he is seen within Descartes' bastion of reason and certainty. God's infinite and all-powerful will proves in the end not to endanger human will and power but, on the contrary, to enable it to achieve a universal mastery of nature. Below this shining facade, however, there are indications that this harmony is artificial and unstable. The Cartesian proof of God's existence and goodness is not entirely satisfying, for his God is an impotent not an omnipotent God, a God who has lost his independence and become a mere representation within human thinking. The wildly omnipotent God of nominalism is thus replaced by a God who conforms to human notions of perfection. At the same time and perhaps more importantly, the human will is conceived as infinite and human freedom is posited as potentially absolute. To preserve man from the thorough skepticism that the omnipotent freedom of the nominalist God seemed to engender, Descartes posits in the human soul precisely that infinite will and freedom that were so dangerous in God. Man is thus granted the capacity for absolute self-assertion against the natural world and ultimately against God himself. The harmony of man and God in Descartes thus seems to depend upon a radical diminution of God and a tremendous exaggeration of man.[69] Underlying the Cartesian project in a way that never becomes entirely explicit is the possibility that man is or at least can become God.[70] In becoming God, however, man also undermines the basis for reason that Descartes attempts to establish.

For the most part, these conclusions are merely implicit in Descartes. The rational or mathematical moment of his thought was preeminent in his lifetime and among his immediate successors, but the ground of this mathematics in the new idea of an infinite and ultimately arbitrary human will became increasingly explicit in the later development of modern thought. The idea of divine omnipotence and the infinity of the human will, however, was suppressed in the period immediately after Descartes' death. Spinoza rejected the idea of an eternal creator altogether, as well as the notion of *creatio ex nihilo*. Divine contingency and arbitrariness thus ceased to be a problem for him. The world or substance in his view is absolute being, and all change in this sense is nothing other than internal rearrangement of this being. The more orthodox Leibniz was deeply troubled by the consequences of the doctrine of the divine creation of the eternal truths. He thus concludes: "By saying that things are not good by any rule of goodness but by God's will alone, it seems to me that one unthinkingly destroys all love of God and all His glory. For why praise Him for what he has done, if He would be equally praiseworthy in doing just the contrary? Where then will be His justice and His wisdom, if there only remains a certain despotic power, if will takes the place of reason, and if, according to the definition of tyrants, what pleases the most powerful is just by that alone."[71]

Malebranche echoes this sentiment: "If God were only omnipotent and not governed by other attributes . . . How could we be certain he would not, on the first day, place all the demons in heaven, and all the saints in hell, and a moment after annihilate all that he had done! Cannot God *qua* omnipotent, create each day a million planets, make new worlds, each more perfect than the last, and reduce each of them to a grain of sand?"[72]

Insofar as Leibniz and Malebranche reject the notion of divine omnipotence that nominalism and Descartes share, and reemphasize other divine attributes such as reason, justice, and goodness, they are able to avoid a radical struggle between man and God. Moreover, because they do not empty God of these attributes they do not have to deify man to regain them. However, insofar as they accept Descartes' science and abandon natural theology, they can scarcely escape the conclusion that in practical affairs reason is only an empty generality of will that is unsatisfying to human thought and potentially quite dangerous to human well-being. The bright facade of Descartes' bastion of reason enthused the seventeenth and eighteenth centuries in large part because it seemed to offer a secure foundation for the reconstruction of rational political and social life after the long years of religious warfare and political instability. The dark foundations of this rationalism, however, were papered over by Cartesians, who recognized the dangers posed by an omnipotent God and a potentially omnipotent humanity. Such a notion of God and man called into question the authority of science, morality, and religion because it removed all natural and rational guides to human action. These dark foundations thus remained largely unperceived. What remained invisible to the Enlightenment, however, was to become all too evident to the nineteenth and twentieth centuries.

Chapter Three

FICHTE AND THE
DARK NIGHT OF THE
NOUMENAL I

"The Speech of the Dead Christ from the Celestial
Sphere That There Is No God"

I lay down once on a summer evening in the sun on a mountainside and . . . dreamed that I awoke in a graveyard. . . . a high and noble form descended from the heights with everlasting pain and all of the dead cried: "Christ, is there no God?" . . . He answered, "There is none. . . . I went through the worlds, I climbed to the suns and flew with the Milky Way through the deserts of heaven; but there is no God. I climbed down as far as being throws its shadow and peered into the abyss and cried, `Father, where are you?' but I heard only the eternal storm, which no one rules, and the shimmering rainbow, which is only essence without a sun that created it, stretched over the abyss and falling into it. And when I looked up to the immeasurable world in search of the divine eye, only an empty eyesocket stared back at me; and eternity lay upon chaos and gnawed at it and chewed upon itself.— Cry out, raise a cacophony, scream until the shadows break, for He is not! . . . Rigid, speechless nothing! Cold, eternal necessity! Insane chance! Do you know yourself? When shall you shatter the world and me? . . . How alone each is in the wide tomb of the all! I am only by myself—oh Father! oh Father! where is your infinite breast, upon which I might rest?—Alas, if each I is its own father and creator, why can it not also be its own avenging angel?"[1]

This nightmarish passage by the early nineteenth-century writer Jean Paul is a literary depiction of the danger that he sees in the teaching of his Romantic contemporaries, whom he calls "aesthetic nihilists."[2] Their nihilism in his view is the result of the assertion that man is an autonomous, self-creating I, free from both God and nature. He sees this view of man and the concomitant desire for absolute autonomy as the result of "the lawless, capricious spirit of the present age, which would egotistically annihilate the world and the universe in order to clear a space merely for free *play* in the void."[3] Its consequences are ominous, for "in an age when God has set like the sun, soon afterwards the world too passes into darkness. He who scorns the universe respects nothing more than himself and at night fears only his own creations."[4] In Jean Paul's view, however, these Romantics are not ultimately responsible for this nihilism— they merely repeat a doctrine enunciated by their teachers, the German idealists.

In his attack, Jean Paul echoes his own teacher, Friedrich Jacobi, and his literary struggle against nihilism is a reflection of Jacobi's philosophic struggle against German idealism and Fichte's critical idealism in particular. In fact, the concept of 'nihilism' first came into general usage as a description of the danger this idealism posed for the intellectual, spiritual, and political health of humanity. The first to use the term in print was apparently F. L. Goetzius in his *De nonismo et nihilismo in theologia* (1733). This work, however, was relatively unknown and apparently played no role in the later reappearance and development of the concept. The term reappeared in the late eighteenth century when it was used by J. H. Obereit and more importantly D. Jenisch, who characterized transcendental idealism as nihilism in 1796 in his *On the Ground and Value of the Discoveries of Herr Professor Kant in Metaphysics, Morals, and Aesthetics.* He uses the term to describe the work not of Kant (or even Fichte) but of the extreme Kantians who teach that the things-in-themselves are nothing for our cognition. While Jenisch employs the term, however, he never really develops a concept of nihilism. This was the contribution of Jacobi, who first used the term in a published letter to Fichte of 1799: "Truly, my dear Fichte, it should not grieve me, if you, or whoever it might be, want to call *chimerism* what I oppose to idealism, which I reproach as *nihilism.*"[5]

More than a decade before his letter to Fichte, Jacobi had been involved in a famous controversy with Herder over Spinozism, the so-called pantheism controversy.[6] Herder had maintained that Spinozism was theism, while Jacobi argued that it was materialism and thus atheism. His argument against Fichte follows a similar path. Jacobi had been an early admirer of Fichte and in the letter from which the above quotation is drawn, he still calls him the messiah of speculative reason. While he was persuaded of Fichte's brilliance and had no doubts about his moral and religious convictions, he was profoundly concerned that Fichte's fundamental principles led him, contrary to his own intention, to atheism.

His letter to Fichte appeared during the time when Fichte was under attack for supposedly teaching atheism. Jacobi's letter was

intended to dispel the illusion that he was either Fichte's supporter
or opponent. His objections to Fichte's system, however, are profound. As he sees it, Fichte's idealism recognizes no truth beyond
consciousness or reason and thus falls into an absolute subjectivism
that is at heart merely an inverted Spinozism. It reduces everything
to the activity of the I, and thus reduces God to a mere creation of
the human imagination. He is repulsed by such a view and turns away
from it as the "most horrible of horrors."[7] If there is nothing beyond
the representations of the I, then the good, the beautiful, and the
holy are merely hollow names.[8]

In place of this philosophy that, in his opinion, claims to make
everything comprehensible but actually reduces everything to nothing, he prefers a philosophy that recognizes that it cannot know the
most essential things and takes its guidance from the inscrutable wisdom of revelation. This philosophy of not-knowing was characterized by the idealists as chimerism, because in their opinion every decision was thereby left up to individual inclination or caprice.[9] While
Jacobi rejects this malicious construction, he believes that even if it
were correct, his thought would still be preferable to idealism, which
is the philosophy of mere appearances and thus of nothing. Man,
according to Jacobi, cannot be his own ground. He depends on
something outside himself, and the attempt to become one's own
ground dissolves everything substantial. Jacobi concludes: "Man has
this choice and this alone: nothing or God. Choosing nothing he
makes himself God; that means he makes God an apparition, for it is
impossible, if there is no God, for man and all that is around him to
be more than an apparition. I repeat: God is and is outside of me, a
living essence that subsists for itself, or *I* am God. There is no third
possibility."[10]

We see in the critique of idealism by Jacobi and Jean Paul the
beginnings of our modern concept of nihilism. This chapter takes the
reception of Fichte's thought by Jacobi, Jean Paul, and the Romantics as the starting point for an examination of the importance of
Fichte's thought for the origin of the concept of nihilism. Nihilism,
as we will see, grows out of the notion of the infinite will that Fichte
discovers in the thought of Descartes and Kant. Fichte, however, radicalizes this notion of the will in a way unacceptable to both Kant and
Descartes, transforming the notion of the I into a world-creating will.
This radicalization leads thinking away from the bright dawn of
Enlightenment that Descartes and Kant proclaimed, into the dark
night of the noumenal I and the nihilism that so alarmed Jacobi and

Jean Paul. Fichtean idealism in this way is the hidden source of the nihilism that becomes increasingly explicit in the nineteenth and early twentieth centuries.

THE HISTORICAL AND INTELLECTUAL BACK-GROUND OF FICHTE'S IDEALISM

Johann Gottlieb Fichte was born in 1762 into a peasant family in Saxony. His intelligence was recognized at an early age by a local aristocrat, who financed his education at the famous boarding school Pforta. Fichte later studied theology and law at Jena, Wittenberg, and Leipzig but, owing to the death of his patron, he was unable to complete his studies. Fichte had long dreamed of a career as a scholar and member of the educated class but, like many other educated men of meager means, he was forced to support himself by working, often under demeaning conditions, as a tutor for noble and bourgeois families.

The French Revolution and the revolution in thinking ushered in by Kantian philosophy gave a new direction to his life. He became a Jacobin and began to dream of becoming a philosopher. He left his job and traveled to Königsberg in 1790 to meet Kant and seek his advice and assistance. To gain Kant's attention, he wrote an essay entitled *Attempt at a Critique of All Revelation,* which he sent to the philosopher. Kant was astonished by the work and convinced his own publisher to bring it out, but the publisher suppressed the name of the author in the first edition. As a result, the work was mistakenly regarded as Kant's long-awaited work on revealed religion and was widely praised. When it was made clear that Fichte was the real author, he became a philosophic celebrity.

Fichte had an illustrious but stormy academic career, in large part because of his uncompromising personality. In 1793 and 1794, he anonymously published two Jacobin pamphlets, the first defending freedom of thought against the restrictive laws of the German princes and the second supporting the French Revolution against the German Burkeans. In 1794, he accepted a position at Jena and published the first edition of his magnum opus, the *Foundation of the Entire Science of Knowledge,* and his *Vocation of the Scholar.* His *Foundation of Natural Right* followed in 1796 and his *System of Ethics* in 1798. In 1799, he was accused of propagating atheism and felt compelled to resign from his position. In 1800, he moved to Berlin and published his *Vocation of Man* and the *Closed Commercial State.* During the

Napoleonic period, he became an ardent German nationalist and urged the German people to assert themselves against foreign domination in his famous *Addresses to the German Nation*. He became head of the philosophical faculty in Berlin in 1810 and served as Rector of the University from 1811 to 1812 before dying of a fever in 1814.

Fichte was extraordinarily important and influential in Germany in the 1790s. Friedrich Schlegel, for example, asserted in his *Athenaeum* that the French Revolution, Goethe's *Wilhelm Meister,* and Fichte's *Science of Knowledge* were the greatest events of his age.[11] He was an extraordinary teacher. In a letter written when he was studying with Fichte, Hölderlin declares that "Fichte is now the soul of Jena and thank God that he is. I know no other man of such depth and spiritual energy."[12] He had an extraordinary impact upon his students and many of them went on to play important roles in German intellectual life. He was the teacher of nearly all the early German Romantics, the so-called Jena Romantics, including Tieck, Wackenröder, Novalis, Friedrich Schlegel, August Wilhelm Schlegel and his wife, Caroline, as well as Hölderlin, Schelling, and later Schopenhauer. His fame, however, was as brief as it was bright. After 1800, he was superseded in the philosophic firmament first by Schelling and then by Hegel. His early work was of decisive importance for Schelling and Hegel and, through their thought, for many of the leading thinkers of the later nineteenth century as well, and his political philosophy had a direct effect upon such diverse thinkers as Carlyle, Lassalle, and Bakunin.[13]

The essential intellectual stimulus of Fichte's thought was Kant's Copernican revolution in thinking. Fichte understands Kant within the horizon of modern thought opened up by Descartes and preeminently represented by Rousseau and the French Jacobins.[14] Kant's thought is clearly an outgrowth of this tradition but it also is a response to the other great tradition of early modern thought, empiricism.

Hobbes spoke for nearly every empiricist when he argued that Descartes had established his system upon a faulty foundation by positing the I as fundamental (*Replies,* AT, 7:171–96; CSM 2:121–37). The I and the whole subjective realm in this view are merely permutations of matter. Consequently, there is no free will. Human beings, like all other beings, are governed by the laws of matter. The supposedly free will is in reality only the last impulse before motion. Moreover, without the certainty of the I, Descartes' demonstration of the existence and goodness of God cannot be maintained. Descartes' God, from the perspective of empiricism, is thus nothing. More importantly, without the certainty of the I and God, Descartes' apodictic science lacks a foundation. Empiricists such as Hume could thus argue that what seemed to Descartes to be causal connections were only regularities of experience. For empiricism, science can only describe such regularities. Its results are thus not certain or a priori but probable and a posteriori.

Kant attempted to save both science and freedom (and thus morality and religion) from the empiricist attack by both deepening and limiting the subjectivistic foundation that Descartes had established. Descartes and rationalism in general had come into disrepute in Kant's view because they laid claim to knowledge that transcends the limits of the human understanding. In order to establish a true ground for science and to open a space for freedom, morality, and religion in the face of skepticism, Kant believed that a thorough critique of reason was necessary.

Hume's skepticism was a frontal attack on rationalism. His demonstration that causality could not be logically deduced or derived from experience dealt an especially grievous blow to rationalist science. Kant perceived the power of this argument and also recognized that it could be extended to other concepts. Such a critique seemed to Kant to undermine the foundations of all knowledge. Kant, however, did not believe that Hume's argument proved that certain knowledge was impossible. It pointed rather to the crucial failure of rationalism to restrain reason to a sphere commensurate with its capacities. This failure necessarily brought reason into contradiction with itself, into what Kant called antinomies.

The discovery of the antinomies was the original impetus for Kant's critical philosophy.[15] Of particular importance was the antinomy of causality (*KrV,* A445/B473–A453/B481). In delineating this antinomy, Kant attempted to show that the notion of causality could not be successfully extended to the infinite without violating the principle of sufficient reason and that it consequently presupposed a first and therefore spontaneous or uncaused cause. Such a causality through freedom, however, contradicted the essential principle of causality that every event has a cause. Kant argued that this contradiction meant that natural science cannot be complete without either divine or human freedom but that such freedom is incompatible with the causal explanation of nature given by natural science.

The antinomy in Kant's view is the result of reason's intrinsic desire to extend itself beyond its own limits in the attempt to comprehend the infinite. This insight led Kant to transcendental idealism, to the doctrine that we do not have knowledge of things-in-themselves but only of their appearances or representations within consciousness. Early in his philosophic career, it had become apparent to Kant that our experience is fundamentally shaped by the forms of the consciousness with which we perceive and understand. Space and time, he argued, are not things-in-themselves but merely forms of our intuition. Thus, we can perceive things only as they appear in space and time, that is, only as phenomena. Similarly, these perceptions are organized not according to their essential natures but according to the categories of our understanding. We may receive an initial impulse from the world that leads us to think, but we understand it only within the structures of consciousness. While we cannot understand the things-in-themselves because we know them only through our own cognitive apparatus, we can know the appearances or representations of these things-in-themselves. The knowledge of these appearances constitutes science or what Kant more characteristically calls understanding.

Kant's starting point is thus fundamentally subjectivistic. What *is* on the most basic level is consciousness *(Bewusstsein)* or experience. *Bewusstsein* for Kant and for idealism in general is a much broader concept than our notion of consciousness. By consciousness, we usually mean a capacity in us for awareness. This is only a small part of the idealist notion of *Bewusstsein*. Kant adopts the term from Wolff, who employed it to translate Descartes' *conscientia*. It is a compound of the adjective *bewusst*, 'known,' 'aware,' from the verb *wissen*, 'to know,' and the verb *sein*, 'to be,' or the noun *Sein*, 'being.' It is thus the togetherness or unity of being and knowing, the being-that-knows and known-being. Thus, it cannot simply be identified with the empirical subject. This empirical I that becomes visible to us in introspection is in fact a mere object of consciousness and not consciousness itself. Consciousness is rather the twofold of subject and object in which man and nature are conjoined. The unity of this manifold arises from a higher subjectivism, from the so-called transcendental unity of apperception, from the "I" that accompanies all of our representations and that is the necessary condition of their possibility. Kant's subjectivism thus embraces all of the human and natural things as we encounter them and leaves open the possibility that those infinite things such as God that transcend our consciousness also *are* in some sense, although he denies that we can ever know them in the same way we know the phenomena.

In Kant's view, such a separation of the natural and the supernatural is the only way to establish a certain ground for an a priori science of nature. Science for Kant and his contemporaries consisted in a system of synthetic truths. Everyone, including Hume, recognized the existence of certain analytic truths, that is, truths in which the predicate can be derived from an analysis of the subject. Such truths are a priori, because they do not require recourse to experience. Everyone also recognized the existence of empirical truths, or truths in which the predicate can be known through perception. These are a posteriori truths. Science, however, depends on the possibility of synthetic truths a priori, that is, truths in which the predicate cannot be logically deduced from the subject but which also do not depend upon the testimony of the senses. Hume believed that there were no such truths. Kant attempted to demonstrate that he was wrong.

The basis for the demonstration of synthetic truths a priori is transcendental idealism. Hume begins and ends with experience, but he does not investigate the structures of experience itself. Kant undertakes such an investigation in order to show that all experience occurs within consciousness and is governed by its laws. If Hume were correct, Kant argued, there could be no experience. For experience to be, it must be a unity as *my* experience. All experience thus is associated with the I and occurs through consciousness. The structure of consciousness thus establishes the limits and laws of understanding.

Kant argued that understanding is the result of judgment and that judgment has a given and unalterable structure that manifests itself in the categories. These categories constitute the basis for an a priori natural science. Such a science, to be sure, cannot tell us a priori what the cause of any particular event will be, but it can tell us that every event has a cause. An a priori natural science of the phenomena is thus possible, but we must recognize that it is a science only of appearances and not of things-in-themselves.

This limitation not only establishes a foundation for science, it also opens up a space for freedom and morality. If the laws of nature applied to the things-in-themselves, human freedom would be impossible and, if there were no human freedom, there could be no moral law, since individuals would not be responsible for their actions. The existence of the moral law is an indication that human beings are free and thus something different from all other natural beings, not mere means or links in the chain of natural causation but ends in themselves, beings who can originate action. The apparent contradiction of nature and freedom that appeared in the antinomy of causality is thus resolved by transcendental idealism. While the laws of nature govern the phenomena, humans are not merely phenomenal beings. They thus have the capacity for freedom and for morality. Within the *Critique of Pure Reason,* Kant is content to demonstrate the possibility of a causality through freedom in addition to a causality through nature. In the *Critique of Practical Reason,* Kant moves in the direction of Rousseau and postulates a free causality as the basis for the moral law.

In contrast to the *Critique of Pure Reason,* the *Critique of Practical Reason* considers not what is but what ought to be. For thinkers such as Bacon and Descartes, who first articulated the idea of a universal science, the question of what ought to be was generally understood in the context of their struggle to assert what was naturally good against the prevailing theological orthodoxy. On a practical level, they were thus principally concerned with man's preservation and prosperity. While Descartes understood the human essence as freedom or will, he did not assert that freedom was the end of human activity or the principle criterion of ethics. It was only with Rousseau that this more radical notion of freedom became explicit and it was this Rousseauian notion of freedom that was decisive for Kant.[16]

For Kant, man is both in nature and above it. As a phenomenal being, he is thoroughly determined by natural necessity through his passions and desires. His will, however, is free, for it can recognize what ought to be and elevate itself above its natural impulses to the ideal. Whether it can realize this ideal, however, is more problematic. To be free means to act rationally, that is, to act according to a universal principle that is indifferent to our particularity. The categorical imperative that one act always so that the maxim of one's action can be a universal law is thus the sine qua non of freedom. Freedom is not the caprice of the passions but their subordination to the moral law. The possibility of free will, however, does not guarantee its efficacy. In fact, Kant had severe doubts that the free will can exercise any causal force in the phenomenal world, for we are not merely free but also governed by natural causality. Man stands between nature and the divine and is pulled by powerful forces in opposite directions. The transcendence of nature through the moral law, however, is the sole legitimate end of human life. Man in other words must strive to manifest the godlike essence within him even if this goal can never be attained.

Many thinkers who were sympathetic to the Kantian enterprise were not convinced that Kant had brought it to a satisfactory conclusion. They found the results of his revolution in the way of thinking difficult to accept, especially because he seemed to leave little space for the constructions of the imagination and speculative reason which they found so enchanting and essential to human life. Kant's world, by contrast, seemed arid and colorless.

Kant was well aware that his critical philosophy was unlikely to satisfy his contemporaries. However, he believed their dissatisfaction was due to the fact that they wanted more than existence had to offer. What man can know is only "an island, enclosed by nature itself within unalterable limits. It is the land of truth—enchanting name!—surrounded by a wide and stormy ocean, the native home of illusion, where many a fog bank and many a swiftly melting iceberg give the deceptive appearance of farther shores, deluding the adventurous seafarer ever anew with empty hopes, and engaging him in enterprises which he can never abandon and yet is unable to carry to completion" (*KrV*, A235/B294–A236/B295).

Kant's warnings notwithstanding, his critics were more prone to interpret their dissatisfaction as a result of the inadequacy of Kant's thought. They were particularly dissatisfied with Kant's supposed resolution of the contradiction of nature and freedom. Hegel, for example, argued that Kant had solved the antinomy of nature and freedom only by transposing the contradiction into consciousness. As he saw it, Kant simply rendered consciousness itself—the highest thing—contradictory.[17] From this perspective, the first and second *Critiques* appeared to be irreconcilable. Transcendental idealism seemed to be not merely a dualism but a contradictory dualism. This apparent contradiction opened Kantianism up to the skeptical attacks of Schulze and others.[18] Kant's admirers had hoped that his third *Critique* would resolve these matters and provide a foundation for the reconciliation of nature and freedom, but they were disappointed with the result. Something more was needed. Reinhold explained that a mere critique of reason was insufficient; what was necessary was a *system* of reason that derived both theory and practice from a single source. It was such a system of reason that Kant's successors attempted to construct.[19]

Descartes opened the door to modernity when he established a bastion of reason in which human beings could be free from the terrifying caprice of the omnipotent God. This bastion was the ground of certainty that shut out the storm of chaos and skepticism that this

God had engendered. Descartes also gave human beings the scientific weapons with which to reclaim the world and reconstruct it according to human measure and for human purposes. Hume's attack, however, opened a breach in the Cartesian walls and threatened the entire enterprise. Kant was able to reconstruct these walls, but only by narrowing their compass. Only if all speculative judgments about God, morality, and freedom were excluded could the consistency of the understanding be guaranteed. Descartes' God was thus banished beyond the realm of the phenomena. However, he was thereby also liberated from the constraints that Descartes had laid upon him.

The bright day of the phenomena that Kant's thought opens up is thus surrounded by an impenetrable night. The thing-in-itself which constitutes the true reality remains merely a dark x. Kant warns us not to enter this night, but he also renders it immensely attractive. He suggests that the noumenal night may in fact be the true world and the day in which we dwell only a representation of this nocturnal reality (cf. *KrV,* A249–A253 [Omitted in B], and A253/B308–A260/ B315). Moreover, he argues that we must take our guidance from the moral imperative that is projected upon us out of this night. Finally and perhaps most importantly, with the idea of practical reason he also seems to open up a breach in the wall of reason that Descartes had so elaborately established.

This breach was an irresistible attraction to Kant's successors, and one after another they passed through it in search of the mystical source of their enlightenment. Kant was reconciled to his island of truth. Everything that one could know could be learned in Königsberg. His successors, however, drew a different lesson from his thought. It taught them that this limited world is radically inadequate as a home for man, for it is a world of finite illusions at odds with man's infinite essence. They were not satisfied with Kant's orderly island of truth and set sail on Kant's stormy seas in search of their true being. One of the first to set sail on these dark seas and explore this nocturnal realm was Fichte.[20]

FICHTE AND THE GROUND IN FREEDOM

It was the conjunction of the French Revolution and Kant's philosophy that propelled Fichte's philosophizing. Fichte has rightly been called "the first legitimate intellectual child of the French Revolution."[21] In his early "Chance Thoughts of a Sleepless Night" (1788), he describes the degeneracy that he sees in the prerevolutionary world. In his view, this world is thoroughly corrupt and the only hope is the individual, conceived as a radically alienated subject, who aims at revolution.[22] In his *The Course of the Present Age* (1804), he describes this time as "complete wickedness" (SW 7:12; see also 7:16–20).[23] He derided the nobility, the Church, absolute monarchy, princes, Jews, the military, the standing orders, courtiers, and conservatives, that is, the whole of the ancien régime. While Fichte supported the ideals of the revolution, however, he deplored its wanton violence. Although the actual revolution in his view was a "horrible spectacle," he expected that it would work some good, if only by convincing the German princes that liberalization was necessary to avoid bloodshed (SW, 6:6).

Given Fichte's Jacobinism, many have concluded that the French Revolution and the philosophic thought that informed it were the principal sources of his doctrine of freedom.[24] While there is little doubt that Fichte was deeply moved by Rousseau's moralism and by the moralistic element of the French Revolution, they cannot have been the sole source of his doctrine of freedom. He was still a devoted determinist in 1790, long after his acquaintance with Rousseau and Montesquieu and well after the outbreak of the revolution.[25] In fact, he did not grasp the true significance of the French Revolution until his "marvelous discovery" of Kantian philosophy and particularly Kant's moral philosophy. It was this discovery on top of the revolution that impelled Fichte to investigate the dark path that led beyond the phenomenal realm in search of a ground for freedom. Kant's Copernican revolution in thinking shattered his determinism and convinced him that freedom was essential. Within this Kantian horizon, the French Revolution became comprehensible as the manifestation of an innate human longing for freedom.[26] As he saw it, Kantian philosophy grounded the sovereign autonomy of man as man, while the French Revolution established the sovereign autonomy of man in a new political and legal order.[27]

Fichte, however, was not satisfied that Kantianism had convincingly established freedom as the ground of the world. While he was initially a whole-hearted Kantian, he came to believe that an unadulterated Kantianism was untenable as a result of his attempt to defend Kant and Reinhold against Schulze's withering critique in the anonymously published *Aenesidemus*.[28] He saw that the emphasis placed upon the thing-in-itself by Reinhold and others was due to the fact that they did not understand freedom. Kant's philosophy in this sense was correct in its results but not in its reasons. In his interpretation of Kant, it thus became his goal to break the enslaving chains of the thing-in-itself and develop a system in which freedom was absolute.[29] He consequently read Kant in a Rousseauian fashion, declaring that his "system from beginning to end is only an analysis of the concept of freedom" and referring to it as "the first system of freedom."[30] Such a system in Fichte's view could be established only by a metaphysical demonstration of the *exclusive* causality of freedom, and this in turn could be achieved only by a deduction of the world as a whole from freedom. Such a deduction was the goal of Fichte's magnum opus, the *Fundamental Principles of the Entire Science of Knowledge.*

Fichte wrote the *Science of Knowledge* as a text for his students after he was appointed professor at Jena in 1794. While it was almost immediately recognized as a work of genius, it was not a final product. In fact, Fichte was never satisfied with the work and continued to revise it throughout his life, adding the two famous introductions in 1797 and significantly reworking the text in 1801. Despite his unremitting efforts, it never attained the clarity that he desired. Nevertheless, it had a tremendous impact upon German intellectual life and played a decisive role in setting the course of speculative idealism and German Romanticism as well as exercising an important if less direct influence upon Left Hegelianism and a number of other intellectual movements of the nineteenth century.

The goal of the work, Fichte tells us in the first introduction, is the propagation of Kant's great discovery. The work in fact is a one-sided development of Kantianism. Given the implicit dualism of Kant's transcendental idealism, two possibilities presented themselves as a basis for reconciling reason with itself. One could emphasize the thing-in-itself as the basis for a transcendental empiricism or one could deny the thing-in-itself and try to establish both nature and freedom on the basis of the autonomous I. Fichte argues that Kant's great discovery was obscured by the dogmatic realists, who insisted that the thing-in-itself provided the grounds for empiricism (*WL,* SW 1:419; *SK,* 3). Following Jacobi, he insists that Kant never seriously advanced this doctrine and that the core of Kant's critical idealism is not the thing-in-itself but the transcendental I. The goal of the *Science of Knowledge* is to demonstrate this fact, to reverse the realist notion that the object determines our cognitive capacity (*WL,* SW, 1:421; *SK,* 4). Such a reversal can be achieved, however, only by more profoundly determining the ground of experience that remains obscure in Kant (*WL,* SW, 1:425; *SK,* 8).[31] For Fichte, this means constructing the system that Kant recognized as necessary but was never able to complete (*WL,* SW, 1:478; *SK,* 51).[32]

The *Science of Knowledge* is an attempt to establish the fundamental principles of such a science. In Fichte's view, the ground on which a science rests cannot be demonstrated within that science and hence presupposes a more comprehensive science, a science of science or science of knowledge *(Wissenschaftslehre),* as Fichte calls it, that can explain everything that we experience. The ground of such a science is necessarily outside all experience and hence absolute (*WL,* SW, 1:428–29; *SK,* 11). Fichte's system attempts to explain everything in terms of this one ground, to reduce all multiplicity to unity.[33]

The *Science of Knowledge* aims at the determination of the primordial, absolutely unconditioned first principle of all human knowledge. Philosophy traditionally recognized the law of noncontradiction as its fundamental principle. Descartes, as we have seen, replaced the principle of noncontradiction with *ego cogito ergo sum.* Fichte accepts this Cartesian principle but radicalizes it in unprecedented ways.

FICHTE'S FUNDAMENTAL PRINCIPLES

Fichte posits three fundamental principles which together comprise the essence of all logic and ontology. The absolutely unconditioned first principle that lies at the basis of all reality is $A = A$ (*WL,* SW, 1:92–93; *SK,* 94). This is the principle of identity. To be real is to be self-identical. While Fichte chooses this beginning because it is a universally accepted truth, he is not content with its supposed self-evidence and attempts to show why it is true.[34] Such a demonstration, however, can be achieved only by going beyond experience. But how is it possible to go beyond experience?

Fichte asserts that we can know the grounds of such principles by means of what he calls intellectual intuition (*WL,* SW, 1:471; *SK,* 44). Here he seems to set himself at odds with Kant, who claimed that such intuition was impossible. Fichte, however, argues that their apparent disagreement is merely terminological, that his intellectual intuition is the same as Kant's intuition of the transcendental unity of apperception or what Kant would have intuited if he had analyzed the consciousness of the categorical imperative (*WL,* SW, 1:472; *SK,* 46).[35]

Fichte tries to come to terms with the ground of this first principle through a consideration of the conditions of its truth. $A = A$,

Fichte argues, only if there is an A; otherwise the principle is false. A exists, however, only because it is posited or established by the I in and for consciousness. With this notion that the object is posited (*gesetzt*) Fichte moves decisively beyond Kant's understanding of the object as given (*gegeben*) in the direction of a philosophy of self-positing freedom. In positing A, the I asserts that A is real and thus that A = A. What, however, are the conditions of the possibility of the I's positing this identity? According to Fichte, this is possible only if the I itself already has the capacity to assert identity. Such a capacity, he argues, can only be the result of the I's recognition of its self-identity, that "I am," or that "I am I," or that "I = I." It is this recognition, according to Fichte, that is the absolutely unconditioned first principle. A = A is merely an abstraction from I = I. A = A is true only if A exists, whereas I = I is true whenever it is articulated, as Descartes had demonstrated (*WL*, SW, 1:100; *SK*, 100). Moreover, since A = A determines what is real, the category of reality is merely the I's projection of its own essential character as the criterion of the reality of objects.

Fichte's point of departure was the intellectual intuition that "The I begins by absolutely positing its own existence" (*WL*, SW, 1:98; *SK*, 99).[36] With this assertion, Fichte brought the pathos of freedom that he had discovered in the conjunction of Kantianism and the French Revolution to its most extreme expression.[37] The I is radically free and absolute in the most literal sense, that is, it absolves itself from all relationships other than those that it itself establishes. Fichte gives voice here to a revolutionary impulse that thinks away all foreign determinations and establishes the I on itself alone.[38]

This act of self-establishment or self-positing constitutes the essence of the I, which is thereby understood not as some thing or object but as a primordial activity (*WL*, SW, 1:440; *SK*, 21). Such a notion of the subject as an activity was already present in Descartes' fundamental principle *ego cogito ergo sum*, but this was obscured by his description of the I as *res cogitans*.[39] This characterization of the I as activity was clearer in Kant, who recognized self-consciousness as the I's own act and nothing more. Fichte, however, goes one step further. While the will for Kant as the transcendental unity of apperception and as practical reason is fundamental, its activities are governed by inalterable laws that arise out of the noumenal realm. Fichte attempts to derive everything from the pure activity of the absolutely unconditioned I. As George Kelly has pointed out, with Fichte we thus enter the realm of Goethe's Faust, who proclaims, "In the beginning was the deed."[40] It is this fundamental act of production that is the basis of all other acts, since it grounds freedom and hence creation itself. Reality is merely a by-product of this creative will that seeks only itself.[41]

Dieter Henrich has argued that this recognition of the I as self-positing was Fichte's fundamental insight. In Henrich's view it is an expression of a new notion of freedom but it also establishes a new notion of self-consciousness. Modern philosophy from Descartes to Kant understood self-consciousness as a reflection or turning of the consciousness with which one ordinarily perceives objects back upon oneself.[42] This reflection theory, however, is beset by a disastrous contradiction: if the I is self-consciousness and self-consciousness is the recognition that "I am I," what is the I that reflects upon itself in the recognition "I am I?" It cannot be self-consciousness because this only occurs as a result of reflection. Nor can it be some sort of pre-reflective I, since the I comes into being only as a result of this reflection.[43] Fichte in Henrich's view was the first to recognize this contradiction and attempt to resolve it by analyzing the primordial activity that produces self-consciousness (*WL*, SW, 1:459; *SK*, 34–35).

Henrich's argument here is compelling and makes clear an important element in Fichte's project. However, Henrich does not appreciate the extent to which a similar argument could be made about Descartes. Descartes' fundamental principle, as we have seen, is an assertion of the will, a self-establishing judgment that grounds all other judgments. Fichte's notion of positing is surprisingly similar to this Cartesian notion of willing. Both understand the act as a self-establishing judgment. For Fichte, the self-positing of the I in the assertion I = I is a thetic or positing judgment. I = I in this sense rests upon the judgment "I am." Kant had argued that such judgments were impossible because being is not a predicate, but Fichte argues that it is akin to what Kant calls an infinite judgment, such as "It is beautiful" (*WL*, SW, 1:117; *SK*, 115). Unlike analytic and synthetic judgments, which either separate or combine two different concepts by attributing a predicate to a subject, thetic judgments leave the concept or subject unrelated to any other concept and thus totally indeterminate.[44] Such judgments are fundamental judgments that posit existence. Existence in this sense is grasped as a product of the will or I. The primordial or absolute I that asserts itself in the judgment "I am" or "I = I" is thus precategorical. As soon as a predicate is attached to it, it ceases to be absolute.[45] Such a judgment is possible only because the I of the "I am" is not a thing or a category but the primordial activity which brings forth all things and categories.

For Fichte's contemporaries, the status of this primordial I was ambiguous. As George Kelly has suggested, it could be interpreted as cosmological or divine, or as the finite human ego or a solipsistic ego, an ambiguity which opened Fichte up to many innocent and willful misreadings.[46] Fichte attempted to clarify this notion of the I and defend his thought against misconstruction in his two introductions to the 1797 edition. He asserts there that his teaching of the absolute I is not a teaching of individualism or egoism (*WL,* SW, 1:517; *SK,* 84). The *Science of Knowledge* begins with the absolute I as an intellectual intuition and ends with the absolute I as a fully articulated idea; as an intuition the absolute I is not yet an individual and as an idea it is no longer an individual (*WL,* SW, 1:516; *SK,* 84). This is further clarified by his assertion in a letter to Reinhold of 21 March 1797 that it was not he who had conceived the *Science of Knowledge* but God or nature acting through him.[47] Similarly, he declared in the 1801 edition of the *Science of Knowledge* that the individual I never acts, "but in me the universe acts."[48]

Insofar as the absolute I posits and therefore wills only itself, that is, insofar as it is only the activity of self-establishment, it remains pure, undifferentiated universality, an infinite plane (to use an analogy that Fichte borrows from Descartes) that is utterly self-same. How, though, can such an undifferentiated I generate a differentiated world of the sort we commonly experience? The answer to this question lies in Fichte's second principle.

Like the first principle, Fichte's second principle is posited absolutely and, consequently, cannot be proven or derived. It is, however, conditioned with respect to its content (although not its form) by the first principle. This principle is that A $\neq$ not-A (*WL,* SW, 1:102; *SK,* 103). This is the principle of negation that is counterposited *(entgegengesetzt)* to the principle of reality, that is, to A = A. Fichte argues, however, that it cannot be deduced from the first principle, since it entails opposition that is completely lacking in A = A (*WL,* SW, 1:102; *SK,* 102). It can arise only because it, too, is posited absolutely by the I. It is an act of the will, a moment of the activity that also posits itself as the I. The capacity of the I to posit such an opposition, that is, to counterposit, must in Fichte's view rest upon the existence of such an opposition or difference within the I itself. A $\neq$ not-A thus rests upon the I's recognition of a not-I and the fact that I $\neq$ not-I (*WL,* SW, 1:104; *SK,* 104).

The origin of such an other for consciousness in Fichte's view is inexplicable. Self-consciousness, however, would be impossible without it. For the infinite and undifferentiated activity of the absolute I to recognize itself as I, there must be an other that impels it to reflect upon itself as other than this other and thus as self-same. Dogmatic idealists thus go astray when they try to deny the reality of the not-I and to show that it is really only a moment of our finite consciousness (*WL*, SW, 1:156; *SK*, 147). Not everything is subordinate to our finite will. We must accept the existence of representations in consciousness that obey an alien law, the law of natural necessity.

The existence of the not-I poses an unavoidable problem for the I. The not-I is the opposite of the I and totally annihilates it. Where the not-I is the I is not. Yet, the not-I is also posited by the I and thus presupposes it. The mutual necessity and mutual contradiction of the I and the not-I is the essence of the problem that manifests itself in Kant's antinomies (*WL*, SW, 1:246; *SK*, 217). For rationalism, the crucial link between the I and the objective world (the not-I) is God.[49] Kant rejects this notion of divine mediation and establishes this relationship upon the dark and obscure transcendental unity of apperception. Building upon this Kantian foundation in a way Kant never intended, Fichte posits an immanent reconciliation or synthesis of the I and the not-I. This reconciliation is posited by Fichte's third fundamental principle, the principle of mutual limitation (*WL*, SW, 1:108; *SK*, 108).

This principle is determined throughout by the other two. Insofar as they limit one another, neither the I nor the not-I is posited as infinite or absolute and both are consequently *something*, that is, finite beings. The absolute I is not something—it is pure activity that is infinite, undifferentiated, and unlimited. The not-I, on the contrary, is the opposite of activity, that is, it is undifferentiated matter. Only with the mutual limitation of the I and the not-I does the world as we ordinarily experience it come into being. The infinite, absolute I which is posited in I = I thereby becomes an individual, empirical I, and the undifferentiated not-I becomes the individual things that constitute the objective world. Fichte, like Spinoza, whom he so admired, thus moves from the indeterminate infinite to infinite determinateness.[50]

All three principles are the result of fundamental judgments of the will. Fichte's first principle is a thetic judgment, his second an antithetic judgment, and the last a synthetic judgment that establishes the basis for the fully articulated natural world and thus for science. As Hegel recognized, this last principle is thus the principle of the ground.[51] Such a grounding synthesis, however, is impossible without the antecedent antithesis, and both in turn rest upon the original thesis. All three principles are therefore mutually necessary and concomitant (*WL,* SW, 1:114; *SK,* 113). This is the basis for the essentially dialectical character of Fichte's thought.

The rest of the *Science of Knowledge* is an investigation of this dialectical reconciliation or mutual limitation of the I and the not-I. It falls into two parts. The first is a consideration of the possibility that the I is limited by the not-I, that is, that the objective world determines all of the structures of subjectivity. This theoretical section corresponds to Kant's *Critique of Pure Reason.* The second part examines the way in which the not-I is limited and determined by the I, that is, the way in which the objective world is informed by subjectivity. This practical section corresponds to Kant's *Critique of Practical Reason.*

THEORETICAL REASON AS IMAGINATION

In the section of his work that pursues a theoretical solution, Fichte attempts to achieve a reconciliation of the I and not-I, of human freedom and natural necessity, by investigating the possible ways in which the not-I limits the I. His goal is to determine whether any of them can serve as the basis for a complete synthesis (*WL,* SW, 1:144; *SK,* 137). These interposed links, which are generated by a dialectical deduction from a consideration of the possible relationships of the I and the not-I, are the categories of the understanding enumerated by Kant. They represent the forms or structures of all possible experience of the world. Kant merely adopted these categories from the table of judgments he had inherited from scholasticism. Fichte attempts to deduce them dialectically from the fundamental structures of judgment itself. What becomes more or less clear in the course of Fichte's torturously obscure deduction is that there is not and cannot be a *theoretical* reconciliation of the I and the not-I. Freedom and subjectivity cannot be explained simply in terms of the laws that govern the objective world. The *Science of Knowledge* thus demonstrates that we cannot understand the I and our subjective experience in the same way we understand the objective world (*WL,* SW, 1:177; *SK,* 164).

This conclusion, in Fichte's opinion, indicates that the Enlightenment notion of reason is inadequate to grasp the infinite essence of the self. The problem of the infinite for discursive reason is not new.

It stretches back to the Greeks and is a central problem in the nominalist-realist debate. Descartes established a new notion of the infinite as a basis for the reconciliation of the finite categories of natural reason with the divine. The antinomies convinced Kant that this notion of the infinite could not unite the finite and the infinite, and he thus settled for the dualism of the transcendental idealism. For Fichte, such a dualism is unacceptable. Reason must be one. He attempts to establish this unity on the basis of the infinite that he discovers in the absolute I. In this sense, he follows the path that Descartes lays out with his notion of an infinite will common to both God and man.

The character of Fichte's I is ambiguous. While it is finite in terms of its concrete existence, it is infinite in terms of its essential activity. Fichte argues that all modes of the I seek to conform to this infinite essence, to the I's own positing, its absolutely free activity (*WL,* SW, 1:205; *SK,* 186). Yet the not-I restricts the I. On the surface, it seems that such a restriction is impossible, since it could occur only if the I were passive rather than active, which is contrary to its essence. If the I is restricted by the not-I, how can it be absolutely free activity? Fichte attempts to dissolve this apparent contradiction by properly distinguishing between the empirical I and the absolute I. The not-I is real and restricts the empirical I, but it does not and cannot restrict the absolute I. While this solution may seem ad hoc, it is justified by Fichte's radical claim that the not-I itself is only an expression of the absolute I. Both the empirical I and the not-I, that is, both individual human subjects and the objective world, in Fichte's view, are expressions of the free activity of the absolute I, of the infinite will that is essential to both God and man.

Since the not-I establishes the limits of the empirical I and is necessary for its existence, the I and the not-I, the infinite and the finite, must be conjoined. The theoretical section of the *Science of Knowledge* considers all the possible ways in which the I can posit itself as determined by the not-I. All, however, prove to be inadequate. No union can be established. These two realms, however, are not totally disjoined. If they were, experience would be impossible, for the I and the not-I must encounter one another for there to be experience. This encounter is made possible by the imagination.

We generally understand the imagination as the capacity for forming images and especially fictitious images or illusions. Fichte recognizes this conventional opinion, but argues that the images produced by the imagination can be deceptive only if there is an objective truth against which they can be measured. Fichte believes he has shown that there is no such truth. In his view, there are no self-subsistent natural forms; all forms are posited (*gesetzt*) by the I. He concludes that all determinate reality is the product of the imagination, which makes the infinite visible in finite images, in forms or categories.

The imagination is able to accomplish this task, according to Fichte, because it has a foot in both the finite and the infinite and wavers between them. The imagination attempts to unite them by producing a unifying image or metaphor that brings the infinite into appearance within the finite, thus allowing the finite to appear as the finite, that is, in opposition to the infinite (*WL,* SW, 1:215; *SK,* 193).[52] The image of a tree, for example, brings into view a finite being but only by differentiating it from the infinity of other things that it is not. It thus makes visible at one time both the finite and the infinite. Within this image, the imagination holds the opposites together without uniting them but also without allowing them to annihilate one another (*WL,* SW, 1:207; *SK,* 187). In its wavering between them, however, the imagination confers reality on them and they become intuitable (*WL,* SW, 1:226; *SK,* 202). The limit established by the imagination creates both the tree and the not-tree. We understand each in terms of the other. As intuitable, they can be abstracted and fixed in the understanding, that is, they can become concepts and categories. Understanding and science in this sense rest upon the creative power of the imagination that establishes the forms and categories of experience.

Contrary to common opinion, Fichte concludes that science depends not upon noncontradiction but upon opposition of the finite and the infinite within the imagination (*WL,* SW, 1:214; *SK,* 192). Knowing is an establishing of boundaries and it is such an establishing that is the essence of all judgment and categories. Boundaries derive their meaning from the fact that they separate each thing from everything that it is not. A boundary, however, is determinate for knowledge only if it can be recognized as a boundary. Understanding is thus possible only if the I is in some sense already beyond the boundary of intuition. The transcendental in other words can be comprehended only by a being who is both transcendent and empirical, who has both theoretical and practical capacities that are in some fundamental sense one (*WL,* SW, 1:278; *SK,* 245).

The image produced by the imagination sets or defines a boundary or limit and separates the finite and the infinite. However, it also unites them by bringing both into view at the boundary. The unity of the finite and the infinite that is embodied in the categories and essential to philosophy and science is thus a product of the boundary established by the imagination. Philosophy and science in this sense are fundamentally dependent upon an imaginative making, upon poetry in the original Greek sense of *poiēsis*. They continue to be defined in Fichte's thought as rational but only by virtue of the fact that reason itself has been redefined as a creative *positing* rather than a passive contemplation of the given or eternal.

Such a poetic science, however, cannot provide a firm foundation for knowing. The infinite activity can never be fully comprehended in any image. The boundary established by the imagination and later stabilized by reason in the understanding is always overturned by the infinite activity of the I itself, which spurns all such limitations. The theoretical resolution of the contradiction of the I and the not-I, of the infinite and the finite fails to establish a satisfying synthesis.

This conclusion was probably inevitable for Fichte. He redefined reason in terms of the imagination as an infinite creative willing that paints finite pictures of its own infinity. That it is never satisfied with the result and constantly begins painting anew is thus hardly surprising.

For Kant, this problem does not arise, because he partitions reason in a way that allows space for both science and morality, for both the finite I and an objective world on one hand and the infinite I and subjective freedom on the other. Fichte, however, believes that he has discovered that Kant's island of truth is itself only an illusion, that there are no fixed and immutable forms, and that everything is merely the projection of the imagination upon the banks of fog where one image gives way to another. This confusion, of course, was exactly what Kant predicted would engulf those who left the shelter of his island. To find his way through these mists, Fichte is driven to desperate and dangerous measures. Since this wavering and frustration would go on forever, the knot of the finite and the infinite "must be cut rather than loosened, by an absolute decree of reason, which the philosopher does not pronounce, but merely proclaims: Since there is no way of reconciling the not-I and the I, *let there be* no not-I at all!" (*WL*, SW, 1:144; *SK*, 137). The continual streaming forth of images by the imagination is insufficient. Because the finite can never embody the infinite, it must be eliminated. Man can be free and come into his own infinite essence only through the elimination of all otherness. Since all forms and categories are illusions, all forms and categories must be eradicated.[53]

Early modern thought was principally concerned with human preservation and prosperity, but even in this context some thinkers recognized that freedom was essential. This was implicit in Descartes and became explicit in Rousseau. The relationship of this freedom to nature, however, was left largely unexamined. Kant faced this problem and tried to provide a ground for their mutual coexistence. In the thought of Fichte, we witness the turn away from coexistence toward the assertion of freedom as absolute and the consequent demand that objective nature be annihilated. Freedom and freedom alone must rule, a pure will or activity that shapes only itself and abides by no laws, that knows in its heart of hearts that it is the source of all laws, of all logic, and of all ontology.[54] The elimination of the not-I, that is, of the objective world and all objective reason, however, entails the elimination of the empirical I, for the empirical I arises only in conjunction with the not-I. The proclamation that the not-I must be eliminated is thus also the proclamation that the empirical I must become the absolute, that man must become an absolutely unconstrained and thus radically free being, must become, in other words, God.

FREEDOM AND THE DARK NIGHT OF THE NOUMENAL I

In the section of the *Science of Knowledge* concerned with practical reason, Fichte attempts to explain in concrete detail the subliminal manner in which the I limits and determines the not-I, that is, to show that the objective world as it appears in consciousness is the result of the unconscious activity of the will and thus a manifestation of freedom. This explanation takes Fichte beyond the realm of consciousness and into the darkness of the noumenal I.

Fichte's goal in the *Science of Knowledge* is the articulation of a unified account of experience that reconciles the I and the not-I. He concluded in the first section of the work that a theoretical synthesis could never accomplish this task, that no account of the world that based itself on the not-I or categorical reason could adequately explain experience. As a result, he concludes that the necessary synthesis requires the elimination of the not-I. This annihilation of the objective world is accomplished by demonstrating that the not-I is immediately determined by the absolute I, that is, that the absolute I is the ground and source of the not-I (*WL,* SW, 1:250, 271; *SK,* 221, 239).

Such a demonstration is possible only on the basis of a deeper examination of the activity of the I, that is, of noumenal freedom. Kant believed that such an examination was impossible, since this realm is not accessible to intuition or understanding. Fichte, on the contrary, believes that we have access to this realm through the imagination, which (imperfectly) portrays it in finite images. While we thus cannot know this realm in the same way we can know the objective world, it is not totally closed to the understanding. Indeed, we can come to understand it by a leap of the imagination, a leap made possible by man's intrinsic freedom (*WL,* SW, 1:298; *SK,* 262).

Fichte identifies the noumenal realm with the subconscious realm of the will, the realm of emotions, instincts, and psychological drives.[55] This realm of the will in his view is the substratum and truth of the world of the not-I. Fichte's understanding of the subconscious, however, differs in essential ways from our own. We generally assume that our emotions, for example, have a physical cause in either our biology or experience. We thus typically understand emotions as passions, that is, as reactions to actions that have their source outside us. On one level, Fichte agrees with this assessment. From the perspective of the empirical I, all emotions are passions. The true source of these emotions, however, is the I itself as an absolute activity, as pure will. Emotions are thus forms of freedom and consequently not reactions but primordial actions. They are the empirical I's experience of its own essence, of the free activity of the absolute I acting on and through the empirical I. Fichte's imaginative construction of this substratum of all experience is the fundamental expression of his doctrine of freedom that attempts to show that the empirical I and the not-I are in fact only moments of the primordial activity or will that constitutes the absolute I itself. It is the will's self-grounding act.

On the most immediate level, this will or activity appears as *striving* (*WL,* SW, 1:261–62; *SK,* 231). The I strives to subordinate the not-I within itself. This subordination, Fichte argues, is demanded by the absolute I in the name of absolute being (*WL,* SW, 1:259; *SK,* 229).[56] Freedom, in other words, establishes this categorical imperative in order that freedom itself be absolute, that freedom absolve itself from all dependence on the other by dissolving the otherness of the other. Striving is the predominant form of the will in the empirical I because this I is not yet absolute. It is the imperfect expression of the pure activity of the will that constitutes the absolute I itself. This notion of pure activity which Fichte employs to characterize the

absolute I is an adaptation of the Aristotelian notion of *energeia*. It is
an activity that is for its own sake and that thus has no end beyond
itself.[57] Striving, by contrast, is always the pursuit of something that
is not present in the activity itself and that presupposes the presence
of the alien other. As a result, it is dissatisfied as long as the other
intervenes, and it aims at the elimination of the other. It is thus a
form of negation that is guided by a half-recognized vision of what it
in essence already is and what it consequently ought actually to be.
As Hegel pointed out, striving for Fichte is what Kant understood as
the ought.[58]

This striving to demonstrate that the not-I is an expression of the
absolute I aims not merely at overcoming and subordinating the
world but also at overcoming the empirical I of every individual (SW,
1:130). It is not merely a Cartesian technological project that seeks
to master and transform nature but also a Rousseauian moral project
that aims at the transfiguration of man himself. Indeed, the subordination of nature is necessary only because it stands in the way of
the absolute unity and freedom of the I. The ultimate goal is thus
not the elimination of the opposition produced by the not-I but the
reconciliation of the I with itself, of the empirical I with the absolute
I. Liberation from nature is merely the means for overcoming alienation, for reconciling the I with itself. Negation thus is always in the
service of self-affirmation. Since the I is itself essentially freedom,
however, overcoming alienation means establishing freedom as
absolute.

From the perspective of the absolute I, the not-I is only an internal disruption in the I itself. The empirical I, however, experiences
this disruption as a feeling. The primordial I, as Fichte understands
it, is both everything and nothing. As pure, unconditioned activity,
it is totally without internal distinctions and encompasses everything
whatsoever. Since it is undifferentiated, however, it is no particular
thing and thus nothing. This pure activity is disrupted by an alien
element that appears within the I. The origin of this alien other,
according to Fichte, is unknowable, but its existence is an undeniable fact of consciousness. This other undermines the self-identity of
the I by establishing a boundary between what it is and what it is not
(*WL*, SW, 1:265, 269; *SK*, 233–34, 237). The I experiences this
boundary as a feeling that curbs its activity. (*WL*, SW, 1:266; *SK*,
235). As a result of this feeling, the I does not want to extend itself
any further in the direction closed off by the boundary. It thereby
ceases to be absolute and becomes merely an empirical I. Thus, it is

this feeling and not an external object that limits the will and the activity of the I.

This limitation of the I is also the source of self-consciousness. The primordial I is a pure activity, a point that wants to become an infinite plane and which consequently does not reflect upon itself. It is pure will. This outreaching, however, is checked at a particular point by the not-I. The will meets a resistance which it cannot overcome. The will is reflected back from this point to its point of origin (*WL,* SW, 1:228; *SK,* 203). The I comes to recognize itself as an I in consequence of its encounter with the not-I or object. In this way, the I becomes self-conscious. The inner experience of the empirical I undergoing this experience is a feeling of incapacity that sets a limit for the I. Insofar as it discovers such an incapacity within itself, the I also discovers that it is a finite thing. By means of an inner experience, the I thus comes to a recognition of itself and its particularity.

Fichte argues that the not-I or object that seems to check the I is really only the occasion or place of the I's self-limitation. This assertion should not be construed as a denial of the ultimate reality of the not-I. Fichte claims that the not-I can affect the I only if the I allows itself to be affected. The not-I thus becomes something for the I only because of a decision by the I itself, because of the feeling that the I has of its own limits. Indeed, without this feeling the not-I would be nothing for the I.[59]

If this is the case, however, why does the I posit the not-I as conditioning the I? The answer to this question for Fichte lies in the impossibility of the I's striving. The I strives for the infinite but the infinite cannot be attained. At some point short of the infinite, the I reaches the limits of its strength, and can go no further. At this point, it is repulsed from the infinite (*WL,* SW, 1:272 and 275; *SK,* 240 and 242). On the emotional level, this is the source of the feeling of incapacity in the I, the feeling that its will is limited, that it is not God. The returning motion of the I from its repulse by the infinite is not grasped, however, for what it is, and the feeling that it engenders is attributed to the object, to the not-I.

The true origin of this feeling is not recognized by the I undergoing this experience because the will of the I that extends toward the infinite and is repulsed by it is not reflected and thus never comes to consciousness (*WL,* SW, 1:235; *SK,* 208). The boundary of intuition, as we have seen, is established by the imagination, which itself in some sense is already beyond the boundary they establish, already in some sense infinite (*WL,* SW, 1:237; *SK,* 210). The fundamental activity of the imagination thus cannot be subject to this boundary. As the source of consciousness, this infinite will thus never appears in or for consciousness.

The absolute activity of such an infinite will can be restrained only by itself. The not-I or other thus must also be a moment of this activity. According to Fichte, it is in fact the same will or motion in the opposite direction, that is, back from the infinite to its point of departure. The I thus consists in two mutually necessary motions, a centrifugal motion that aims at the infinite and a centripetal motion that returns to the I (*WL,* SW, 1:274; *SK,* 241–42).

From this perspective, it becomes apparent that the primordial activity of the I has two components. On one hand, it is an infinite practical striving to fill out the infinite, an endless self-assertion that aims at the subjection of the world to absolute freedom. On the other hand, it is a theoretical drive to reflection in which the reflective element forgets itself because it itself is not reflected (*WL,* SW, 1:308; *SK,* 269).[60] These two drives are equally primordial and mutually necessary. Reflection is the basis for the I's going forth outside itself, since it is only because of reflection that there is limitation and thus an outside and an inside. The demand that it exhaust the infinite is the basis for its striving after causality in general and thus the source of the activity that passes beyond the boundary. It thus makes the boundary comprehensible as a boundary and the I comprehensible as an I (*WL,* SW, 1:276; *SK,* 243). There could be no striving for the infinite without reflection and no reflection without such a striving for the infinite.

Practical reason thus can never achieve its goal. This goal, however, remains as the eternal spur to further activity. In Fichte's view, this goal of absolute liberation and reconciliation floats like a vision before us drawing us onward, but it is never attained (*WL,* SW, 1:270; *SK,* 238). This fact points to the truly primordial character of this will as *longing.* Longing, as Fichte understands it, is a drive toward something unknown which reveals itself through need, discomfort, and a void (*WL,* SW, 1:303; *SK,* 265). Only through longing does the I issue forth from itself and posit something. It is thus the activity through which the external world is revealed within the I (*WL,* SW, 1:303; *SK,* 266). Because of the feeling of separation and emptiness, the I reaches out beyond itself in search of what it lacks. This alienation is the source of the infinite striving that gives birth to both the not-I and the empirical I.

Longing is thus the original, wholly independent manifestation of the will that lies at the core of the self (*WL,* SW, 1:304; *SK,* 267). It is the source of the striving which is the essence of freedom. As such, it is the deepest ground of the activity of the I. It is, in other words, the noumenal ground of reality. As Hegel recognized, longing for Fichte is thus divine.[61] Substantively, longing is the drive toward a change of feelings, and that means toward a reinterpretation of the objective world, a subordination of that world to the I (*WL,* SW, 1:320; *SK,* 280). As we have seen, the I experiences the not-I as a boundary that reflects the I's own feeling of incapacity, which itself arises as a result of its inability to attain the infinite. A change of feelings thus can occur only as a result of an extension of our capacity for filling out the infinite. Longing is the attempt to attain the infinite that is simultaneously aware of its own limits. Insofar as it is aware of these limits, however, it already is in some sense beyond them. Longing in this sense is the activity of the infinite, absolute I as it manifests itself within the finite, empirical I. It is the original source of both the drive to fill out the infinite and the drive to reflection and thus of both the theoretical and the practical will.

Longing arises out of a dissatisfaction with the limits of the I, that is, out of its feeling of incapacity. This feeling arises, however, because in longing the I is already in some sense beyond its limitations and thus feels the contradiction between what it is as an absolute activity and what it is as an empirical being. What the I should be, however, is unclear to the I undergoing this experience. It knows only that it is dissatisfied with what it is, with the feeling that constrains it. Longing thus turns against this feeling, against feeling x, and wills its opposite, that is, feeling not-x, without any idea of the substantive character of this new feeling (*WL,* SW, 1:305–6; *SK,* 268). This is accomplished by a reconstruction of the world by the imagination according to the imperative of the I. The imagination thus projects a new image that sets up a new boundary between the finite and the infinite. The substantive structure of this image and the new world it establishes, however, arise not from the I itself but from a negation of the old world, of the old feeling x.

The new image engenders a new boundary and a new feeling of limitation (*WL,* SW, 1:323; *SK,* 282). This in turn leads to a new dissatisfaction and a new longing. The I does not realize that what it really longs for is the abolition of all limitations and thus of all feeling. As a result, it is driven forward from one image to the next along a dialectical path by the repeated negation of successive realities. At each moment of liberation, "harmony exists and a feeling of *incli-*

nation ensues, which in this case is a feeling of *contentment,* of reple-
tion, of utter completeness," but this harmony "lasts only a
moment, . . . since the longing necessarily recurs" (*WL,* SW, 1:328;
SK, 286).

This process in Fichte's view is endless. Drawing upon Kant, he
argues that the attainment of the highest unity in the unimpeded
activity of the absolute I would be possible only in a completed infinity (*WL,* SW, 1:217–18; *SK,* 195). For this reason, man can never
actually be an absolutely free and infinite being. This fact does not
remove or weaken the moral imperative to strive for such an end. On
the contrary, it presents human beings with the endless task of pur-
suing an ideal that can never be attained. With his radical separation
of nature and freedom, Kant saved human beings from such a fate.
Any reconciliation of nature and freedom in Kant's view can come
about only as the result of teleological forces beyond our control.
Human freedom thus plays no role in shaping human history. At
best, it can serve as an imperative for individual action, and even on
this level it may be subordinate to the natural force of the passions.
Thus, we can be morally satisfied if we are motivated by a good will,
even if we cannot transform the world or our own desires to conform
to it. For Fichte, by contrast, the human will can change the world,
and moral satisfaction thus comes only from the constant use of one's
freedom to effect such a transformation. The end of this transformation is the completion of freedom, that is, the liberation of the empirical I from all constraints. Because this goal can never be attained but
only approached, striving always has a moral goal. Fichte's thought
thus establishes an ideal that can never be attained as a spur to an
activity that can never be completed.

In this way, Fichte brings man before the infinite abyss of his own
being, the noumenal night that Kant argued understanding could
never master. In his view, man can only listen to the voice of conscience that spoke out of this abyss. Fichte by contrast argues that it
is man's moral duty to eradicate all finite forms that separate him
from this infinity, for these are barriers that separate man from himself. Through this destruction of the not-I, man struggles to realize
his own infinity, his own infinite freedom. Such a struggle brings light
into this darkness, for it reveals more and more that this abyss is only
the interior of man's own self. Fichte in this way sets man on a course
toward the infinite and thus toward the divine. He little suspected the
danger, which became all too clear to Nietzsche, that man would
shipwreck on this infinite (*M,* KGW V 2:335).

THE TOTALISTIC POLITICS OF FREEDOM

As we shall see, this Fichtean notion of freedom had a great impact on early German Romanticism, Left Hegelianism, and Russian nihilism, each of which proclaimed in its own way a politics of freedom. The character of such a politics, however, is already evident in Fichte's own political philosophy.

While Fichte's thinking about political matters underwent considerable change from his early attachment to the principles of the French Revolution to his later advocacy of a hyper-German nationalism, he always sought a politics that could realize his vision of absolute freedom. He was never satisfied, however, that he had found such a politics. The extreme measures he adopted in the course of his search, though, are an indication of the dangers of trying to realize such a notion of freedom.

While the *Science of Knowledge* examines freedom from the perspective of the absolute I, this I remains outstanding in our actual experience of the world. Practical life is characterized by the confrontation of the empirical I and the not-I, of individual human beings and nature. Each individual is driven by an intrinsic longing for freedom and attempts to demonstrate that the external world is only an expression of his own creative will. He thus strives to liberate himself from the limitations imposed by the not-I and become absolute. Put in another way, each seeks to realize the universal essence of humanity in himself.[62]

The individual, however, cannot achieve such a transformation on his own. In fact, according to Fichte, he cannot even become self-conscious and recognize himself as an I, that is, as a free being, by his own powers. Self-consciousness depends upon the encounter with another free consciousness. Consciousness in the first instance is what it perceives. Originally, it confronts the not-I, the unfree world of nature, and is absorbed in it. It can become conscious of itself as a free being only if it encounters a being that is both free and other, that is, only through the encounter with another I (*NR*, SW, 3:29, 4:218). This other I is a thou, an other that is like us. Contrary to Rousseau, Fichte believes that "man is determined to live in society; he shall live in society; he is not a whole, completed human being and contradicts himself, when he lives in isolation" (*BG*, SW, 6:306).

The recognition of one's freedom is thus simultaneously the recognition of the freedom of others. In contradistinction to Hegel, the individual does not have to prove his freedom by proving that

everyone else is unfree. The I asserts itself in opposition to the not-I
by conquering it and subordinating it as its property, but other individuals cannot be treated as property, as a mere means, but must be
treated as ends in themselves. It is possible to treat others as a means
only by denying that they are free beings, but such a denial is also a
denial of one's own freedom.

Not all men, however, are capable of freedom, for many remain
determined by the not-I in the form of natural desire. Already in the
first introduction to the *Science of Knowledge,* Fichte argued that
there were two types of human beings, those who had raised themselves to the consciousness of freedom and those who had not (*WL,*
SW, 1:433; *SK,* 15). Only the former act uniformly according to their
moral will. The others must be constrained to act morally. Kant
argues that we are morally obligated to treat all men as ends in themselves. Fichte qualifies this position. He believes that we are morally
obligated to treat all men as ends in themselves who are indeed ends
in themselves, that is, who are free beings, and that we are also obligated to help others become free by liberating them from the tyranny
of the not-I. Thus, coercion may be employed to modify the behav-
ior of individuals who are driven by caprice *(Willkür)* rather than by
moral will.

Morality for Fichte, however, is not politics. Indeed, he widens the
gulf that Kant had opened up between them. He adopts Kant's
notion that morality is the realm of freedom, and politics the realm
of desire, but rejects Kant's conclusion that freedom is powerless to
change the world. Freedom in fact can transform man and the world
to make politics superfluous. In the initial period of the French Revolution, Fichte believed that such a radical transformation was imminent, but he increasingly came to see that it was at best a long-term
project. He also came to realize that politics itself could play a significant role in helping to bring about such a transformation. Political
authority, however, could be legitimately established only as a system
of right, and such a system must be based on freedom.

Political freedom, however, cannot be absolute, because those
who are driven by desire cannot be trusted to treat others as ends in
themselves. They must be restrained. Since there is no a priori means
of distinguishing such men from those who obey their moral will,
every man must suspect every other man and protect himself against
them. The result is a war of all against all.[63] Rational individuals in
Fichte's view will thus consent only to a political order that can guarantee that no one's freedom will now or at any point in the future be

endangered by the capricious action of others. Therefore, the communal life of free beings requires that the capricious freedom of all individuals be limited in all futures.[64] Freedom can therefore be secured only by total administration and total education. Fichte's state is thus necessarily totalitarian.[65]

The state in Fichte's view is a creation of human will and is established by universal consent. In contradistinction to the moral law which is binding on all individuals, the principles of right established by the state constrain only those who freely accept them. The will that is thereby established is akin to Rousseau's general will and subordinates the will of the individual to the general moral will of the community, but in contrast to Rousseau, Fichte argues that the individual has the right to leave at any time he pleases. The state for Fichte is in this sense a purely voluntary association.

The state aims at the realization of human freedom through the destruction of the not-I. The principal way in which this goal is achieved is through the institution of property.[66] Property for Fichte is *Eigentum,* what is my own, subordinate to the I. Fichte's notion of property, however, differs in many ways from ours. The end of life in Fichte's view is not satisfaction or happiness, but freedom, and this requires not concrete things but the right to free, unimpeded activity. The right to property is thus not the right to physical things, but to one's own powers and pursuits (*NR,* SW, 3:210; SW, 6:117–18, 177–78.[67] Physical objects may be necessary to this end but, their ownership is always conditional and is limited by the needs others have for property to exercise their own powers. Property is thus constitutive for the individual in the same way that freedom is for the I (*BG,* SW, 6:292). It is freedom made concrete.

As the ground of freedom, property cannot be left to the determination of the market, for the market is governed by the not-I, by a blind mechanical necessity.[68] It is nothing other than the realm of desire, of unfreedom. The government must regulate the economy and professions to guarantee the individual's free exercise of his powers and to organize society for the technological conquest of nature. These are the goals of Fichte's closed commercial state. This state coordinates all the different sectors of the economy. It controls the size and activity of the various occupations, allowing the individual to choose his own profession. However, it does not guarantee that he will be able to practice this profession.[69] In addition to controlling the size and activities of various occupations, the state also has the right to control the income and expenditures of its members, to prevent dislocations of labor and unemployment that the free expression of consumer preferences would produce. Moreover, to make such a controlled economy possible the state in Fichte's view can and indeed must shut out foreign trade and isolate the society from the world economy.

On the surface, this extensive reliance on coercion seems to undermine Fichte's goal of universal human emancipation, but from Fichte's point of view this conclusion is mistaken, for coercion is employed against only the not-I, not the I, against only unfreedom, not freedom. Primarily, this is the coercion of brute nature by technology. Secondarily, it is the use of coercion against nature as it manifests itself as caprice or desire within the individual human being. Our humanity is thereby not constrained, but set free. In Rousseauian fashion we are forced to be free.

Even if such coercion is compatible with freedom, one might legitimately wonder if Fichte is not overly optimistic about the morality of the leaders who will guide men to freedom. How can we be certain that they themselves will not act capriciously? What is to prevent them from becoming tyrants who will use the enormous, totalistic powers of the state to satisfy their own desires under the pretext of securing human freedom? Fichte is opposed to the separation of powers characteristically employed in such circumstances to prevent these kinds of abuses. In his early thought, he argued that usurpation could be avoided by establishing an Ephorate that would oversee the rulers, but he increasingly came to realize that such an institution would be ineffective. Such organizational constraints also limit the state's powers to do good. In any case, Fichte is ultimately convinced that such constraints are unnecessary, because the ruling class will be a noble cadre of scholars virtuously devoted to the cause of freedom.

The foundation of Fichte's political theory is his argument for the rule of scholars. Indeed, this class makes his state possible. The goal of universal human emancipation requires the comprehensive administration of things and total education of human beings. The latter is the key to overcoming the contradiction between absolute freedom and universal coercion. The scholarly class is crucial to this system of education not only because they possess the necessary technical knowledge to bring it about but because they alone have the requisite moral character to put the general good ahead of their own individual interests. The scholar embodies the goal of universal freedom that he seeks to establish for all human beings. "In the Divine Idea [the scholar] carries in himself the form of the future age which one day must clothe itself with reality . . . It is the business of the scholar so to interpose in this strife as to reconcile the activity with the purity of the idea [in each new age]" (SW, 6:350–403). He sees further into the future and therefore better understands what needs to be done to promote the goal of universal freedom (*BG,* SW, 6:331–34). The moral superiority of this class is a product of their activities. They have a more general perspective because they are not subject to the social division of labor that produces one-sided human beings. They thus constitute what Hegel was later to characterize as a general or universal class.

In his early thought, Fichte imagines that this vision of a ruling scholarly class is essentially egalitarian because the inequality between this class and the rest of the society is a result of the respect of the masses for the scholar. In his later thought, however, Fichte increasingly comes to accept the essential elitism of this notion and grants the scholars a special status and freedom as a result of their moral superiority. While this class may be an elite, it is vastly different from the old aristocracy, for it is part of a new organic social structure at odds with the corporate fragmentation of the ancien régime.[70] The moral equality of all men sanctions social inequality based on the functional needs of interaction and coordination.

The end of right and government for Fichte is the establishment of universal moral freedom in which the particular natural will in each individual is subordinated to the general will of the absolute I. This can be achieved only by the abolition of the not-I through the collective efforts of humanity. "This war [against nature] can never end, if we do not become gods; but it can and should make the influence of nature weaker and weaker, the rule of reason stronger and stronger . . . what the individual could not do is made possible by the united powers of all. Each battles individually, but the weakening of nature occurs through the collective struggle, and the victory that each individual achieves in his part comes to all" (*BG,* SW, 6:315–17).

Fichte's practical goal is a radicalization of the Cartesian and Baconian project for the conquest of nature that has as its end not the physical well-being of individual human beings but the liberation of humanity from nature altogether and the consequent establishment of a realm of universal human freedom and power. This goal for Fichte can be achieved only by the organized mass of laborers under the leadership of an educated elite of scholars. The goal of politics is thus not preservation or prosperity but a liberation from nature, and that means an internal liberation from nature as well, that is, from the desire for preservation and prosperity. Although this political project requires coercion, as society advances and the not-I plays an increasingly less important role in human life, the need for coercion will diminish. In contrast to his humanistic contemporaries, Fichte thus believes that the golden age lies not in the past but in the future and can be attained through the mastery and control of nature by science and technology (*BG,* SW, 6:335–46). Indeed, this final goal of moral freedom is the only thing that can justify the coercion that is intrinsic to Fichte's politics.

In his late thought, Fichte defended a form of hypernationalism because he came to believe that love of the fatherland might replace coercion as a means of social and moral transformation. In this formation of an egalitarian national community based on patriotism, Fichte also hoped to overcome the contradiction between elite and mass that characterized his earlier thought. While patriotism might reduce the need for internal coercion in the narrow sense, however, such patriotism could itself be established and maintained only by an even more totalistic system of education. The state, for example, would have to separate children from parents at an early age and subject them to compulsory education and military service (*RDN,* SW, 7:428–44).

Each nation in Fichte's view has its own character and system of right. History itself must be understood in these nationalistic terms. Indeed, in his *Science of the State,* Fichte locates the origin of the distinction between those who are capable of freedom and those who are dominated by nature in different original races (SW, 4:470–77, 489–96). From this perspective, society has its origin in armed force backed by spiritual terrors of a superior race under the leadership of divinely inspired dictators *(Zwingherren)* (*RDN,* SW, 7:565, 576). This race aims at human liberation and it is its sacred duty to coerce others. Fichte argued that the advancement of this task in each epoch falls to a particular nation and believed that Germany was the inheritor of this destiny in his age.

This view is not simply chauvinistic. The triumph of Germany in Fichte's view is in the interest of humanity.[71] The German nation is for the human species what the scholarly class is for a given society, the agent of freedom creating a rational social and political order. In its assertion of its unique creative freedom Germany merely follows the universal moral law (*RDN,* SW, 7:277–95). The German nation thus is the savior of earth: "If it sinks, so humanity will sink with it, without hope of a single reconstitution" (*RDN,* SW, 7:499; cf.

7:486, 503). National self-assertion from this perspective is a kind of humanitarianism and the good patriot is the good cosmopolitan (SW, 7:571–73).

Fichte's political philosophy reflects the moralistic utopianism of the *Science of Knowledge*. Fichte recognizes the apparent contradiction of this utopian element with the practical goals of his thought, but he believes that it is ameliorated by the possibility of coming infinitely nearer the ideal. This modification, however, does not reduce the practical danger of such an approach. Fichte assumes that nature or the not-I is infinitely malleable by the human will. However, if nature and especially human nature should prove more resistant to change than Fichte believes, then greater coercion and tyranny may be necessary. Moreover, such tyranny can be morally justified, with torture interpreted as the means to emancipation. Indeed, given Fichte's admission that the goal of moral striving can never be obtained, such an outcome is likely. While clearly this totalitarian element is more apparent in his later nationalistic thought with its emphasis on superior peoples whose sacred duty it is to save humanity, and dictatorial leaders sent by God, it is equally present in his earlier more socialistic thought. As we shall see, it is a side of the notion of freedom and absolute will that becomes increasingly explicit during the nineteenth century.

FICHTE AND THE DEVELOPMENT OF NIHILISM

It is generally believed that nihilism originated in the late nineteenth century. However, the crucial turn onto the path that leads to the nihilism of the nineteenth and twentieth centuries begins with Fichte's rejection of the Enlightenment notion of reason in favor of an absolute subjectivism that attempts to derive all reason from the infinite will of the absolute I. This rejection leads to the dark night of the noumenal I and to an adulation of the striving and longing that are the manifestation of this subconscious will. While Fichte draws upon the thought of Descartes and Kant, he ultimately chooses a different and more dangerous path. This path leads, as Jacobi realized, to the death of God and the deification of man.

The history of Fichte's influence has generally remained unperceived. In what follows we will try to make apparent his importance for the development of nihilism. Modernity began with Descartes' attempt to construct a bastion against an utterly omnipotent and thus transrational God. To build such a bastion, however, Descartes had to posit a similar omnipotence and irrationality in man. This was the essential freedom of the human will. Rousseau and Kant made this element in man explicit and fundamental. With Fichte, however, it first becomes philosophically revolutionary and turns against all actuality in the name of absolute freedom and omnipotence. This philosophical revolution both heralds and informs the social and political revolutions of the nineteenth and twentieth centuries. At the end of modernity, man awakens from his long dream of freedom and reason to discover that he has become the monster he sought to slay.

Chapter Four

THE DAWN OF THE DEMONIC

Romanticism and Nihilism

The Tyger

Tyger tyger burning bright,
In the forests of the night:
What immortal hand or eye
Could frame thy fearful symmetry?

In what distant deeps or skies.
Burnt the fire of thine eyes?
On what wings dare he aspire?
What the hand, dare seize the fire?

And what the shoulder & what art,
Could twist the sinews of thy heart?
And, when that heart began to beat,
What dread hand? & what dread feet?

What the hammer? What the chain,
In what furnace was thy brain?
What the anvil? What dread grasp,
Dare its deadly terrors clasp?

When the stars threw down their spears
And water'd heaven with their tears:
Did He smile His work to see?
Did He who made the lamb make thee?

Tyger tyger burning bright,
In the forests of the night:
What immortal hand or eye,
Dare frame thy fearful symmetry?[1]

—William Blake

Blake's magnificent and unsettling poem offers us a profound insight into the connection of Romanticism and nihilism in its articulation of the idea of what we will call the demonic. The full meaning of this term will become clearer as we examine the material pre-

101

sented in this chapter, but in a preliminary way we might say that the demonic names a dark and powerful but essentially negative will underlying the phenomena, a will that may arise out of the divine but is opposed to it, and that empowers and liberates certain individuals but also catapults them beyond the bounds of conventional morality into what is simultaneously an exalted state of superhumanity and a degraded state of bestiality. They are rebels against God and are willing to accept whatever penalty he exacts, unafraid, doing what they will, taking what they will, destroyers, conquerors, revolutionaries.

Blake's poem is especially effective in evoking this demonic force in all of its power and mysteriousness by posing it as a question. Nowhere in his poem is the demonic described or even named. Instead, the fourteen questions which constitute the poem circumscribe its terrifying possibility. The question of the demonic arises in the poem from the consideration of two forms. The first is the awesome tiger with the eyes of fire who inhabits the ominous forests of the night. The other is the even more terrifying, dreadful, and mysterious creator of the tiger.

The tiger is a destroyer, a creature from hell or from a hellish heaven, born out of and filled with an all-consuming fire. The tiger, however, is not merely a destroyer, it is a sublime destroyer; it attracts us in the same moment that it terrifies us. The formless and ever-changing fire that constitutes its essence is embodied in a fearful symmetry that is beautiful and alluring. Despite its dangers, the tiger thus cannot be condemned. Indeed, it is precisely the danger of the tiger and the thrill of the danger, the tiger's demonic joy in destruction, that attracts us.

Sublimity, however, is hardly sufficient to justify destruction. The deeper reason the tiger cannot be condemned is the possibility that it was created by the same power that created the rest of nature, including Blake's beloved lamb. If this is the case, saying yes to the lamb would require saying yes to the tiger.[2] It would also mean that the creative force responsible for both the lamb and the tiger is contradictory and thus incomprehensible. The very existence of the tiger points to this conclusion, since the creator of the tiger is necessarily the creator of the destroyer.

This conclusion leads to the further suspicion that it is the tiger not the lamb who most fully resembles the creator, for in the creation of the death-dealing tiger this creative will reveals its deepest truth, the awesomeness of its power, its freedom from the laws of contradiction and thus from all notions of good and evil.[3] Blake only points to this possibility with a question which expresses his horrifying suspicion that this creative power may have smiled and thus affirmed this destroyer, named it his own, sanctified it. This possibility remains a question for Blake because it transcends man's understanding, but it arises as a question because he himself is attracted to this destroyer.[4] Thus, Blake finds in himself an apparently irresistible admiration for the tiger and, as a result, is forced to confront the possibility that God himself may be more tiger than lamb, more a destroyer, more pitiless and demonic than is generally acknowledged.

This insight leads to the fundamentally disturbing conclusion that the highest evil may be a moment of the highest goodness, that God may be not merely indifferent but malicious, or that the demonic is the truest and most complete manifestation of God and his omnipotent freedom.[5] Blake's poem in this sense reveals the fatal attraction of the question that draws much of Romanticism in its disparate and often antagonistic forms into nihilism. The demonic, however, is seen here only as through a glass darkly, only as the demonic creative force behind the tiger. The tiger itself remains alien, inhuman, incapable of speech, a nightmare vision of an incomprehensible engine of destruction. The demonic is thus something still at one remove from human life, a force that evokes fascination and fear but that does not yet exercise power over actuality.

This chapter is an investigation of the great attraction that this demonic force exercised upon the early nineteenth-century imagination. This fascination impelled the thinkers of this period to develop an increasingly concrete and comprehensive notion of the demonic that brought it ever more centrally into human life and politics. Blake's poetic tiger in this way becomes a practical and ultimately terrifying political and social force. This transformation was achieved not only by those who were most attracted to the demonic but also by those who most feared it, including many of the most profound and powerful thinkers of the period. They tried to refute or reshape this notion of the demonic, but even they were ultimately unable to reject it. Indeed, it was precisely these opponents of Romantic nihilism who unwittingly and unwillingly became its most powerful advocates, and it was their efforts to check this nihilism that served to enthrone it.

ROMANTICISM AND NIHILISM:
THE DEMONIC HERO

Nominalism emphasized the supremacy of divine will and established it above reason. Early modern thinkers, on the contrary, sought to construct a bulwark against the potential caprice and chaos of such a divine will. Descartes' conception of the impregnable self-certainty of consciousness, empiricism's notion of an infinite natural causality, and Kant's assertion of the rationality of practical reason all helped to constrain the power and scope of divine caprice and irrationality. The absolute I that Fichte established, however, seemed to embody and empower it. Like the nominalist God and Descartes' evil genius, the creative capacities of the absolute I transcend natural reason. The traditional God of Christianity in this sense became superfluous. In the early nineteenth century, this notion of the absolute I was itself replaced by the idea of a demonic force that informs and guides human history and the natural world. Romanticism in general and German Romanticism in particular brought about this transformation.[6]

The idea of the demonic has its origins in the Greek term *daimon* or *daimonion*. For the Greeks, daimons were intermediate spirits between gods and heros. In some accounts they occupy the realm between gods and human beings, in others they are indwelling spirits. Socrates' famous daimon in this sense is an indwelling spirit or genius that is the progeny of some divinity. Moreover, great heros were thought to become daimons after their deaths and were often worshiped as such. This notion of an indwelling but also superhuman spiritual power is essential to the later notion of the demonic. Within the monotheistic world of Judaism and Christianity, however, such spirits were first interpreted as angels, but then more negatively as evil spirits or agents of the devil. The Romantic notion of the demonic retains many of these negative connotations, but it also has a more positive meaning. The revival of this more positive or heroic notion of the demonic is associated with a decline in Christianity. The Romantic notion of the demonic, however, is not simply a return to the ancient "heroic" notion of the demonic, because of the continuing recognition that however great such powers may be they are at heart still evil.

The spiritual father of Romanticism was Rousseau, who articulated a conception of freedom and will that provided the foundation not only for the political radicalism of the French Revolution but also for Romantic inwardness and emotionalism. This notion of freedom, which found a dual expression in the idea of the general will of the *Social Contract* and the inner will of the *Confessions* and the *Solitary Walker*, arises out the Cartesian and Christian voluntarist traditions. While the Jacobins were guided by the notion of the general will in their political revolution, the Romantics took their bearings from the notion of the individual will of natural man in their opposition to the cultural and spiritual degeneracy of bourgeois society. The new man that Romanticism envisaged was not everyman, but the man who turns into himself and finds in his own psyche a heroic will that struggles to free itself from the constraints of social life and find a way back to a more natural existence.

Romanticism discovers this will not only in man's psyche but in the natural world. Nature, for the Romantics, is not merely the orderly motion of matter according to the categories of creation but the expression of a mysterious and largely incomprehensible will, a will that does not appear to the senses but that can be grasped by the feelings, a passionate, subconscious, and subrational will which acts in enigmatic and unpredictable ways. Byron's Manfred, for example, speaks for almost all Romantics when he proclaims that "the Tree of Knowledge is not that of Life."[7]

This will is seldom identified as divine and is more characteristically understood as demonic, the will of Satan, the rebel against God, or the will of some other demonic spirit. It is the dark underworld of will that the bright heaven of Christian reason conceals.[8] Blake's poem is only one of many examples of this Romantic notion, but it points to the profound problem that arises for Romanticism in its confrontation with this primordial will.

Blake himself was little influenced by the metaphysical concerns that were so important to Fichte and others. The language within which he thinks is indirectly influenced by philosophic thought but is drawn largely from his theosophistic reading of the Bible and other religious works which give a wide-ranging role to the demonic. This was generally true, although to a lesser extent, for many of the other English Romantics. While many German Romantics were intimately acquainted with theosophy, they were also generally well trained in academic philosophy. Tieck, Novalis, and the Schlegels, for example, were thoroughly schooled in the philosophical systems of the day. While they too were entranced by the demonic, they saw it not only in the theological light of a theosophistic Christianity or a pagan pantheism but in the metaphysical half-light of Fichte's murky vision of the absolute I. This is hardly surprising, since they were almost all Fichte's students and were deeply influenced in their early creative years by his thought.[9] Moreover, this Fichtean foundation helped them resolve the obscure relationship we noted between Blake's tiger and the mysterious creator of the tiger. The basis for this resolution was the Fichtean connection of the absolute I and the empirical I. The demonic God who stood behind Blake's tiger reveals himself in their work as the concealed essence of the human psyche. The dreadful creator of the tiger is thus none other than man himself. Man, however, thus ceases to be man: empirical I becomes absolute I, human becomes superhuman.[10]

It was precisely for this reason that Jacobi characterized Fichte's philosophy and idealism in general as *nihilism*. For similar reasons, Jacobi's student and follower, Jean Paul, characterized the German Romantics as poetic nihilists. Jean Paul believed these Romantics posed a real danger to civilized life because their subjectivism was so distant and isolated from reality that it left man surrounded by nothingness. Like their political cousins, the Robespierrites, these poetic nihilists rejected nature and God as standards in favor of reason and the I. Jean Paul feared that "in an age when God has set like the sun, soon afterwards the world too passes into darkness. He who scorns the universe respects nothing more than himself and at night fears only his own creations."[11]

In this attack, Jean Paul may well have had in mind Ludwig Tieck's William Lovell, who has been called "the first European nihilist."[12] Lovell is in fact the elder brother of a whole family of German Romantic heros that includes Hölderlin's Hyperion, Brentano's Godiwi, and Brüchner's Danton. He is also a not so distant cousin of such famous Romantic heros as Byron's Don Juan, Shelling's Prometheus, and Stendhal's Julien Sorel, as well as Pushkin's Eugene Onegin and Lermentov's Pechorin. Lovell is particularly important, however, not merely because he is a more radical Romantic hero but because he becomes such a complete egoist, so utterly absorbed by the demonic potentialities of the I. He is a "complete Fichtean."[13]

At the beginning of the novel, Lovell is a dreamy young gentleman at ease in English society. He embarks on a grand tour of the Continent at the request of his father, leaving the idyllic country life of England for the urbane and corrupt life of Paris, Florence, and ultimately Rome. The external voyage is emblematic of his deepening inner voyage. With every stage of his journey, he is drawn more profoundly into himself. The veneer of civilization that hitherto formed and limited his being is gradually worn away, and he gives himself over to an exploration of his own ego, thereby uncovering his demonic essence. Subjectively, this is experienced as the liberation and glorification of a self that society conceals and restrains. Objectively, it is a decline into libertinism and evil.[14] Lovell's development is thus a mixture of triumph and degradation, a meteoric flight of genius that is likewise a precipitous decline into immorality and decadence.

This path is clearly antagonistic to the mores of traditional society. Lovell repudiates his dearest friends, leaves his father to a lonely death, seduces an innocent peasant girl, murders her fiance, abandons her, attempts to poison his best friend, seduces and abducts this friend's sister, and abandons her to a remorseful death. His career is as despicable as that of any other literary villain of the eighteenth and nineteenth centuries. Indeed, he is even more resolutely evil than his literary model, Richardson's Lovelace. What is striking and revolutionary about Lovell, however, is that he is not a villain. He is rather a hero, motivated not by a pernicious desire for his own pleasure or advantage but by a thirst for freedom and the knowledge of his hidden inner self and the inner forces that govern all men. The knowledge he wants, however, is the demonic knowledge that is denied to men who live under the moral law.

Immorality and sensualism are the means of his liberation. He rejects guilt and shame because they are barriers to his knowledge of his inner self and the inner self of the world. These feelings limit the will. To be free means to overcome not merely external but more importantly internal constraints. Lovell's sensualism is not mere hedonism but a hubristic self-assertion that in Sadistic fashion investigates the deepest and most profound truths about the world as they are reflected in his feelings. Libertinism is the way of liberation.

In a Fichtean fashion, he recognizes that the external world is derivative; it is merely the not-I which arises out of the I itself, out of the subconscious and infinite will of the absolute I. To know and thereby become one with this concealed will, Lovell must overturn the conventions that constitute him as a limited being. These limits seem to be set by the external world, but in Fichte's view the external world is merely an expression of the will of the absolute I, and we experience this will on the most primordial level through our feelings. The empirical I thus can come to know itself and the world only through its feelings, which indicate its limits and thus the shape of the not-I, of the objective world. To come to a deeper understanding of the absolute I that lies at the ground of both the empirical I and the not-I, it is necessary to overcome these feelings and the limitations that they establish. This means overcoming both the not-I and the empirical I, becoming one with the absolute I, with the underlying creative will that is the source of all things. Lovell's repeated and ever deepening journey into a brutal sensualism is nothing other than a heroic and ultimately tragic striving to become one with this absolute will, a striving for the infinite, for absolute freedom. His life is an attempt to tear away the philistine veil of traditional European life and to reveal in all its truth the demonic subjectivism, the lust and caprice that lie at its heart. His example is meant to demonstrate that the primordial will at the heart of the world is not the will of the lamb but the will of the tiger, or at least that it is only the tiger whose will can penetrate to the truth of existence and attain real freedom.

This knowledge does not bring Lovell satisfaction. Freedom is not happiness. His striving catapults him against all limits, against all horizons, and yet when he has transcended each horizon, a new one always surrounds him. From a Fichtean perspective he can never be happy, because he seeks freedom and autonomy, and such freedom can never be attained. He is therefore continually frustrated. The infinite is unreachable. When each new veil is torn away he always faces only another veil. Striving to become a god, he instead becomes a beast or, more correctly, a beast-god.

Tieck recognizes this dark, hubristic side of Lovell's actions but does not condemn them. For Tieck, there is something intrinsically admirable about this striving. Lovell's fate is not intended as a warning against hubris but as a clarion call to assault the walls of heaven, even if they ultimately cannot be overturned. Thus, if Lovell does not become God, he does become one with the demonic rival of God and thus something superhuman.

For Tieck and the other early German Romantics, Lovell's career was noble and tragic. It brought to light the demonic essence of man. His "crimes" are not despicable deeds but the tragic price he has to pay for the elevated freedom he attains. Immorality becomes a badge of freedom and greatness. To Jacobi and Jean Paul, it seemed that the lure of idealism and subjectivism led Lovell into nihilism. Jacobi points to this dark possibility: "I know that superstition in itself goes so far that it will let itself be worshipped. It believes in nothing above or below; it has . . . only itself alone, it sees itself . . . determined as the tool of fate; it does not will, but discovers itself to be the agent of the will that wants the most horrible things to be brought to light, things which previously have only appeared in dark legends."[15]

Tieck too recognized the horrors that an absolute subjectivism entailed, but was unwilling to condemn it because the philistine alternative was so unattractive to him. As Tieck portrays him, postrevolutionary man is confronted with a choice between cultured banality and demonic profundity.

The attractiveness of this demonic alternative should not be underestimated. Even Jean Paul, one of demonism's harshest critics, presents a nihilistic hero, Roquairol, in his novel *Titan*. While this work is a critique of Romantic nihilism, it also makes clear the attraction that it exercised on Jean Paul. This is not surprising. Jean Paul, like his mentor Jacobi, believed in a God beyond man's capacity to understand or control. Their God was akin to the nominalist God and in this sense not so different from the demonic force behind Blake's tiger. The Fichtean and Romantic attempt to locate this force in the I, however, was anathema to them.

In *William Lovell*, we see the birth of nihilism out of the spirit of a Romanticism that is decisively informed by the thought of Fichte. Fichte was not the spiritual inspiration of Romanticism in general or even of German Romanticism, but his influence on the early German Romantics was crucial for the transformation of Romanticism into nihilism because it made possible the notion of nature as a mere projection of the I. For Rousseau, the relationship of freedom and nature remains ambiguous. He develops a notion of human will or freedom as a capacity to rise above nature and its laws, but he does not develop a corresponding theory of nature as a projection of freedom or the human will. Similarly, while many Romantics had strong pantheistic sentiments, few were willing to argue that nature as a whole was the expression of human freedom. Mainstream Romanticism, to be sure, typically glorifies the inner life of feelings and deemphasizes the power of conscious thought and reason, but it does not take the Fichtean step of reducing nature itself to a manifestation of the will.

Lovell's fate is an indication of the consequence of Fichtean subjectivism. The attempt to base human life in the absolute autonomy of the I is a revolt against traditional morality and marks the beginning of a radical transformation of European intellectual life. It destroys the basis for all objective standards and undermines reason itself, establishing the supremacy of the transrational, of emotions and feelings, and a growing concern with and belief in the supernatural, the miraculous, and the magical. In rejecting the rational order

of nature and a mathematical natural science, this absolute subjectivism in nominalistic fashion turns to an utterly arbitrary and potentially irrational will, a will, however, no longer of an inscrutable God
but of an absolute I. Idealism and Romanticism in this sense signal
the death of the traditional Christian God, who is reduced to a mere
concept, and the advent of the overman, who is guided by his subliminal instincts.

Within Romanticism, however, this overman remains indistinct,
and is characteristically more underman than overman. The most
famous of these god-beasts is certainly Frankenstein's monster, but
such demonic figures are widespread in Romantic literature.[16] The
works of E. T. A. Hoffman, Edgar Allan Poe, and many other
Romantics are filled with such unsettling figures. The concern with
the supernatural in this sense is the initial and still unself-conscious
consideration of the superhuman.

A DEAL WITH THE DEVIL:
GOETHE'S FAUST AND THE INEFFICACY OF EVIL

Nihilism makes its first appearance on the European stage between
1789 and 1807 and is bound up with the fundamental political and
spiritual transformation that swept across Europe during this period.
While this movement exercised considerable influence over the
German and the wider European imagination, it did not come to predominance at that time or indeed until the end of the nineteenth century. During the intervening years, it disappeared so completely that
many later scholars came to believe, for example, that Turgenev had
invented the term. How are we to explain this eclipse of nihilism?
While it was due in part to the waning of revolutionary passions, it
was equally if not principally the result of the overwhelming intellectual influence of Goethe and Hegel.

Goethe once remarked that "Classical is healthy, Romantic is
sick," and much of his work was devoted to demonstrating the truth
of this proposition.[17] Goethe had such keen insight into the
Romantic soul because he himself had followed a similar Romantic
path during his early *Sturm und Drang* period. Hence, his rejection
of Romanticism was in part a rejection of the Romantic element of
his own soul, an attempt to exorcise his own demons.[18] This attempt
is already clear in his early *The Sorrows of Young Werther,* but it is also
apparent in his *Faust.*

Faust was written over a period of sixty years, and the circumstances of its composition and publication are important for understanding its reception and influence. Although an original version of the work, the *Urfaust,* was written between 1773 and 1775, nothing appeared in print until Goethe published *Faust: A Fragment* in 1790. The first part of the work as it now stands was not published until 1808 and the second part was not completed until a few days before Goethe's death in 1832 and was published in the same year. The *Fragment* met with considerable enthusiasm, especially among the Romantics. *Faust: Part One* was less well received but still widely read and studied. The reception of *Faust: Part Two* was much more problematic. It is obscure and convoluted. The Helen episode, which was published separately in 1827, was generally admired, but the rest of the second part baffled readers and led critics to conclude that it was the product of genius in decline.[19]

At the beginning of the play, Faust is a thorough Romantic. Nothing can satisfy him. He asserts that he has mastered all of the traditional forms of human knowledge—philosophy, law, medicine, and theology—and has learned only that we cannot know, that is, he sees that he has knowledge of the appearances of things but not of what lies behind them. As a result, he turns to magic in the hope of mastering these demonic powers that rule the world. His encounter with the first of these demonic spirits, the spirit of the earth, terrifies and humbles him, for he recognizes it as a being completely beyond his power to comprehend or control. This spirit is the spirit of nature itself out of which everything comes and within which everything revolves. All opposites, ebb and flow, life and death, are contained in this spirit and woven together. It is an infinite and eternal sea of unending movement that can be neither grasped nor emulated. Faust himself is but a part of this spirit and can never be one with it. It terrifies and overawes him.

With the failure of this attempt to attain the absolute in one leap, Faust turns back to the finite, hoping to attain the satisfaction that has eluded him through a demonic sensualism. To this end, he strikes a deal with Mephistopheles to obtain his services with the stipulation that he will become Mephistopheles' servant if he ever attains satisfaction, that is, if he ever says, "Linger moment, you are so beautiful." Faust, in this sense, follows the same sensualistic path as Lovell and the other Romantic nihilists in pursuit of freedom and knowledge of the hidden forces that govern the world.

In the first part of the work, Faust regains his youth and seduces an innocent young girl, Gretchen, whom he impregnates and abandons. Her mother dies from a sleeping potion Gretchen administers at Faust's direction; Faust kills her brother in a duel; their child is drowned; and Gretchen is condemned for its murder. Driven by a mixture of love and remorse, Faust attempts to save her, but she refuses the aid of his demonic power and chooses instead death and salvation. Faust is shattered. This was the story the early nineteenth century knew and admired.

The second part of the work is more allegorical and less accessible. Faust is cured of his suffering by the restorative powers of nature. He then offers his services to the king, but is entranced by the vision of Helen that he conjures up, and sets off in search of her. He investigates the mythological background of the ancient world and protean powers of human nature. He then attempts to synthesize Romantic and classical art, symbolized by his marriage with Helen. This is a failure. Their offspring, the demonic Euphorion, destroys himself, and Helen herself dissolves. Faust is borne away in a golden cloud. He returns to earth many years later and after watching the endless ebb and flow of the tides determines to build great dikes against the sea to open up new land in order to found a new state. To complete this project, however, he allows an old couple who stand in his way to be murdered by Mephistopheles' minions. With the project near completion, he hears digging and imagines his magical workers are raising the last walls. In his physical and spiritual blindness, however, he does not realize that they are in fact digging his grave. In this moment of delusion, he has a magnificent vision of a free land and a free people and declares that he could say to such a moment, "Linger, you are so beautiful." With this proclamation he dies. Mephistopheles lays claim to his soul, but this claim is denied by angels who bear Faust's soul up to heaven. Despite his crimes, Faust is thus saved.

His criticism of Romanticism notwithstanding, Goethe is ultimately unwilling simply to condemn Romantic nihilism. This unwillingness was in part certainly due to his strongly held opinion that the demonic forces that ruled the world were finally good:

> Although the demonic can manifest itself in all bodily and non-bodily things . . . it stands in the most wondrous connection preeminently with man. . . . When it comes forward in overpowering fashion among men . . . a monstrous power goes out from them and they exercise an unbelievable power over all creatures, indeed even over the elements, and who can say, how far their influence reaches? All of the unified powers of the community cannot resist them . . . they can be overcome by nothing except the universe itself with which they have entered into

competition; such observations may have led to the strange but monstrous maxim: *Nemo contra deum nisi deus ipse* [None against God save God himself].[20]

These demons, as Goethe see it, "are finally all dependent upon a God."[21] While the actions of individuals who are dominated by this demonic power may seem to be evil, Goethe concludes that this is not simply the case. Their demonic striving is akin to the striving of God himself. As the chorus of angels at the beginning of *Faust* makes clear, God is responsible not merely for the harmony of the world but for its raging chaos as well. God's infinitude encompasses this contradiction. The demonic natures that Goethe admires are in this sense part of God and thus also transcend nature and reason.

This demonic transcendence is evident in Faust's turn to magic, for magic, as capacity to create out of nothing, is a manifestation of the most radical freedom. It is a means by which man can transcend nature and free himself from the not-I. It is thus also the means by which Faust establishes himself on a plane with the divine. The master of magic in *Faust* is not Faust, however, but Mephistopheles. Mephistopheles, in fact, is Faust's poetic genius, a demonic will that makes possible his magical, or more correctly his poetical, creations. Mephistopheles describes himself as

a part of that force, / That always wants evil, and always produces good. / . . . I am the spirit, that always negates! / and that with right: for all that comes to be, / is worthy of perishing; / therefore it would be better, that nothing came to be. / So then everything, which you call sin, / destruction, in short evil / is my ownmost element. / . . . I am a part of a part, which in the beginning was all, / a part of darkness, that gave birth to light, / the proud light, that now contests mother night's / rank and position. (1337–52)[22]

He is the spirit of negation but is capable only of determinate and not absolute negation. Thus, Faust responds to him: "You cannot negate at large so you begin with what is small" (1360–61). Mephistopheles, and thus by extension Faust, is evil only in the small sense, that is, under the hegemony of an almighty God who has arranged the world in such a way that all attempts to do evil produce only goodness. Mephistopheles implicitly denies this with his claim that darkness gave birth to light, but he is probably disingenuous here. In *Poetry and Truth,* Goethe describes the theological understanding that is the basis for this account: God creates Lucifer and Lucifer creates the angels in his image. He and some of the angels then rebel against God and are cast out of heaven. They become mat-

ter. God then creates light to counterbalance darkness, and the mixture of light and darkness then constitutes the finite things of our
experience.[23] Mephistopheles here represents a position similar to
Fichte's that attempts to explain everything in terms of the action of
absolute freedom understood as absolute negativity. Goethe himself
denies this beginning in negation and asserts instead the supremacy
of the positive force of God.

This point is explicitly made in the second prologue to the play, the
"Prologue in Heaven," which takes the form of a dialogue between
Mephistopheles and God. Mephistopheles begins the conversation by
recounting the multiple ways in which men torment themselves on
earth. In response to the implicit claim in this assertion that the world
was created imperfectly, God points to his servant Faust as a coun-
terexample. Mephistopheles suggests that Faust serves God in strange
ways, for he arrogates everything to himself and still is never satisfied.
God responds that though Faust serves him in a perplexed manner,
he will soon act more clearly. Mephistopheles claims that he can
seduce Faust if God does not interfere. God responds that this is not
forbidden as long as Faust is on the earth, because, "Man errs as long
as he strives" (318). Indeed, the devil is necessary to promote human
activity: "I have never hated your sort; / Of all those spirits that
negate, / The rogue is the least burdensome to me. / Human activity goes to sleep all too easily; / Man soon falls in love with uncondi-
tional ease. / Therefore, I gladly give him up to the fellow, / Who
entices and works and as devil must create" (337–43).

The great danger to man is that he fall into lethargy, that he
become satisfied with life and cease striving. He can be lifted out of
this laziness only by the attractiveness of evil or, more correctly, by the
attractiveness of what *appears* to be evil, since God insures that such
apparent evil is actually part of a higher and more all-embracing
goodness. Thus, while Faust commits many crimes, they cannot be
condemned and in fact are part of the enormous energy which is
intrinsically good. Because he strives, he errs necessarily and unavoid-
ably.

As a result, Faust can never be damned. As his soul is borne to
heaven, the angels sing, "The noble member of the spiritual world is
saved from evil, he who always motivates himself to strive we can
redeem" (11,934–11,937). This Faust who relies on the demonic
powers of negation is thus never beyond the sphere of the good and
can never really do evil. He is no Macbeth, and he is not even a
William Lovell. In contrast to the Romantic vision of the radically

free individual embodied in Blake's tiger, Faust is tame; if not harmless, he is also neither awesome nor terrifying.

Goethe's domestication of Faust was not the result of his misunderstanding of this type of human being. Indeed, he reflected upon these demonic characters perhaps more deeply than any of his contemporaries, but he concluded that their enormous energies were fundamentally life-enhancing. Moreover, he was convinced that they were not subject to the laws of nature and convention which governed ordinary human beings. The reason that Faust is not terrifying thus has little to do with Faust himself. It is rather the consequence of the place he occupies in Goethe's cosmos. He is a primordial force, but such forces are arranged by God for the ultimate good of humanity.

While Goethe labeled Faust a tragedy, it is thus at best a sentimental tragedy.[24] In this neo-Platonic world ruled by a beneficent and omnipotent God, there can be no real evil and therefore no real freedom. Mephistopheles and the forces of negation are always frustrated. This fact is nowhere so evident as in Mephistopheles' great speech after Faust's death. He believes he has won his bet and that his work is *vollbracht,* 'completed,' 'brought to its end.' But the chorus asserts that it is only *vorbei,* 'past,' 'gone by.' Mephistopheles is enraged: "Past! a dumb word. Why past? / Past and pure not: completely one and the same! / What then is the purpose of eternal creation? / To tear away the created into nothing? / It is as good, as if it had never been, / and drives itself around in a circle, as if it were! / I would therefore rather love the eternally empty" (11,598–11,605).

Negation is itself always negated and the great negator himself is subject to his own laws, leaving only the circle of becoming, eternal transition, and therefore eternal frustration, but also an eternal spur to further activity. In the end, Goethe is thus closer to Mozart than to the Fichtean Romantics: in Faust, Blake's tiger becomes the lion, drawing Sarastro's chariot of reason into battle against Sarastro's consort and enemy, the queen of the night.[25]

HEGEL AND THE DIALECTICAL SUBORDINATION OF THE DEMONIC

Like Goethe, Hegel recognized the danger of Romantic nihilism and attempted to overcome it by showing that the principle of freedom or negation did not lead to meaninglessness and despair but to absolute knowledge and a thoroughly rational ethics and politics. Hegel began with the same contradiction that Fichte and the Romantics faced but ended in a rational spiritual and political order directly at odds with their subjectivistic irrationalism. He rejected Fichte's attempt to construct all of existence on the basis of the absolute subject and sought instead to reconcile subject and object, and thus freedom and nature, through a more profound conception of consciousness. This reconciliation depends upon the dialectical demonstration that the nothingness of contradiction is the highest reason.[26]

Like Fichte, Hegel begins with the Kantian antinomy doctrine, but instead of positing the priority of freedom over nature he seeks their reconciliation. The basis for this reconciliation lies in the antinomy itself. For Kant, the necessity of contradiction in the antinomy is an intellectual disaster. For Hegel, on the contrary, it is the source of salvation, for if the contradiction is *necessary,* as Kant had demonstrated, then there is a necessity that is implicit in the contradiction that can serve as the basis for reconciliation, that indeed *is* the reconciliation. This speculative synthesis of contradictions is the basis of Hegel's idealism. It allows him to develop a comprehensive system that avoids the unmitigated subjectivism of Fichte and the Romantics as well as the unbending objectivism or materialism of empiricism and natural science.

Hegel was able to achieve this reconciliation, however, only by accepting the implicit nihilism that lay at the heart of transcendental idealism. Kantianism in his view made nihilism inevitable.[27] As he saw it, the choice was between a false nihilism that posited a transcendent and inscrutable God, and a true nihilism that recognized and participated in the absolute. False nihilism, represented by Jacobi, results in the disheartening recognition that reason does not rule the world. It thus subjects human beings to an arbitrary and willful God. Hegel's own form of nihilism, which follows a Fichtean path, rejects capricious divine omnipotence in favor of the true omnipotence and dialectical rationality of absolute spirit.

Whether such a nihilism can serve as the ground for reconciliation, however, depends upon the rationality of the absolute itself. Hegel's absolute spirit, like Fichte's absolute I, is based upon negativity. As a dialectical movement, it is both contradictory and unitary, both a tearing apart and a setting together. It is becoming. Becoming for Hegel, however, is absolute negativity:

> Becoming in essence, its reflected motion, is thus the *motion from nothing to nothing and thereby back to itself.* The transit or becoming overcomes itself in its transit; the other, that becomes in this transit, is

not the non-being of a being, but the nothing of a nothing, and this being the negation of a nothing, constitutes being. —Being is only as the motion of nothing to nothing, so it is essence; and this does not *have* its motion *in itself,* but rather is it as absolute appearance itself, pure negativity, with nothing outside of itself that negates it, but that negates itself through its negative itself, that only is in this negating.[28]

The absolute, as Hegel understands it, is the nothing that negates itself, the annihilation of annihilation. To accept this and to recognize its necessity, Hegel believes, is to overcome it. Out of this "abyss of nothing . . . the feeling: God is dead . . . The highest totality in its complete seriousness and out of its deepest ground, at once all-encompassing and in the most joyful freedom of its form can and must arise."[29] Nihilism taken to its extreme in Hegel's view rebounds upon itself and reconstitutes itself as the most comprehensive order.

If freedom is the transcendence of the natural world of finite or determinate being, then freedom is essentially nothing and as such always a negation of being. Absolute freedom must in this sense be absolute negation. Absolute negation, however, must be self-negation, therefore, the negation of negation, and consequently the source of being. This is the path that Hegel's argument follows in his attempt to demonstrate the impossibility of utter nihilism. He shows that the ground of all being is in nothingness and that this nothingness is accessible to human reason. Indeed, he reconstructs all reason and science on the basis of this self-negating nothingness. This is the essence of his notion of dialectic. This nothingness, however, is freedom. The self-negation of nothingness is thus freedom's self-limitation and consequently the establishment of a system of rational necessity.

For Hegel, this self-establishing and self-limiting freedom is the motive force of human history. History is the dialectical development of this freedom from pure consciousness through self-consciousness, reason, and spirit to absolute knowledge. The *Phenomenology of Spirit* is the account of this great human voyage. It describes the unconscious process by which this freedom lifts itself to complete self-knowledge and a fully mediated unity with itself in absolute knowledge.

Hegel in this sense takes a profound and fateful step beyond Kant and Fichte. Kant and even Fichte believed there was an unbridgeable abyss that separated man from the absolute. For Kant, all speculative knowledge is thus impossible. Science is merely phenomenal, that is, merely the knowledge of the appearances or representations of the thing-in-itself, and we cannot understand the ultimate ground of our being. In the moral realm, this means that there is no scientific knowledge of good and evil. We do, however, have immediate access to moral truths through the moral law. Practical reason tells us what we ought to do. To speak metaphorically, we cannot know God but we can know what God wants from us. Fichte, as we have seen, tried to construct a unified system of science by expanding Kant's notion of practical reason, but even he concluded that absolute knowledge was unattainable. Man is morally obligated to strive for such knowledge and freedom, but he also can never attain the goal he is obliged to pursue.

For Hegel, the absolute is not absolute I but absolute spirit. Fichte and Kant in his view were unable to bridge the gap between knowledge and the absolute because they remained too entwined in a defective philosophy of consciousness. They understood everything *only* from the perspective of the I. This subjective beginning with consciousness was essential to a correct understanding of the world, but it was ultimately insufficient because it did not recognize that all individual consciousness is merely a moment of general consciousness or spirit. History in this sense is the process by which spirit comes to consciousness of itself as absolute. It is also the reconciliation of all the moments of spirit in a speculative synthesis. For individual consciousness, this means the growing recognition that it is a moment of general consciousness or spirit, that is, part of the social whole. It is also the ultimate recognition in absolute knowledge that spirit is absolute, that is, that spirit is divine. Absolute knowledge in this sense is the speculative reconciliation and synthesis of the individual, society, and the divine. In contradistinction to Kant and Fichte, Hegel thereby bridges the gap between man and God by attributing absolute reality not to man *or* to God but to spirit.

This attribution of ultimate reality to a self-moving and self-developing spirit opens up history as the preeminent realm of human being. Morality ceases to be a problem since individuals are no longer imagined to be separate and absolute ends in themselves but moments of a larger social whole. Morality does not become superfluous but is subordinated to ethics and politics. Actions are judged not on a moral standard but by their conduciveness to the establishment of a fully rational ethics and politics in which the individual is integrated in the spiritual whole.

This means that all standards of good and evil are relative to the particular task of spirit in any given historical epoch, and all individual human beings are mere moments of spirit. The greatest of these are the world-historical individuals. These human beings are the unconscious agents of the absolute, who carry out its highest and most profound tasks. They are the first cousins of Goethe's Faust—tigers, demonic destroyers and negators, conquerors who seek only dominion and glory. However, like Faust and unbeknownst to themselves, their striving, as a result of "the cunning of reason," is in the service of the "divine," and like Mephistopheles their negation always serves only the good, whether they will it or not. Napoleon's fate is a perfect example. As long as Napoleon acted in the general interest he was successful, but once he had realized the aims of spirit, he became superfluous and was removed from the European stage.[30] Like Goethe, Hegel thus turns the demonic destroyer of Romantic nihilism into an agent of reason. The conquering tiger becomes the servant of the lamb; the irrational is made rational, the demonic subordinated to the divine.

Such a transformation, however, depends upon the realization of the rational order, upon reason being more cunning than unreason, upon reason making itself absolute. Hegel's entire *System of Science* is the attempt to demonstrate this fact. From a practical point of view, the most important part of this argument is his demonstration of the attained rationality of ethics and politics in his *Philosophy of Right*.

In the preface to the *Philosophy of Right*, Hegel asserts that "the rational is actual and the actual is rational."[31] This has often been interpreted as a quietistic justification for the prevailing political order. In fact, the political order that Hegel describes in the *Philosophy of Right* was decisively at odds with the states of his day. His assertion must instead be understood in the context of his notion of the development of spirit. In an earlier lecture version of the work, he wrote, "The rational becomes the actual and the actual becomes the rational."[32] What he points to is the reconciliation of reason and actuality, the recognition in absolute knowledge that the apparently meaningless suffering of what he called "the slaughter bench of world-history" is redeemed by the rationality of the state that it ultimately brings into existence, that is, that the demonic force that manifests itself in world-historical individuals is recognized finally as the unconscious manifestation and working out of dialectical reason. To show this, Hegel must demonstrate that the tiger does indeed become the servant of the lamb. The *Philosophy of Right* describes the final and insuperable form of rational ethical and political life made possible by spirit's reconciliation with itself in absolute knowledge.

Without examining the structure of this rational state in detail, it is sufficient for our purposes to note that it is a state which has completely bound and harnessed the demonic. There are no more world-historical individuals. They are no longer necessary or possible. Spirit or reason in its cunning has come to fruition and no longer needs to depend upon the unconscious actions of individuals. The historical task of demonic men is complete because humanity has finally become conscious of its end.

Hegel does not mean by this that all individuals become fully and perfectly rational. Rather one class, the so-called universal class of civil servants or bureaucrats, serves as the *conscious* agent of spirit within the state and orders ethical and political matters in keeping with reason. These bureaucrats constitute a universal class because they participate immediately in absolute spirit. They are educated in philosophy and look to the general good in making decisions. They are guided by their rational will. The demonic tigers and William Lovells of the world are tamed by dialectical reason, which shows them that their will to freedom can ultimately be satisfied only within the rational state. Their negation, Hegel argues, is ultimately a self-negation, a negation of negation that produces being and that comes to realize the impossibility of absolute negation and absolute freedom. The demonic tiger is thus transformed into the considerate civil servant in whom "a dispassionate, upright, and polite demeanor becomes customary."[33]

This transformation does not mean that all human conflict disappears. War and warriors continue to play a role within the rational state, but their connection to the demonic disappears. Wars are fought not for glory or conquest but to defend the autonomy of the state. Structurally, they serve to maintain the internal unity of the state versus the centrifugal forces of bourgeois society. As a result, wars become civilized and less violent.[34]

After the long years of strife, Hegel's system provided the basis for reconciliation. It consequently had an extraordinarily broad and deep appeal. It thus provided a bulwark against the nihilism that had first appeared in Fichte and the early German Romantics.[35] However, this new bastion of dialectical reason rested on an uncertain foundation. Hegel's ingenious solution to nihilism was based on the same negativity that constituted the core of nihilist thought, and this accounted in no small measure for its success. However, his transformation of negativity into rationality and negation into affirmation was possible *only* on the basis of his speculative synthesis of the absolute. This synthesis, however, was suspect from the beginning and ultimately proved unconvincing not only to Hegel's critics but also to many of his own students and followers.

The eclipse of the Hegelian system was due in part to the forced retirement of Hegel's friend and supporter, Baron von Altenstein, as the Prussian minister of culture in 1838 and the ascension of Frederick William IV, an ardent Romantic nationalist, to the throne of Prussia in 1840. Schelling was called to fill Hegel's chair in Berlin and told to "root out Hegelianism." The failure of the Revolution of 1848 was also a severe blow to Hegel's identification of the rational and the actual. Whatever the sources of dissatisfaction with Hegel's system, the very fact that it failed to persuade the succeeding generations is an indication that it was defective, since it predicts its own success.

Whatever the philosophic truth of Hegel's system, it ultimately failed in its efforts to restrain the longing for absolute freedom that had manifested itself in the French Revolution and Romantic nihilism. Hegel believed that the attempt to attain absolute freedom necessarily led to disaster and tried to redirect this longing toward a more limited, rational freedom. The course that Hegel laid out for humanity, however, rested on a speculative synthesis that mystified his contemporaries and an identification of the rational and the actual that outraged many of them. Hegel was thus no more successful than Kant in persuading his successors to be content on his island of truth. The captains of human thought who succeeded Hegel set sail over treacherous seas in search of the elusive land of absolute freedom.

MANFRED AND THE TRAGEDY OF THE I

Goethe's completed *Faust* was never adequately understood or accepted by the Romantics. They were perplexed and dissatisfied with the finished work and preferred instead the *Fragment* of 1790. Grillparzer, Hebbel, Mörike, Keller, and C. F. Meyer were openly hostile to the second part of the work, which seemed to them little more than a bizarre allegory.[36] The ending in particular provoked the Romantics' wrath. That Faust should be saved seemed the height of absurdity.[37] In their view, Faust was an imperfect hero, insufficiently devoted to absolute subjectivity and freedom, too concerned with a reconciliation with the world, too banal in his ultimate aspirations, and finally too petty in his evil to serve as their model for a higher humanity.

The Romantics' disenchantment with the completed *Faust* was matched only by their enthusiasm for Manfred, Faust's not-so-distant cousin. Indeed, for many Romantics, Manfred was the hero that Faust should have been, the realization of the young Goethe's brilliant conception that the old Goethe had corrupted. In part, this was certainly the result of timing. Byron completed *Manfred* in 1817 and it was published in the same year. It thus fell between the publication of the first and second parts of *Faust*. There is no doubt that Byron was greatly influenced in his composition of *Manfred* by Goethe's great work, but it is also clear that the intention of his work is fundamentally different than that of *Faust*.[38] Both Faust and Manfred seek to become something more than human, both come under the spell of the demonic, both are dominated by it, and both are driven into the vilest iniquity. Despite his crimes, Faust can be saved because the spirit of negation which entices him is always in the service of the good. Manfred, on the contrary, is doomed beyond all hope of redemption because the demonic force that empowers him is inextricably linked to evil.

Like Faust, Manfred recognizes the inadequacy of all traditional knowledge and seeks a deeper understanding of the world through magic. Such knowledge is attained not through the observation of the natural world or the deductions of logic but through immediate intuition of feelings which are connected to the "spirits of the unbounded universe" (1.1.29). Such intuition, however, is constrained by social mores, and it is thus only when these bonds have been broken that we can grasp the truth. Only then can we feel truly. Manfred attains such superhuman knowledge and freedom but only at a terrible price. To know the world in all its depths, he must shatter its most sacrosanct barriers. His knowledge thus grows out of the most heinous crime, the rape of his sister and her suicide. These events form the background of the play.

On the surface, the play seems to be about the remorse of a man tortured by guilt for an unnamed deed. However, while Manfred feels guilt, he does not regret what he has done and indeed would do it again. He reaches out to embrace his sister's ghost, crying out "I will clasp thee, and we again will be—" when the ghost vanishes (1.1.190–91). His desire is infinite and leads him beyond all limits. This is the source of his superhuman freedom. He knows what his greatness costs and is willing to pay the horrible price, willing to bear the tremendous guilt that his crime entails. Faust flees from the death of Gretchen and is preserved by a forgetfulness induced by nature. Manfred lives in the constant consciousness of his deed. Indeed, he must keep the recollection of the deed before him, because it is the knowledge of his crime that is the source of his freedom, his knowledge, and his greatness. The height that he has attained can be sustained only by a constant recurrence to the abysmal depths out of which it has arisen. He avoids slipping into the everyday by dwelling in the vicinity of this horror. In contradistinction to Faust, Manfred is not blind to the horrible truth but dwells within it.

The character of Manfred's crime is not accidental. It is the utmost expression of his being, the denial of otherness, the attempt to eliminate all boundaries and convert everything into the I. Manfred thus violates the most sacred law of difference, the injunction against incest, that draws a line between those things that are nearest to one another. This is especially important in his case because Astarte is not merely his sister but his twin in every respect save one: she is gentler and more tender. Manfred sees himself in her and loves her with a thorough self-love, annihilating her independence. "I loved her, and destroyed her!" (2.2.117). Even love, the preeminent source of reconciliation, becomes an engine of destruction when it is put in the service of the self-willing I.

The spirit of Manfred's sister makes clear the consequences of violating this law: "By thy cold breast and serpent smile, / By thy unfathomed gulfs of guile, / By that most seeming virtuous eye, / By thy shut soul's hypocrisy; / By the perfection of thine art / Which passed for human thine own heart; / By thy delight in others' pain / And by thy brotherhood of Cain, / I call upon thee! and compel / Thyself to be thy proper Hell!" (1.1.242–251).

Faust is purged of guilt, renewed, able to achieve a kind of reconciliation with the world. Manfred is thoroughly isolated from the world and other men. He is his own hell, and a hell that he cannot escape or even want to escape, because escape can be achieved only by sacrificing his superhuman freedom and knowledge, by giving up the supremacy of the I that his crime established.[39] He thus rejects a witch's offer to cure him, if he will swear obedience to her will (2.2.157–59). His suffering is great but greater still is his superhuman pride.

Manfred's greatness is the model for a new type of tragic hero whose titanic nobility was hitherto scarcely imaginable. He looks down upon even the demons who come to claim his soul:

Manfred: my past power / Was purchased by no compact with thy crew, / But by superior science—penance, daring, / And length of watching, strength of mind, and skill / In knowledge of our Fathers— when the earth / Saw men and spirits walking side by side, / And gave ye no supremacy: I stand / Upon my strength—I do defy—deny— / Spurn back, and scorn ye!—

Spirit: But thy many crimes have made thee—

Manfred: What are they to such as thee? / Must crimes be punished by other crimes, / And greater criminals? —Back to thy hell! / Thou hast no power upon me, *that* I feel; / Thou never shalt possess me, *that* I know: / What I have done is done; I bear within / A torture which could nothing gain from thine: / The Mind which is immortal makes itself / Requital for its good or evil thoughts,— /Is its own origin of ill and end— / And its own place and time: its innate sense, / When stripped of this mortality, derives / No color from the fleeting things without, /But is absorbed in sufferance or in joy, / From the knowledge of its own desert. / *Thou* didst not tempt me, and thou couldst not tempt me; / I have not been thy dupe, nor am thy prey— / But was my own destroyer, and will be / My own hereafter. (3.4.113–40)[40]

It is not God who rules here but the self-creating I. Manfred claims to stand above the demons and above God himself, to be an immortal mind that makes itself and its world, that lives within itself and enjoys or suffers from itself. In this respect, he echoes Fichte and the Jena Romantics. Manfred, however, comes to recognize what Fichte never imagined and the early Romantics only suspected: to be one's own creator is to be one's own judge, jury, and executioner.

Camus and others have argued that this inner torment that is so typical of Romanticism arises out of the will's immense desire for liberation at any cost and its concomitant inability to free itself from its moral scruples.[41] Such an interpretation does not understand the shattering truth that Manfred reveals. If he is his own world, then his crime lies not in the injury he does to another but in his destruction of the other within himself. His rape of his sister is the rape of himself and her death the death of his gentler and more tender self. His crime is its own punishment. He has become as his sister's spirit predicted, his own proper hell. His great freedom and knowledge were attained only by brutalizing himself; by cutting off all connection to anything outside himself and thus confining himself to the empty sphere of the self. His freedom in this sense is the freedom of the void, and he has become a superman only by becoming an underman.

Faust, as we noted, is at best a sentimental tragedy. *Manfred,* on the contrary, is the supreme tragedy of Romanticism, the tragedy of the I in its search for absolute freedom and knowledge. This tragedy is not the result of some dark and incomprehensible fate, nor is it the result of some flaw of character. Manfred wills his tragedy, wills his suffering and destruction. He and no one else makes him a monster. It is precisely this willed character of his fate, however, that reveals the height of the new possibility for greatness that he represents. This new excellence so surpasses our understanding that it can be indicated only by the suffering that Manfred is willing to endure to attain it. Beyond this point Romanticism cannot go.[42] In Manfred, Blake's tiger and the mysterious creator of the tiger have become one; they become the chimera.

Goethe never attained this height or this depth and tried to warn mankind about the dangers of such a path. Goethe, however, could not ultimately provide the kind of warning that was necessary, because he loved the heroic striving of those who climbed this treacherous peak and fell into this dark abyss. He thus cannot finally condemn Faust. Goethe, however, at least sensed the danger of such a journey even as he was irresistibly drawn toward it. At the end of his autobiography, *Poetry and Truth,* Goethe describes how after reaching one of the supreme decisions of his life, he rejected a last appeal to reconsider. Filled with passion and enthusiasm, he cries out the words he put into the mouth of his most demonic hero Egmont: "Child, child! no further! As if whipped by invisible spirits, the sunstallions of time bolt away with the light chariot of our fate; and there remains nothing that we can do other than to hold onto the reins courageously and guide the wheels now to the right and now to the left, away from a stone here, away from a precipice there. Whither it goes, who knows? He can scarcely remember whence he came."[43]

By contrast, Goethe's successors, the enthusiastic nineteenth-century riders on the tiger, were often so engrossed in their journey that they were unwilling or unable to recognize their abysmal destination.

LEFT HEGELIANISM AND THE ADVENT OF POLITICAL NIHILISM

While Hegel was more successful than Goethe in his attempts to combat nihilism during his lifetime, in the period after his death it was his students and followers who were principally responsible for nihilism becoming a world-historical political force. Hegel attempted to provide a bulwark against nihilism by reconciling freedom and natural necessity. Neither the Left nor the Right Hegelians, however, were interested in maintaining the speculative synthesis that was crucial to Hegel's thought. The Right Hegelians favored a conservative, theological interpretation of his thought that fastened upon the unity of God and the state within the absolute. They originally hoped to see this unity realized in a liberal Germany but, after the failure of the Revolution of 1848, they turned increasingly to Romantic nationalism.[44] The Left Hegelians rejected Hegel's speculative solution out of hand and turned his dialectical methodology against the existing political order in an attempt to bring about social justice.[45]

The Left Hegelians employed Hegel's principle of negation in their critique of the existing social order and his dialectical methodology in their attempt to delineate the rational goal of political change. Such a critical and prospective methodology is foreign to Hegel's thought, which is essentially retrospective and conciliatory. Contradiction in his view must always be understood from the perspective of completed reconciliation, not as a signpost to a necessary future.

The Left Hegelians rejected the theological element of Hegel's thought, which in their view was bound up with the repressive authoritarianism of existing political structures. This is already apparent in Ludwig Feuerbach, who argued that "*the divine essence is nothing other* than the human essence or better: *the essence of man,* purified, freed from the limitations of the individual man, objectified, that is, *contemplated* and honored as another, differentiated from him, but still his own essence—all *characteristics* of the divine essence are thus human characteristics."[46] Romanticism rebelled against God and reason in the interest of individual autonomy. The Left Hegelians reduce God and reason to a reflection of the human spirit or a projection of human needs in order to secure human omnipotence. Feuerbach asserts that "what the individual man does not know and cannot do all of humanity together knows and can do. Thus, the divine knowledge that knows simultaneously every particular has its reality in the knowledge of the species."[47] The development of Left Hegelian thought represents a continuing radicalization of this notion of human autonomy and omnipotence that fastens upon and ultimately universalizes the Hegelian principle of negativity.

Left Hegelianism is thus essentially un-Hegelian. In fact it is a concealed reversion to Fichteanism.[48] This Fichteanism, however, was transformed by the historical and political philosophy of Hegel.

Hegel had attempted to turn the Fichtean principle of negation back upon itself by reconciling the dialectical antitheses in a higher speculative synthesis. The Left Hegelian rejection of the speculative moment in Hegel's thought was a return to a notion of unreconciled dialectical development. It was thus a return to Fichte, but a return that took place within a fundamentally Hegelian view of history and politics. For Hegel, history is the dialectical unfolding of human social life. The agents who bring about this change are the world-historical individuals. At the end of history, these individuals are superseded in the rational state by the universal class of civil servants.

The Left Hegelians argued that this state is imperfectly rational and that the so-called universal class is universal only in name, since each of the individuals has a particular class interest that is at odds with the universal. In their view, a further transformation is thus necessary to bring a class to power that is substantively and not merely formally universal. The agent of such a transformation, however, is no longer understood to be a single world-historical individual, but is seen as a world-historical party or class. In the case of Marx, this is the Communist party that will overthrow the capitalist system and establish the rule of the proletariat. The goal that Marx sees so clearly before him, however, recedes into the more distant future in later Left Hegelian thought, reachable only by repeated revolutionary transformations. The Fichteanism that Hegel had sought to overcome thus ironically becomes the essence of latter-day Hegelianism. It is through this Left Hegelian misappropriation of Hegel's principle of negation that nihilism becomes a world-historical political program.

THE ROMANTIC DEMONS OF REALISM

The liberation of the negative element in Hegel's thought from its Hegelian chains occurred only gradually as successive thinkers reluctantly turned to ever more radical forms of negation when less radical alternatives proved ineffective. While these hesitant nihilists remained critical of those not merely to their right but also to their left, they found it difficult to resist moving toward the doctrine of absolute negation implicit in their critical stance toward the existing order. Criticism becomes critical of every stable form and order. Freedom, understood in terms of negation, finds itself limited by every limit. Once one has abandoned the circular course of Hegel's "good infinity," one is almost ineluctably drawn toward the "bad

infinity," that is, toward Fichte's infinite striving for a boundless freedom. Such freedom is possible, however, only as the result of the
repeated negation of orders continually established, that is, only
through permanent revolution. One of the first steps on this path was
the realist critique of Romanticism.

This critique, which began in the 1830s, was led by members of
the so-called Young Germany movement.[49] The name, 'Young
Germany,' was created by state authorities in 1835 to link together a
group of young writers and thinkers, including Heinrich Heine and
Karl Gutzkow, who stood in general opposition to the regime. They
did not all know one another, nor did they have an explicit program.
But while they were united only in this superficial way, they did all
reject Romanticism as a result of the growing awareness of poverty
and the cold authoritarianism of industrial entrepreneurs and the
bureaucratic state. They were also all deeply influenced by Left
Hegelianism and particularly by the notion of negation as the basis of
social critique. Indeed, it was their emphasis of this negative element
that led to the characterization of them as nihilists in the late 1840s.

This nihilism is portrayed by Karl Gutzkow himself in his novella
The Nihilists.[50] The work is set in an unnamed German principality
and most of the action takes place in the months immediately preceding the 1848 Revolution. The story turns upon the attraction of
a young woman, Herta Wingolf, to two different men, Konstantin
Ulrichs and Eberhart Ott. All three are nihilists and their nihilism is
an extension of their Left Hegelianism. When we first encounter
Herta, she is reading a passage from Feuerbach which the narrator
quotes at length: "Practical cognition is a tainted cognition,
besmirched by egoism. With it I observe a thing not on its own
account, but to appropriate it, as when a man loves a woman only for
sensual purposes. Practical cognition is not satisfied in itself, only theoretical cognition is, it is joyful, it alone is sacred; for it the object of
love is an object of wonder" (*N,* 183).

This passage articulates the distinction on which the novella and
its evaluation of nihilism turn. Two different forms of nihilism are
represented in the novel by the two men, and the relative value of
each is reflected in Herta's love for first one and then the other. The
development of her love and understanding, however, is in fact only
the working out of this Feuerbachian distinction between practical
and theoretical cognition.

Gutzkow in this way exposes extreme nihilism as a radical egoism
that manifests itself as the Mephistophelian spirit of criticism and

negation. At the same time, he defends a moderate nihilism that is critical and negative but also interested in constructing a better world.Konstantin Ulrichs represents that form of nihilism that corresponds to Feuerbach's practical cognition, the Mephistophelian moment of pure negation or radical criticism (*N,* 271). He is witty, charming, always the center of attention, always master of the most current thinking on issues of science and politics. He is a Left Hegelian who speaks in the spirit of Ruge and Bruno Bauer and is described by the reactionary Baron Hans von Landschütz as a Communist (*N,* 237). This makes him and his brand of nihilism immensely attractive in the heady days immediately preceding the Revolution of 1848 (*N,* 201).

Herta is attracted by Konstantin's charisma because it seems to promise a new life. There is another side to Konstantin, however, that she does not see, "a rampant egoism" (*N,* 194). The "doubly demonic Konstantin," as the narrator describes him, entrances her with his speeches, most of which he himself does not believe, since he is a cynic. He is a man of words who opposes everything, but his opposition does not proceed from a vision of a better world but from a desire to rise above every world, above every content. His spirit is thoroughly critical and negative.

Herta comes to understand this fact during her stay with Konstantin's family, where she comes to know his sister Frida. Frida, as Eberhart describes her, is a "wild child of nature" (*N,* 232). She is proud to the point of vanity and has no concern for the feelings of others. She wants above all else to command and, if this is not possible, then at least to overthrow those who do command. She is the spirit of negation incarnate. She constantly speaks but never listens, she is always critical but generally has no knowledge of what she opposes. As Herta ultimately realizes, her genius is the genius of the "laughing destroyer, of the negative, like the genius of her brother" (*N,* 241–42). Through the sister and the rest of the family, Herta comes to understand the superficiality of Konstantin's merely negative nihilism.

Konstantin himself is incapable of moderation. He wants either Cato or Caesar, either America or Russia. This absolute criticism allows him and those like him to rise above every content, since they never have to affirm or create anything. They believe themselves to be "the gods of the earth, who declare spirit to be phosphorus, Romanticism to be nonsense, free will to be a fairy tale; and there was a titanic sweeping gesture in their assertion that what a man would be, he must be entirely, and that he must always act only according to his own nature" (*N*, 238). Konstantin's negativity is enormously powerful, and Herta is the only one who stands up to him, pointing out that his constant appeals to the brute force of nature are a denial of all human progress. In her view, this constant juxtaposition of absolute alternatives can do no good. It is much better to seek mediation and reconciliation, the marriage of right and duty and of strength and weakness, because civilization as a whole rests on mutual restraint and pity for human fallibility (*N*, 243). Her criticism, however, falls on deaf ears, and Frida and Konstantin deride her as pedantic and backward-thinking.

Eberhart Ott is a nihilist of a different stripe. He too is a Left Hegelian and is opposed to the existing order, but he is not an egoistic negator and does not have to condemn everything to destruction to assuage his own ego. Eberhart is tall, quiet, and sincere, and wins every heart that is attracted to the inner and not the outer man. He is self-sacrificing, other-directed, and constructive. He tirelessly organizes political groups and programs to support reform. The difference between him and Konstantin is the difference between theoretical and practical cognition. Konstantin wants to know things in order to possess them, to bend everything around him so that he can be the center of creation. Eberhart follows the Stoic maxim that one lives not for oneself but for others. He believes that "passions and egoism as a rule corrupt everything" (*N*, 224). He is not a glittering orator like Konstantin, but asserts that the test of a man is not his words but his deeds and his impact on history.

He soon becomes Herta's ideal. He possesses everything she admires in Konstantin and lacks everything she finds objectionable. She realizes finally that she loved not Konstantin himself but only his understanding and that this is more fully developed in Eberhart. What particularly attracts her to Eberhart, however, is his love of Agnes. Agnes was previously engaged to Konstantin, but when Konstantin met Herta, he sent Eberhart to break off the engagement. Out of pity for her suffering, Eberhart comes to love and ultimately marry her. This is something incomprehensible to Konstantin and Frida, who value only those things that gratify their own desires. It is this concern for others, however, that endears him to Herta and, as a result, she decides to leave Konstantin.

The outbreak of the revolution changes everything. Konstantin seems to be transformed. Everything that had been wavering in him becomes solid. He is active everywhere and takes the lead in everything. Herta is carried away. Konstantin's passion, anger, and hatred become her passion, anger, hatred (*N,* 238). They are constantly active, constantly in motion. Herta, however, cannot stand this life of continual negation. She becomes seriously ill and retires to Switzerland to recover. She hears less and less from Konstantin and begins to realize that he has changed. They grow apart.

The failure of the revolution brings about a sea change. Agnes dies in childbirth. Frida marries the reactionary Junker, Baron von Landschütz, and Konstantin marries the Baron's sister and takes a position with the government as prosecuting attorney. Their actions reveal Frida and Konstantin as pure egoists. Eberhart and Herta, by contrast, live much more constructive and meaningful lives. Herta takes over the care of Agnes's child and Eberhart becomes a public defender. The destructive nihilists are unable to accomplish anything of value and are content with social position and a fading renown. They live within the Romantic illusion that they possess a unique genius that sets them above the crowd, and have nothing but contempt for the constructive nihilists who have begun to build a new world.

The difference between the two forms of nihilism becomes clear in the concluding section of the novella, in which Konstantin prosecutes Herta's father for his role as a member of the constitutional assembly. He is defended by Eberhart. Konstantin argues that before the revolution he himself and his sort of nihilist had come to despise the world and work for its negation because they believed the world could be easily made anew. When they saw the result of many contradictory efforts at reform, however, they were disgusted. This was not the utopia of pure freedom that absolute negation was to bring about. This half-finished world could not satisfy a spirit that had always demanded all or nothing, Cato or Caesar, America or Russia. Unable to attain perfection immediately and effortlessly, they concluded that the time was not ripe and returned to the old order, embraced it, and became a part of it. We see in this statement all of the egoism and self-centeredness of Konstantin and his brand of nihilism. They are merely negative spirits with nothing to offer. The failure of their absolute negation to produce the millennium leads them to abandon negation altogether and seek only personal gratification within the existing order.

Eberhart and Herta represent a different position that comes to light in Eberhart's speech. The powers of negation in his view can be tamed and turned in a constructive direction. Absolute negation which has brought about ruin everywhere gives way to determinate negation which does not seek to criticize and negate everything but to bring negation to bear to transform the present order, slowly and tentatively, into something better. Their limited success, however, is despised by the extreme nihilists who deride anything short of perfection as valueless, because they themselves are nothing but opposition and destruction. They spoil the world for everyone else. Eberhart consequently concludes that moderate reformers "are to be more highly esteemed than those who go over to the enemy kit and caboodle" (*N,* 269).

In the end, the moderate nihilists find happiness with one another in building a new life together. Herta explains to Eberhart how she had fallen in love with him for his noble fulfillment of his duty. They decide to marry, and Herta's father responds to this good news with the hopeful Left Hegelian phrase that sums up Gutzkow's opinion of moderate nihilism: "The times and men all go in a circle, but the eternally same circulation climbs upward in a soft line like a spiral and our hopes go with it" (*N,* 274).

On one level, Gutzkow is a critic of nihilism or at least of the most extreme form of nihilism. This critique, however, is part and parcel of his defense of a moderate nihilism that employs determinate and not absolute negation in its methodical efforts to attain the absolute. This nihilism is not egoistic and rampantly self-interested but virtuous and self-sacrificing, dedicated to duty and to the steady improvement of the human condition. Gutzkow's depiction suggests that this form of nihilism is grounded in a true interpretation of Left Hegelian thought. In this way, he seeks to turn Left Hegelianism away from the revolutionary abyss of 1848 toward a more constructive political engagement in the postrevolutionary world.

There is no denying that this moderate nihilism is more appealing than the absolute nihilism of Konstantin, but it is not without its dangers. At first glance, Gutzkow's moderate nihilism seems to be identical with traditional liberalism—it assumes a legalistic form and rejects radical measures. However, this moderate nihilism still follows the Left Hegelian path of negation and is in fact more resolute than extreme nihilism: it does not strive to transform the world in one great moment of apocalyptic negation and then retreat into quietism when this fails, but recognizes the magnitude of its task and adopts a strategy of continual determinate negation that will lead to a successful conclusion. It is more easily reconciled with reality and can construct a home in the world, but this reconciliation is always only tentative, always only with a world that still needs to be negated and transformed.

One might also wonder whether such a doctrine of negation is compatible with a constructive approach to the world. In the context of the novella, this arises as the question of the plausibility of the characterization of Eberhart and Herta. Are such human beings possible? Can they hold such opinions about the crucial necessity for autonomy and still be satisfied with only moderate reform? If they sincerely believe that absolute freedom is essential to happiness, can they be as happy as they are portrayed in a world of limited freedom? Here one has to wonder whether freedom and duty can be as easily combined as Gutzkow would have us believe. This was the problem that tormented German idealism and that found an answer only in Hegel's speculative synthesis. It was precisely this synthesis, however, that was rejected by the Left Hegelians and Young Germany. On what basis then do they reestablish this combination of freedom and duty? The general Left Hegelian response is to argue that there is a duty to secure freedom, that is, a duty to espouse and practice criticism, negation, revolution. The basis for any other sort of reconciliation is lacking in Gutzkow's work, and the reconciliation that he portrays thus seems to be ad hoc or to rest on a poorly comprehended and therefore unstable foundation. This leads to the further suspicion that Gutzkow's moderate nihilism is in fact unstable and likely to degenerate into the extreme nihilism he criticizes. The history of the latter half of the nineteenth century also strongly points in this direction.

Finally, one must wonder whether the self-sacrificing nihilism of Herta and Eberhart is ultimately preferable to the egoistical nihilism of Frida and Konstantin. On the surface, self-sacrificing action seems to be preferable to egoistic action. However, this is the case only if the goal for which the sacrifice is made is itself desirable. In the context of the novella, self-sacrifice is essentially motivated by pity, and pity itself legitimated by the aesthetic judgment that it is beautiful. Herta's love for Eberhart, for example, arises out of the image that preoccupies her of Eberhart comforting Agnes in her despair. The self-sacrifice of the moderate nihilists, as it is portrayed in the novella, is noble but its nobility arises out of its end. If such ends, however, are merely the product of feelings, then there is a real danger that self-sacrifice will in other circumstances prove to be perverse. Insofar as the motive for positive as opposed to negative action resides in feelings, we are faced with the same danger that we saw in William

Lovell. Where feelings rule, sadism is near at hand. Giving oneself up to the cause is laudable only when the cause is just. If the justice of the cause is determined only by our feelings, however, we constantly run the danger of giving ourselves up to perversity and fanaticism. This reliance on self-sacrifice and feeling opens the door to the demonic in a new and even more dangerous form, for the demonic here appears not in the individual but in the collectivity, not in the William Lovells of the world but in the party and the people, and its consequence is not the degradation of the individual but of humanity. Gutzkow's rejection of egoistical nihilism in favor of a self-sacrificing nihilism in this sense prepares the ground for a perverse nihilism that engages the hearts of multitudes not merely against their own interests but against the better interests of mankind. Martyrs in the service of morality, these nihilists become the unwitting agents of perversity.

——Chapter Five——

THE DEMONS UNBOUND
Russian Nihilism and the Pursuit
of the Promethean

We have examined the extraordinary attraction that the demonic exercised upon the early nineteenth-century imagination. Another figure closely akin to these demonic heros of Romanticism was Prometheus. As Goethe presents him in his poem "Prometheus," he is a valiant being who stands face-to-face with the gods and defies them, aware of their power and the suffering they can cause, but unwilling to bow down to them. In one sense, he is even superior to the gods, for he is self-sufficient while they are dependent upon their worshipers. Goethe's Prometheus is the great advocate of this world, spurning the effortless joys of heaven for the painful struggle of earthly life. His willingness to bear this pain elevates him above the gods and is the source of his great pride. The poem, which is addressed to Zeus, concludes with the following stanza: "Here I sit, forming men / In my own image, / A race, that is like me, / Made to suffer, to weep, / To take pleasure and to enjoy itself, / And to pay no attention to your kind, / Like me."[1]

Goethe's Prometheus seems to be another instance of the Romantic fascination with the demonic. He is, however, something more. The demonic is the negation of the divine or, in the case of Goethe and Hegel, a negative moment of God or world-spirit. The Promethean, by contrast, antedates or is contemporaneous with the divine. It is not defined merely through negation, nor is it simply a negative power. Prometheus is not subject to divine law, but lives according to laws of his own that compete with those of the gods. Satan is justly thrown down from heaven and his assertion of autonomy is always immoral and guilt-laden. Prometheus has been bound to his rock unjustly, because of his generosity to men. His assertion of autonomy is thus accompanied not by guilt but by righteous indignation.

The Promethean and the divine, however, are not altogether distinct. As the last stanza of Goethe's poem makes clear, the chief

135

activity of Prometheus is the creation of man in his own image. While the Promethean moves beyond the negativity of the demonic, it does so only by usurping to itself the powers that the Christian tradition attributes to God. Prometheus in this sense is not an immoral violator of a beneficent divine law but a rebel against divine despotism. He is the source of autonomy and the agent of human liberation. While Blake's demonic tiger contained an all-consuming divine fire, Prometheus steals this fire from the gods and brings it down to men.

This chapter attempts to show how important the idea of the Promethean is for Russian nihilism. Russian nihilism has been generally understood as a repudiation of idealism and Romanticism in favor of materialism and populism. As we shall see, this nihilism was characterized by a longing for the Promethean, for a new kind of human being who rises above the level of humanity in search of autonomy. This vision of the Promethean is thus fundamentally dependent upon the notions of will and freedom that are inherited from idealism and Romanticism. This means that the nihilistic vision of a new superhumanity beyond all gods is in fact decisively dependent upon the old God against which it rebels. Russian nihilism in this sense is only a further and more radical permutation of the idea of absolute will whose development we have traced from nominalism through Descartes to Fichte and the German Romantics.

THE BACKGROUND OF RUSSIAN NIHILISM

Russian society of the early nineteenth century rested upon the twin pillars of autocracy and orthodoxy and was maintained by a repressive police apparatus that employed censorship, exile, and simple brutality to eliminate all opposition. Some Russian liberals sought to reform this regime, but they found little support in Russia itself. The failed Decembrists' Conspiracy of 1825 is indicative of the difficulties confronting liberal reformers. Moreover, in its aftermath most critics of the regime were forced to emigrate, and they often lost touch with what was happening in Russia. For them, Russia became more an idea than an actuality, and words replaced deeds as the means of political reform.

This tendency toward a politics of words was intensified by the aristocratic backgrounds of early revolutionaries such as Vissarion Belinski, Nikolai Nekrasov, and Alexander Herzen who believed in the power of rational argument and spilled tons of ink in an effort to achieve reform. Their audience, however, was small, and while they had much to say, little was heard and even less accomplished.

These radicals were indebted to English liberalism and German idealism for their philosophical ideas. Their attraction to the airy heights of idealism was partly a result of the stultifying political atmosphere of the autocracy, but it was also an unintended consequence of Czar Nicholas I's attempt to Prussianize Russian society. Their flight from the harsh reality of everyday life into the ideal was prepared on an intellectual level by the theosophy of free masonry, which exercised great intellectual force in Russian at the time, especially among those whose intellectual education had been shaped by the Böhmian mysticism of the radical orthodox sects, the so-called Old Believers.[2] The importance of this theosophistic movement for the reception of Schelling's Romantic idealism, for example, can hardly be exaggerated, and helps to explain the millenarian character it assumed in Russia. Peter Chaadaev's suggestion that Russia overleap the materialistic West and establish a spiritual kingdom in the interest of all Christian civilization was typical of Russian Schellingians and indicative of their debt to Böhme and theosophy.[3] It is also evident in the thought of the Romantic critic Nadezhdin, the leading Russian Schellingian, who dreamed of a revolutionary transformation to bring about a new classical age.

This theosophistic background also gave Hegelianism a more mystical tone in Russia than it had in Germany, as is evident in the case of Nikolai Stankevich, who was particularly important for the propagation of the thought not only of Hegel but also of Kant and Fichte.[4] The response of his young follower Mikhail Bakunin was typical. Hegel's philosophy seemed in a mystical fashion to lift him above the subjectivism of Romanticism. He wrote, "My *personal I* has been killed for ever, it no longer seeks anything for itself; its life will henceforth be life in the absolute; but in essence my *personal I* has gained more than it has lost . . . My life is now a truthful life."[5] Among opponents of the regime such as Herzen and Bakunin, however, Right Hegelianism quickly gave way to Left Hegelianism or to a combination of Left Hegelianism and the thought of Saint-Simon. This turn to the Left Hegelians and Saint-Simon was a turn away from the divine and toward man as the central world-historical force. The hopes that had hitherto been placed in God or the world-spirit as the agent of transformation and reconciliation were henceforth placed in man. The earliest groups inspired by Saint-Simon thus had a quasi-religious character, but it was a religion with man at its center. However, these early Russian radicals disagreed with Saint-Simon's emphasis on industrial production and looked not to the workers but to the peasants for their models of the Promethean supermen of the future.

It was this apotheosis of man that outraged the Schellingians and led them to characterize Russian Left Hegelianism as nihilism. In an attack on Herzen and Belinski, for example, Mikhail Katkov argued, "If one looks at the universe, and has to choose one of two extreme attitudes, it is easier to become a mystic than a nihilist. We are everywhere surrounded by miracles."[6] In his view, Hegelian dialectic was lifeless, merely a virulent expression of the negative tendencies that are present everywhere and always. His attack is in fact an extension of Jacobi's and Jean Paul's attacks on Fichte and the Romantic nihilists. Katkov and other Russian Schellingians were aware of the work of Jacobi and many were acquainted with Jean Paul's literary criticism. Their critique of Left Hegelianism focuses on the Fichtean moment of dialectical negativity, mirroring in this respect Schelling's attempt to "root out Hegelianism" in Germany. The Russian debate over nihilism is thus an extension of the German controversy.

THE NEW MEN AND THE ORIGIN OF THE NIHILIST MOVEMENT

The Russian political and intellectual horizon was decisively reshaped in the latter half of the nineteenth century by the failure of the revolutions of 1848 and the ascension of the liberal Czar Alexander II to the throne in 1855. For Russian Westernizers, the failure of the revolutions in Germany and France were shattering. The liberals' perceived betrayal of the other classes undermined the argument for a class coalition that the Westernizers had been developing since the Decembrist insurrection. It also hardened the autocracy's position vis-à-vis the intellectuals.

The ascension of Alexander II and the period of liberalization that ended with the emancipation of serfs on 19 February 1861 seemed to be the answer to the Westernizers' prayers. Here at last was a czar who could reconcile the various elements of an irrational society into a new unity. However, the czar's reforms were limited and were seen by the radicals as a duplicitous trick to avoid real change. They concluded that there was only one way to deal with the autocracy, the way of negation, of revolutionary transformation under the leadership of "new men."

These new men in their view would have to be fundamentally different from the radical leaders of the past, not men of words but men of deeds, not aristocrats already compromised by their backgrounds, but "men of different ranks"; not "superfluous men," but irresistible men with implacable wills. Real change, according to Herzen, would require "giving first place to practical action rather than theory."[7] Only a new Prometheus could bring this about, and the goal of the nihilist movement was to liberate him from the autocratic rock to which he was bound.

Russian nihilism is often identified with the spasm of negation that shook the country from 1858 to 1863, but this period of negation is only the most visible manifestation of nihilism. It is, however, a good starting point for our consideration of the phenomenon, since it marks the moment when nihilism passed from the realm of ideas into actuality. This period witnessed the attempt by a large segment of Russian youth to free itself from autocracy and orthodoxy. For the most part, they were not aristocrats but the offspring of doctors, lawyers, and other professionals, often with similar training of their own, and they rejected the older, aristocratic leadership of the radical movement. Their hopes lay not in reform but in a complete clearing of the ground for a new beginning.

This nihilist movement was essentially Promethean. Ivan Turgenev's Arcady Kirsanov defines a nihilist as "a man who does not bow down before any authority, who does not take any principle on faith, whatever reverence that principle may be enshrined in" (*FAS,* 17).[8] Herzen expands upon this definition:

> Nihilism is logic without structure, it is science without dogmas, it is unconditional submission to experience and the resigned acceptance of all consequences, whatever they may be, if they follow from observation, or are required by reason. Nihilism does not transform something into nothing, but shows that nothing which has been taken for something is an optical illusion and that every truth, however it contradicts our fantastic ideas, is more wholesome than they are, and is in any case what we are duty bound to accept.[9]

It has often been argued that Russian nihilism is little more than skepticism or empiricism. While there is a certain plausibility to this assertion, it ultimately fails to capture the millenarian zeal that characterized Russian nihilism. These nihilists were not skeptics but passionate advocates of negation and liberation. Moreover, their methodological rejection of traditional authorities was bound up with a naive faith in their own enlightenment, entirely at odds with scepticism, which manifested itself as a thoroughgoing disdain for the opinions of their opponents.

Sergey Kravchinsky came closer to capturing this element when he described nihilism in 1883 as "a passionate and powerful reaction, not against political despotism, but against the moral despotism that weighs upon the private and inner life of the individual."[10] This points to the central demand of nihilism for radical autonomy. While such autonomy required the negation of all institutions of repression, the nihilists were convinced that a shining world of freedom waited on the other side of this sea of destruction. The destructive moment of nihilism is merely the prelude to a new reconstructive phase of human life. Even an opponent of the radicals, Peter Boboriukin, recognized that the principles and tendencies of nihilism "are much more positive . . . than negative. If the Nihilists began with a destructive criticism, it was only to enable them to introduce with greater enthusiasm and a more ardent belief their own rules and doctrines into every part of their teaching."[11]

There are problems with such a constructive interpretation of Russian nihilism. First, the positive or constructive side of nihilism was never clearly defined. For some radicals, it was vaguely socialist, based on the idea of the village commune *(mir)*. Others saw a managerial class as the basis for the new order. Most nihilists, however, were convinced that this positive goal could only be properly formulated when the chains of repression had been broken. The uncanny attraction that nihilism exercised upon Russian youth thus cannot be explained as simple utopianism. However, it also cannot be explained as a mere rejection of the actual world. Negation for the nihilists is never mere negation, but is always understood in Fichtean or Hegelian fashion as the ground of freedom. This freedom is both negative and positive, a freedom from the autocratic restraints of the past and a freedom for the as yet unimagined wonders of the future. It combines revulsion and negation with a faith that a better world waits just beyond the horizon.

It is also questionable whether a constructive program of any sort is compatible with the radicals' longing for universal negation, that is, whether the Promethean fire can be turned into a productive force in the service of civilization once it has been unleashed in the service of destruction. Gutzkow was skeptical that such a reconciliation of destructive and constructive nihilism was possible, but this skepticism found little echo among the Russian radicals.

Russian nihilism drew heavily upon Left Hegelianism in general and Feuerbach in particular. However, in contradistinction to the development of German Left Hegelianism, which accepted the *necessity* of the dialectical development of history and consequently a severe limitation on the freedom and power of human will, Russian nihilism attributed to man an almost absolute power to transform his social and political existence. The theoretical basis for this nihilist view was the belief that history was determined not by immutable laws but by free individuals. Russian nihilism in this sense is more Fichtean than German Left Hegelianism. This is especially evident in the thought of Bakunin, who was introduced to Fichte by Stankevich in 1836 and profoundly influenced by his ideas of freedom and negation for the rest of his life. According to Bakunin, Fichte was the true hero of our time.[12] This Fichtean transformation of Left Hegelianism was also due to the influence of the French utopian socialists, including Considerat, Leroux, Fourier, and above all Saint-Simon, Comte, and Proudhon, who generally attributed a greater causal capacity to freedom than the German and Polish Left Hegelians.

This belief in the causal power of human freedom was essential to the radicals' Prometheanism and reinforced their view that Russia might follow a different path of development, by-passing capitalism and moving directly into socialism. This view, which was shared by Comte, Marx, and many Russian conservatives, was nurtured by the widespread belief in the socialist character of the Russian commune. This notion also helps to explain the populist form that Russian nihilism assumed.

The belief in such a unique opportunity lent an air of desperation to the nihilist enterprise. A direct transition to socialism was possible, but this opportunity would not last forever. The development of capitalism, many believed, would destroy the *mir* and place Russia in the hands of efficient but immoral industrial managers. Radical reform thus had to take place immediately.

This focus on the socialist character of the peasant commune has led many scholars to the mistaken conclusion that nihilism was merely one element in a broader socialist movement. Many nihilists were neither populists nor socialists. Even among the nihilists who were populists, not all were socialists. Moreover, among those who were populists or socialists, many were only secondarily so. Their principal aim was negation that aimed at liberating man's Promethean powers. This goal was crucial, for if Prometheus was liberated, everything else would follow but if not, everything would be in vain. For this reason, the radicals were willing to trust future generations to determine the shape of social and political life. The unbinding of Prometheus, however, required negation and nihilism.

This Promethean view of human freedom established a moral imperative for the radicals. If history is driven by powers beyond human control, as Marx had argued, then no one is really responsible for or obligated to do anything about the evil in the world. If, on the contrary, man is free to shape his own destiny, then revolutionary activity is a moral duty. N. K. Mikhailovsky thus argued that anything that delays progress "is immoral, unjust, harmful, irrational."[13] Economic and political ills, from this perspective, are the result of the moral failings of the body social and will disappear with social reform.[14] Dedication to revolution thus became the highest moral imperative, and commitment to the cause absolved all personal failings.

If the reconstruction of human society depends only on human will, then, the nihilists concluded, such changes can be achieved immediately. This conclusion points to a chiliastic or even apocalyptic element in nihilist thinking. Nikolai Dobrolyubov, for example, argued that it would be necessary to wait only approximately a night for the social transformation they expected.[15] The basis for this belief in the imminence of the new world was the nihilists' naive faith that the entire truth about nature and man had been discovered and could be employed in the cause of human liberation. While this notion harkened back to Hegel, it was based on a radical materialism quite at odds with his idealism. This turn to materialism was not unique to the Russian nihilists—the Left Hegelians had followed a similar path—but the Russian nihilists were more ardent and less critical materialists than their German cousins. Drawing heavily on the German materialists Jacob Moleschott, Karl Vogt, and Ludwig Büchner, the nihilists argued that the natural sciences were preparing the way for the millennium. This turn to materialism was also bound up with the growth of atheism. Nihilist atheism was rooted in Left Hegelian thought, but it was given a concrete reality by materialism, especially in combination with the Darwinism that became increasingly popular among the nihilists. In theology lectures, for example nihilists often shouted "Man is a worm," as an attack upon both idealism and religion.[16]

The leaders of the nihilist movement were connected to two competing journals. The most important of these was the *Contemporary,* edited by Nikolai Chernyshevsky and Dobrolyubov. Both of these men had been destined for the priesthood, but after reading Hegel and Feuerbach, they abandoned religion and turned to radical social reform. They were dedicated to peasant socialism and attacked the Decembrists, the revolutionaries of 1848, and the liberals who secured the emancipation of the serfs not merely as superfluous men but as corrupt and duplicitous politicians. Liberalism in their view was merely a deception for enslaving people under the banner of rights. What was needed was not liberal reform but radical revolution. Such a revolution, however, could be fomented only by a new type of humanity, men of deeds versus the men of words who had characterized the previous generation. Chernyshevsky thus held up Robespierre and Louis-Auguste Blanqui as models for the nihilists. In this respect, he was probably closer to Carlyle than to Marx. He had little understanding of economics and believed that the course of history was determined not by abstract economic forces but by great men.

The other wing of the nihilist movement, led by Dmitri Pisarev and his journal, *Russian Word,* was less populist than the *Contemporary* group.[17] Pisarev believed that Russia could be transformed only by an intellectual elite. He was influenced by the Left Hegelian notion of a leading, universal class, but he drew even more heavily on Comte's idea of a ruling scientific elite.[18] Such an elite, however, could come into being only as the result of the universal negation of the existing order: "In a word, here is the ultimatum of our camp: what can be smashed must be smashed; whatever is able to withstand, let it stand; whatever flies into pieces is rubbish; in any case hit right, hit left, from that no evil can nor will come."[19] Pisarev was convinced that only the strong would withstand such destruction and that an elite would thereby come to rule. His followers were dedicated to this negative path, and Varfolomey Zaytsev and Nikolai Sokolov, for example, became disciples of Bakunin after Pisarev's death.

While the two leading nihilist groups disagreed on details, they both sought to liberate the Promethean might of the Russian people by destroying the existing order. Neither of these groups was politically effective, however, because neither was really interested in political reform. This strange lack of concern was apparently the result of their belief that politics was linked to an outdated stage of humanity. Men were free and could shape their own destinies in the most radical way. If they had not already done so, it was because they were morally depraved. With such men, no compromise was possible. A new beginning required the overthrow of these men and their institutions. Revolution was a moral imperative.

Morality thus comes to inform an ideological politics that is driven not by the desire for power but by a missionary zeal that is willing to use any means to convert the heathen and secure salvation. Inspired by Chernyshevsky, a small underground organization, Young Russia, had already come into being under the leadership of P. G. Zaichnevsky in 1860. Its immediate aim was "a bloody and implacable revolution, which shall radically change the whole foundation of contemporary society."[20]

Such a missionary politics points to the fact that nihilism is not a simple doctrine of negation but a new kind of religion, what Comte called a religion of humanity. Even as dedicated an opponent of the nihilists as Katkov recognized that nihilism was "a frustrated religion, filled with internal contradictions and nonsense, but none the less a religion, which can have its own teachers and fanatics . . . the religion of negation is directed against all authorities, but is itself based on submission to authority. Everything that has a negative character is *eo ipso* indisputable dogma in the eye of these sectarians."[21] Katkov saw the danger in this new religion in its vast exaggeration of the power of the human will, but it was precisely this Prometheanism that made this movement so attractive.

The nihilists believed that the prototypes of this new Promethean humanity already existed in the cadres of the revolutionary movement itself. These Promethean cadres were called "new people" by Chernyshevsky, the "thinking proletariat" by Pisarev and Nikolai Shelgunov, "critically thinking personalities" by P. L. Lavrov, and "cultural pioneers" by others. N. K. Mikhailovsky called them *intelligentsia*.[22]

The intelligentsia was thus conceived as the new universal class, like Fichte's scholars, Hegel's civil servants, and Marx's proletariat. For Pisarev and others, they were the Promethean heros guiding world history. Hegel had argued that the age of world-historical individuals was over because history was at an end. Humanity thus required only a rational civil service to maintain the order that had been established. The Left Hegelians argued, on the contrary, that history had not yet reached its end and would do so only when the truly universal class, in Marx's case the proletariat, came to predominance. Hegel's notion of the world-historical individual in the hands of the Left Hegelians becomes the notion of a world-historical class. The Russian nihilists followed this path but replaced the proletariat, which was almost nonexistent in Russia anyway, with the peasantry.

Neither the proletariat nor the peasantry, however, could act without first coming to recognize itself as a class, and this could be achieved only under the leadership of world-transforming supermen. Marx believed these leaders would arise from the proletariat and the bourgeois ideologists who joined the proletarians in their world-historical struggle with the bourgeoisie. The Russian nihilists believed these leaders would come from the intelligentsia, whom they conceived as members of a kind of monastic order ready to give up their lives in the service of the great moral crusade of human liberation.[23] In their view, this class would create a new superhumanity and then merge with it. The revolutionary leaders were thus no different from those they would produce; they were simply more heroic because of the difficulties they had to face. The heroism of the intelligentsia was also the source of their tragedy, for as an essentially negative force, they could only lay the groundwork for this new world through universal negation. The intelligentsia was thus doomed to perish, or as Herzen put it, to be devoured by the world they were creating.[24]

TURGENEV'S *FATHERS AND SONS*

The most famous literary depiction of these new men was the protagonist of Turgenev's *Fathers and Sons,* Eugene Bazarov, and it is in his character that we can begin to see the hidden relationship of the Promethean nihilist to the demonic hero of Romanticism and the absolute I of idealism. *Fathers and Sons* is set in a provincial context, but the action concerns the most important intellectual and political issues of the day. The principal events all take place during the period of the agitation over the question of emancipation. It is a story of the conflict between two generations: the older Romantics and idealists; and their children, the nihilists of the 1860s. The two children, Arcady Kirsanov and Bazarov, are students returning home for the summer. They first visit the Kirsanov family, which includes Arcady's father, Nicolai, Nicolai's young mistress Phenechka, and Arcady's aristocratic uncle Pavel. The father and uncle discover that under the tutelage of Bazarov their son has become a nihilist and that he now views them as hopelessly behind the times in their Romanticism and liberalism. Nicolai is disheartened by this charge but believes that it is probably true. Pavel, however, contests the matter, first with his brother and then with Bazarov. In this context, Bazarov and Arcady are called upon to define and defend nihilism. They do not convince Pavel, and it becomes clear that there is an unbridgeable gap between Pavel and Bazarov, the leading representatives of their generations.

Arcady and Bazarov leave the Kirsanov estate and travel to the local town where, after an encounter with Bazarov's supercilious disciple Sitnikov and the ridiculous new woman Kukshin, they meet the beautiful and wealthy widow Odnitsova, who invites them to her estate. As the Kirsanov estate was the site for the presentation of the theory of nihilism, the Odnitsova estate is the place where it is tested. Bazarov, who has hitherto declared all Romanticism to be bosh and all romantic attachments to be physiological disorders, falls madly and hopelessly in love with Odnitsova. While she is attracted to him, she draws back when he declares his love. He is mortified not by her refusal but by his own romantic desires that stand in manifest contradiction to his nihilism.

The remainder of the novel details the disintegration and collapse of Bazarov. He and Arcady visit his doting parents, but he can find no peace, for he is constantly tormented by his hopeless love and the contradiction between this love and his principles. The rest of the novel is a series of misadventures. He nearly comes to blows with Arcady; he misguidedly agrees to a short and ultimately quite embarrassing visit to Odnitsova's; he returns to the Kirsanov estate, where he is not wanted; he tries to seduce Nicolai's mistress and is drawn into a duel with Pavel; he returns home and falls into ennui; and he finally cuts himself while performing an autopsy on a cholera victim, contracts the disease, and dies, although not until after a final visit from Odnitsova.

Bazarov is one of the most enigmatic characters in Russian literature, a strange combination of opposites that evokes both loathing and admiration. He is dedicated to the good of his fellow man but is himself in many ways inhumane. He is tall and strong, astonishingly self-assured, filled with pride, a "bottomless pit of self-conceit," which leads him at one point to liken himself to a god (*FAS*, 86). At the same time, he befriends almost all of the simple people he meets.

He claims that he is studying natural science in order to become a physician, but this is only half true, because he really wants to understand human nature. As he tells two peasant boys, he dissects frogs to better understand men, since the two are essentially the same. Human beings are organisms and can be understood only generically: "A single human specimen is sufficient to judge all the rest. People are like trees in a forest; no botanist would think of studying each individual birch tree" (*FAS*, 66). Their individual personalities are irrelevant. He thus rejects Romanticism and idealism, which focus on the subjective elements in man. Chemistry is twenty times more useful than poetry in revealing the truth about man: "What does matter is that two and two make four, and the rest is all nonsense" (*FAS*, 33). Through medicine and physiology, he means to comprehend humanity.

Bazarov wants to be useful to society and "at the present time negation is the most useful of all" (*FAS*, 39). Nihilists destroy, Arcady explains, "because we are a force . . . [and] a force is not to be called to account" (*FAS*, 41). Bazarov's aim, unstated by Turgenev because of the censorship, is, of course, revolution. Nothing is worth saving, everything must be repudiated, including the village *mir* and the peasant family (*FAS*, 39). All social institutions are corrupt and only universal destruction can make a decent future possible. What this universal negation will produce, however, is unclear. Bazarov proclaims: "That's not our business now. . . . The ground has to be cleared first" (*FAS*, 39). He expects something magnificent: "Reform society and there will be no diseases . . . in a proper organization of society, it will at least be absolutely the same whether a man is stupid or clever, wicked or good" (*FAS*, 66–67).

The important thing is hate and negation. Bazarov declares: "We want to smash other people!" (*FAS*, 148). This hate is directed at times even against those he loves. In the midst of a quarrel, Bazarov's face appears to Arcady to be "so vindictive—there was such a menace in grim earnest in the smile that distorted the lips and in his glittering eyes, that he instinctively felt afraid" (*FAS*, 105). Even as Bazarov expresses his love to Odnitsova, his face is almost bestial. Odnitsova "had forced herself to go up to a certain point, forced herself to glance behind it, and had seen behind it not even an abyss, but a void . . . or something hideous" (*FAS*, 83). Bazarov expresses his loathing in unequivocal terms: "I hate so many" (*FAS*, 103).

He finds it impossible, however, to live up to his principles. He falls in love with Odnitsova and is forced to admit the importance of the subjective side of life he so decidedly rejects. He also finds he cannot simply ignore Romantic codes of honor, for his pride will not let him refuse when he is challenged to a duel by Pavel. Finally, he discovers that the power of negation is not an omnipotent force but is itself subordinate to the powers of life itself. As he lies dying he proclaims, "Go and try to disprove death. Death will disprove you—and that's all!" (*FAS*, 157). His fate is tragic, but his unwillingness to repudiate his principles even in the face of death makes him heroic.

Turgenev's own opinion of Bazarov was ambivalent: "Did I want to abuse Bazarov or extol him? *I do not know myself,* since I don't know whether I love him or hate him!" (*FAS,* 184; cf. 190). Bazarov is a negative but extremely powerful character, precisely the sort of man Turgenev was attracted to: "I prefer Prometheus, I prefer Satan, the type who revolts, who is an individual."[25] In order to understand the peculiar attraction of Bazarov, we must examine his character more fully.

Bazarov is one of the most Promethean revolutionaries in modern literature. Turgenev claimed that he "dreamt of a figure that was gloomy, wild, huge, half grown out of the ground, powerful, sardonic, honest—and doomed to destruction nevertheless—since he nevertheless still stands only at the threshold of the future—I dreamt of some sort of strange *pendant* to Pugachev" (*FAS,* 186).[26] Bazarov's greatness is unquestionable and was never doubted by anyone other than the board of *Contemporary.* Katkov complained that if Turgenev did not apotheosize Bazarov, he at least set him on a very high pedestal (*FAS,* 173). Turgenev himself remarked, "I portrayed the fellow too heroically, too idealistically" (*FAS,* 189).

This general impression, however, is hard to justify on the basis of Bazarov's words or deeds. We are convinced of his greatness, however, not by anything he does but by the way others act toward him.[27] This aspect of Bazarov's character led one commentator to remark that Turgenev seems abashed in his presence, not so much to dislike as to be afraid of him.[28] Another revealingly argued: "Bazarov is the antithesis of the cowardice of the crowd. That is the secret why we love him."[29] The negative character of Bazarov's greatness, however, is part and parcel of his nihilism. As he himself admits, he does not stand for anything. He wants merely to clear the ground. He thinks very highly of himself but is also highly self-critical. When he falls in love with Odnitsova, he directs his enormous disdain against himself. He is a monster of negation and of freedom, both Prometheus and the eagle that tears at Prometheus's liver. His greatness and his tragedy in this sense are bound together. As a nihilist, he stakes out a position against not merely autocracy but nature itself, including his own human nature.

Viewed from this perspective, one might conclude that *Fathers and Sons* was an attack on nihilism, as the *Contemporary* board believed. Such a conclusion, however, is doubtful. To be sure, Turgenev had little use for Chernyshevsky and Dobrolyubov. He considered them literary Robespierres and was disgusted by their arrogance and elitism.[30] Moreover, he believed that they exercised a pernicious effect on literature, trying to replace art with seminary principles. Finally, he was enraged by Dobrolyubov's malicious attempt to show that his *On the Eve* was a call to revolution. In his characterization of Bazarov, Turgenev clearly imitates the language and personal characteristics of the radical leaders, but this does not mean that his hero is a parody or a critique of them.[31] Turgenev always employed living models. While Bazarov resembles Chernyshevsky and Dobrolyubov, he also resembles Pisarev, Belinski, and Bakunin and perhaps even the young unknown doctor whom Turgenev mentions in his own article on *Fathers and Sons*.[32]

What is striking about Turgenev's portrayal of nihilism is the extent of his attraction to a way of thinking that he himself sees as so defective. Bazarov with all his faults remains strangely and immensely alluring to Turgenev and many others. Pisarev, for example, argued that Bazarov was a positive model for the new men.[33] He admitted that it would have been more pleasant if Turgenev had concealed Bazarov's rough places, but asserted that the character would then have been less true to reality.[34] This roughness, however, should not blind us to his greatness.[35] Pisarev saw him as the model for the hardened elite he believed was necessary to transform Russia. In fact, he raised the specter of a hundred Bazarovs, of a revolutionary elite that was growing with every hour.[36]

Turgenev himself argues that "Bazarov is empty and barren [but still magnificent]. Perhaps my view of Russia is more misanthropic than you suppose: in my mind he is the real hero of our time. A fine hero and a fine time you'll say. But that's how it is" (*FAS*, 182). Turgenev alludes here to Mikhail Lermontov's Romantic novel *A Hero for Our Time* and its Byronic protagonist, Pechorin. At first glance, Turgenev's connection of Bazarov to the Romantic Pechorin seems misplaced. Pechorin is one of the superfluous men that the nihilists despised. How can Turgenev compare Bazarov to Pechorin? The answer to this question leads us to the hidden connection of Romanticism and Russian nihilism.

BAZAROV AS A ROMANTIC ANTI-ROMANTIC

On the surface, it seems improbable that Bazarov is in any way a Romantic. There are few literary characters more critical of Romanticism than Bazarov. He is portrayed as drab and mundane, a collector of frogs, not hearts. Moreover, his chief antagonist in the novel,

Pavel Kirsanov, is clearly constructed on the Byronic model. These objections to a Romantic Bazarov, however, focus on the superficial. Bazarov in fact is a Romantic anti-Romantic, and the antagonism between Bazarov and Pavel is not the antagonism of a realist and a Romantic but of two generations of Romantics.

Needless to say, Bazarov is not a traditional Romantic hero. His materialism and realism cannot simply be dismissed as superficial gloss. Turgenev suggests as much in a draft of *Virgin Spring:*

> There are *Romantics of Realism* . . . They long for a reality and strive toward the ideal. In reality they seek not poetry—that is ludicrous for them—but something grand and meaningful; and that's nonsense: real life is prosaic and should be so. They are unhappy, distorted, and torment themselves with this very distortion or something completely inappropriate to their work. Moreover, their appearance—possible only in Russia, always with a *sermonizing* or educational aspect—is necessary and useful: they are preachers and prophets in their own way, but complete prophets, contained and defined in themselves. Preaching is an illness, a hunger, a desire; a healthy person cannot be a prophet or even a preacher. Therefore, I put something of that romanticism in Bazarov too, but only Pisarev noticed it.[37]

Bazarov is a Romantic but he does not live in an ideal, literary world of his own. Rather, he wants to transform reality into the ideal, to realize the rational in the actual. Bazarov like the typical Romantic does not fit in his world, but rather than flee into the ideal or live the life of a demonic criminal, he proclaims the moral order of the world itself to be irrational and criminal. His negation is thus the negation of a negation in the service of the ideal. He is a preacher of this ideal and thirsts for it but believes that it can be attained only by the negation of the unjust and immoral world. Hence, he is a Romantic, but a Romantic who seeks to negate the irrational actuality.

In constructing Bazarov, Turgenev drew on several Romantic models. Perhaps the most important of these was Faust. In his early review of Vronchenko's translation of Goethe's *Faust,* Turgenev described the Romantic hero: "He becomes the center of the surrounding world; he . . . does not submit to anything, he forces everything to submit to himself; he lives by the heart, but his own solitary heart—not another's—even in love, about which he dreams so much; he is a romantic and romanticism is nothing more than the apotheosis of personality. He is willing to talk about society, about social questions, about science; but society like science, exists for him—not he for them."[38]

While Turgenev came to see Faust as an egoist for whom there was no Romantic solution, there is still an essential element of Faust in Bazarov. It is most fully captured in the idea of the "apotheosis of personality." Like Faust, Bazarov refuses to submit to anything and forces everything to submit to him. He too lives by his heart, a heart that Turgenev describes at the end of the novel as passionate, sinning, and rebellious. He, too, sees himself not as the servant of society and science but as their master. Moreover, if he cannot quite become the god he imagines himself to be, he can at least despise himself from a divine height for failing to live up to his own impossible aspirations.

A second model for Bazarov was Byron's *Manfred*. At an early age, Turgenev was an enthusiastic admirer of Byron. His early work *Steno* was in fact little more than a paraphrase of Manfred. He later ridiculed this youthful enthusiasm, but his mature work owes much to *Steno* and thus to Manfred.[39] Bazarov like Manfred is a supreme egoist whose egoism is essentially tragic because he measures himself against a superhuman standard and imposes a superhuman punishment when he does not live up to this standard. Like Manfred, he is his own harshest judge and proves in the end to be his own jury and executioner as well.

A third Romantic model for Bazarov was Hamlet.[40] Hamlet was on Turgenev's mind when he wrote *Fathers and Sons*. Shortly before writing the work he had completed his famous essay on Hamlet and Don Quixote, which seemed to identify the nihilist revolutionaries of the 1860s with Don Quixote and the superficial men of the 1840s and 1850s with Hamlet. This, however, is a misinterpretation. For Turgenev, Don Quixote and Hamlet represent two different types of human beings. Quixote is naive and lives according to principles independent of himself. By contrast, Hamlet is completely egoistical, concerned not with morality but with the problems of his own life. His power is the power of negation, and he consequently doubts everything and negates everything.[41] Like Hamlet, Bazarov is certain of only one thing, that "something is rotten," and that this rottenness must be obliterated. His negation like that of Hamlet is thus always the negation of negation and his struggle is a struggle against evil which is only marginally concerned with the substantive character of the good. Hamlet's powers of negation, however, destroy first those he loves and then Hamlet himself. Bazarov's similar path leads to self-negation. Like Hamlet, Bazarov comes fully into his negative essence in death. His final "Now . . . darkness . . ." is powerfully reminiscent of Hamlet's "The rest is silence."

What is surprising is not that Turgenev portrays Bazarov as a Romantic, but that Turgenev's Romantic Bazarov came to define the image of the new men. What attracted the nihilists to Bazarov? Bazarov's principal characteristic is his egoism. He considers it unnecessary to lay any restraints on himself, because he considers himself superior to man and nature. He believes that he is truly autonomous, a self-creating being. As a result, he seems to hang in limbo. He has a past but seems to have no relationship to it, to have repudiated it. He also seems to have no determinate future, despite the fact that everyone in the novel is convinced he can be whatever he wants to be.[42] He is in this sense the Fichtean I that constantly but always unsuccessfully strives to subordinate the not-I to itself. Pisarev recognized this in Bazarov: "Bazarov, everywhere and in everything, does only what he wishes or what seems to him to be advantageous or convenient. He is ruled only by his whims or his personal calculations. Neither over himself, nor outside himself, nor within himself does he recognize a moderator, a moral law or principle; ahead—no exalted goal; in his mind—no high design, and yet he has such great capacities."[43]

This egoism is not a damaging characteristic but a moment of the Romantic dilemma that encompasses him. Pisarev saw this as well:

> Bazarov is exceedingly full of self-esteem, but this self-esteem is unnoticeable as a direct consequence of his vastness. He is not interested in the trifles of which commonplace human relationships are composed; it would be impossible to insult him with obvious disdain or to make him happy with signs of respect; he is so full of himself and stands so unshakably high in his own eyes that he is almost completely indifferent to other people's opinions. Kirsanov's uncle . . . calls his self-esteem "satanic pride." This expression is well-chosen and characterizes our hero perfectly. In truth, it would take nothing short of a whole eternity of constantly expanding activity to satisfy Bazarov, but to his misfortune, Bazarov does not believe in the eternal existence of the human personality.[44]

Bazarov's egoism does not offend us because it is not tinged with even the least trace of vanity. He lacks all smugness and self-satisfaction; pride brings him no joy.[45]

Turgenev was more moderate in his portrayal of the egoism of the nihilists than the more conservative antinihilist authors. In fact, the conservative P. V. Annenkov complained that Turgenev did not give Bazarov enough of the "burning, diseased egoism" that, for example, characterized Chernyshevsky.[46] Even when this egoism does break through, Bazarov like Faust and Manfred does not become vain. He does not revel in his ego but suffers from it. His egoism is as much a curse as a blessing. It drives him to ceaseless activity and ceaseless criticism, but it leaves him with nothing solid or certain, without a home, without family or friends.[47]

Bazarov is in rebellion against the world and indeed against life itself. Like Fichte's I, he is a monster of will but his will has no object other than freedom. He is thus a creature of pure negation, a destroyer and revolutionary, Blake's tiger in the shape of a man. As sheer negativity, this will cannot construct a positive new reality. Bazarov himself tells us that there is an empty void in his life that he is stuffing up with hay, for "we would stuff it up with anything rather than have a void" (*FAS*, 148). This emptiness is bound up with Bazarov's nihilism. His nihilism is identical with liberation and that means with the absence of all external and internal constraints. It is a measure of Bazarov's greatness that he attempts to live and ultimately chooses to die according to this doctrine. An early twentieth-century commentator insightfully remarked: "He is Aggression, destroyed in his destroying."[48]

Whether this negativity exhausts his character, however, is doubtful. Despite his cavalier treatment of his parents, for example, he sincerely loves them. Moreover, in his duel with Pavel he demonstrates that he is not entirely the destroyer he claims to be as he rushes to aid his wounded opponent.[49] Bazarov's negativity is learned and not intrinsic. He is a good man who has been transformed by his adoption of the ideology of negation. Like Faust, two souls dwell in his breast and, like Manfred, he has a gentler side, a good "Astarte" that appears from time to time. This more humane element in his soul, however, has been brutalized and repressed by the ascendent Mephistophelian moment.

As the agent of negation and freedom, Bazarov attempts to establish the preeminence of I over the not-I but learns that the not-I has a reality of its own, that the Fichtean interpretation of the natural world as the not-I is insufficient, that in fact the I in all of its strength arises out of the not-I, out of nature, and is thus ultimately subordinate to it.

Bazarov believes he is an autonomous, self-creating being, a Prometheus who has freed himself from the rock of political and the-

ological despotism. In this respect, he embodies the Fichtean essence
of Russian nihilism, its heroism and its nobility. Turgenev, however,
tries to show us that this heroic Prometheanism is essentially tragic
because it rests upon a faulty understanding of man and nature.
Bazarov's greatness, in Turgenev's view, is an expression of nature
itself. N. N. Strakhov had argued already in 1862 that "Bazarov is a
titan, rising against mother earth; no matter how great his force it
only testifies to the greatness of the forces that begot him and fed
him, but it does not come up to mother earth's force."[50] Bazarov's
belief in his own autonomy leads him to violate "natural laws" and he
must pay the price that nature exacts. Like Pavel and Odnitsova, who
also try to rise above nature, he is sterile. He replaces their pure for-
malism with negation but the result is the same. His desire for autonomy leads him to neglect his family and makes it impossible for him
to have a family of his own. Bazarov says that he does not depend on
time, but time on him. He learns, however, that everyone depends
on time.[51]

Bazarov's nihilism is tested by his love for Odnitsova. This test
takes the form of a great battle in Bazarov's soul between his desire
for autonomy and his love for Odnitsova, but it is a struggle he cannot win without ceasing to be human and becoming either a beast or
a god. This battle is entirely internal and is almost completely invisible, since Turgenev only rarely reveals anything of Bazarov's inner
life. Its consequences, however, are evident throughout the latter half
of the work: his restlessness on his first visit home, his abandonment
of his work, his flirtation with Phenechka, his duel with Pavel, his
despair when he returns home again. It is a battle that he loses at
every turn. In the end, he is driven to the most desperate measure,
intentionally failing to cauterize his cut when performing an autopsy
of a cholera victim. This is the ultimate demonstration of his heroic
egoism, of his willingness to enter into what Hegel called "the life
and death struggle" to demonstrate his freedom, but it is also the
moment of his defeat, for he contracts the disease and is destroyed by
it.[52]

At the beginning of the novel, Bazarov believes and proclaims
himself to be a veritable Prometheus defying man and nature.
Bazarov's love for Odnitsova, however, forces him to confront his
own being, and he discovers that he is not thoroughly autonomous
but bound by nature in ways he cannot overcome. This is the source
of his pathos. His tragedy is not the loss of self-identity, as some have
suggested, but the recognition of the price of such a Promethean

identity.[53] Bazarov comes to see that his Prometheanism places him in conflict with nature itself. He abandons his belief that the world can offer little resistance to his self-assertion. This apparent loss of self-identity, however, is in fact a reaffirmation of his identity as a nihilist in the full knowledge of all this entails, that is, in the face of the necessity of his death. It is only in this moment that he ceases to be a man of mere words like those superfluous men of the previous generation and attains a tragic greatness and authenticity. He wills and affirms his nihilism by willing and affirming his own death.

Turgenev tells us that he conceived of *Fathers and Sons* backward from the death of Bazarov. His death is the result of the assertion of his autonomy from nature but it is also the basis for his reconciliation with nature. Facing death, he does not bewail his fate but fights to the last to demonstrate his autonomy. Nature may destroy him but it cannot subdue him. He does, however, send a message to Odnitsova that he is dying, and she comes to pay him a last visit. He says to her, "I didn't kiss you that time . . . Breathe on a dying image-lamp, and let it go out" and after she kisses his forehead he responds, "And that is enough! . . . Now . . . darkness—" With his request and her kiss, the battle is brought to a conclusion, for on the verge of death, of utter self-negation, he is able finally to affirm the natural affection that has arisen in his own soul. There is a moment of light—if only the light of a dying lamp—that reveals the limited character of individual existence, but also all of its beauty, which is embodied in Odnitsova and which Bazarov not merely admires but accepts with her kiss. After that, all is sheer negation, darkness, the absence of form, perfect freedom, the final realization of all Bazarov's ideals. The horror of this realization is redeemed by the momentary acceptance of the beauty of this world, of the limited and finite. Bazarov sees that "that is enough!" Odnitsova's finite beauty does not induce him to abandon his Promethean struggle for autonomy, but it does reconcile him to the ultimate sacrifice that this struggle entails.

This reconciliation is reflected in the surprising last paragraph of the work: "No matter how passionate, how sinful and rebellious the heart that has hid itself in the grave, the flowers growing thereon gaze untroubled at us with their innocent eyes; it is not solely of eternal peace that they speak to us, of that great peace of 'indifferent' nature; they speak, also, of eternal reconciliation and of life without end." The paragraph seems to be almost a parody of Bazarov's views, but this is not the case. This life without end points to earth, not to heaven.[54] Both Bazarov's longing for autonomy, for the formless infinite that shatters all limits, and his love for Odnitsova, for the limited in all its shapeliness and beauty, arise out of and are reconciled in nature. The limited and therefore the beautiful, represented here by the flowers, grows out of the sheer negation of death. To employ the language of Hegel, whom Turgenev studied and admired, Bazarov's negation in the end is not absolute but determinate negation, a negation of negation. His striving does not bring the world to its end but rejuvenates the soil so that a new world can germinate and grow.

This final reconciliation is thus neither Fichtean nor Left Hegelian and consequently does not rest on the negativity of the absolute I or the dialectical movement of spirit. Turgenev presents rather a Goethean or Hegelian argument against nihilism that tries to show that the nihilist's war against nature in the name of freedom is doomed to failure because freedom itself arises out of nature. Bazarov is a rebel to the end, but his rebellion is itself only an affirmation of the natural force against which he rebels. Like Faust, he errs as long as he strives, and like Mephistopheles his negation ends only in affirmation.

Turgenev, like his mentors Goethe and Hegel, thus denies the existence of real freedom and real evil in the world. As a result, he is unable to condemn nihilism despite all of the dangers that it represents. It is a form of human striving that springs from the source of all striving, and that source is good. Moreover, because his is a preeminent form of striving, Bazarov is not only not an evil man, he is a great one. He is energy and this energy, regardless of its form, is life-enhancing. Turgenev like Goethe and Hegel is entranced by the superlative but tragic power that reveals itself in his contradictory hero. Like them, he gazes entranced at the fire that this Prometheus brings to humanity and cannot finally decide whether it will enlighten his benighted world or ignite a conflagration.

THE NIHILIST ALTERNATIVE: CHERNYSHEVSKY'S *WHAT IS TO BE DONE?*

Franco Venturi has argued that we can learn little about the nihilist movement in Russia by examining the literary works of writers such as Turgenev.[55] In his view, literature is entertainment and not a real attempt to understand or portray historical actuality. Such a view of literature, however, is misguided. Literature for most cultures plays a much more important role than Venturi is willing to admit. This was particularly true in nineteenth-century Russia. Because of the censorship, literature was one of the few places where political debate could take place, and it consequently became the site for public reflection about the character of society and politics. This was especially true in the case of *Fathers and Sons,* as the great debate that followed its publication makes eminently clear.

Fathers and Sons was attacked by the *Contemporary* board and other nihilists, but because of the censorship they could not simply present alternative models of revolutionaries. Hence, they sought to portray them in literary works of their own. The most important of these was Chernyshevsky's *What Is to Be Done?* It was a direct response to *Fathers and Sons* that presented an alternative vision of the new men. The book propounds a new ideal of love, family, and social life that is predicated on the absolute independence of the individual.

The work is the story of a young girl, Vera Pavlovna, who escapes a bad family and the threat of an even worse marriage with the assistance of a "new man," Lopukov, who gives up his aspirations to be a physician in order to marry her. They live together on an equal basis, like brother and sister. He works as a tutor and she organizes a sewing shop on generally socialist principles. She and Lopukov, however, are not suited for one another emotionally, and she falls in love with her husband's friend, Kirsanov. When this becomes evident to Lopukov, he pretends to commit suicide and leaves Russia with the help of the heroic Rakhmetov. Vera Pavlovna marries Kirsanov, Lopukov returns several years later to marry another young woman, and all are happily reunited. The book ends with the whole group and a mysterious lady in black waiting for the return of an unnamed man, presumably Rakhmetov.

The work bears many resemblances to Gutzkow's *The Nihilists,* and it is possible that Chernyshevsky was familiar with this work. In contrast to Gutzkow, however, Chernyshevsky presents only good and not bad nihilists. The chief protagonists in both works are women who have become disciples of Feuerbach through an encounter with new men. Vera Pavlovna, like Herta Wingolf, is driven by a desire for autonomy, to live as she pleases: "I only know that I do not want to be anybody's slave! I want to be free! . . . The main thing is liberty; to do what I please; to live as I please, not asking anybody for anything."[56] Like Eberhard Ott and unlike Konstantin Ulrichs, Lopukov is willing to sacrifice his career for the good of someone he loves. He asserts that this is the result of rational egoism, but this is an egoism devoid of all selfishness. This sort of action is typical of Chernyshevsky's new men: "Every one of them is a man, dauntless, firm, unwavering, capable of undertaking any matter; and if he undertakes it, he sticks so resolutely to it that it cannot slip out of his grasp . . . each one of them is a man of irreproachable integrity, so much so that the question never even enters our mind, 'Is it possible to rely on this person unconditionally?'"[57]

These people, according to Chernyshevsky, are not unusual. They are only what all men would be if they were not deformed by corrupt social institutions. Jealousy and all the other emotions that degrade human nature are the result of the corrupt "order of things," that is, the existence of private property.[58] He suggests that in a properly ordered society the ill-tempered will all become kind because it will not be contrary to their interests to be kind.[59] Because of the censors, the vision of this new age is presented merely as a dream that comes to Vera Pavlovna.

The dream describes the woman of the future who embodies all the perfections of the past and adds to this complete freedom:

> There is nothing loftier than man; there is nothing loftier than woman . . . Vera Pavlovna saw. It was her own face, kindled with the brightness of love; more beautiful than all ideals left to us by sculptors of ancient time and by the great artists of the great age of art. . . . She is more beautiful than all the beauties of the past. . . . I have all the enjoyment of sense, which Astarte had; . . . I have the rapture at the sight of beauty no less than Aphrodite had; I have the reverence for purity which "chastity" possessed. But in me it is not as it was in them, but fuller, loftier, keener . . . till I appeared, people had no idea of perfect enjoyment of freedom.[60]

What makes this new human being possible is the generally socialist order of this new world. It is a world of aluminum and glass, a communal world in which almost all work is done by machines and in which there are few old men and women since they remain healthy and youthful until shortly before they die. There is only freedom, satisfaction, and enjoyment, "an everlasting spring and summer, an everlasting joy."[61]

In Chernyshevsky's view, such a world can come to be only through a revolutionary transformation of society, and such a transformation can be brought about only by truly extraordinary men and women. Chernyshevsky portrays such a man in Rakhmetov, a dedicated and heroic revolutionary who is the true nihilist rival to Bazarov. He has superhuman strength and powers of concentration. He understands that his revolutionary commitment will require great sacrifices, and sleeps, for example, on a bed of nails to prepare himself for torture. He is, as Chernyshevsky himself admitted, a "titanic being," a true Prometheus.[62] Lopukov asserts that "Rakhmetov belongs to a different species. They take hold of common affairs in such a way that the necessity of it fills their existence; for them it even forms a substitute for personal existence. But for us . . . this is unattainable. We are not eagles, like him; we can only live our personal lives."[63]

His dedication to the revolution is all-consuming, overshadowing his human qualities. He has a gentle soul but appears to be a gloomy monster because in times such as these, "a man, with such burning love for good, cannot help being a gloomy monster."[64] The deformation of his character is tragic but it is the necessary consequence of his abysmal task of universal negation. Chernyshevsky is unsparing in his praise of such men:

> There are few of them, but through them flourishes the life of all; without them life would become dead and putrid; there are few of them but they will help all people to breathe; without them people would suffocate. The mass of honest and kind people is great but people like these are few; but they are in the midst, like theine in tea, like the bouquet in fine wines, from them come their fruit and fragrance; it is the flower of the best people; they are the motive power of motive powers, they are the salt of the salt of the earth.[65]

What Is to Be Done? presents a much more positive vision of nihilism than *Fathers and Sons,* but the two views are not as different as they first appear. Both focus on the Promethean in man and both emphasize the importance of autonomy. Chernyshevsky is much more optimistic than Turgenev because he has a greater faith that human freedom can transform the world. Turgenev is skeptical because he is impressed with the immense power of nature, both in the physical world and in the human soul, to derail man's efforts to construct a new and better world. It is not surprising that Chernyshevsky's vision was more satisfying to the young nihilists than Turgenev's and consequently exercised greater influence on the nihilist movement at the time.[66] However, it was not the bright and hopeful image of Vera Pavlovna that was ultimately to triumph, but the darker form of Rakhmetov and a Rakhmetov that increasingly came to resemble his rival Bazarov. Confronted with the harsh realities of an autocratic regime, the positive populistic nihilist gave way to the great destroyer.

THE FAILURE OF NIHILISM
WITH A HUMAN FACE

The humanistic strain of nihilism failed for several reasons. First, all the experimental communes founded on the model of Vera Pavlovna's sewing shop collapsed either because their founders acted dictatorially or because weak leadership led to anarchy. The nihilists' neglect of politics, which they believed to be outdated, proved in this case to be their undoing. A second and more important reason for the failure of this form of nihilism, however, was the inability of the movement to win any concessions from the state. These two factors together with Dobrolyubov's death in 1861 and Chernyshevsky's arrest in 1862 severely undermined populist nihilism.

The failure of populist nihilism drove the movement to abandon public campaigns and turn to conspiratorial politics and terrorism. This change represents a turn from Vera Pavlovna to Rakhmetov. The turn to Rakhmetov, however, is essentially a return to Bazarov and to the elite revolutionary Prometheanism of Pisarev and others. This strain of nihilism first appeared in the Young Russia group in 1860. More politically significant was the conspiratorial Land and Liberty group founded by N. A. Serno-Solovevich and destroyed by the authorities by 1863. More effective was N. A. Ishutin's conspiratorial group Organization, inspired by Chernyshevsky, and its terroristic subgroup Hell, which was organized as a quasi-religious order. Recruited heavily from seminarians, these revolutionaries abandoned all traditional ties to devote themselves fanatically to revolution. One of the members of the group, V. A. Fedoseyev, even planned to poison his father to obtain funds to support their revolutionary activities.[67]

The prototypical advocate of conspiratorial politics was Bakunin. He began his intellectual career as a Right Hegelian but moved to Left Hegelianism and finally to anarchism and terrorism.[68] His development mirrors the development of the nihilist movement as a whole. In the 1860s and 1870s, he came to see that the unity of church and state, which he had advocated in his Right Hegelian phase, was the highest form of repression and concluded that atheism and anarchism were the only answer. "If God is, man is a slave; now, man can and must be free; then, God does not exist. . . . [Therefore] it will be necessary to eliminate, first of all, this fiction of God, the eternal and absolute enslaver."[69] This religious notion in his view had become so deeply embedded in the human soul and social institutions that total revolution and total destruction were necessary.

Bakunin, however, remained determined by what he rejected. While he became an atheist, Satan was his prototypical revolutionary. Satan's powers of destruction, however, are mystically blended with divine powers of creation: "Let us trust the eternal spirit which destroys and annihilates only because it is the unfathomable and eternally creative source of all life. The passion for destruction is a creative passion, too."[70] This revolutionary mysticism owes a great deal to the Fichtean and Left Hegelian notion of negation. Its full meaning is even clearer in a passage from 1848: "The star of revolution will rise high and independent above Moscow from a sea of blood and fire, and will turn into a lodestar to lead a liberated humanity. You should devote yourselves entirely and unequivocally to the Revolution. You must burn like a flame in order to perform a miracle."[71]

The constructive side of Bakunin's anarchism which might have helped counteract the organizational centralism of later socialism was overshadowed by this mystical emphasis on the powers of negation. This apocalyptic element in Russian nihilism isolated it from the rest of the European revolutionary movement, as Marx's victory over Bakunin for control of the First International made unmistakably clear. Shut off from public activity in Russia by the autocracy and from participation in the international movement by Marx and his followers, the Russian revolutionaries were driven to extreme conspiratorial measures. These measures at first horrified the populists, who remained wedded to their religion of humanity, but they gradually became more acceptable as the only remaining means of revolutionary activity. The man who did the most to put into practice the doctrines that Bakunin preached was Nechaev.

In contradistinction to most of the radicals of the 1860s, Sergey Nechaev was not a member of the intelligentsia but came from the lower classes. He was attracted to revolutionary activity by Ishutin's Hell group. In 1868, he joined a revolutionary group through which he met Petr Tkachev, who had earlier helped write "Young Russia." Together they set down their plans for organizing a revolt in *A Program for Revolutionary Action*. Their goal was to win "full freedom for a renewed personality" by creating revolutionary prototypes. They adopted many of Ishutin's conspiratorial methods, including the hierarchical organization of the revolutionary group, and terrorism. They believed that previous groups had relied too heavily on the people and that a successful revolutionary organization required professional revolutionaries who were willing to dedicate themselves to radical activity.[72] Their *Program* takes this logic of revolutionary activity to its extreme.

Nechaev, however, lacked any standing among his fellow radicals. To remedy this situation, he traveled to Switzerland and presented himself to Bakunin as a representative of a secret conspiratorial organization. Bakunin was delighted with him and together they rewrote the *Program* into the famous *Catechism of a Revolutionary*. It was this work and the actions that it inspired that were the source of Nechaev's importance for the nihilist movement. They laid out a plan of revolutionary organization and discipline, a revolutionary Jacobinism, that was to become the backbone of the radical movement in Russia.

While the principles of conspiratorial organization that their plan laid out were monstrous, the vision of the revolutionary that they developed was awe-inspiring. This vision draws upon the Prometheanism of Turgenev's Bazarov and Chernyshevsky's Rakhmetov, but radicalizes them in a way that Turgenev and Chernyshevsky would have deplored. The revolutionary according to Bakunin and Nechaev is a doomed man and must treat himself and his fellow revolutionaries as capital to be expended in the service of the revolution:

> The revolutionary is a man set apart. He has no personal interests, no emotions, no attachments; he has no personal property, not even a name. Everything in him is absorbed by the one exclusive interest, the one thought, one single passion—the revolution. In his innermost being he has, not only in words but in deeds, broken every bond with the present-day society and with the whole civilized world including all its laws, customs, conventions and morality. If he continues to live in it, he does so as its implacable enemy for the sole purpose of destroying it. . . . Anything assisting the triumph of the revolution is for him moral, anything hindering it is immoral and criminal. . . . All the gentle and enfeebling sentiments of kinship, love, gratitude and even honor must be suppressed in him by the single cold passion for revolution. . . . In the unflinching pursuit of merciless destruction he must be prepared to perish himself or to destroy with his own hands everything standing in the path of revolution.[73]

This revolutionary is an avenging angel. Utterly immoral in a conventional sense, he is fanatically moral as a revolutionary. His commitment, like that of Prometheus, turns against all gods, religions, and political institutions. These have only suppressed human freedom. In fact, this revolutionary transcends the mere defiance of Prometheus and orchestrates a devastating attack upon actuality. Because he is opposed by the enormous state power, he must operate in secret and adopt harsh and merciless methods. He employs murder, extortion, blackmail, sex, whatever is necessary to his ends. He deceives and sacrifices family, friends, and fellow revolutionaries to secure the success of the revolution. His greatness resides in the fact that he like Bazarov applies the same merciless standards to himself. This is also the source of his tragedy.

The gripping force of the *Catechism* probably owes more to Bakunin than Nechaev. Bakunin turned the *Program* into the *Catechism* by employing a formula derived from the philosophy of Fichte and the Left Hegelians: the hatred that was so important to Bazarov, for example, is expressed not in political terms but in absolute formulas drawn from the Hegelian idea of negation.[74] Hatred in this sense is given an ideological and metaphysical, if not quasi-theological, justification. The *Catechism* is a preeminent expression of the doctrine of freedom and negation that arose with Fichte's notion of the absolute I and that was concealed in Left Hegelianism. It is a catechism of a religion of revolution in service of the dark god of negation.

In contradistinction to almost all of his predecessors and Bakunin himself, Nechaev was a man of action. Fanatically dedicated to revolution, he was willing to sacrifice everything and everyone to that end. He was also a prodigious conspiratorial organizer. With the meagerest of resources, he began to set up a conspiratorial organization in Russia that aimed at realizing the goals outlined in the *Catechism*. In order to bind the revolutionaries more tightly to the organization, he involved them in various crimes, including the execution of one of their own members. This was his downfall. The accidental discovery of the body led to the arrest of everyone except Nechaev.

The trial of the Nechaevists, however, was a disaster for the state. As one defendant after another denounced the autocracy and defended the humanitarian goals of their organization, public opinion began to turn in their favor. The prosecution was able to turn opinion around only by entering the *Catechism* into evidence. One of the police agents present at the trial recognized the state's mistake:

> The trial represents a milestone in the life of the Russian people . . . At the present moment there is scarcely a spot in all our wide fatherland

where Nechaev's manifestoes are not being read among uneducated
masses who naturally give their particular attention to those points
where there is talk of the suffering of the people and of the men
responsible for it. One must be very shortsighted to believe that an
uneducated man who considers himself to be oppressed will fail to feel
warm sympathy for people who pretend to protect him and to care for
his interests. . . . The trial has encouraged discussion among people
who have never taken an interest in politics, and many have seen with
great sorrow what deep roots social theories inimical to our law and
order have taken in our youth.[75]

The ineptitude of the state thus turned Nechaev's terroristic religion
of negation into a world-historical force.

Nechaev himself was captured in Switzerland, returned to Russia,
and imprisoned. Applying his principles within the prison, he sub-
verted his guards, established contact with the revolutionary underground, and assumed virtual control of the prison. In the midst of
plans for escape and the abduction of the czar and his family, his work
was accidently discovered, the guards imprisoned, and Nechaev con-
signed to utterly solitary confinement and death.

Nechaev's vision of the revolutionary horrified not merely the
conservatives and liberals but most revolutionaries themselves. The
populists thought him a monster and even Bakunin was disgusted
when he saw their ideas carried out in all their intrinsic ruthlessness.
The immediate effect of the propagation of these ideas was to
strengthen antinihilist sentiments in Russia. The intelligentsia, which
had been generally sympathetic to nihilist aims, began to view the
movement with increasing suspicion. This was particularly apparent
in literature. In "The Plague," Avenarius characterizes nihilism as
madness. Dostoevski has Raskolnikov dream of a similar plague that
makes people go mad in *Crime and Punishment*. In his *The Possessed*,
the nihilists appear to be filled with evil spirits, and in Pisemsky's *In
the Whirlpool* they are portrayed as men driven by uncontrollable passions.[76] The antinihilist novels generally try to show that nihilist ideals fail in practice and that the nihilists do not really understand society. This is brilliantly portrayed in the nihilist hero Polojarov, who
incites a group of boys to cry "Rez' publika!" which means both
"Republic!" and "Slaughter the public!"[77] This antinihilist sentiment, however, was more than matched by a growth in underground
revolutionary activity.

THE TRIUMPH OF TERRORISM

Most radicals rejected Nechaev's Jacobinism as incompatible with their faith in the wisdom and institutions of the people. They were also revolted by his lack of morality and by his willingness to deceive and murder his fellow revolutionaries. The revolutionary movement in the early 1870s was still by and large dedicated to the religion of humanity and had not yet adopted the religion of terrorism and revolution.

At the center of this religion of humanity were the Chaikovskists. Turning away from what they saw as the Jesuitical principles of Nechaev, they sought purity through total self-sacrifice. N. V. Chaikovsky, however, was himself arrested and deported to his native Orel, where he abandoned revolutionary activity in favor of what he called deo-humanism. M. F. Frolenko, a later conspiratorial radical, described his development in somewhat ironic terms: "There was no need for conspiracies, secrecy, revolution and revolts. It was enough to free oneself of shortcomings and vices, to feel oneself a God-man, to believe that one was this. He believed it with an absolute faith."[78]

While Chaikovsky in Fichtean fashion found the superhuman in himself, his followers and many other young Russians went in search of it among the peasantry during the To the People Movement of 1873–74. The peasantry had long been an object of Romantic fascination among the populist nihilists, but most had no real understanding of the people. The aim of the To the People Movement was to take the cause of revolution to the people themselves. With this end in view, thousands of young people left St. Petersburg and Moscow in the summer of 1874 to organize the peasantry in the countryside. The movement had a hopeful, evangelical air but was an utter failure. The peasantry were not only unwilling to follow the lead of the young intellectuals but often denounced them to the police. While this attempt to organize the peasantry failed, it did alarm the autocracy, which acted decisively to end such agitation. Over four thousand people were arrested, imprisoned, deported, or harassed by the police. This action crushed the populist element in the nihilist movement and brought the open phase of the movement to an end. The populists failed because they did not take politics seriously, since it seemed to them that politics was hopelessly behind the times, still attached to the metaphysical epoch of world history that had already come to an end.

The recognition that the people were not the enchained

Promethean beings the intelligentsia had imagined them to be threw the revolutionaries back upon the Jacobin elitism of Bazarov and Nechaev. The new Prometheus was to be found not in the people but among the revolutionaries themselves. Following this logic, the revolutionaries entered into a battle with the autocracy to determine whose laws should prevail.

The first of these Promethean efforts was undertaken by the second Land and Liberty group. A number of its members were drawn from the circle around Nechaev and were deeply influenced by his methods. They struck at the leading figures in the autocracy. The first of these attacks was the attempted assassination of General Trepov by Vera Zasulich in January of 1878 for his flogging of the radical Bogolyubov (A. S. Emelyanov). Brought to trial, she was acquitted in March 1878 and rushed out of the country before the police could imprison her. As a result of this acquittal and the strong support for the verdict in the press, the radicals came to believe that they enjoyed widespread support and thus intensified their activities. In August 1878, General Mezentosov, the head of the police, was assassinated by Sergey Kravchinsky; in February 1879 Alexander Kropotkin, governor of Kharkov, was assassinated by Grigory Goldenberg; in March, Leon Mirsky attempted to assassinate Drenteln, the new head of the police, and in April, Alexander Solovev attempted to kill the czar.

The autocracy was greatly alarmed by these events and declared martial law. The repression took its toll on the Land and Liberty group and brought about a split between those concerned with the division of the land and those dedicated to liberty. The former became the Black Partition, the latter the People's Will. The formation and organization of the People's Will by Andrey Zhelyabov marked a major step within the radical movement toward the acceptance of Nechaev's vision of the Promethean revolutionary and his conspiratorial principles of revolutionary organization. The group was dedicated to the assassination of the czar. Its members were clever, courageous, hard-working, and relentless. No sacrifice was too great, and all had long since accepted Nechaev's fundamental axiom that their lives were already forfeit. In them, Bazarov and Rakhmetov came to life. Despite several daunting failures and arrests, the members of the People's Will continued their feverish attempts, sacrificing themselves one by one to achieve their goal. They blew up trains, dug tunnels, planted bombs in the Winter Palace, killed police spies, and even planted a spy of their own in police headquarters. Ultimately and against all odds, they prevailed: on the first of March 1881 they blew up the czar.

As dedicated as they were, they were not thoroughly ruthless. Their bombs, for example, were constructed for use at close range, and they understood that the thrower would probably be killed with the victim, but they believed this was necessary to minimize injury to innocent bystanders. At his trial, the conspirator Zhelyabov claimed with great sincerity that "the essence of the teachings of Jesus Christ . . . was my primary moral incentive."[79] The members of the People's Will were driven not by hatred but by a quasi-religious principle. Like Bazarov and Rakhmetov, they were essentially good men and women who had given themselves over to a nihilist ideology that required a life of negation and destruction. While Nechaev to his very core had embodied the desire for merciless destruction, they still hoped for the triumph of reason and an end to violence. After the assassination, they thus appealed to the new czar to end repression so that they would not be driven to further acts of terrorism.

The new czar, however, had no intentions of giving in, and used the state's instruments of repression to destroy the revolutionary movement. Only a handful of revolutionaries remained, and they took on the name the Terrorist Faction of the People's Will. Their goal was the assassination of the new czar. Less well organized than their predecessors, they were discovered, arrested, and brought to trial. Included in their number was a brilliant and saintly young student of the natural sciences, Alexander Ulyanov. Like Chernyshevsky, whom he read with great admiration, Ulyanov considered the intelligentsia the flower of the best people and believed it was his moral duty to serve the cause of liberation. At his trial, he tried to protect his fellow conspirators by taking all of the blame upon himself. The state, however, was relentless, and he and his fellow conspirators were dealt with in the harshest fashion.

With the failure of this assassination attempt and the execution of the conspirators, the last active revolutionary organization in Russia itself was extinguished. All the significant revolutionary leaders had been driven out of Russia, and all hopes of a popular revolt had been crushed. The populistic religion of humanity that had dominated the revolutionary movement in the 1860s thus gave way to conspiratorial politics and Jacobinism. The future belonged not to the Vera Pavlovnas of the world but to the Bazarovs, the Nechaevs, and last, but certainly not least, to the younger brothers of the Alexander Ulyanovs, the Lenins.

THE PROMETHEAN ESSENCE
OF BOLSHEVISM

The Russian revolutionary movement underwent important changes in the twenty-five years before the Revolution. Populist sentiment waned and Marxism grew, especially in conjunction with Nechaevist Jacobinism. The growing importance of Marxism in Russia was due in part to the dependence of the exiled Russian revolutionaries on the predominately Marxist European socialist movement, but it was also due to rapid industrialization and concomitant dislocations within Russia itself. A small but growing proletariat sprang up in crucial national and provincial centers. Torn out of traditional life and subjected to a whole series of new class distinctions and forms of social repression, this new proletariat became a potentially revolutionary class to rival the intelligentsia.

What form of Marxism could appeal to this class and to other radicals, however, was unclear. The Legal Marxists renounced terrorism and revolution, but their parliamentary course did not appeal to the intelligentsia or the new proletariat. By contrast, Grigory Plekhanov argued that Russia was ripe for revolution. In his important essay *Our Differences,* he maintained that Russia did not need to pass through a capitalist and liberal phase but could move immediately from feudalism to socialism because the whole struggle between the bourgeoisie and the proletariat took the form in Russia of the rich versus the poor peasants. A revolution fought on these grounds in his view could by-pass liberalism entirely. Here Plekhanov struck a chord that had been central to the radicals since at least 1848. Plekhanov, however, was opposed to terrorism. He had left the Land and Liberty group to form the Black Partition when the terror-oriented People's Will faction gained predominance within it. His brand of Marxism was thus less appealing to the radicals who had been inspired by Bakunin and others. The third and most important development within Marxism at the turn of the century was Bolshevism, which accepted Plekhanov's notion of Russian exceptionalism but practiced a revolutionary Jacobinism, arguing that a revolution could succeed only if led by a class of professional revolutionaries, organized into conspiratorial cells. Bolshevism in this respect drew more heavily than all other forms of Russian Marxism upon the nihilist tradition.

This connection is especially evident in the life and work of Lenin. While Lenin was a Marxist, his Marxism was shaped by his previous attachment to Russian nihilism. In his early years, Lenin was actually critical of the radicals. His favorite author was Turgenev and he was deeply influenced by his critique of nihilism.[80] His brother's arrest and execution changed all of this. Lenin was astounded to discover that his brother was a revolutionary. In his attempt to discover what motivated him, Lenin reread Chernyshevsky's *What Is to Be Done?* He saw in it a profound critique of liberalism and a blueprint for revolutionary action. As he himself admitted, the work "ploughed me over again."[81] Indeed, Chernyshevsky's novel became his sacred book. Lenin described Chernyshevsky as the "great Russian Hegelian and materialist" and placed him as a philosopher on the level of Engels.[82] Of all Chernyshevsky's characters, the Promethean revolutionary Rakhmetov made the greatest impression on Lenin, and he determined to emulate him. He turned to Chernyshevsky's other works in the *Contemporary* and from there to the work of Dobrolyubov and Pisarev, immersing himself in the thought of Russian nihilism.[83]

Lenin, however, always saw Chernyshevsky in terms of the terrorist movement of which his brother had been a part. Lenin knew about the censorship at first hand and recognized that all authors and Chernyshevsky in particular had to write between the lines. Lenin read Chernyshevsky with this in view and came to see him as an advocate of conspiratorial politics and terrorism. This new understanding of Chernyshevsky led Lenin to reevaluate Turgenev. He began to discard his original understanding of him as a critic of nihilism and to see him instead as an apostle of revolution. From Dobrolyubov's review, he learned that Turgenev's *On the Eve* could be regarded as revolutionary and began to see that the same might be true of *Fathers and Sons*.[84] Turgenev's heros, and Bazarov among them, became his models and he drew much of his thought and revolutionary language from them.

Lenin's Marxism developed within this horizon. At nineteen, he read Marx's *Capital* and Plekhanov's *Our Differences* and became a dedicated Marxist. His understanding of Marx, however, was heavily influenced by his reading of Plekhanov. Thus, he accepted the idea of dictatorship of the proletariat in its most dogmatic form. Similarly, on matters of revolutionary tactics he was deeply influenced by *On Agitation,* written by A. Kremer and Julius Martov, which was not Marxist but Bakuninist in its program.[85] Lenin did abandon some of the central nihilist theses, but they often sprang up in new ways in his interpretation of Marx. He rejected Chernyshevsky's concept of rational egoism, for example, but then employed it as the interpretative model for the idea of class interest.[86]

It has often been argued that Lenin was directly influenced by Nechaev or Tkachev, but there is little evidence to support this contention. The Mensheviks started this rumor, but they were anxious to point out Lenin's nihilist connections for their own, self-interested reasons. More convincing is the fact that the Bolsheviks themselves drew attention to this connection in the early 1920s but then discarded and suppressed it during the inner party struggles of the later 1920s and 1930s.[87] Even this, however, is only indirect evidence. Linking Lenin to Nechaev and Tkachev, however, adds little to what we already know with much greater certainty about his connections to the earlier nihilist tradition and about his one-sided interpretation of Marx.

This connection to nihilism and its Prometheanism remained central to Lenin's thought and activity. Rosa Luxemburg noted with irritation this distinguishing characteristic: "Here is the 'ego' of the Russian revolutionary again! Pirouetting on its head, it once more proclaims itself to be the all powerful director of history—this time with the title of His Excellency the Central Committee of the Social Democratic Party of Russia."[88] This Promethean element is particularly evident in a Bolshevik pamphlet of 1906 which argued that man is destined to "take possession of the universe and extend his species into distant cosmic regions, taking over the whole solar system. Human beings will become immortal."[89]

This nihilist Prometheanism was also an important element of surrealism, futurism, and other intellectual movements of the early twentieth century. Nicholas Berdyaev, for example, wrote: "Every creative artistic act is a partial transfiguration of life. In the artistic concept man breaks out through the heaviness of the world. . . . Beauty saves the world . . . beauty as being itself, that is the transformation of the chaotic deformity of the world into the beauty of the cosmos."[90] Similarly, P. D. Uspensky argued that there was a seventh dimension of the pure imagination (in addition to the three spatial and three temporal dimensions) that takes one beyond the three ways of godliness typified by the fakir, monk, and yogi.[91] And finally, Leo Shestov argued that "only one assertion has or can have objective reality: that nothing on earth is impossible."[92] The most extreme Prometheans were probably the Cosmist and Blacksmith groups, who spoke of the imminent transformation of the entire cosmos: "We shall arrange the stars in rows and put reins on the moon. We shall erect upon the canals of Mars the palace of World Freedom."[93] In a similar vein, the futurist opera *Victory over the Sun* proclaimed freedom from all traditional order in the world.[94]

This sense that mankind was on the verge of a new Promethean age was bound up with a belief in the imminence of apocalyptic change. Diaghilev, for example, wrote in 1905: "We are witnesses of the greatest moment of summing-up in history, in the name of a new and unknown culture, which will be created by us, and which will also sweep us away."[95] Such apocalypticism was especially strong in Bolshevism. In *Faust and the City*, Anatol Lunacharsky declared that the idea of immortal God was only an anticipation of what the might of men shall be.[96]

This Promethean apocalypticism reached its apogee in the "God-building" movement, which aimed at transferring to the urban proletariat the attributes of God. This movement, which was led by Lunacharsky and Lenin's friend Maxim Gorky, saw physical labor as a form of devotion, the proletariat as the congregation of true believers, and the spirit of the collective as God. Gorky ends his *Confession* (1908) with a prayer to the almighty and immortal people: "Thou art my God and the creator of all gods, which thou hast fashioned from the beauties of the spirit in toil and struggle of thy searchings. And there shall be no other gods in the world but thee, for thou art the one God that creates miracles! Thus do I believe and confess!"[97] Some contemporary critics called this demotheism. It is driven by a vision of the "fusion of all peoples for the sake of the great task of universal God-creation."[98]

The failure of the revolution to bring this new Promethean humanity into being shattered the naive nihilist belief that this transformation of humanity could be accomplished in the space of a night. This recognition led on one hand to the idea of permanent revolution and on the other to the attempt to build this paradise in one country. The idea of permanent revolution represents a recognition of the supremacy of negativity at the heart of the whole nihilist and revolutionary movement, a recognition that one can be free only through continual negation. Where negation ends, tyranny and degeneration begin. The idea of permanent revolution in this sense rests upon the identification of freedom and chaos. This is especially clear in Eugene Zamiatin's assertion that "revolution is everywhere, in everything; it is endless, there is no last revolution, no last number. Social revolution is only one of innumerable numbers: the law of revolution is not social, but infinitely greater—a cosmic and universal law."[99]

The most powerful proponent of this view was Trotsky, who argued that through permanent revolution man would be able to "raise himself to a new plane, to create a higher social biological type, or, if you please, a superman. . . . Man will become immeasurably stronger, wiser, subtler; his body will become more harmonized, his movements more rhythmic, his voice more musical. The forms of life will become dynamically dramatic. The average human type will rise to the heights of an Aristotle, a Goethe, or a Marx. And above this ridge new peaks will rise."[100] In Trotsky's Promethean vision, we see a further unfolding of Fichte's dream of absolute freedom. The attempt to make this dream a reality, however, produced a nightmare from which we have only recently awakened.

Stalin too believed in the apotheosis of man, but it did not assume the intellectualized form for him that it did for Trotsky or Zamiatin. Stalin's Prometheanism drew heavily upon the crude theology of his youth. The most obvious example of this is his deification of Lenin, which resonated so deeply with his own theological training and that of Bolshevik leaders such as Molotov, Khrushchev, and Mikayan. While this form of expression was derided by party intellectuals, its liturgical character appealed to the peasantry and their traditions and made revolutionary Prometheanism comprehensible to them. Stalin similarly adopted and transformed the notion of the intelligentsia. The intelligentsia had hitherto been seen not merely as the agent of social change but as the prototype for a future superhumanity. For Stalin, the intelligentsia no longer needed to be concerned with destruction and liberation, but had to focus their attention on the construction of a new way of life. The new intelligentsia thus had to be a technical eilte to construct the new socialist order. This meant that the older humanistic intelligentsia would have to be eliminated and their doctrine of liberation and negation replaced by a positive doctrine of authority.[101]

On the surface, it seems that Stalin transforms the nihilist doctrine of negation into a positive doctrine of progress and reform. Permanent revolution seems to be replaced by socialism in one country. The Prometheus who broke his chains and overthrew the gods, can at last, it seems, turn his attention to the construction of the aluminum and glass paradise of human freedom that Chernyshevsky had foreseen and to the formation of the superhumanity that socialist realism portrayed.

The underlying reality, however, was something altogether different. The powers of negation and destruction could not be so easily subdued, either in Stalin's psyche or in the Bolshevik party as a whole. Although Trotsky was eliminated and his doctrine of permanent revolution declared heretical, the nihilistic core of Bolshevism remained. In a disguised form, it reappears as a demand for internal purification. In his famous speech at the "Congress of Victors" in 1934, Stalin declared that the revolution was over and all external enemies subdued. This did not mean, however, that the state could wither away. Rather, now the elimination of internal enemies could begin. The means of purification were only a further adaptation of the means which Lenin and Trotsky had adopted from their nihilist predecessors: negation as liberation, terror as the path to universal human freedom.

The Russian revolution has been called the god that failed. This mistaken conclusion is the consequence of a fundamental misunderstanding of the theological and metaphysical essence of the revolutionary movement in Russia. The Russian revolution is in fact the story of the god who triumphed, but this god was not a god of light who inhabits cities of aluminum and glass but a dark god of negation who lives within the secret souls of the Bazarovs and Rakhmetovs of the world and enters into actuality in the form of Nechaev, Lenin, and Stalin.

What we discover in the afterglow of this great event is that the fire this new Prometheus brings down to earth is not the hearth flame that is the center of the home but a conflagration that consumes civilization. The fiery heart of Blake's demonic destroyer when liberated from its animalistic shell does not assume a symmetry and humanity of its own but remains the formless force of chaos, an essentially negative will. At the end of modernity, the dark God of nominalism appears enthroned within the bastion of reason as the grim lord of Stalin's universal terror.

Chapter Six

FROM THE DEMONIC
TO THE DIONYSIAN

At the end of modernity is inscribed an account of the last and great-est assault upon Descartes' shining citadel of reason. Scrawled in mighty letters across the ruined wall it reads: "Dionysus versus the Crucified." This inscription proclaims *in nuce* the downfall of this magnificent fortification of modern rationality and the advent of a twilit world in which the dark noumenal beyond has been reunited with the pure light of phenomenal reason.

"Dionysus versus the Crucified" was the last sentence of Friedrich Nietzsche's last work. It is a summary of his life-long confrontation with the moral and philosophical tradition that has characterized the European world since Plato, a tradition that Nietzsche generally calls "Christianity." This confrontation began with his juxtaposition of Dionysus and Socrates in *The Birth of Tragedy* and ended with his opposition of Dionysus and the Crucified in *Ecce Homo*. Nietzsche's concept of nihilism was born out of this confrontation. Nihilism for him is the result of the fact that the highest values devalue them-selves, that God and reason and all of the supposed eternal truths become unbelievable. All of this is summed up in Zarathustra's famous assertion "God is dead." The meaning of nihilism for Niet-zsche, however, can be grasped only in the context of the dichotomy of Dionysus and the Crucified that constitutes the framework within which his thought unfolds.

While there is general scholarly agreement about the importance and meaning of Christianity for Nietzsche, there is considerable debate about the significance of the Dionysian. Nietzsche's earliest interpreters accepted his claims at face value and portrayed him as an antimetaphysical thinker, interested in establishing a new mythology with Dionysus at its center.[1] This vision of a "mythologizing" Niet-zsche, which played such an important role in the development of Fascist and Nazi ideology, was challenged by Martin Heidegger, who argued in a series of lectures and articles in the 1930s that Nietzsche was not the great alternative to the philosophical tradition but its culmination. Indeed, according to Heidegger, Nietzsche's core doctrine of the will to power is nothing other than the final form of the subjectivistic metaphysics of modernity. Nietzsche thus does not overcome nihilism but remains entangled in its essence, in what Heidegger calls the onto-theological essence of metaphysics.

While Heidegger's reading of Nietzsche was extraordinarily influential, it was not without its problems. In particular, Heidegger neglected most of Nietzsche's published works because he believed they were a mere antechamber to the great metaphysical system that dimly shone forth in *The Will to Power*. The apparently metaphysical structure of this supposed work, however, was the creation of Nietzsche's editors. Moreover, Nietzsche had already decided not to publish most of the fragments included in the work and actually tried to dispose of many of them.[2] Even if we overlook these facts, Heidegger's interpretative strategy is questionable, because he does not even consider all of *The Will to Power*, neglecting in particular many antimetaphysical fragments. His interpretation is thus one-sided. Of particular importance, he mentions Dionysus only once in his Nietzsche lectures (amounting to less than a page in his two-volume *Nietzsche*), and then misconstrues the notion, arguing that it can only be understood metaphysically as the conjunction of the will to power and the eternal recurrence.[3] This conclusion is directly contrary to Nietzsche's own claim that Dionysus is the alternative to Christianity and metaphysics.

Heidegger's interpretation shaped much of the post–World War II reading of Nietzsche and led to the general neglect of the crucial idea of the Dionysian. Nietzsche was seen not as the forerunner of a philosophy of the future but as a philosopher of subjectivity and will who represented the culmination of a failed philosophical tradition.

This reading of Nietzsche also helped shape much of American Nietzsche scholarship, which sought to discover a consistent philosophical position in his thought. The work of F. A. Lea, Arthur Danto, Richard Schacht, and J. P. Stern is characteristic. In contrast to Heidegger, many of these American scholars were trained in analytic philosophy and focused on Nietzsche's nominalism and positivism, but like Heidegger they rejected the more "mythological" reading of Nietzsche's thought. Although Walter Kaufmann recognized the limitations of this Nietzsche, he did not question the general claim that Nietzsche was a part of the philosophical tradition. Thus, while he saw that the Dionysian was an important element of

Nietzsche's thought, he sought to show that it was compatible with previous philosophy. This effort, however, only distorted and trivialized the concept. He argued, for example, that Goethe and Socrates were Nietzsche's archetypes for the Dionysian man, although Nietzsche himself claimed in *Twilight of the Idols* that Goethe did not understand the Dionysian.[4]

Since the late 1960s, postmodernist thinkers in both France and the United States have sought to overturn Heidegger's metaphysical reading of Nietzsche. At the center of this attack is a vision of a more Dionysian Nietzsche, who is not the culmination of metaphysics but its destroyer, who explodes all logic and subjectivity and opens man up to the manifest otherness of existence. Such thinkers as Jacques Derrida, Gilles Deleuze, Michel Foucault, Pierre Klossowski, Bernard Pautrat, Jean-Michel Rey, and Sarah Kofman have thus taken the problem of the Dionysian in Nietzsche more seriously than Heidegger. They have done so, however, not in order to spell out a positive Dionysian alternative but to attack the strictures of metaphysical thinking that they see degrading human existence.[5] Christianity for them is bound up with the philosophy and politics of identity. The triumph of Dionysus over the Crucified is thus a triumph of otherness or difference over identity.

Deleuze's reading of Nietzsche is typical. He sees Nietzsche as the great liberator from the philosophical tradition that has found its last refuge in dialectics: "The opposition of Dionysus or Zarathustra to Christ is not a dialectical opposition, but opposition to the dialectic itself . . . Nietzsche's philosophy has a great polemical range; it forms an absolute anti-dialectics and sets out to expose all the mystifications that find a final refuge in the dialectic."[6] Michel Haar argues in a similar vein that Nietzsche seeks to destroy all logical and dialectical seriousness, the goal of which is to establish identities and reveal the one absolute identity.[7]

Such an interpretation of the Dionysian leads to a view of Nietzsche as a deconstructive thinker who preaches a doctrine of radical liberation. It assumes that Nietzsche did not and could not formulate a positive doctrine, because such a doctrine would have been incompatible with his project of radical liberation. For Deleuze, Nietzsche's thought is thus the dawn of the counterculture because it resists all efforts to establish a stable system or code. It is a nomadic war machine that repeatedly opposes itself to the despotic administrative apparatus of traditional philosophic systems from Plato and Hegel to Marx and Freud. Nietzsche, in contrast to Marx, thus provides a doctrine for revolution that does not degenerate into bureaucratic despotism.[8] Deleuze admits that there is a metaphysical element in Nietzsche's thought, especially in the idea of the will to power, but he argues that it is not the will to power but the eternal recurrence that is Nietzsche's most fundamental teaching, and that the eternal recurrence is always a manifold and never a unity. At the heart of Nietzsche's thought, he therefore always finds diversity.[9] The adequacy of Deleuze's interpretation is questionable for reasons we will consider below, but we can gain a preliminary insight into its problems by comparing his claim that Nietzsche's thought is nomadic and anti-imperial with Nietzsche's own claim that the *imperium Romanum* was the noblest structure ever built on earth (*AC*, KGW VI 3:243).[10]

Although one might disagree with the use that postmodernism often makes of Nietzsche, the core of this postmodern reading cannot simply be dismissed. Other interpreters have also pointed to the antimetaphysical character of his thought. Karl Jaspers, for example, argued more than fifty years ago that Nietzsche's thought rested upon contradictions that could not be reconciled or resolved.[11] More recently, Wolfgang Müller-Lauter has asserted that at the heart of Nietzsche's thought there is only a contradictory plurality that makes any comprehensive interpretation of his thought as a metaphysical system impossible.[12] Jean Granier, who attacks Deleuze's reading of Nietzsche, also comes to the conclusion that Nietzsche's idea of perspectivism is a defense of ontological pluralism, demonstrating that the essence of being is to show itself according to an infinite number of viewpoints.[13] Even Eugen Fink, who was quite close to Heidegger, suggests that the antimetaphysical idea of the Dionysian is Nietzsche's most important contribution.[14] Henning Ottman sums up this position with his observation that we have underestimated how much the Dionysian for Nietzsche is the counterimage to the technological reason of subjectivity that Heidegger saw in Nietzsche.[15]

The Dionysian element in Nietzsche's thought thus cannot be neglected, but we also cannot simply assume that Nietzsche's thought is as antimetaphysical as the postmodernist reading of the Dionysian would suggest. While this view has much to recommend it, it too easily dismisses the concealed connection of Nietzsche and the Dionysian to the metaphysical tradition that Heidegger uncovers.[16] It is this question of the connection of Nietzsche to the metaphysical tradition that is crucial for evaluating his account of nihilism. Heidegger argued that Nietzsche was still entwined in metaphysics and nihilism, but because he did not consider the Dionysian, he did not confront the most profoundly antimetaphysical moment in Nietzsche's thought. Heidegger's Nietzsche was thus a straw man, and postmodernist scholars have rightly revealed him as such. It does not follow from this, however, that Heidegger's basic insight into Nietzsche was incorrect. If we want to come to terms with Nietzsche's account of nihilism, however, we will thus have to go beyond Heidegger and come to terms with this "Dionysian" Nietzsche.

NIETZSCHE'S CONCEPTION OF NIHILISM

Contrary to the conventional wisdom, nihilism is not the central question of Nietzsche's thought. Indeed, the term does not even appear in his notes until 1880 or in his published work until 1886 (*NL,* KGW V 1:445,457–458; *JGB,* KGW VI 2:17).[17] While Nietzsche was concerned with the death of God and the related complex of problems he later characterized as nihilism, none of the terms he used to define them exactly corresponds to the concept of nihilism.[18] Moreover, even when the concept of nihilism does appear, it does not play a central role in his published work and only briefly does so in his notes.[19] The belief that nihilism is central to Nietzsche's thought is largely derived from its role in *The Will to Power* and the mistaken belief that this work was his magnum opus. In this way, the antimetaphysical or postmetaphysical moment of his thought that is associated with Dionysus is overlooked.

In the first instance, nihilism for Nietzsche means Russian nihilism. The concept of nihilism apparently first came to his attention as a result of his reading of Turgenev, but many different Russian writers, including Dostoevski, Chernyshevsky, Bakunin, Herzen, and perhaps Peter Kropotkin were instrumental in shaping his understanding of the concept.[20] His use of the term, however, differs considerably from that of his Russian predecessors in large part because he wrongly believed that the Russian nihilists were Schopenhauerians.[21] He thus sees Russian nihilism as a manifestation of the same spiritual malaise that produced German pessimism and the nervous irritability of the French and Italians. This malaise was a consequence of Romanticism and also positivism, which Nietzsche understood as disappointed Romanticism (*NL,* VIII 1:128–29). In either case, nihilism is the result of the belief that existence has been rendered meaningless by the death of God (*NL,* KGW VIII 1:215–21; 2:60–62, 73–74, 156–57; 3:56–57, 327).[22]

Nietzsche suggests that this conclusion is a peculiarly Christian overgeneralization (*NL,* KGW VIII 2:205–6, 288–92). The Christian comes to believe that nothing is true when faced with the death of God because it was only the belief in such an absolute that made his life bearable. In contrast to all of his predecessors from Jacobi to Turgenev, Nietzsche thus sees nihilism as the consequence of human weakness and not as the result of a Promethean striving for the super-human. Indeed, for Nietzsche, the superhuman is not the cause of nihilism but its solution.

From his late notes, it is apparent that Nietzsche briefly considered writing a history of European nihilism. In his sketches for this history, he first distinguishes what he calls incomplete and complete nihilism. The former is characterized by the attempt to escape from nihilism without replacing contemporary values with new ones. He includes here positivism, St. Petersburg nihilism, and Parisian materialism.[23] Complete nihilism, in Nietzsche's view, is either active or passive nihilism. Passive nihilism is a form of resignation in the face of a world without God. It is characterized by an increase in pity and is thus akin to the Buddhism that destroyed Indian culture (*NL,* KGW VII 1:220; cf. *AC,* KGW VI 3:184–85). Active nihilism, by contrast, is not content to be extinguished passively but wants to extinguish everything that is aimless and meaningless in a blind rage; it is a lust for destruction that purifies humanity (*NL,* KGW VII 1:221, 2:76–79, VIII 2:14–16). The Russian nihilists are its clearest manifestation, but they are only one instance of a larger revolutionary movement. Active nihilism is driven by the same sense of futility and despair as passive nihilism. Both are forms of negation, of no-saying. Thus, the apparent energy of active nihilism is not a measure of its health. In fact, "the unhealthiest kind of man in Europe (in all classes) furnishes the soil for this nihilism" (*NL,* KGW VIII 1:220). They are puritanical fanatics who despair of life (*JGB,* KGW VI 2:17).

Active nihilism does have an instrumental value. It levels the ground for a new creation by instituting a monstrous logic of terror that destroys European morality (*FW,* KGW V 2:255). Nietzsche thus concludes,

> Nothing would be more useful or more to be encouraged than a thoroughgoing *practical nihilism.* . . . What, on the other hand, is to be condemned in the sternest terms is the ambiguous and cowardly compromise of a religion such as Christianity: more precisely, such as the church: which instead of encouraging death and self-destruction, protects everything ill-constituted and sick and makes it propagate itself—

. . . through continual deterrence from the *deed of nihilism*, which is suicide—It substituted slow suicide; gradually a small, poor but lasting life; gradually an entirely ordinary bourgeois, middle-class life, etc. (*NL,* KGW VIII 3:14)

Active nihilism in this sense is authentic nihilism. Passive nihilism deflects the convulsive self-obliteration that active nihilism seeks by putting in its place a doctrine of universal pity. It wants to go out not with a bang but a whimper. This is the path of the Crucified. Active nihilism, in Nietzsche's view, is more desirable because it brings itself and the Christian world to a more expeditious end. Russian nihilism in its destructive rage thus has more greatness of feeling than the incomplete nihilism of British utilitarianism (*NL,* KGW VII 2:236, VIII 2:14). However, it is not for this reason something affirmative and healthy.[24]

As forms of negation, both active and passive nihilism must be distinguished from the affirmative stance toward life that characterizes the Dionysian man. The Dionysian man grows out of nihilism but he also overcomes it (*NL,* KGW VIII 2:61). In one sense, he therefore represents the most extreme form of nihilism, which Nietzsche describes as a divine way of thinking (*NL,* KGW VIII 2:18, 440). However, he also passes beyond nihilism because in contrast to the Christian, he does not need to believe that all values are absolute values. His stance toward life is not reactive, it is not driven by the spirit of revenge or by resentment, and it is thus not a form of negation. Nevertheless, the Dionysian man recognizes the tragic character of human life and affirms pain and suffering. While he is not cruel and destructive out of weakness or resentment, he may be cruel and destructive out of a superabundance of strength: "What must not be confused with [the no of active nihilism or pessimism]: pleasure in saying no and doing no out of a tremendous strength and tension derived from saying yes—peculiar to all rich and powerful men and ages. A luxury, as it were; also a form of bravery that opposes the terrible; a sympathetic feeling for the terrible and questionable because one is, among other things, terrible and questionable: the *Dionysian* in will, spirit, taste" (*NL,* KGW VIII 2:332; cf. *NL,* KGW VII 3:269; VIII 2:52, 62, 90, 288–91).[25]

The path of the Dionysian thus has much in common with active nihilism, but active nihilism is ultimately a manifestation not of joy and superabundance but of negation and despair. The Dionysian or tragic man can affirm the active nihilist but the active nihilist cannot affirm the Dionysian stance toward life. Indeed, he cannot even affirm himself. His action is always reaction, and his reaction is always rejection and negation. While the active nihilist clears the ground in an act of convulsive self-destruction, he creates no future. The Dionysian man may be a destroyer but he is an innocent destroyer, untouched by the spirit of revenge.[26]

In his notes, Nietzsche speculates that nihilism will blossom during the next 200 years (1888–2088) (*NL,* KGW VIII 2:431). This period will be characterized by three great affects, disgust, pity, and a lust for destruction, which will produce the catastrophe that will usher in a thousand-year Dionysian *Reich* (*NL,* KGW VIII 2:41, 313). In place of modern men, Christians, and nihilists, the man of this future age will step forth as the antichrist and the victor over God, as the antinihilist and victor over nothing (*GM,* KGW VI 2:352; *EH,* KGW VI 3:298; *NL,* KGW VII 3:199, 308–9).

In his mature thought, Nietzsche sees the preeminent form of passive nihilism in the thought of Schopenhauer and especially in his doctrine of resignation.[27] This asceticism, in Nietzsche's view, is the final manifestation of the European devotion to the Crucified. In this very will to nothingness, however, Nietzsche believes he discerns the possibility of a wonderful reversal and self-overcoming. At the extreme, the will does not cease to will but continues to will by willing nothing. This willing nothing is active, Russian nihilism. The very destructiveness of this will indicates that there is thus something unkillable, invulnerable in it. The weakening of the will produces nihilism but the spasmodic violence of active nihilism indicates, in Nietzsche's opinion, that this weakening has reached its limit and that now a new and more powerful form of the will, a new god, may be coming into being (*FW,* KGW V 2:263; *GM,* KGW VI 2:352). The Schopenhauerian will that is the final expression of Christianity thus is the ground out of which the great Dionysian will may arise.[28] Nietzsche's conception of the confrontation of Dionysus and the Crucified which establishes the horizon for his understanding of nihilism is thus crucially dependent upon the thought of Schopenhauer. In order to come to terms with Nietzsche's account of nihilism, we thus must examine his reception and understanding of Schopenhauer.

NIETZSCHE'S RECEPTION OF SCHOPENHAUER

Nietzsche grew up in the confused intellectual milieu of the latter half of the nineteenth century. Left Hegelianism, late Romanticism, materialism, positivism, neo-Kantianism, revolutionary socialism, and nationalism presented alternative perspectives for the inquiring mind. Nietzsche's father and both his grandfathers had been Lutheran pastors, and Nietzsche himself was intended for such a career. After his father's early death, Nietzsche was educated at Naumberg and Pforta and went on to study theology at Bonn. He was soon dissatisfied and turned to classical philology, first at Bonn and then Leipzig. It was here that he became a devoted Schopenhauerian and met Wagner. Nietzsche was an extraordinary student and at twenty-four was offered the chair in classical philology at the University of Basel. He renewed his acquaintance with Wagner, who lived in the vicinity at Tribschen, and quickly became a valued member of the Wagner circle. His first book, *The Birth of Tragedy*, was published in 1872. It was harshly criticized by many philologists for its unscholarly character, its obvious debt to Schopenhauer, and its effusive praise of Wagner, but it was admired by many nonprofessionals for some of the same reasons. The scholarly criticism, however, was a severe blow to Nietzsche's career. His *Untimely Meditations* that followed in 1873–76 were scarcely noticed by the scholarly community and were less enthusiastically received by the general intellectual world. Nietzsche's succeeding works were read by a few friends but received little public attention during his productive life. Due to ill health, he retired from teaching in 1879 and lived principally in Switzerland and Italy until his breakdown in 1889. He was cared for first by his mother and then his sister until his death in 1900.

The seminal philosophic event of Nietzsche's life was his discovery of Schopenhauer's *The World as Will and Representation* in a used-book store in 1865. It is thus surprising that relatively so little attention has been paid to the relationship of Nietzsche and Schopenhauer.[29] Nietzsche almost immediately became an ardent Schopenhauerian. Even at his most enthusiastic, however, he was never uncritical of Schopenhauer. In his early thought, for example, his differences with Schopenhauer are as apparent as his borrowings. His critique of Schopenhauer becomes more open in *Human, All-Too-Human* and is even sharper in his later works, where Schopenhauer is characterized as the supreme decadent and nihilist.[30]

This critique of Schopenhauer has led many scholars to believe that Nietzsche's early infatuation with Schopenhauer did not have any lasting philosophical significance. Curt Paul Janz, for example, voices a widely held opinion that it was not Schopenhauer's philosophy but his personality, his creative morality, and his uncompromising struggle for truth that appealed to Nietzsche.[31] Nietzsche himself suggests as much in *Schopenhauer as Educator.* He is almost certainly disingenuous here, however, since he takes great pains to distance himself from Schopenhauer in ways that disguise his continued dependence on Schopenhauer.[32] This interpretation places too much weight on Nietzsche's rejection of Schopenhauer's moral teaching and fails to see how much of the rest of Nietzsche's thought is indebted to Schopenhauer. Nietzsche, for example, still praises Schopenhauer's atheism in *Ecce Homo* (KGW VI 3:316). The young Nietzsche saw Schopenhauer as the philosopher of a regenerated Germany who could reawaken German Hellenism and provide the philosophic foundation for a new tragic age (*NL,* BA 4:213). In fact, Nietzsche's critique and rejection of Schopenhauer are in many respects merely a reversal: Schopenhauer's absolute negation and resignation became Nietzsche's absolute affirmation (*GT,* KGW III 1:14).[33] Nietzsche attacks Schopenhauer so vehemently precisely because Schopenhauer is so close to him. No where is this kinship so apparent as in the concept of will that they both employ.

Nietzsche's concern with the will antedates his knowledge of Schopenhauer. He first considered the question at eighteen in two essays that dealt with its relation to fate and history (*NL,* MusA, 1:60–69). In these surprisingly sophisticated essays, the young Nietzsche argues that free will and fate are antagonistic but mutually necessary forces. He concludes that "fateless, absolute freedom of the will would make man God, the fatalistic principle would make him an automaton" (*NL,* MusA, 1:69). What is striking about the concept of will that Nietzsche employs in these essays is that it remains within the general orbit of German idealism and is much less radical than his later notion of a Dionysian will to power. This radical transformation was the consequence of his encounter with Schopenhauer.

Most scholars recognize that Nietzsche drew his notion of the will to power from Schopenhauer, but most also argue that he gave it a different and at times opposite meaning because he deployed it in a different framework for different purposes.[34] While there is much to be said for such an interpretation, it misconstrues Nietzsche's reversal of Schopenhauer's notion of will and thus conceals the essential elements of this notion that Nietzsche adopts.[35] We thus need to consider more carefully whether Nietzsche's notion of the Dionysian will to power is as decisively opposed to Schopenhauer's notion of the will to life as Nietzsche himself claims. In order to answer this question, we will have to examine Schopenhauer's account of the will more fully.

SCHOPENHAUER'S EARLY INTELLECTUAL DEVELOPMENT: THE THING-IN-ITSELF AS WILL

Schopenhauer grew up in the midst of the revolution in the way of thinking that Kant initiated and Fichte, Schelling, and Hegel completed. He was an unlikely philosopher. His father was a businessman and wanted his son to pursue a similar career. His mother, by contrast, was a novelist and a member of the Goethe circle who had little time for her son and did little to help and much to hinder his intellectual development. Schopenhauer began a career in business but quickly became disenchanted with his work. When his father died, he decided to study philosophy and went to Göttingen to work with Gottlob Ernst Schulze. Schulze sought a middle way between a subjective-idealist and a dogmatic-realist interpretation of Kantian critical philosophy.[36] Schopenhauer admired this attempt but was revolted by the general degeneration of the philosophy of his day into a sophistical juggling of concepts that lost touch with the world. In search of a teacher who could help him break through this conceptual web, Schopenhauer transferred to Berlin in 1811 to study with Fichte.[37]

He was vastly disappointed. After only a few weeks, he began to suspect that Fichte was not an antidote to the empty conceptualism he abhorred, but one of its foremost proponents.[38] He found Fichte's lectures incomprehensible (HN 2:37).[39] He began to suspect that Fichte was playing him and the other students for fools and was soon convinced of this. He wrote in the margin of his notes on Fichte's lecture on the *Science of Knowledge,* "raging madness," "insane chatter," and "It is madness but there is method in it" (HN, 2:123). This harsh view of Fichte and idealism never softened and if anything grew and intensified. In the *World as Will and Representation* he remarks:

> Fichte was the first to grasp and make vigorous use of this privilege [of using obscure language which Kant had legitimized]; Schelling at least equalled him in this, and a host of hungry scribblers without intellect or honesty soon surpassed them both. But the greatest effrontery in serving up sheer nonsense, in scrabbling together senseless and maddening webs of words, such as had previously been heard only in madhouses, finally appeared in Hegel. It became the instrument of the most ponderous and general mystification that has ever existed. (*WWV,* 1:548–49; *WWR,* 1:429)

Schopenhauer argues that Fichte's principal error lies in trying to deduce the world from the subject. For Fichte, "the I is the ground of the world or of the not-I, the object, which is just its consequence, its product. . . . Fichte makes the not-I result from the I as the web from the spider (*WWV*, 1:68–69; *WWR*, 1:33). In this way Fichte, Schelling, and Hegel empowered the subjective spirit and overturned Kant's judicious limitation of human reason. In Schopenhauer's view, this philosophy of reflection is only a cognition of cognition which leads to a fruitless doubling and a search for a new immediacy.[40]

For Schopenhauer, Fichte and the other speculative idealists are simply sophists.[41] They do not begin with questions that arise out of their own existence but with the conceptual problems they find in books (*WWV* 1:67; *WWR*, 1:32). They are not interested in truth but in securing their academic positions and salaries. Their work is empty and dishonest, unworthy of consideration.

In opposition to the speculative idealists, Schopenhauer holds up Kant as a model of philosophical probity. Kant's thought, however, was not without its own problems. Indeed, as we have seen, speculative idealism arises as an attempt to reconcile the fundamental disjunction that Kant establishes between the phenomenal and noumenal. Schopenhauer tears this reconciliation to pieces and returns to the Kantian beginning. In his early thought, this appears as the distinction of "empirical consciousness" and "better consciousness." What the substance of this consciousness is, however, is unclear to the young Schopenhauer. His great breakthrough is the recognition that the substance of "better consciousness" is will, that Kant's thing-in-itself, his unknown x, is nothing other than the will experienced in one's own body. The notion that the will is the thing-in-itself is a radicalization of Kant, as Schopenhauer himself admits, but he argues that Kant's idea of autonomy clearly points in this direction (*WWV*, 1:539–40; *WWR*, 1:422).

Despite its similarities to the idea of will in speculative idealism, Schopenhauer maintained that he came to this view of "better consciousness" not though his encounter with Fichte but through his consideration of the old Indian religion (HN, 1:380).[42] Whether and to what extent Schopenhauer's claims can be believed depends upon an examination of his mature thought and especially his magnum opus, *The World as Will and Representation*.

SCHOPENHAUER AND THE DEMONIC: *THE WORLD AS WILL AND REPRESENTATION*

For Schopenhauer as for Fichte, Schelling, and Hegel, the central problem for philosophy was the relationship of freedom and natural necessity, and like them he too believed that this problem had been given its explicit formulation by Kant in his Third Antinomy of Pure Reason. In this Antinomy, Kant lays out the central contradiction of the modern age between nature and freedom and thus between natural science and morality, by demonstrating that causality through nature and causality through freedom are mutually necessary and mutually contradictory. Kant's solution to this antinomy, as we have seen, was transcendental idealism. The speculative idealists rejected this solution and attempted to find another means of reconciliation.

Schopenhauer was dissatisfied with their solutions because they merely papered over the real and enduring diremption in existence. Indeed, in Schopenhauer's view Kant himself did not draw the contradiction radically enough because he still assumed that reason in some sense governed both the phenomenal and noumenal realms. He thus left open the possibility of bridging this disjunction. His failure to recognize and articulate the essential irrationality of the will made the frivolous solutions of the speculative idealists possible.[43]

The phenomenal realm, or what Schopenhauer following Kant calls representation, is ruled totally and without exception by the principle of sufficient reason. His dissertation, *On the Fourfold Root of the Principle of Sufficient Reason,* was meant to demonstrate this. Eliminating eleven of Kant's twelve categories as redundant, Schopenhauer argues that the phenomena are governed solely by causality. This position was reiterated in the first book of *The World as Will and Representation.* All events and human actions are governed by a rigid necessity. He thus closes off even the possibility of the free causality of the human will, which Kant had postulated in his moral philosophy.

This unalterable necessity has its origin in the will that Schopenhauer sees underlying the phenomena. This will is Kant's thing-in-itself properly understood. Kant failed to grasp this fact in Schopenhauer's opinion because he was still entwined in a Cartesian philosophy of consciousness. The will, however, cannot be grasped by consciousness, for it is the ground of consciousness. It rules us through our bodies and thus can be understood only through the body. On this point, Schopenhauer sees himself at odds with speculative idealism as a philosophy of consciousness and reflection. Schopenhauer rejects reflection and argues that the truth can be attained only through the immediate intuition of the will in our own bodies (HN, 1:209). The noumenal realm of thing-in-itself is thus not inaccessible, as Kant had maintained, but can be known through the inner experience of our passions and drives.[44]

Such a view, as we have seen, was characteristic of Romanticism, but Schopenhauer goes one step further: we do not merely know the will through our bodies; our bodies are nothing other than the objectification of this will (*WWV*, 1:160; *WWR*, 1:107). The penis, for example, is nothing other than the objectification of the sex drive. We are thus not merely something upon which the will operates, for we would then have at least a rudimentary ontological independence. We are nothing other than the will as it is manifested in the phenomenal realm. The tyranny of the will thus is grounded in our very being.

The identity of the body and the will, which Schopenhauer calls a miracle, is a fundamental principle that can never be demonstrated or deduced. It can only be raised to consciousness. While such intuition gives us no power to change our fundamental condition, it makes possible the knowledge of man's true essence and knowledge of the world as well, for the will that I perceive in my body is not merely my will, it is the will that governs all phenomena, the thing-in-itself, the world-soul, or what the Indians called Brahma (*WWV*, 1:163–64, 226–27, 640; *WWR*, 1:110, 162, 505). I discover in the immediate intuition of my own feelings, drives, and so on, the concealed essence of all things, a will that governs the motions of all things, from the motion of my hand to the motion of the stars in the most distant galaxy (WWV 1:173; *WWR*, 1:117).

Following Kant, Schopenhauer argues that the phenomenal realm exists only in and through the forms of consciousness, that is, within space and time. As a result, we perceive only individual beings surrounded by other beings. The phenomenal world is governed by the *principium individuationis* and is thus always a multiplicity or plurality. As the thing-in-itself, however, the will is beyond the phenomenal realm and its laws. It is therefore not subject to the *principium individuationis* and is thus one and indivisible (*WWV*, 1:174, 216; *WWR*, 1:119, 153).[45]

The will does not manifest itself uniquely and indiscriminately in the world but objectifies itself in the forms or species that constitute the natural world. Each of these in Schopenhauer's view constitutes a different level of objectification of the will. Why this occurs is unknowable, a vagary of the incomprehensible world will. That it occurs, our aesthetic contemplation and understanding make apparent. Schopenhauer in this respect follows his first teacher, Schulze, in attempting to unite Kant and Plato. These forms or ideas are interposed between the will and representations. The will, according to Schopenhauer, thus reveals itself as fully in one oak as in a million. Individual things and individual human beings are consequently irrelevant. The form of everything, of every rock, plant, and animal, thus speaks of the essential will that lies behind it in a language more precise and perfect than any constituted by mere words. On this basis, a kind of science of nature is possible, for in contrast to Plato, who was always puzzled by the question of the relationship of the ideas to one another, Schopenhauer argues in a scholastic manner that they are hierarchically organized. The higher the objectification of the idea the greater its individuality. Thus, for example, gravity, at one of the lowest levels of objectification, lacks all individuality, while human beings at the opposite extreme are preeminently individual.

Man is thus characterized not by reason but by individuality. In fact, the capacity for thought, that is, for representation, arises only when it becomes expedient for preservation, and its use corrupts the user (*WWV,* 1:213–14, 383; *WWR,* 1:151, 292). With the emergence of the capacity for representation, the certainty and infallibility of the will's manifestations are almost entirely lost. Unlike all other forms of life, man does not hear everywhere and always the voice of the will welling up out of his body. Instinct withdraws and man finds himself constantly struggling to keep afloat and find his way in a swirling sea of representations (*WWV,* 1:214; *WWR,* 1:151).

As the one and indivisible source of all things, the will is absolute: "The will is not only free, but even almighty" (*WWV,* 1:358–59; *WWR,* 1:272). Every phenomenal thing is bound by the strictest necessity and individual human beings thus are never free. The will as the thing-in-itself, however, is not subject to phenomenal laws and is thus absolutely free and omnipotent (*WWV,* 1:166, 376, 401; *WWR,* 1:113, 286, 307). There is nothing behind it; it is groundless.

Romanticism had articulated a similar notion of a world-spirit underlying the phenomena. For the Romantics, however, this spirit had goals and purposes. It was essentially poetic and was guided in its *poiēsis* by a specific goal or end. By contrast, Schopenhauer's will has no goal and is in fact little more than a blind drive: "It always strives, because striving is its whole nature, to which no attained goal can put an end. Such striving is therefore incapable of final satisfaction" (*WWV,* 1:402–3; *WWR,* 1:308–9; cf. *WWV,* 1:229; *WWR,* 1:164).[46] It has no goal because it is bereft of all reason. "*The world* as *thing-in-itself* is a great will, that doesn't know what it will; for it doesn't *know* and only *will,* just because it is a will and nothing else" (HN

1:169).[47] All previous thinkers in Schopenhauer's view have gone astray in trying to understand the will on the basis of their own experience of willing. They imagine that because they have purposes in willing, the will itself has some purpose. This view, however, is incorrect, for while "every individual act has a purpose or end; willing as a whole has no end in view" (*WWV,* 1:230; *WWR,* 1:165). Life as a whole is meaningless.

Unfortunately, this pessimistic conclusion does not begin to exhaust the abysmal reality of human existence, as Schopenhauer sees it. Because the will always manifests itself only in individual beings, it is irreconcilably alienated from itself. Each thing strives under the domination of the will for life to preserve itself and grow. Because there is insufficient material within the phenomenal world for the complete manifestation of the will, however, the will must feed on itself. All beings as egoistic manifestations of the will are thus constantly in conflict with one another. Life, as Hobbes clearly recognized, is the war of all against all:

> Thus everywhere in nature we see contest, struggle, and fluctuation of victory [and this is the result of] that variance with itself essential to the will. . . . Thus the will-to-live generally feasts on itself, and is in different forms its own nourishment, till finally the human race, because it subdues all others, regards nature as manufactured for its own use. Yet . . . this same human race reveals in itself with terrible clearness that conflict, that variance of the will with itself, and we get *homo homini lupus* [man is a wolf for man]. (*WWV,* 1:208; *WWR,* 1:146–47; cf. *WWV,* 1:432–33; *WWR,* 1:333)

All willing is injury and war; it is crime, an inflicting of suffering on others; and all suffering is thus just punishment for the suffering that our very existence inflicts upon others.[48]

The world in Schopenhauer's view thus has a demonic heart of darkness at odds with human happiness. At eighteen, Schopenhauer asked himself if God created the world and concluded that the world was in fact the work of the devil.[49] This opinion was tempered in his later thought but still reflects a profound moment of his fundamental insight. Eichenwal, a Russian Schopenhauerian, described this element of Schopenhauer's thought in 1910: "Something meaningless and lawless lurks in the world's foundation—hence, the world cannot but lie in evil."[50] Will is not the magic word that unlocks the world, but the name of the enemy of truth and happiness. The will constantly tortures itself without rhyme or reason. It is a monstrous inhuman force that through its blind and aimless activity makes this

world into a hell. And even more monstrous is the fact that we ourselves are nothing other than this self-torturing will, that we ourselves in our heart of hearts are this dark, malevolent god (*WWV,*
1:377–79; *WWR,* 1:296).

Standing atop the various objectifications of the will as the most
fully individual being, we are the masters and possessors of nature.
We live on other beings; their existence is sacrificed to our comfort
and enjoyment. However, we are not the happiest but the most mis-
erable of beings. As the most individual being, we are the greatest
enemies of our own happiness. Knowledge which shows us so clearly
how to attain what we desire shows us as well the infinity of other
desirable things that are concealed from beings who live only by their
instincts. Each individual seeks only his own aggrandizement and is
willing to sacrifice not merely all of nature but all of his fellow human
beings to this end. Man, the master of nature, cannot master himself
and thus repeatedly inflicts the most terrible suffering upon himself
and his fellows.

Human beings have tried to solve this problem. The formation of
the state, as Hobbes pointed out, is an attempt to harmonize all interests and wills in the interest of human happiness and prosperity
(*WWV,* 1:453–54; *WWR,* 1:349–50). In Schopenhauer's view, however, there is no political solution, since politics itself is always
employed as an instrument of torture by egoistical individuals striving to aggrandize themselves. Moreover, even if a political solution
in this conflict were possible, it would not produce happiness, for
peace and prosperity lead only to a "life-destroying boredom, a lifeless longing without a definite object, a deadening languor" (*WWV,*
1:230; *WWR,* 1:164). Life, as Schopenhauer sees it, is thus a constantly prevented dying, and the alertness of man a constantly post-
poned boredom. There is no way out; the life of every man is a
tragedy (*WWV,* 1:419; *WWR,* 1:322).

REDEMPTION THROUGH ART
AND RESIGNATION

Human happiness, according to Schopenhauer, is an impossibility.
Certain individuals, however, can transcend suffering either by ceasing to be an individual, that is, a self or ego, or by ceasing to will. The
former is the path of the artist, the latter the path of the saint.

In his youth Schopenhauer asserted, "Philosophy has been sought so long in vain because man has sought it by the path of science rather than the path of art."[51] Science is always in the service of individual happiness. Art wants to know, not to will, and is concerned only with the eternal forms of things, not with individuals. Ideas can become the objects of knowledge, however, only through the abolition of the knowing subject. The subject forgets himself, loses himself in the object. The artist's eye becomes purely objective and he becomes the pure reflection of world, of the will and its manifestations. In this way, individuals can escape from the will, throw off its yoke, and exist simply as a mirror of the world. They become will-less, painless, timeless knowing. The capacity for such knowing in Schopenhauer's view lies in all men but it is actualized only in men of genius, in great poets, painters, and composers.

There are significant differences among the arts because they represent various ideas at different levels of objectification and individuality. For Schopenhauer, however, music is unique, for it is not the copy of any particular idea but of the will itself and as such constitutes a universal language: "Music is as *immediate* an objectification and copy of the whole *will* as the world itself is, indeed as ideas are . . . Therefore, music is by no means like the other arts, namely a copy of the Ideas, but a *copy of the will itself* . . . For this reason the effect of music is so very much more powerful and penetrating than is that of the other arts, for these others speak only of the shadow, but music of the essence. . . . Accordingly, we could just as well call the world embodied music as embodied will" (*WWV,* 1:341, 346; *WWR,* 1:257, 262).

The truth about the will is thus ultimately revealed to mankind by musical geniuses who have purged themselves of their individuality and become perfect mirrors of the will that manifests itself in their bodies as feelings, drives, and passions. They make the truth evident to the rest of humanity. Indeed, it is their art and not science that is the true source of wisdom. To give a sufficient philosophical explanation of music in concepts would thus constitute a sufficient repetition and explanation of the world; it would be the true philosophy (*WWV,* 1:349; *WWR,* 1:264). Such an aesthetic philosophizing helps to prepare human beings for Schopenhauer's moral solution.

The second and higher means of human redemption in Schopenhauer's view is resignation. This is the path of religious asceticism and rests not on the disinterested contemplation of the eternal forms but on an engaged experience of the suffering of others. This is what

Schopenhauer calls *Mitleid,* 'pity' or literally 'suffering-with.' The capacity for pity is present in all of us and is the source of all morality, but as in the case of the artist, some human beings have an extraordinary capacity to grasp and act upon this truth. These individuals are saints, geniuses of pity. They bear the pain and suffering of their fellow human beings and thus recognize the futility and immorality of willing. They thus reject all willing and lead thoroughly ascetic lives: "This is the ultimate goal, and indeed the innermost nature of all virtue and holiness, and is salvation from the world" (*WWV,* 1:215; *WWR,* 1:152). The saint rejects the will in all of its forms but especially in those forms that are the most essential to the preservation of life and propagation of life. Symbolically, this takes the form of the promise that the holy man will not be born again (*WWV,* 1:461; *WWR,* 1:356).

This path cannot be chosen. To choose is to will and the individual cannot will not to will. Even suicide is not an answer, for suicide is a self-interested flight from suffering. The saint acts against his interests, fleeing life's joys. Such a superhuman feat in Schopenhauer's view can occur only if the will itself wills it. It is the will's self-renunciation, contradictory and unimaginable from the finite human point of view but possible as a result of the will's omnipotent freedom.[52] The individual attains this height only through an exceptional accident or miracle of grace (*WWV,* 1:519; *WWR,* 1:404). How he has done so is incomprehensible, but the fact that he has done so is the a posteriori proof that such renunciation and freedom is possible.[53] The saint is thus absolved from the guilt of existence: absolute negation produces rapture (*WWV,* 1:526; *WWR,* 1:410).

Schopenhauer thus ends with the exaltation of what Nietzsche was later to call nihilistic or Buddhistic negation. Schopenhauer, however, calls it liberation: "We freely acknowledge that what remains after the complete abolition of the will is, for all who are still full of the will, assuredly nothing. But also conversely, to those in whom the will has turned and denied itself, this very real world of ours with all its suns and galaxies, is—nothing" (*WWV,* 1:528; *WWR,* 1:411–12).

At the end of Schopenhauer's "demonodicy" there thus appears a spark of divine light. His gnosticism, however, does not impel him to proclaim war upon the darkness or to raise armies of light, for this "divine" light is in fact only a vanishingly small spark produced by the darkness itself. Some few may be warmed by its lambent flame, but beyond their circle there is only a cold and uncaring night.

SCHOPENHAUER'S CONCEALED DEBT
TO SPECULATIVE IDEALISM

Until the end of his life, Schopenhauer lived in the shadow of speculative idealism and he defined himself in large measure by his opposition to it. He claims that his thought is superior to speculative idealism because it rests on a true Kantian foundation and considers
concrete reality rather than the empty heaven of concepts which speculative idealism constructed. Almost all interpreters of Schopenhauer, including Nietzsche, have accepted these claims and his assertion that his thought is decisively at odds with speculative idealism.
Are these claims, however, believable? Does Schopenhauer in fact
offer a fundamental alternative to speculative idealism?

It is necessary to ask this question because on the surface
Schopenhauer's thought bears many similarities to that of Fichte and
Schelling. Schopenhauer himself admits that there are such similarities, especially with Schelling's famous assertion that "will is primal
being," but he maintains that these similarities are merely the result
of their mutual point of departure from Kant.[54] An analysis of
Schopenhauer's thought that treats his own claims more skeptically,
however, reveals a deep debt to speculative idealism and in particular to Fichte. Schopenhauer's explanation of this relationship, as
Martial Gueroult has shown, is a smokescreen that conceals his deep
and direct debt to speculative idealism.[55] The text and structure of
Schopenhauer's arguments attest to the fact that he borrows his doctrine from his predecessors and especially from Fichte, Schelling, and
Reinhold.[56] While Schopenhauer rejected the algebraic form of
Fichte's thought, Gueroult demonstrates that he found the direct
source of inspiration for his notions of will and representation in
Fichte's thought in general and in the *Vocation of Man* in particular.[57]

Most contemporary scholars believe that Schopenhauer's universal will to life that manifests itself in and through the body was a decisive rejection of the idealist philosophy of consciousness. Is this, however, the case? Speculative idealism understands will within the
Kantian framework as practical reason. As we have seen, Fichte tried
to reconcile the contradictory dualism of transcendental idealism on
the basis of an understanding of the thing-in-itself as practical reason
or will. He concludes that the I is the thing-in-itself. This I, of course,
is not the I of an individual human being but the absolute I that is
perfectly autonomous. Indeed, this I posits these laws and is only its

own self-positing. Fichte in this way established the existence of both the subjective world and the objective world on the basis of the radically free and omnipotent will of the absolute I.

The result of such a notion is the alienation of the empirical I from the absolute I because of the limitation imposed on the empirical I by the not-I. Fichte's solution to this problem, as we have seen, is the ever more comprehensive annihilation of the not-I. However, even this radical alternative offers the individual no final satisfaction, but only an infinite progress toward oneness with the absolute I. A real reconciliation is impossible. For Fichte, this conclusion means that human beings will always have the opportunity for moral activity and progress. The failure to achieve complete reconciliation and freedom is thus not disheartening but ennobling.

In his critique of Fichte, Schopenhauer argues that Fichte derives everything from the I and establishes the subject as absolute. Schopenhauer, however, conflates the empirical and the absolute I. The absolute I for Fichte is the unity of the empirical I and the not-I, and Fichte's thought is thus not subjectivistic in the way Schopenhauer claims. It is true that the distinction was less apparent in Fichte's earlier work, and Fichte himself even characterized this thought as absolute subjectivism. This ambiguity led many of Fichte's students and critics to misunderstand his thought. However, in Fichte's later work, which Schopenhauer knew well, this distinction is more clearly drawn. Fichte argues there that the absolute I is antecedent to the distinction of subject and object and the presupposition of both. Therefore, his philosophy is not the absolute egoism or transcendental Napoleonism that Schopenhauer claims it is, and Schopenhauer almost certainly knew this to be the case.

Schopenhauer's notion of the will to life is in fact derived from Fichte's notion of the absolute I. This debt is already apparent in his earliest formulation of the notion as "better consciousness," which almost certainly derives at least terminologically from Fichte's "higher consciousness" or "higher intuition."[58] In *The World as Will and Representation,* the interpretation of the will in terms of consciousness disappears, but the structural similarities are still apparent. Both the absolute I and the will to life are conceived of as will. Both are understood as pure activities. Both are described as radically free. Both are activities that take place behind the empirical subject in a way that the subject for the most part cannot comprehend. Both manifest themselves in empirical subjects and empirical objects. Both produce a striving for a goal that can never be attained. All of these similarities go beyond anything that one could readily attribute to their mutual origin in Kant.

Even Schopenhauer's supposedly most original contribution, the beginning with the body, has its antecedents in speculative idealism. Fichte developed a philosophy of the body and brought it into a central position in his *Natural Right and the Doctrine of Ethics,* which Schopenhauer knew from Fichte's lecture notes.[59] The I as practical reason or will embodies itself in its efforts to transform the world to restore primal absoluteness. This moment of idealist thinking was summarized by Schelling in the well-known claim that the body is the spirit made visible.[60] Even the hated Hegel developed a doctrine of the embodiment of will in the *Philosophy of Right.* These thinkers, of course, do not begin with the intuition of our bodily experience of drives, passions, and desires, and this leads to crucial differences between them and Schopenhauer; but Schopenhauer's discovery of the will through the body decisively depends on their theory of the body as the incarnation of will. Schopenhauer is also probably indebted to Fichte for his notion of representation, and the transition from will to the intelligence follows the same path as Fichte's "Deduction of the Willing I" in his *System of Ethics* (1798), but these similarities could possibly be the result of a common origin in Kant's thought.[61]

His borrowings from Fichte notwithstanding, Schopenhauer is not a plagiarist, for he uses Fichte's notions for radically different purposes. His transformation of these doctrines is shaped by his moral revaluation of the will. For Fichte, the central human problem is alienation and the central human goal is the struggle for freedom and reconciliation. Schopenhauer agrees with Fichte but argues that this goal can never be achieved. He is dissatisfied with Fichte's notion of an infinite progress toward reconciliation, focusing not on the lessening distance between man and the absolute but on their continuing separation. The lure of infinite progress seems to him only a deception of the will that spurs man on to ever greater suffering and misery. What Fichte sees as an eternal moral task is eternal frustration for Schopenhauer.

Schopenhauer found himself even more thoroughly at odds with Hegel. Hegel, in contrast to Fichte, argued that man's separation from the absolute is not eternal and necessary. Indeed, their final reconciliation is at hand, for "the rational is actual and the actual is rational." For Hegel, this reconciliation is possible because man and the absolute are always already subliminally united in and as moments of self-consciousness. Man finds the same reason in the world and in the divine that he finds in himself and realizes finally that all three are only moments of a deeper, all-comprehending unity. For Schopenhauer, the misery of human existence is the result of the continuing separation and isolation of these moments under the tyranny of the will. The absolute will is not the source of reason and freedom but of unreason and slavery which can be overcome only by escaping its all-throttling grasp. Such an escape, however, is possible only for a very few. No general solution is possible because man is also the will, because man discovers in the world and in the "divine" the same irrationality that he finds in himself, in his bodily passions, drives, and desires. Schopenhauer too recognizes a deeper unity of all things, but this is not a moment of joy but of despair; not the moment of greatest human magnificence but of greatest degradation; not man's apotheosis but his annihilation. The will for Schopenhauer is a titanic demonic force, Descartes' evil genius released from the fetters of self-consciousness, who deceives us, enslaves us, and drives us to make senseless and purposeless war upon ourselves. Speculative idealism's great Ode to Joy in Schopenhauer's hands thus becomes a *Dies irae*.

How can these differences be explained? Bartuschat argues that Schopenhauer simply radicalizes Schelling's thesis when he teaches the total irrationality of the will.[62] There is certainly an element of truth in this claim, but what must be explained is not Schopenhauer's debt to the earlier idealists but the reason for his revaluation of their notion of will. Some scholars have sought to trace this transformation to psychological factors in Schopenhauer's childhood. While there is considerable support for this contention, it is ultimately insufficient because at best it explains only his general dissatisfaction with the world and not the form that this dissatisfaction took. In fact, the particular form of Schopenhauer's dark vision owes much more to Fichte's students, the Jena Romantics, Wackenröder, Friedrich Schlegel, Novalis, and above all Ludwig Tieck. They gave direction to his rejection of the dialectical optimism of speculative idealism.

Decisive in this respect was Tieck's *William Lovell*, which Schopenhauer read many times as a young man.[63] This nightmarish vision of man, which we examined in chapter 4, plays a crucial role in Schopenhauer's normative revaluation of life. He follows Lovell's path, sees its ineluctable necessity, and is revolted by its conclusion. For Schopenhauer, however, Lovell is not an exception, but all men; and it is not they who are responsible for the evil they cause, but the demonic will that turns them into both torturers and victims. His turn to the notion of a demonic will thus grows out of the peculiar interpretation of Fichte's thought propagated by the Jena Romantics. Schopenhauer consequently sees the world in a Fichtean framework but comes to decidedly un-Fichtean conclusions. As Eichenwal pointed out, this vision of the heart of darkness at the center of the world

> distinguishes Schopenhauer not only from the panlogician Hegel and from Schelling, but also from Fichte, whose absolute ego really constitutes will, but a radiant will identical in its inner essence with reason. Hegel's world arises from silence and clarity, from measure and logical order; life is born in the quiet bosom of the idea, and all that is actual is rational. For Schopenhauer all existence in its mindless urges to struggle comes out of some gloomy abyss of wild and indomitable forces. In this manner the philosophy of Cosmic Disorder regards the primal essence of being as the seed of tragedy. The world is not an idyll of spontaneously developing rationality, but it is rather an eternal tragedy, and suffering is not a chance occurrence, but an inescapable element.[64]

Schopenhauer in this sense represents the philosophic triumph of the demonic, and the collapse of the last bulwark of the citadel of reason.[65] Speculative idealism had constructed this final fortification out of the rubble left by Hume and Kant. For a variety of reasons that we have examined, Schopenhauer found these walls indefensible and capitulated to the demonic force they were meant to repel. For him, there remained only a vague passive disobedience and even this only for a few fortunate souls singled out by a vagary of the all-mastering will for salvation.

TRANSFIGURING THE DEMONIC

Nietzsche recognized that the bastion of reason had fallen: God and all of the eternal truths that rested upon this God were dead beyond all hope of resurrection. While the immediate consequences of this event in his view were cataclysmic, the future was not simply dark, for the death of God also contained within it the seeds of a new dawn (*FW*, KGW V 2:255). The God who had died was only the tame, rational God of Christianity, and with his departure new gods might appear, gods previously relegated to a realm beyond the walls of human understanding. In his early years, Nietzsche believed that the demonic will that Schopenhauer had discovered was one form such gods might take. He later came to see this will as a degenerate form of Christianity that culminated in nihilism, and engaged in a life-long effort to bring forth a different and ultimately more affirmative god. He sought such a god not as the basis for a new rationality but a new beauty, not on behalf of science but of art, and not to secure a liberal or democratic politics but to found a tragic culture and a new tragic age.

The question of the demonic was deeply rooted in Nietzsche's experience. This is clear from a chilling note he wrote as a young man: "What I fear, is not the horrible form behind my chair, but its voice: also not the words but the inarticulate and inhuman tone of that form that sets loose an uncontrollable shuddering. Yes, even when it speaks as human beings speak."[66] Under the influence of Schopenhauer, Nietzsche interpreted such experiences metaphysically. Describing a thunderstorm, he wrote to a friend: "What was man and his restless will to me! What was the eternal 'Thou shalt,' 'Thou shalt not' to me? How different lightning, the storm, hail, free powers without ethics! How happy, how powerful they are, pure will without dulling through the intellect!"[67]

Such a view of the world led him to the conclusion that "instinct is what is best in the intellect."[68] In light of this experience of a dark hinterworld, it is not surprising that he was drawn in his youth to the Romantics and their struggle to liberate and control the demons within their souls. He was particularly attracted to such figures as Byron's Manfred, the mythological Prometheus, and the semilegendary Ermanarich. Nietzsche, too, sought to liberate and control this demonic force. His struggle with the demonic, however, was not merely a personal struggle but a struggle to determine, in the words of Zarathustra, "who shall be lord of the earth" (*Z*, KGW VI 1:394).

In Nietzsche's view, the demonic power at the heart of the world may degrade man by driving him into the purposeless pursuit of self-preservation and pleasure that characterizes the last man, or it may elevate him by providing the foundation for a new tragic culture and a new type of human being, the overman. Already as a schoolboy, he joined several friends to form a "Germania Club" to combat spiritual flattening. His concern with spiritual elevation and cultural renewal also played a role in his choice of classical philology as a discipline of study. The study of Hellenic culture, he believed, might help to transform German culture.

Politics, in his view, offered little hope. German conservatives sought to expand the power of the state at the expense of cultural life. Liberals and socialists, by contrast, preached the value of man and work, but this teaching, in Nietzsche's opinion, only perpetuated a meaningless life under the deception of will (*GS*, KGW III 2:258). Liberals assume that human beings actually control their own fate when in fact they are driven by the same demonic force that drives the rest of nature. We moderns believe in the value of work and existence because in modern times it is slaves who control public opinion. Real value is found only where the individual goes beyond himself and no longer seeks or works for his individual preservation.

In his early thought, Nietzsche was convinced that liberation from the will to life was possible only through the establishment of an aesthetically grounded, agonistic culture like that of the Greeks. In Nietzsche's view, such a culture presupposes inequality and slavery. In opposition to liberal and socialist thought, he thus concludes that the general suffering of mankind will have to be increased rather than lessened in order to make it possible for a small number of Olympian men to produce the superior art that can transfigure the demonic will to life into something higher (*GS*, KGW III 2:258–60).

In *The Future of Our Educational Institutions* and his *Untimely Meditations*, Nietzsche described in some detail the kind of spiritual aristocracy he believed was necessary to carry out this struggle to transform German culture. Contemporary education, in his opinion, was promoting exactly the opposite goals. Instead of producing the genius who could revitalize culture, it was teaching young men to be money-earning beasts wholly subservient to the will to life (*UB*, KGW III 1:384). As Schopenhauer had pointed out, such men seek art only as an escape from boredom and not as an elevating force (*UB*, KGW 1:385). Nietzsche attacked these cultural philistines and their ruination of German culture. Hegel had earlier declared that a people without a metaphysics was an absurdity.[69] Nietzsche claims that a people that lives by mere historical imitation is really a nonpeople, because they do not create their own existence but are merely passive spectators without a real unity.[70] In his view, only art that is generated out of the people can save man, and only the genius can produce this art.

In the absence of art and culture, the demonic force that rules the world leads us to banality. The artist lifts us above this banality not because he overpowers the demons, but because he is the agent of the life-force in its greatest form.[71] He is more intensely alive, more vital, more powerful, healthier than other men because he is possessed by this force at its flood while ordinary men are a reflection of this force at its ebb. He reshapes and ennobles life just as the ordinary man banalizes and degrades it. When we are ruled by genius, Nietzsche concludes, we are happy and courageous, and when it deserts us, we become timid and afraid, suffering from all existence (*M*, KGW V 1:311).

The genius, for Nietzsche, is thus the be-all and end-all of human life. The value of every other human being is greater or lesser to the extent that his activity consciously or unconsciously serves the genius. Man as such has no value: "Only as a fully determined being serving unconscious purposes can man justify his existence" (*GS*, KGW III 2:270). Nietzsche was fully cognizant of the great dangers that such genius poses. Drawing on Emerson, he argues that "when the great God lets a thinker come to be on our planet, everything is in danger. It is as if a conflagration had broken out in a great city and no one knows what is certain and where it will end" (*UB*, KGW III 1:422). However great this danger, Nietzsche believed humanity had to follow this path because all other paths lead only to degradation.

Nietzsche's concept of the genius was decisively shaped by his reception of Schopenhauer. Schopenhauer's question whether existence has any meaning was earthshaking for Nietzsche (*FW*, KGW V 2:282). While he was later to see Schopenhauer's answer to this question as juvenile, the young Nietzsche was impressed and deeply moved by Schopenhauer's statement of this problem and by the solutions he developed to it. He was particularly attracted to Schopenhauer's aesthetic solution. In his view, Schopenhauer, like Goethe, recognized that there was a demonic force in the world but also saw that there was beauty in it (*M*, KGW V 1:164). While a happy life thus might not be possible, he concluded that a heroic life was still within man's grasp (*UB*, KGW III 1:369).

The genius can transform the will to life into something sublime, however, only if he gives up the pursuit of happiness that characterizes the rest of humanity; for as long as man strives for mere happiness he has not risen above the level of animality (*UB*, KGW III 1:374). Those who follow this heroic path thus bear the greatest burdens and endure the greatest suffering but are also the highest human beings. These artists, saints, and philosophers are in fact the only true human beings, the only ones who are no longer animals. The sole legitimate task of society is thus to produce and support these three heros (*UB*, KGW III 1:376, 378). Only they can lift human beings above the banality of the will to life by founding a tragic culture in which human suffering is made beautiful and thus redeemed.

The young Nietzsche believed that his friend and fellow Schopenhauerian Richard Wagner was such a hero.[72] Wagner revealed the tragic structures of the will in the most profound way. Moreover, he too hoped to transform German culture by giving the Germans their mythology in a new and mighty form. This was to be achieved through great festivals of musicdrama, akin to the ancient Greek religious festivals. This new mythology would be the foundation for a new German culture that would transcend the petty political differences among states and unite them in a transcendent cultural enterprise.

Nietzsche's first published work, *The Birth of Tragedy Out of the Spirit of Music,* was an integral part of this enterprise, an attempt to show how music could elevate German culture to tragic heights. In formulating this argument, he drew heavily on Schopenhauer. For Schopenhauer, music was the immediate manifestation of the will. Nietzsche accepted this notion in toto (*GT,* KGW III 1:102).[73] If the world in its essence is music, then music might change the world; a musical genius such as Wagner might reveal new depths and new heights and lift Germany above the banality of bourgeois life into a magnificent tragic age.

While Nietzsche's initial enthusiasm for Schopenhauer is unmistakable, he had already begun to see the deficiencies of Schopenhauer's thought as early as 1867.[74] In his view, what is original in Schopenhauer is the notion of the groundless, unknowing will. He argues that if we subtract everything from Schopenhauer that he derives from Kant, what is left can be brought under the word 'will' and its predicates. This will, however, rests upon a new foundation, for Schopenhauer was able to put the will in place of Kant's x "only with the help of a poetic intuition and the attempted logical proof can satisfy neither Schopenhauer nor us" (*NL,* MusA, 1:394). Nietzsche recognizes that Schopenhauer in fact had no alternative: standing before the riddle of the world he could only guess and hope that his answer was correct. Thinking what is not an object as if it were an object is as difficult as hanging bright clothes on an ungraspable x. All of the predicates of will are borrowed from the world of appearance: unity from manyness, eternity (timelessness) from temporality, and freedom (groundlessness) from causality (*NL,* MusA, 1:392–98). Thus, while Schopenhauer's poetic intuition about the will may be correct, he can only define it negatively, through the negation of the realm of representations. If the will is radically different from the phenomena, however, how can it appear among the phenomena? How can it be known? In Schopenhauer's account, the intellect is tertiary, presupposing not merely the will but the body and the *principium individuationis*. Therefore, either the intellect rests on a predicate that is eternally conjoined with the thing-in-itself, which Schopenhauer denies, or there can be no intellect, because an intellect could never come to be. But there is intellect and, therefore, it can never be the instrument of the world of appearances that Schopenhauer wants it to be but must be the thing-in-itself, that is, the will. Nietzsche concludes that "the Schopenhauerian thing-in-itself thus becomes both *principium individuationis* and the ground of necessitation, that is, the present-at-hand world. He [Schopenhauer] wanted to find an equality to x and his calculation indicated that it = x, that is, he did not find it" (*NL,* MusA, 1:400).[75]

What troubles Nietzsche about Schopenhauer's notion of will is the central problem we noted above, that is, the radical disjunction of will and understanding that seems to make understanding impossible and will unknowable. This disjunction is the result of Schopenhauer's rejection not merely of Hegel's speculative synthesis but also of Kant's interpretation of the will as practical reason. For Schopenhauer, the will is thoroughly irrational and demonic. Nietzsche tried to resolve this problem not through a return to consciousness or dialectical reason but through a Schopenhauerian turn to art. In Nietzsche's view, this aesthetic path, which Schopenhauer himself regarded as insufficient, was the truly productive moment of Schopenhauer's philosophy that needs to be separated from the Kantian conceptual framework. Schopenhauer's own insight into the will was an essentially aesthetic or poetic insight, but he either did not recognize this or was unwilling to admit it. According to Nietzsche, he would have done better to abandon the Kantian framework altogether and rest his entire philosophy on will understood as art or *poiēsis*. This is the path that Nietzsche follows (*GT,* KGW III 1:42).[76] It is his new bridge between the world of the phenomena and noumena, between representations and the will, and it is ultimately the ground for his abolition of this separation altogether. He names this primordial unity Dionysus and sees in this figure the great alternative not merely to Schopenhauer but to Christianity and the entire European tradition since Socrates. As we shall see, however, the idea of the Dionysian is not as radically new as Nietzsche believes, nor is it as clear an alternative to the Crucified as he suggests. Indeed, in crucial respects the Dionysian is indebted to German idealism and a doctrine of will that has its origin in the nominalist idea of God.

Chapter Seven

DIONYSUS AND THE
TRIUMPH OF NIHILISM

For Nietzsche, the will to life that Schopenhauer described and bourgeois society embodied was the culmination of the Christian tradition, of the long decline that ended in nihilism. In opposition to this declining nihilistic will, Nietzsche juxtaposes an ascending will to which he gives the name Dionysus. Dionysus is his great alternative to Christianity and to nihilism. But who is Nietzsche's Dionysus? This question is not easy to answer. His discussion of Dionysus is complicated and obscure. Moreover, there are subtle but important differences between the Dionysus he presents in his early thought and the Dionysus of the later period. In order to determine whether Dionysus really is an alternative to Christianity and the solution to nihilism, we thus need to investigate the development of this concept in Nietzsche's thought.

THE DEIFICATION OF THE DEMONIC WILL:
DIONYSUS IN *THE BIRTH OF TRAGEDY*

Nietzsche first formulated the idea of the Dionysian in 1868 in a series of public lectures on Greek tragedy and philosophy. These lectures formed the basis for *The Birth of Tragedy Out of the Spirit of Music*. This work was part of Wagner and Nietzsche's project of cultural renewal. It sought to show how the tragic culture of the Greeks had come into being out of the spirit of music, and how German culture could be renewed and ennobled by a similar spirit. Schopenhauer also recognized such a power in music, but he believed that it led only to resignation. Tragedy in his view teaches us that the world can give no satisfaction and is not worthy of affection. Nietzsche rejects this vision as the product of a weak or sick will. The strong or healthy will aims not at self-preservation but at self-overcoming. This overwill Nietzsche ultimately calls the will to power. It is no longer understood as a demonic will but as the will of an overdemon who can transform man's suffering into joy through the power of his music and thus give birth to a tragic culture and a tragic age. Nietzsche's name for this overdemon is Dionysus (*NL*, KGW VIII 2:19, 99, 122–23).

In his later preface to *The Birth*, Nietzsche tells us that the fundamental question it seeks to answer is: "What is the Dionysian?" (KGW III 1:6). Put in the context of Schopenhauer's thought, this is the question "What is the form of the will which can affirm rather than deny life in the face of the greatest suffering?" Nietzsche believed that the answer to this question could be found in the will of the Greeks that manifested itself in tragedy, that suffered not from exhaustion but from overfullness, and was pessimistic not from weakness but from strength. It was the "sharp-eyed courage that tempts and attempts, that *craves* the frightful as the enemy, the worthy enemy against whom one can test one's strength" (KGW III 1:6; cf. *NcW*, KGW VI 3:423–24). It is possible only for one who adopts a Dionysian perspective on life.

Nietzsche knew that Schopenhauer had rejected such a possibility. Schopenhauer remarks that

> a man who had assimilated firmly into his way of thinking the truths so far advanced [that we are determined by the will to life], but at the same time had not come to know, through his own experience or through a deeper insight, that constant suffering is essential to all life; who found satisfaction in life and took perfect delight in it; who desired, in spite of calm deliberation, that the course of his life as he had hitherto experienced it should be of endless duration or of constant recurrence; and whose courage to face life was so great that, in return for life's pleasures, he would willingly and gladly put up with all the hardships and miseries to which it is subject; such a man would stand "with firm, strong bones on the well-grounded enduring earth" and would have nothing to fear. (*WWV*, 1:372–73; *WWR*, 1:283–84)

This heroic being, whom Schopenhauer identified with Goethe's Prometheus, would not be frightened by death or suffering, for he would know "that he himself is that will of which the whole world is the objectification or copy" (*WWV*, 1:373; *WWR*, 1:284). He would, in short, be a god or at least regard the world from a divine point of view. Schopenhauer rejected this possibility because he believed that it rested on the mistaken assumption that life was essentially good. Nietzsche, by contrast, tried to imagine a being who would affirm life even if he were aware of its abysmal character.[1] In the Greeks and their love of tragedy, Nietzsche believed he had found a people who recognized the inevitability of such suffering but nonetheless cried out *de capo.* They were able to utter such a "Once more!" because of their devotion to Dionysus.

Janz argues that beginning from Schopenhauerian metaphysics Nietzsche sought a replacement for Christianity and found it in the myth of Dionysus cut to pieces, the primordial unity fragmented into all of its individual fates in the Apollinian world of appearance.[2] Janz correctly sees the connection of the Dionysian to Schopenhauer's concept of will, but he does not understand that Dionysus is the *deification* of this will.

> Against the theory that an "in-itself of things" must necessarily be good, blessed, true, and one, Schopenhauer's interpretation of the "in-itself" as will was the essential step; but he did not understand how to *deify* this will: he remained entangled in the moral-Christian ideal. Schopenhauer was still so much subject to the dominion of Christian values that, as soon as the thing-in-itself was no longer "God" for him, he had to see it as bad, stupid, and absolutely reprehensible. He failed to grasp that there can be an infinite variety of ways of being different, even of being god. (*NL,* KGW VIII 2:18–19)

Dionysus is the deification of the will in its strength, not as life-denying but as life-affirming, not as resignation but as ecstasy and rapture.

In *The Birth,* the Dionysian is contrasted with the Apollinian. This polarity mimics Schopenhauer's polarity of will and representation. The Apollinian and Dionysian are not intellectual constructions but manifestations of the fundamental life-force. As such, they exercise a power over us that we cannot control. Under the influence of Apollo, man has an unshaken faith in the *principium individuationis,* that is, in the individual existence of all things, including himself. Under the influence of Dionysus, on the contrary, "everything subjective vanishes into complete self-forgetfulness"; the union between man and man is reaffirmed, as well as the reconciliation of nature with its lost son, "as if the veil of *maya* had been torn aside and were now merely fluttering tatters before the mysterious primordial unity" (*GT,* KGW III 1:25).

Nietzsche claimed that his predecessors had understood the Greeks as an Apollinian people, a people of order and form, whose underlying cheerfulness produced what Hegel and his contemporaries called "beautiful ethical life." Nietzsche tried to expose the dark and violent Dionysian will behind this cheerful facade. The Dionysian, in his view, was originally an Asiatic principle (*GT,* KGW

III 1:25). In the orgiastic oriental festivals of Dionysus, all order was abolished and everything was dissolved into the primordial unity. The Dionysian principle played a similar role in the pre-Homeric Greek world, where we see "only night and horror, in the productions of a fantasy accustomed to grimness . . . a life ruled by the Children of Night, strife, deception, death . . . revulsion in the face of existence, existence as punishment, the identity of being and guiltiness . . . Orient" (*HW,* KGW III 2:279).

Drawing on Schopenhauer, Nietzsche argues that there are only two ways out of the Dionysian condition, the path of the saint and the path of the artist (*DW,* KGW III 2:62). The oriental peoples followed the former, the Greeks the latter. Greek culture rested on a Dionysian foundation, but rather than immerse themselves in these depths as oriental cultures had done, or flee from them as European culture was to do, the Greeks transformed this experience into something sublime. This was the great triumph of Homeric culture, which established itself over the Dionysian powers of the pre-Homeric world, over the measureless hubris and excess of the Titans and the barbarians (*GT,* KGW III 1:36). The Greeks thus discovered a way to moderate the pure Dionysianism of the Orient, drawing upon its power without being consumed by it.

The Greek experience of the Dionysian terror of existence, according to Nietzsche, is epitomized in Hesiod's account of the world coming into being out of *chaos,* 'the abyss.' This view of the world sees all individuality arising out of and returning to a mysterious primordial unity. The power that this insight exercised over the Greeks is made clear, in Nietzsche's view, by the statement attributed by Greek folk wisdom to Dionysus's companion Silenus that the best thing for man is never to be born and the second best thing is to die soon. To be born is to be an individual, to be severed or alienated from the whole. This experience produces suffering, and the only way to relieve this suffering is to cease to be an individual, that is, to die and return to the original unity. The Greeks, in contrast to Schopenhauer, were able to bear the burden of such pessimism and transform it into something glorious through their construction of dream illusions, that is, through an Apollinian art which interposed between them and life the radiant dream birth of the immortal Olympian gods, who represented the triumph of the individual over the titanic and barbaric Dionysian forces of nature (*GT,* KGW III 1:32, 36). In and through the Apollinian as the *principium individuationis,* the primordial unity thus attained its goal and preserved the individual from despair through the pleasure of mere appearance.

This Homeric victory, however, was ephemeral because the Greeks themselves remained rooted in the Dionysian, in the primordial unity of the will that dissolves all Apollinian individuality. Thus, the Gorgon's head that Homeric culture employed to frighten the Dionysian into submission could not long subdue the overpowering terror of the Dionysian itself. This second assault of the Dionysian was contained only by the Doric state and Doric art which established a permanent military encampment against the Dionysian. But this triumph too was short-lived, and the fall of Doric culture gave rise to the final and greatest struggle at the heart of Greek culture, the struggle that produced Attic tragedy and the tragic age.

The Dionysian poet who led this final assault, according to Nietzsche, was Archilochus. Archilochus identified himself with Dionysus, with the fractured primordial unity, and reproduced it as music. Under Apollinian dream inspiration, this music revealed itself as a symbolic dream image, showing him his identity with the heart of the world as a dream scene that embodied the primordial pain and pleasure of mere appearance. In Schopenhauerian terms, the Dionysian artist becomes one with the great self-contradiction and suffering that characterizes the will through the immediate intuition of the will in his own body, that is, through his feelings, affects, and desires. Expressing these feelings in his music, he becomes the perfect mirror of the will and its pain. This music, however, is combined with Apollinian images drawn from the realm of representation: "The images of the *lyricist* are nothing but *his very* self, and as it were, only different projections of himself, so he, as the moving center of the world, may say 'I': of course, this self is not the same as that of the waking, empirically real man, but the only truly existent and eternal being at the basis of things, . . . [It is] a vision of the genius, who by this time is no longer merely Archilochus, but a world-genius expressing his primordial pain symbolically in the symbol of the man Archilochus" (*GT*, KGW III 1:40). The Dionysian poet is thus not an individual human being but the will itself, that is, Dionysus.

Man is consequently not the author of the world, not the master and possessor of nature as Descartes proclaimed him, but the medium of the will's self-expression and self-creation:

Insofar as the subject is the artist, however, he has already been released from his individual will, and has become, as it were, the medium through which the one truly existent subject celebrates his release in appearance. . . . we may assume that we are merely images and artistic projections for the true author, and that we have our highest dignity in our significance as works of art—for it is only as an *aesthetic phenomenon* that existence and the world are eternally *justified*—while of course our consciousness of our own significance hardly differs from that which the soldiers painted on canvas have of the battle represented on it. Thus all our knowledge of art is basically quite illusory, because as knowing beings we are not one and identical with that being which, as the sole author and spectator of this comedy of art, prepares a perpetual entertainment for itself. Only insofar as the genius in the art of artistic creation coalesces with this primordial artist of the world, does he know anything of the eternal essence of art; for in this state he is . . . at once subject and object, at once poet, actor, and spectator. (*GT,* KGW III 1:43)

The Dionysian poet is the genius who identifies himself with the will and becomes its medium of creation, who is possessed by it. The artist and the world itself, as they are known by the understanding, are not something in themselves or something merely for us, but only something for the primordial will, the primordial self that lies at the heart of the world.[3] This primordial self is Dionysus, and man and the world are thus justified only through his reconciliation with himself, as the products of this great cosmic artist's self-creation.[4]

Nietzsche believed that Dionysian music had given birth to the tragic age of the Greeks that culminated in the great tragedies of Aeschylus and Sophocles (*GT,* KGW 1:109; *NL,* KGW III 2:41). Its decisive beginning, however, lay in the poetry of Archilochus. He was the inventor of the folk song, which was the basis for the songs of the satyr chorus out of which tragedy arose. This chorus in Nietzsche's view remained the center of tragedy, generating the tragic vision with dance, tones, and words. The Dionysian reveler saw himself as the satyr; and as the satyr he saw his god, that is, Dionysus, the primordial unity. The individual was thus nullified by the Dionysian folk wisdom of this chorus and plunged back into the primordial unity. Dionysian excess was thus sought not for any hedonistic purpose but because it tears aside the veil that conceals the abyss at the heart of reality.[5]

Looking into the cruelty and destructiveness of nature, the Greek individual is saved from the Buddhistic negation of the will, that is, from the path of the Crucified, by the Apollinian joy in appearance: "Art saves him, and through art—life" (*GT,* KGW III 1:52). Dionysus adopts Apollo's veil to avoid becoming Oedipus.[6] The satyr and the chorus represent nature in opposition to the lie of culture, parallel in this sense to the thing-in-itself and the world of representation. The satyr chorus proclaims the musical relation of these two. Music in this way annihilates the cultural philistine's Apollinian individuality, because it reveals a deeper form of wisdom, a Dionysian wisdom of the primordial unity. And yet this wisdom is presented through Apollinian illusions that foster joy and save man from despair.

This Dionysian vision of the primordial unity is monstrous and unbearable because it reveals not a ground but an abyss.[7] Man is saved from the madness that this vision entails by tragedy, for "tragedy is the natural healing power against the Dionysian" (*NL,* KGW III 3:69). The Apollinian interpretation of this revelation creates a distance from the Dionysian abyss that allows us to view it without being consumed by it (*DW,* KGW III 2:60; *NL,* KGW III 3:349). It thus sets the abyss at a distance, making it beautiful and therefore bearable, providing us in this fashion a way back to everyday life (*GT,* KGW III 1:128; *DW,* KGW III 2:59; *NL,* KGW III 3:72, 75, 157, 370).

This account of tragedy in the central section of *The Birth* calls into question Nietzsche's original assertion of the independence of Apollo. Strictly understood, the Dionysian as the primordial unity does not allow a second principle outside itself. The Apollinian element thus must be a projection of Dionysus himself, of the primordial unity that itself brings forth the *principium individuationis* (*GT,* KGW III 1:40; *NL,* KGW III 3:214, 330).[8] In fact, Apollo from this point of view is a moment of and metaphor for Dionysus which conceals and thereby makes bearable the primordial pain of existence (*GT,* KGW III 1:150–51).[9] He is a mask projected by Dionysus, the god of masks (*GT,* KGW III 1:22–23, 30, 36, 52–53, 99, 104).[10] This mask, however, is not something negative, for it is only in and through this Apollinian mask that the primordial will is able to ennoble, affirm, and thus redeem its pain. The goal of the Dionysian is thus not to end individuation, but to allow this fractured unity to shine forth out of the individual. This individuality, however, is thereby comprehended as a moment of the primordial unity itself, the moment of its own self-overcoming.

With the articulation of the concept of the Dionysian, Nietzsche moves decisively beyond Schopenhauer. For both thinkers the primordial will is characterized by pain and contradiction. Both believe the will is made manifest by art in general and music in particular. For Schopenhauer, however, this artistic presentation leads to despair and

resignation, because man comes to recognize that his individual existence is fundamentally tragic. Nietzsche, by contrast, sees the will not
as inimical to man but as ennobling. Indeed, in its artistic heights and
working through the musical genius, it can make man *even in his
greatest suffering* something sublime. This transfiguration of man,
however, is nothing other than the self-transfiguration of the will.
Tragedy sanctifies "the hubris of the tragic hero as the hidden activity of the very power against which the hero has set himself."[11] The
experience of tragedy thus justifies existence and is a source of joy
because it is the recognition that individual existence with all of its
suffering is a moment of the divine, that we are this will, that we are
Dionysus (*GT,* KGW III 1:105, 137, 148–49).[12]

Nietzsche hoped that this Dionysian wisdom which had been the
ground of Greek culture could serve as the ground of a future German culture, growing in a similar manner out of the German folk
song and culminating in the music of Beethoven and Wagner.
Through music and a renewed dedication to Dionysus, he believed
that the tragic *pathos* might be transformed into an *ethos.*[13] Like the
Greeks, the Germans might be able to reconstitute themselves and
overcome the banality of bourgeois life.

Such a transformation was possible, Nietzsche believed, because
the faith in reason that had posed the greatest barrier to tragic culture was coming to an end. In *The Birth,* he argues that this faith
originated with Socrates, who rejected tragedy and music in favor of
science. Dionysian wisdom was thus replaced by a comprehensive
conceptualization of the relations between all things (*GT,* KGW III
1:79).[14] This Socratic rejection of Dionysus was an attempt to overcome the contradictions of a tragic world by subordinating everything to reason. The rest of European thought down to Kant, in
Nietzsche's view, is nothing other than the working out of this project.

Nietzsche does not give a detailed account of this history in *The
Birth* and in particular does not discuss the role that Christianity plays
in this project. In his later "Self-Critique," he suggests that the work
treats Christianity with inimical silence (KGW III 1:12). The role
that Nietzsche believes Christianity plays in the history of European
rationalism, however, is spelled out in his later works in much greater
detail. Christianity, in his view, had an oriental origin akin to that of
Buddhism, but it was transformed by the Socratic faith in reason.
Through Plato and the other Socratics, Socrates' dream of a rational
"real" world beyond the pain and suffering of the actual world had a

broad and profound impact. It proved especially appealing to those least able to bear the pain and suffering of life, the slaves and oppressed peoples of the ancient world. It thus provided the intellectual foundation for what Nietzsche called the slave revolt in morals, the foremost manifestation of which was Christianity.

Nietzsche does not identify Christianity with Christ. In his view, the historical Jesus did not reject this world or pursue vengeance against the ruling classes; he preached a doctrine of universal innocence and acceptance that sought to liberate human beings from guilt and the spirit of revenge. Nietzsche admires this Christian spirit and portrays it as an intrinsic element of his vaunted overman in *Zarathustra*. Jesus, however, was not the true founder of Christianity. As Nietzsche succinctly puts it, the last Christian died on the Cross (*AC*, KGW VI 3:209–10). Christianity as a world-historical force was the creation of the apostle Paul and focused not on the moral precepts of Jesus but on his crucifixion, on the God on the Cross, on the Crucified. In Paul's hands, Christianity was refashioned into a religion of pity and revenge, an expression of the resentment of the lower classes, a slave revolt against the master morality of antiquity, a revolt against sexuality, power, and self-assertion that in Platonic fashion sought the quiescent peace of another world in which all debts are paid and all punishments meted out.[15] It is consequently a religion that sees all life as suffering and preaches universal guiltiness and asceticism.[16]

The faith in reason that characterizes the modern world is an outgrowth of Christianity. In Nietzsche's view, the Christian demand for truth bent back upon Christianity itself. The result was the rejection of the Ptolemaic vision of the world in favor of the Copernican perspective. This cosmological revolution transformed man's vision of himself as well. He came to see himself as a self-determining being, free from the constraints of tradition and religion. He was able to attain this new status, however, only by giving up the vision of himself as the God-man in the center of creation and recognizing instead that he was only a minor piece of matter adrift in an infinite universe. The Christian demand for truth undermined the cosmological and anthropological foundations of Christianity itself. This gave rise to the Enlightenment. The demand for truth that produced the Enlightenment, however, could not be satisfied with its conquest of superstition; it also turned against the logical and ontological foundations of the Enlightenment itself. The resulting skepticism culminated in critical philosophy which led to the recognition that the highest truth is contradiction. With this recognition, the long tyranny of reason came to an end.

The faith in reason ends, Nietzsche argues in *The Birth,* when reason is forced to recognize its limits: "When they see to their horror how logic coils up at these boundaries and finally bites its own tail—suddenly the new form of insight breaks through, *tragic insight* which, merely to be endured, needs art as a protection and remedy" (*GT,* KGW III 1:97). Nietzsche refers here to the antinomies that Kant articulates and that play such an important role in the thought of Schopenhauer. These antinomies demonstrate the limits of understanding and point to a noumenal realm that science can never comprehend: "The extraordinary courage and wisdom of *Kant* and *Schopenhauer* have succeeded in gaining the most difficult victory, the victory over the optimism concealed in the essence of logic—an optimism that is the basis of our culture" (*GT,* KGW III 1:114). Through the antinomies, the concealed contradictions in the foundations of the European tradition become explicit and therefore a question. Reason, the highest value, devalues and overcomes itself.

Kant, according to Nietzsche, was the first to recognize the antinomies, but he was unwilling to accept the death of God that they entailed. He thus tried to preserve the theocentric perspective of Christianity by delimiting the realm of critical reason, thereby leaving room for morality and religion. His efforts, however, were unsuccessful—transcendental idealism could not contain skepticism and pessimism. While Kant tried to avoid the conclusion that God and reason were dead, Schopenhauer proclaimed it from the mountaintops.

Schopenhauer's pessimism in Nietzsche's view was an authentic response to the experience of the negative will he saw manifested in all things. This will, however, was in fact only the petty will of the present, the will of the last man, of democratic society that sees the principal goal of human life as preservation and prosperity. The denial of suffering, however, is a denial of life in its greatest and highest moments. The desire to preserve oneself subverts the desire to overcome oneself. The morality of pity that the Crucified represents has its high or sublime moments, for example, in the victorious negative will of asceticism; but in the end, it becomes a democratic doctrine that produces the petty philistine, the last man who no longer has any appreciation for what is great and beautiful, and the pessimist who sees pity as the sole legitimate stance toward a life that is nothing more than suffering and delusion. Such a morality ultimately becomes incapable of sustaining the God after whom it is named. God thus dies out of pity for man, that is, because man became too weak to sustain the belief in God. The morality of pity that grows out of a Platonized Christianity is the source of the death of God and consequently of nihilism. Indeed, nihilism is Christianity's self-destruction (*EH*, KGW VI 3:309). The bastion of reason at the heart of the Enlightenment is thereby overthrown, revealing the fundamental mysteriousness of existence. In this way, a space is opened up for the birth of a new god. The death of the God of reason produces nihilism, but nihilism prepares the ground for a new revelation. The god that Nietzsche believes will be born or perhaps reborn out of nihilism is Dionysus.

Nietzsche argued in *The Birth* that the Dionysian spirit was slowly awakening in the modern world, rising like a demon from the unfathomable depths of the German spirit (*GT*, KGW III 1:123, 124).[17] He hoped that this demonic spirit would make possible a rebirth of tragedy and a tragic age. When he wrote *The Birth*, he conceived of Wagner as the vehicle for such a rebirth. In the following years, however, he became increasingly disenchanted with Wagner. The first Bayreuth Festival solidified this disenchantment not merely because of its manifest failure to achieve the cultural transformation that Nietzsche longed for, but also and perhaps principally because of Wagner's courtship of the hated philistines. Nietzsche concluded that he and Wagner had never really wanted the same thing. As a result, he came to believe that cultural renewal could not be brought about either through the theater or through the epic form.[18]

In spite of this terrible disappointment, Nietzsche did not abandon his hopes for establishing a tragic culture and a new tragic age. Nor did he abandon Dionysus. Wagner's failure, in Nietzsche's opinion, was due to the fact that he had not ultimately freed himself from Christian values, that is, from the Crucified. He did not appreciate the significance of Kant's and Schopenhauer's destruction of the universality of reason. What was needed was not merely a musical genius but a musical genius who was also a philosopher. This seemingly contradictory being is the enigmatic figure that Nietzsche refers to in the latter sections of *The Birth* as the "Socrates who practices music," a tragic philosopher who combines the Dionysian insight into the primordial ground with the dialectical knowledge of the conceptual order of individual things (*GT*, KGW III 1:92, 107).[19]

While the form of this tragic philosopher was vastly overshadowed by Wagner in *The Birth*, it was no mere afterthought. During the same period, Nietzsche was working on *Philosophy in the Tragic Age of the Greeks* and on an Empedocles drama, both of which were intended to present models of such philosophers.[20] Heracleitus is the preeminent example of the tragic philosopher in the unfinished former work, but it was apparently Empedocles whom the young Nietzsche considered the best model for own age (*NL,* KGW III 3:122).[21] Nietzsche's Empedocles is a disciple of Dionysus. He is wise but he is also devoted to the god. In contrast to Oedipus's attempt to cure the plague of Thebes through a Socratic investigation, Nietzsche's Empedocles treats the plague that overwhelms his city with a "great drama, a Dionysian bacchanalia" (*NL,* KGW III 3:246). He is pessimistic, but his pessimism versus that of Schopenhauer produces action, not quietism (*NL,* GA 19:194; *FW,* KGW V 2:303). The historical Empedocles offered the Greeks a philosophic solution to the contradictions of their lives that was compatible with their adherence to Dionysus. Indeed, if Socrates and the Socratics had not misled them, the Greeks in Nietzsche's view might have come to understand their own existence with all its unreason and suffering through such thinkers as Empedocles and Democritus (*NL,* KGW IV 1:183–84). The future Empedocles or musical Socrates that Nietzsche envisaged would play a similar role in creating a tragic culture. He would not reject music and myth but would unite them with philosophy to complete and unify a culture. These new myths would stand as the demonic guardians of the young's education and thus of the mores of the society (*GT,* KGW III 1:141). Nietzsche thus imagined a kind of unification of the Dionysian and the Socratic akin to the Greek unification of the Dionysian and the Apollinian.[22] The historical Empedocles was a crisis figure who stood between the Dionysian age of myth and the age of philosophy. Nietzsche's Empedocles was meant to be a similar figure standing between the Socratic culture of the present and the tragic culture of the future.[23] Like Bazarov, however, he was merely a transition figure, able only to reach the threshold, at home in neither the old world nor the new.

Nietzsche never finished this Empedocles drama. In part, this failure was due to Empedocles' inability to mitigate his tragic vision of the fractured primordial unity. Pity thus drove him to throw himself into Aetna (*NL,* KGW 3:122–23, 169). He did not understand finally how to make contradiction and suffering sublime. He was a philosopher and peered into the abysmal depths of existence, but he was not an artist, or at least not artist enough, and thus was unable to transfigure this suffering into something sublime. Nietzsche tried to develop this idea more fully at this time but was dissatisfied with the results.[24] He did not, however, abandon this project. In fact, the development of Nietzsche's thought after *The Birth* is in large measure a series of attempts to represent such a tragic or Dionysian philosopher.

THE CONCEPT OF THE DIONYSIAN IN NIETZSCHE'S LATER THOUGHT

One of the perplexing features of Nietzsche's thought is the disappearance of the Dionysian from 1878 to 1886 and its reappearance and preeminence after 1886. Nietzsche's apparent abandonment of Dionysus is connected to his break with Wagner and his rejection of Schopenhauer and the artists' metaphysics he employs in his early thought (*NL,* KGW IV 2:559). From *Human, All too Human* onward, he rejects all otherworldliness and is unwilling to countenance a truly existing subject behind the apparent world.[25] Metaphysics gives way to a critical science that attacks the idealism of traditional philosophy, religion, art, and morality.[26] It is not the artistic genius or the saint but the free spirit who is Nietzsche's new hero.

The extent to which Nietzsche actually abandons his earlier concept of the Dionysian, however, should not be exaggerated. While Nietzsche declares the artists' metaphysics untenable, he never explicitly rejects the Dionysian and continually returns to the questions that he raises in *The Birth* (*EH,* KGW VI 3:312).[27] Moreover, toward the end of the middle period of his thought he begins to salvage a number of features of his earlier artists' metaphysics by stripping them of otherworldliness and locating them in the human psyche.[28] Even the free spirit who is presented as the antagonist of all of the ideals of metaphysics during the middle period of Nietzsche's thought is in a certain sense only a modification of the saint, the artist, and the philosopher who were the heros of his early thought. He is the self-conscious saint, artist, and philosopher who recognizes that he himself has projected his god into the heavens. He is free not because he is scientific, but because he uses science as a means of liberation from ideals. Science is thus a mask that conceals a new man who does not bow before god but recognizes god as his own projection, who is stronger and more capable of *deifying* than modern men.[29]

Nietzsche's rejection of the Romanticism of Schopenhauer and Wagner is not a rejection of the Dionysian but a rejection of the metaphysical interpretation of the Dionysian. This turn has its own

Romantic core and is reminiscent of Bazarov's anti-Romantic Romanticism. Nietzsche employs his positivistic tools not to construct a new form of thinking or new values but to destroy the ideal world that previous philosophy had constructed in opposition to the actual world. This attempted destruction of all previous ideals, however, is nothing other than the expression of the power of negation that was so central to the idealist and Left Hegelian enterprise. As Detwiler has pointed out, it is not in the interest of progress or prosperity that Nietzsche turns to science but as the disciple of a hidden Dionysus who drives men ruthlessly to experiment with themselves, dismembering not merely their ideals but their very souls.[30]

Nietzsche's vision of a musical Socrates that appears fleetingly in *The Birth* becomes ever more explicit in his succeeding works. In *The Untimely Meditations,* this genius takes the form of an idealized Schopenhauer and an idealized Wagner; in his early aphoristic works he is the free spirit, Prince Vogelfrei; later Zarathustra, the antichrist; and ultimately Nietzsche himself.[31] Behind all of these forms, however, is Dionysus. Nietzsche remarked in *The Birth* that before Euripides, all the heros of Greek tragedy were really only masks for Dionysus (*GT,* KGW III 1:67). The same might be said of his own thought: all of his heros in fact only conceal the god who is constantly torn to pieces and constantly reborn. This hidden Dionysus gradually reappears in Nietzsche's work after *The Gay Science.* His reappearance begins with the development of the concept of the will to power, and its deployment in his work beginning with *Zarathustra* represents a step away from the antimetaphysical stance he adopts in his works from *Human, All Too Human* to *The Gay Science.* In his early thought, Nietzsche treats Dionysus as the metaphysical ground. In the works between *Human, All Too Human* and *The Gay Science,* by contrast, Dionysus appears as the god cut to pieces, dispersed, and concealed beneath the mask of the *principium individuationis.* Nietzsche's studies during this period focus on the individual, on his passions and drives, his self-deception, his subordination to his own illusions. From *Zarathustra* onward, Nietzsche also attempts to describe the all-embracing life-force that expresses itself in and through all of these individual passions and perspectives. He calls this life-force the will to power, but this will is itself merely the metaphysical mask of Dionysus.[32]

The appearance of the will to power in *Zarathustra* marks the beginning of the reconstitution of the primordial unity, of Dionysus himself not as a metaphysical beyond but as the principal motive force of nature. This will, however, has not yet deified itself; has not yet revealed itself as divine, as Dionysus. Put another way, Dionysus is still on the way, still masked. Thus, he appears as the demon in *The Gay Science* who imparts the heaviest thought of the eternal recurrence (KGW V 2:250). In *Zarathustra*, he is the vintager with his diamond knife, the great deliverer, for whom only future songs will find names (KGW VI 1:276).[33] He reappears under his own name near the end of *Beyond Good and Evil*, where he is described as the genius of the heart, and again at the end of *Twilight*, where he appears as Dionysus the philosopher, who in turn is enthroned as the great opponent of the Crucified in *Ecce Homo* (*JGB*, KGW VI 2:247–49; *GD*, KGW VI 3:154; *EH*, KGW VI 3:372).

There is a corresponding transformation in Nietzsche's portrayal of himself. During his middle period, he typically characterizes himself as an atheist or free spirit. His alter ego, Zarathustra, is cut from the same mold: until his great revelation of the eternal recurrence, he repeatedly characterizes himself as "Zarathustra the godless" (KGW VI 1:267). In the aftermath of this revelation and with the abandonment of the expanded Zarathustra project, however, there is a significant change in Nietzsche's self-portrayal. At the end of *Beyond Good and Evil*, *Twilight*, and *Ecce Homo* Nietzsche thus describes himself as the last disciple of the philosopher Dionysus (*JGB*, KGW VI 2:248; *GD*, KGW VI 3:154; *EH*, KGW VI 3:310). In the end, he portrays himself as the vessel of Dionysus who aims at the transfiguration not merely of German culture but of Europe as a whole. As Fleischer has pointed out, Nietzsche "holds tightly onto Dionysus. His name can stand for Being itself, for the will to power, which is creative and destructive, and whose desire for creation outweighs its suffering. . . . Dionysus who is so two-faced in *The Birth of Tragedy* proves again to be such in the end and allows Nietzsche to articulate the ultimate limits of his philosophy."[34]

DIONYSUS AND THE CRUCIFIED

Nietzsche's later concept of the Dionysian is intimately related to his concept of the Crucified. Both, however, can be understood only in conjunction with the idea of the will to power. The will to power is a complicated and much disputed concept. It clearly owes its origin to Nietzsche's encounter with Schopenhauer's concept of will, but it goes beyond this concept in a number of decisive ways. Heideggerians see the will to power as the final form of modern subjectivistic

metaphysics, akin to the Schopenhauerian will to life, the Hegelian
notion of self-moving spirit, and the Spinozistic notion of substance.[35] Postmodernists, by contrast, seek to minimize the role of
will in Nietzsche's thought, arguing, for example, that there is no will
as such for Nietzsche, no center, but only a plurality of elemental
wills.[36] Some go further, arguing that Nietzsche aims to eliminate not
merely the notion of a universal cosmic will, but will as such, replacing it with a notion of power.[37] At its most extreme, the postmodernist reading of Nietzsche argues that Nietzsche replaces the notion
of the will to power with the doctrine of the eternal recurrence
understood as the thought of the nonidentical that renders every
identity different at every moment.[38]

There is clearly some support for this postmodernist reading in
Nietzsche's work. Nietzsche occasionally suggests that "there is no
such thing as the will" (*NL,* KGW VII 1:693–95, 705; VIII 2:55–56;
3:186). However, he means by this something different from what
his postmodernist interpreters would have us believe. It is the traditional notion of the will as a psychological capacity that in his view
does not exist (*NL,* KGW VIII 2:296, 3:170–71). The supposed
individual will is in fact a collection of impulses that are either chaotic
or ordered by the predominance of one over all the others. We call
the disorder of these impulses a weak will, their organization a strong
will (*NL,* KGW VIII 3:186). Willing in this sense is not desiring or
choosing but commanding (*NL,* KGW VIII 2:296).

The will to power for Nietzsche is thus the metaphysical interpretation of what is. At its heart, the world is chaos. While this chaos
lacks all order, arrangement, form, beauty, law, and purpose, each of
its moments is governed by a commanding impulse or necessity, by a
will to power (*FW,* KGW V 2:145–47). The will to power, however,
is not merely the motivating force in all things; all things *are* only *as*
moments of the will to power and therefore only in and through their
antagonistic relationships to all other things. The will to power, like
Schopenhauer's will to life, is thus a universal will that is divided
against itself; but in contrast to Schopenhauer's will, it is not some-
how beyond the world or more than the moments that make it up
(*NL,* KGW III 3:7, 12; VIII 2:278–79). Each of its moments constantly strives to become master over all other moments. At any given
time, each moment is thus either waxing or waning, becoming master over others or subordinate to them. Nature is thus characterized
not by cause and effect but by the struggle of becoming with itself
(*NL,* KGW VIII 1:321). As moments of this all-encompassing will,

human beings constantly are at war with themselves, with each other, and with all other beings, constantly in pursuit of mastery but also constantly in danger of falling into slavery.

Each moment of this will, however, is frustrated in its pursuit of power by the apparently insuperable obstacle of the past, by the fact that the will always seems to be subject to an antecedent causality, always indebted and thus subservient to a previous form or moment of the will. The pursuit of power thus runs aground on the rock of the past, on what Zarathustra calls the "it was" (KGW VI 1:175–78). The "it was" presents the will with its greatest problem. How can the will truly will and create itself, if it is always only the product of a previous creation? Self-creation would be possible only if the will could will backward.

The idea of the gods offers at least a partial solution to this problem. They are fundamental powers that order the cosmos as a whole and as such constitute the *togetherness* of all things (*NL*, KGW VII 3:51). They are thus the embodiment and summation of all antecedent causality. Humans can thus attain a kind of power over the "it was," by identifying themselves with that god who created it.

While the idea of the gods plays an important role in Nietzsche's thought, he is not a religious thinker in the traditional sense. All gods in his view are human creations (*FW,* KGW V 2:323; *EH,* KGW VI 3:276–79). The gods, as they have traditionally been understood, thus do not exist (*NL*, KGW VIII 2:277, 300). Nietzsche, however, is not simply an atheist. Although the gods are human creations, they are not *merely* human creations.[39] Human beings, in Nietzsche's view, are moments of the will to power, and it is this cosmic force that determines their place and direction in the disorder of becoming. Their attempts to master and understand the whole are moments of the will's own impulse toward self-understanding, toward self-mastery and reconciliation. They create gods not because they want to but because they must, because of the drive to create, the torture of needing to create (*NL*, KGW VIII 1:114). The gods for Nietzsche are thus projections of the will to power. They are the way in which the will to power projects an image of itself through man, the way in which it "deifies" itself. Man's production of gods is the will's attempt to overcome its particularity and reconstitute itself as a whole. "Around the hero," Nietzsche argues, "everything turns into a tragedy; around the demigod, into a satyr play; and around God— what? perhaps into 'world'?" (*JGB,* KGW VI 2:99).

While the projection of the gods is the work of the will to power, this will always acts through a particular people. Each god is an unself-conscious expression of a people's will to power. A god is thus rooted in the people's way of life and represents the goal or ideal that binds them together and sets them in opposition to their neighbors (*Z*, KGW VI 1:70–72; *NL*, KGW VII 1:203). The nation and the god are inextricably bound together, and the death of a nation's god or the introduction of new gods thus betokens the collapse of a people (*NL*, KGW VIII 2:393).

The problem of the past is concretely experienced by a people as a sense of debt to its ancestors. The members of primitive tribes feel indebted to the founders who established the conditions which make the tribe's particular form of life possible. The founders' will lives on in the tribe's institutions and the founders themselves are even imagined to be present among the living, who, for their part, reserve places of honor for them at banquets, present them with sacrifices, and so forth. The goal of such sacrifices is to placate the ancestors and to gain their support. The longer the tribe endures and the more successful it is, the greater the debt to the founders and the fear of them becomes, because their foresight and prowess grow in direct proportion to the increase in the tribe's power. If such a tribe thrives over a long period of time, its founders are transfigured into gods (*GM*, KGW VI 2:343–45).

The form the gods take depends upon the character of the particular people and its will to power. Zarathustra, for example, speaks of a thousand different peoples and wills to power (KGW VI 1:70–72).[40] While all of these peoples have different substantive goals, they are fundamentally distinguished by the strength or weakness of their will. A strong people considers itself free and looks forward to the future, finding in its past a justification for its conquest and mastery of others. A weak people sees itself constrained by the past and seeks in its gods a redemption from the "it was." A strong people is filled with a thankfulness for its success and believes it can count on its gods in the future. Such a people enjoys life and blesses existence, even when it is hideous or terrible. A weak people, by contrast, is dominated by the spirit of revenge, or what Nietzsche later called resentment. Such a people hates life because it suffers from it and has no goal that can justify its suffering; a weak people thus rejects the actual world in favor of a transcendent beyond or afterlife.

The character of the various peoples and their gods in Nietzsche's view is determined by the relative strength of their will to power. Using this measure, Nietzsche defines a continuum of peoples and gods stretching between two extremes, which he calls Dionysus and the Crucified. Dionysus is the god projected by the most powerful form of the will to power, the Crucified by the weakest or neediest. All other forms of religion—including Roman polytheism, Hinduism, Islam, Judaism, and Buddhism—fall between Dionysus and the Crucified and are intelligible only in relation to these extremes.

This continuum is also a measure of the relative truthfulness of various religions. The chaos of existence, according to Nietzsche, is a tremendous psychological burden that few can bear. For most, this unmitigated Dionysian vision produces paralysis and despair. Hamlet, in Nietzsche's view, is the archetypal example of the stupefying consequences of such a vision (*GT,* KGW III 1:52–53). Life can be sustained only by a greater or lesser denial of this chaos, by establishing horizons within which human beings can survive and thrive. Lies in this sense are generally more valuable to life than truth. Only the strongest form of life can face the terrifying truth that existence is chaotic and meaningless. Thus, the stronger and more vital a people is, the more it will be able to grasp the truth and express that truth in its god. The strongest people will consequently produce the truest god, and this god will be the most comprehensive reconciliation of the will to power with itself.

Dionysus, according to Nietzsche, is the god of the highest form of the will to power (*NL,* KGW VIII 2:7, 193). He is the most successful attempt to grasp and transfigure the chaos of existence into a whole, for he represents the affirmation of this existence with all of its inconsistencies and contradictions. He is, in other words, life's fullest projection of itself. All other religions need to negate or repudiate the chaos they cannot bear. Thus, they distort life. The whole that they recognize is a simplification, a lie made necessary by their weakness. The Dionysian man, by contrast, is able to affirm the chaos and contradiction of existence absolutely. Through Dionysus, he can will the past entirely by willing the whole. This great yes-saying is achieved by recognizing and affirming what Nietzsche calls the eternal recurrence of the same.

The eternal recurrence is another name for Dionysus (*NL,* KGW VII 2:1; VIII 3:347, 397). The recognition and acceptance of the eternal recurrence is the affirmation of the whole understood as chaos or the will to power, or, put another way, it is the moment in which the will to power constitutes itself as a whole. This whole is not a systematic or noncontradictory whole. It is what it is, but whatever it is, it is that thing as a whole eternally. Although it may be a chaotic

series of moments or forms of the will to power that express themselves entirely only over an incredibly vast stretch of time, it is not
incomplete or fragmentary, or eternally different from itself. It
repeats itself time and again, ceaselessly. It is thus always at its beginning and always at its end. In willing forward, in saying yes to everything to come, one thus also wills everything that has been, wills
everything glorious and everything abysmal. Such an affirmation,
however, is possible only for the most powerful human being,
because only such a man can bear the abysmal moment of this truth.
Therefore, the idea of the eternal recurrence in Nietzsche's view is
also a hammer which tests the strength of humanity and separates the
weak from the strong (*EH*, KGW VI 3:346–47; cf. *Z*, KGW VI
1:316; and *NL*, VII 1:637, 2:73; VIII 1:130). As such, it is a means
of breeding and selection (*NL*, KGW VIII 2:6–7). The weak will be
crushed by it, and the strong will be strengthened, for they will be
liberated from their indebtedness to the past.

In willing the eternal recurrence, the strongest man wills the will to
power as a whole, becomes the will to power as a whole, and wills
through it all things. He becomes the one true being, supremely powerful, thoroughly autonomous, and self-creating. He becomes Dionysus. In and through this unification with Dionysus, he is liberated from
the spirit of revenge and delivered over to a new innocence. Like
Christ, Dionysus thus frees human beings from guilt and sin. This
Dionysian liberation, however, is not redemption in the Christian
sense. The Christian is saved by a God who takes the punishment the
Christian deserves upon himself. Dionysus, by contrast, takes upon
himself not the sinner's punishment but his guilt or debt (*GM*, KGW
VI 2:349–51). From the Dionysian perspective, the individual does not
have a free will and is thus not responsible for his actions. He is rather
a piece of fate, of the world-game that is the self-creation and self-
destruction of Dionysus, of the eternal struggle of the will to power
with itself (*NL*, KGW VII 3:338–39). In becoming one with Dionysus, the Dionysian reveler is thus filled with *amor fati*, with a love of
fate that affirms and in a sense creates the past, thus absolving him from
the spirit of revenge. Dionysian faith in this respect is a faith in life as a
whole, a faith in the inexhaustible fertility of life, in what Nietzsche in
Twilight calls the eternal recurrence of life through procreation (KGW
VI 3:152–54; cf. *NL*, KGW VII 1:213, VIII 3:16, 32, 58).

Dionysus thus liberates human beings not merely from guilt but
also from shame. Humans feel shame, Nietzsche suggests, because
they are dependent beings, indebted to others for their very being.

They come out of others, are created by others. Their claims to autonomy and individuality are thus ontologically suspect. The revelation of man's procreative nature is consequently something shameful because the male and female genitalia reveal the apparently insuperable debt all human beings owe to the past. Humans can be liberated from this shame only by learning how to will their past and thus how to create themselves. Dionysus makes this liberation possible and his nakedness is a symbol of this new freedom and independence. Dionysus, however, does not stop at a mere liberation of man from shame. Sexuality is not merely permitted, it is holy. Dionysus is the exuberant fertility of life that triumphs over suffering and death, the capacity for love and self-overcoming that makes the yes to life, to the chaos of existence, possible. He is thus not merely the naked god, he is the god of the upright penis, of sexual ecstasy, of the orgiastic, and his worship is a bacchanalia, a glorification of the self-overcoming of life through procreation (*FW,* KGW V 2:140–41, 197; *JGB,* KGW VI 2:248–49; *GD,* KGW VI 3:152–54). Dionysus means

> *eternal* life, the eternal return of life; the future promised and hallowed in the past; the triumphant Yes to life beyond all death and change; *true* life as the over-all continuation of life through procreation, through the mysteries of sexuality. For the Greeks the *sexual* symbol was therefore the venerable symbol par excellence. The real profundity in the whole of ancient piety. . . . Here the most profound instinct of life, is experienced religiously—and the way to life, procreation, as the *holy* way. (*GD,* KGW VI 3:152–54)

This Dionysus differs from Nietzsche's early Dionysus, who offered a kind of metaphysical solace and forgetfulness in the face of suffering and death. The later Dionysus offers not solace but the vitality of life itself that transcends the death of all individuals, that reproduces individuality in the face of death and the dissolution of individuality.

This Dionysus stands at the opposite end of Nietzsche's continuum from the Christian God:

> The tragic man affirms even the harshest suffering: he is sufficiently strong, rich, and capable of deifying to do so. The Christian denies even the happiest lot on earth: he is sufficiently weak, poor, disinherited to suffer from life in whatever form he meets it. The god on the cross is a curse on life, a signpost to seek redemption from life; Dionysus cut to pieces is a *promise* of life: it will be eternally reborn and return again from destruction. (*NL,* KGW VIII 3:58–59; cf. *NcW,* KGW VI 3:423–24)[41]

Dionysus is the god of life at its most powerful, the god of conquerors, of the masters. The Crucified, by contrast, is the God of
slaves (*NL*, KGW VII 1:231). The disciple of Dionysus affirms life,
the Christian slave repudiates it. Even in his repudiation, however,
the slave is driven by the will to power, but it is a sick or diseased will
to power. Because his will is weak, he is unable to master either himself or others by imposing an order of rank, by *ruling* or *commanding* in the traditional sense.

The Christian discovers the solution to this problem in faith.
Faith, according to Nietzsche, is a weak form of the will that achieves
power through an incredible narrowing of existence, by a vast oversimplification of life that eliminates all ambiguity and contradiction,
in Socratic fashion constructing a rational real world over against the
chaos of actuality (*GM*, KGW VI 2:346–47). Faith is thus a form of
fanaticism through which even the weak can become strong (*FW*,
KGW V 2:263–65). In this way, the man of faith is higher than the
last man, for the last man has no discipline or constraint. Indeed, he
is really only a collection of disordered drives. He is so self-satisfied
that he cannot even recognize his own insignificance. The man of
faith can at least look down upon himself in disgust.

The Christian God in Nietzsche's view began as the god of the
people of Israel. This god was powerful and demanded obedience. As
long as his people followed him, they were triumphant, but when
they fell away and honored other gods they perished. The history of
the Jews is the story of their repeated degeneration and reconstitution. Ultimately, the Jewish will to power waned and the Jewish state
was destroyed by the Romans. In the process, the god of the Jews was
transformed from a god who wanted the greater glory of the Jewish
people into a good and universal God who sought to aid the weak
and infirm regardless of their nationality. The noble god of Israel
became the lowly God of slaves (*AC*, KGW VI 3:181–83).

The Christian God, however, was not imagined by the Christians
to be the weakest God. Rather he was imagined to be the only God,
the creator of the world, supremely powerful but also supremely
good. Therefore, human suffering was not God's fault but man's, the
consequence of sin, but of sin that could be redeemed, that he in fact
had already redeemed. This God was thus the promise of salvation
and ultimate victory for all of those who believed in him. He was the
great counterconcept to the greatest empire of all time, the expression of the slave's resentment against Rome, and thus against life

itself at its greatest. The will that found expression in this God thus aimed not merely at preservation, but at conquest and power, at the destruction of Rome by convincing the strong and healthy that they were evil and sick, and the weak and infirm that they would inherit the earth. The Christian God in Nietzsche's view is thus the deification of a disease of the will (*NL*, KGW VII 2:231).

This sickness proved infectious and spread beyond its beginnings with the Jews and Roman lower classes. Its seduction of the ruling class was decisive. The strong were made to feel guilty and the will to power which had carried them to such heights was accounted a crime and an affront to humanity. The fanaticism of Christian faith in the face of death, which was really only a hatred of life, seemed to the Roman ruling classes to be a new and incomprehensible form of courage, and the Romans increasingly came to rely on it as their own will to power waned. The later success of Christianity in converting the northern tribes was similarly due to their weakness and the impotence of their god-forming powers (*NL*, KGW VIII 3:321). This weakness drove them to rely on the same kind of fanaticism that had attracted the Jews and later Romans. Commensurate with the further declines in the will to power of the Germanic peoples, this Christian God was increasingly attenuated and disembodied. He was transformed by scholasticism into a concept and by the Reformation into a mere spirit. This final Christian God, in Nietzsche's view, is the lowest concept of god ever attained on earth, the greatest repudiation that the world has ever known, since it is able to encompass everything only by emptying everything of all significance (*NL*, KGW VIII 3:300). All of the living ambiguity and contradiction of existence is eliminated. Procreation and sexuality are declared unclean, and the desire for glory and power is proclaimed a sin (*GD*, KGW VI 3:152–54). This God is the contradiction to life instead of its clarification and affirmation; he is antinature par excellence, the deification of the beyond, the nothing (*EH*, KGW VI 3:371–72; *FW*, KGW V 2:99). Christianity thus ends in nihilism (*NL*, KGW VIII 3:321; cf. *GM*, KGW VI 2:279–80).

Christianity, however, contains within itself the seeds for a new birth. Because religions are moments of the will to power, they *are* only as the striving to overcome opposition, and without opposition they cease to exist. Thus, a monotheistic religion such as Christianity can survive only by creating another, opposing god out of itself (*FW*, KGW V 2:168–69; *NL*, KGW VII 1:72). "The devil," Nietzsche argues, is thus "merely the leisure of God on that seventh day" (*EH,* KGW VI 3:349; cf. *NL,* KGW VII 3:352). In the idea of the devil, Christianity keeps alive its own opposition, although this opposition appears only in a distorted fashion through the dark glass with which Christianity interprets and delimits the world.

The death of the Christian God opens up the possibility of a return of other gods. In "the refutation of God," Nietzsche argues, "actually only the moral God is refuted" (*NL,* KGW VII 3:354). If the moral God is refuted, however, so is the devil, insofar as the devil is understood as the negation of God (*JGB,* KGW VI 2:52). If, however, the devil is understood as an alternative to God, the death of God leads to the devil's liberation and transfiguration (*NL,* KGW VII 1:23, 3:355–56). While the defenders of the old God may continue to characterize this new force as the devil or antichrist, he becomes something much more, an independent divine power in his own right (*NL,* KGW VII 1:80).

The character of this new god, however, is uncertain. Nietzsche recognizes the possibility of a further decline into a Buddhistic or Schopenhauerian negation of life. In opposition to this possibility, he holds up Dionysus, the furthest extreme from the Crucified (*NL,* KGW VIII 3:321). Why though should the death of God be followed by a rebirth of Dionysus rather than any of the intervening gods between the two extremes? Nietzsche's reasoning in this case is circumstantial and probabilistic. He believes that the death of God obliterates all horizons, reveals the chaos of existence which undermines all standards, and leads to the realization that if nothing is true, everything is permitted. The result is universal terror and world war. These wars may lead to further collapse, but Nietzsche believes they may also lead to a new order of rank in which the weak are subordinated to those who are driven by the greatest will to power. These supremely powerful individuals will be able to bear the most terrifying truths and will thus produce a different god, for they will be stronger and more robust, more capable of loving and creating, and thus, more capable of *deifying* than the men of today. The god that such people call into being, according to Nietzsche, will be beyond good and evil.[42] The death of the Christian God may thus really be a transfiguration: "You call it the self-destruction of God: it is rather only him shedding his skin:—he sheds his moral skin! and you shall soon see him again, beyond good and evil."[43]

The Dionysus who arises from the ashes of Christianity is not the Dionysus that Nietzsche described in *The Birth.* The earlier Dionysus wore an Apollinian mask. The new Dionysus wears a Socratic mask, but it is the mask of a Socrates whom Nietzsche has rethought and reinterpreted (*JGB*, KGW VI 2:248; *GD*, VI 3:154). He is no longer merely the destroyer of tragedy; he is also the savior of life in the face of the unadulterated Dionysianism of the later Greek world (*GM*, KGW VI 2:396). Without this Socrates, the Greeks in Nietzsche's view would have destroyed themselves. He preserved them, however, only by turning the powers of the Dionysian against itself.[44] This Socrates was not an ascetic but a great erotic whose thought was triumphant because he captivated Athenians with a new kind of *agon* (*FW*, KGW V 2:340; *GD*, KGW VI 3:65). In contrast to Christianity, he did not deny the orgiastic but sought to subordinate it to reason. Even here, however, the Dionysian plays a central role, for the ascent from the actual world to the rational world—at least as Socrates describes it in the *Symposium*—is achieved by means of a ladder of love.[45] In the *Republic* as well, Socrates recognizes eros as a universal principle. This erotic element was eliminated in the Christian appropriation of Platonism and replaced by a doctrine of original sin that explicitly condemned sexuality. While Christianity was thus Platonic in one sense, the Plato they drew on was very much at odds with the erotic Socrates that Nietzsche describes.

The similarities of this erotic Socrates and Dionysus are apparent in Nietzsche's later work. Dionysus, he argues, is "the tempter god and born pied piper of consciences whose voice knows how to descend into the netherworld of every soul; who does not say a word or cast a glance in which there is no consideration and ulterior enticement" (*JGB*, KGW VI 2:247). The similarity to Socrates, the "mocking and enamored monster and pied piper of Athens, who made the most arrogant youths tremble and sob," is unmistakable (*FW*, KGW V 2:249–50).[46] The erotic element central to both is at odds with the cool and distant individualism of Apollo. Both attract and capture their disciples not by means of beautiful dream images but by the drunken, sirens' call of their philosophical song.[47]

This Socratic Dionysus is related to the musical or Dionysian Socrates of *The Birth*. Indeed, he is the god revealed and worshiped by the musical Socrates. As we saw above, Nietzsche was unable to fully articulate this vision of a philosophic counterpart to the tragic poet in his early work because he was unable to solve the problem of pity. The god of this philosopher remained at heart a tragic god, more a god of primordial pain and alienation than of reconciliation. The musical philosopher, Nietzsche came to believe, must be able to look into the abyss in Socratic fashion and yet not lose faith in life, not end his life like Socrates owing a cock to Asclepias, or like Empedocles compelled by his pity to throw himself into Aetna. Nietzsche's Zarathustra wrestles with the problem of pity, but even he does not entirely solve it. He waits instead for one who is higher, an overman. This overman, however, remains distant. Even at the end of *Zarathustra,* it is only Zarathustra's "children" who are near, and they must yet mature, for it is only in their maturity that they will finally become overmen, who are capable of producing the overgod Dionysus.

This Socratic Dionysus is more profound than the Apollinian Dionysus of Nietzsche's earlier work. Poets, Zarathustra claims, lie too much. They lie because they are not strong enough for the truth. They create false horizons that preserve and enhance human life. The free spirit of Nietzsche's middle period hates these lies and constantly seeks to reveal them as falsifications. However, he reveals chaos and thus produces madness. The musical philosopher is stronger than both the poet and the free spirit. He too lies, but he does not lie too much. Most importantly, he does not lie to himself about his lies. In contrast to the free spirit, however, he is content to live by these lies, because he knows they are the closest approximation to the truth in a chaotic world. This musical or Dionysian philosopher is able to grasp chaos philosophically *and* to establish a horizon around it poetically. He is thus the greatest moment of the will to power, the moment in which the will conquers and unifies itself. His greatness is not diminished by the fact that he achieves this end by means of a lie or fiction. It is the greatest lie and the truest fiction because the Dionysian philosopher is the most powerful man (*NL,* KGW VIII 2:436). It is the lie of the eternal recurrence of the same, which is the closest approximation of becoming to being (*NL,* KGW VIII 1:320). The later Nietzsche is thus not the disciple of an Apollinian Dionysus who creates a dream image of unity. He is rather the disciple of a Socratic Dionysus who reveals the abyss and the fundamental chaos of existence but is also able to transfigure it through his art into a beautiful whole.

Nietzsche never fully describes the character of this new philosophic Dionysus, but a few remarks in his published works and more extensive comments in his notes give us some insight into his character. Nietzsche's earlier conception of Dionysus was bound up with a rebirth of tragedy and a new tragic age in which human beings would be lifted above the banality of democratic society. His later, more philosophic Dionysus is no longer merely a god of tragedy. He has a comic or satiric side, as well.[48] Moreover, the new age he establishes will be characterized not merely by the high seriousness of tragedy but also by the high foolishness of comedy.

This transformation in the meaning of Dionysus is evident in one of Nietzsche's late notes where he lists a title for a proposed work, "*Dionysos philosophos:* A *Satura menippea*" (*NL*, KGW VIII 1, 228). The story of Dionysus the philosopher is a Menippean satire. Menippean satire was invented by the Cynic Menippus of Gadara, developed by his Roman follower Varro, and perfected, as Nietzsche himself points out, by Petronius, who "more than any great musician hitherto, was the master of presto in inventions, notions, words."[49] It was a combination of philosophy and poetry that aimed at the transmission of philosophic truths through a satiric exaggeration of life. It was directed on one hand at a broad popular audience and on the other at the few among them who could understand the philosophic truth behind the popular facade. It was thus written like Nietzsche's *Zarathustra* "for all and none."

Zarathustra, in fact, is an excellent example of this type of musical philosophy which combines satiric exaggeration and philosophical profundity (*NL*, KGW VIII 1:321). The central problem for Zarathustra is the creation of the overman. This task, however, presupposes his liberation from the spirit of revenge, from the "it was." This liberation is achieved by affirming the eternal recurrence of the same. The new culture that Nietzsche dreams of establishing is based on this model. It is not simply the tragic culture of his earlier thought that is made momentarily bearable by the individual beauty of the gods and the heros. The recognition of the eternal recurrence transfigures existence. Death is not a final end, for life is lived eternally, but it is always this life and part of an eternally self-recapitulating whole. The highest and the lowest are thus necessarily bound together. From the Schopenhauerian point of view represented by the Soothsayer in *Zarathustra,* this vision of the whole leads to despair and ultimately to suicide. Zarathustra himself, however, is able to say yes to this whole because he can laugh at the Soothsayer, because from the perspective of the eternal recurrence, the Soothsayer's teaching is a parody, a fact that the Soothsayer himself begins to understand under Zarathustra's tutelage near the end of the work. That this comic moment is a signal advance over Nietzsche's earlier vision is evident in the profound differences between Empedocles and Zarathustra. Empedocles like Tristan is swallowed up by the night; Zarathustra waits for the great noon.[50]

The key to overcoming despair for Zarathustra is laughter, which, he tells us, is the greatest slayer (*Z*, KGW VI 1:45, 225, 388). Comedy, satire, and parody free one from the spirit of gravity, Zarathustra's archenemy. Laughter is possible for Zarathustra and for Nietzsche because of the recognition that this individual life with all its suffering is only a moment of the exuberant fertility and extravagance of life itself. This recognition, however, is the recognition of Dionysus; it is the truth of the mysteries of Dionysus and thus the Dionysian foundation for the triumph over Nietzsche's earlier tragic vision.

As we have seen, Nietzsche's later Dionysus is the god who reveals the truth of life not merely in death but in procreation and rebirth. As such, he teaches human beings to laugh at the foolishness of individuals who believe they pursue their own purposes when they are in fact entwined in the mysteries of procreation. This laughter is a reflection of the exuberant experience of the procreative will to power, in which one feels oneself swept away by the exhilarating wave of life. Dionysian foolishness is thus a means of convalescence, of overcoming suffering and shame (*GD*, KGW VI 3:124).[51] The later Dionysus thus does not conceal the abyss but teaches man to dance over it.[52] Through his gloriously enrapturing song, we experience a paroxysm of joy even in the face of the destruction of the noblest forms, for we recognize the inexhaustible fertility of life itself; we are one with life, with Dionysus.

Nietzsche calls this new Dionysian philosophy *la gaya scienza* and *gai saber*, 'gay science' or 'joyful wisdom' (*NL*, VII 3:202, 275).[53] He explains the meaning of this new way of thinking in the 1886 preface to *The Gay Science*. This new form of philosophy, he argues, is a celebration of convalescence, of the powers of life that overcome all sickness and suffering. It is a philosophy that is playful, filled with foolishness and merrymaking, a saturnalia of the spirit, a renewed faith in the future, the recognition of open seas, of new goals. It is, in other words, the celebration of the procreative powers of life. Death and suffering are present but they are coupled with birth and regeneration. Thus Nietzsche suggests that his *gaya scienza* is as much a comic as a tragic wisdom, a unification in fact of tragedy and comedy (*FW*, KGW V 2:13–14). In the language of *Zarathustra*, it is the metamorphosis of spirit that produces the child, a new innocence and beginning, a first turning of the wheel (*Z*, KGW VI 1:27). It is thus playful and cheerful. It does not pursue truth to bring everything to the light, for this leads only to despair and retreat from the world, but respects what remains hidden, that is, nature itself, as Heracleitus pointed out. Nature or life is thus the great concealed one, the one whom Nietzsche elsewhere identifies as Dionysus (*JGB*, KGW VI 2:247). Playfully, Nietzsche leaves Dionysus concealed in this preface behind the mask of Baubo, his female counterpart.[54]

Nietzsche's Dionysian philosophy is thus a return to what he characterizes as the superficial profundity of the Greeks, but it is a return that combines philosophy and music more fully than his earlier thought.[55] It is aware of the chaos of existence, but it allows this truth to remain concealed behind a beautiful facade. The wisest man, Nietzsche argues, does not seek the truth; he always seeks only Ariadne (*NL*, KGW VII 1:127). Love of the mysterious surface rather than knowledge of abysmal depths leads wisdom to new heights, leads man to overcome himself but thus like Theseus to perish. The necessity of death is concealed by love, by the frenzy of the urge to create, to overcome oneself. Having created beyond oneself, however, one must also step aside for one's heir. The beautiful surface, "woman," draws man upward to his doom, as Nietzsche suggests in a late note:

> "Ariadne," said Dionysus, "you are a labyrinth. Theseus lost himself in you. He had no more string; what does it benefit him now that he was not eaten by the Minotaur? What eats him is worse than the Minotaur." "You flatter me," answered Ariadne, "but I am tired of my pity. In me all heros should shipwreck: that is my love for Theseus. I condemn him to perish." (*NL*, KGW VIII 2:66)

The *gaya scienza* of Dionysus that Nietzsche presents is a combination of music and philosophy. We have examined the philosophical structure of this Dionysian philosophy. We must now examine its musical character.

NIETZSCHE'S MUSICAL PHILOSOPHY

The importance of music for Nietzsche has long been recognized, but we have only recently begun to understand its philosophic significance for his thought.[56] In his early thought, Nietzsche sought in a halting and incomplete way to develop an artists' metaphysics that was essentially musical. Ontologically, this metaphysics treats music as the thing-in-itself, prior to and behind all phenomena. While this conception of music resembles that of Schopenhauer, there are important differences between them. Schopenhauer saw music as the mirror of the will to life. Nietzsche, by contrast, argues that while music may appear as will, it cannot *be* will. "Language," he declares, "can never adequately render the cosmic symbolism of music, because music stands in symbolic relation to the primordial contradiction and primordial pain in the heart of the primordial unity, and therefore symbolizes a sphere which is beyond and prior to all phenomena" (*GT,* KGW III 1:47). For the early Nietzsche, will is thus merely the Apollinian interpretation of truly primordial Dionysian music.[57] This reversal of Schopenhauer allows Nietzsche to solve the problem we noted in Schopenhauer's thought of explaining the relationship of knowing and willing, for it provides a common source and connection for both in primordial music.[58]

The connections between these two realms are defined in Nietzsche's early artists' metaphysics by a musical logic. Music, he believes, is a universal language which is related to universal concepts as they are related to particular things. All possible effects, excitements, manifestations of the will, all feelings may be expressed by the infinite number of melodies (*GT,* KGW III 1:101; cf. *FW,* KGW V 2:111–24; and *NL,* KGW VIII 2:159). Music incites symbolic intuition and allows symbolic images to emerge in their highest significance. In this way, it gives birth to both myth and philosophy. Both Apollinian images and Socratic concepts arise out of a world that has already been formed musically. They consequently do not represent an independent source of form but are interpretations of the musical form that already infuses nature. The tones themselves symbolize different ways of pleasure and displeasure without accompanying representations. Thus, "the will and its symbolism—harmony—both are in the final analysis *pure logic!* . . . harmony is the symbol of the pure essence of the will" (*NL,* KGW III 2:66; cf. 4:23).[59] Tones, for Nietzsche, constitute the essence of all the various things in the world. Tones, however, also stand in precise geometric proportions to one another. The qualitative differences between discrete things in this sense become quantitative differences that can be treated mathematically. This mathematical treatment, however, is itself essentially musical, for mathematics, like all other language, for Nietzsche is born out of music (*NL,* MusA, 3:376).

Nietzsche clearly draws upon the Pythagoreans in formulating this musical logic and they also played an important role in shaping his cosmology. It was their great insight that "the entire essence of the world whose image was music, although played only on one string, might be expressed purely in numbers" (*NL,* GA, 10:118; cf. *WS,* KGW IV 3:302; and *NL,* KGW III 3:73). This Pythagorean vision of the cosmos in Nietzsche's view was part of the Dionysian revelation received from the orient.[60] Moreover, while the Pythagoreans were the first Greeks to grasp this idea, it was only fully developed by Heracleitus, who Nietzsche argues was the most Dionysian of all philosophers (*NL*, GA, 10:119). Heracleitus was able to grasp the process of coming-to-be and passing-away

> under the form of polarity, as the diverging of a force into two qualitatively different opposed activities that seek to re-unite. Everlastingly, a given quality contends against itself and separates into opposites; everlastingly these opposites seek to re-unite. . . . the limited human mind . . . sees things apart but not connected [but this is not the case] for the con-tuitive god. For him all contradictions run into harmony, invisible to the common human eye, yet understandable to one who, like Heracleitus, is related to the contemplative god. (*PTZG*, KGW III 2:318–19, 324)

It was this Heracleitean vision of harmony in diversity that informed Nietzsche's musical cosmology with its emphasis on the great struggle of becoming in its unending cycles of generation and destruction.

For the early Nietzsche, ontology, logic, and cosmology were thus construed musically. The same is true for Nietzsche's early theology and psychology, which we examined in our earlier discussion of *The Birth*. Within Nietzsche's artists' metaphysics, the whole of life is thus grasped as an aesthetic phenomenon, as the expression of Dionysian music. We also experience the tragic or fractured whole itself through music.

> We are for a brief moment primordial being itself, feeling its raging desire for existence and joy in existence; the struggle, the pain, the destruction of phenomena, now appear necessary to us, in view of the excess of countless forms of existence which force and push one another into life, in view of the exuberant fertility of the universal will. . . . In spite of fear and pity, we are the happy living beings, not as individuals, but as the *one* living being, with whose creative joy we are united. (*GT*, KGW III 1:105)

Through music, we can not only understand the relationships between things but also participate in the primordial unity out of which all things arise. Music, in other words, overcomes the alienation of individual existence and is thus the ground of all reconciliation. All things are nothing but the expression of primordial music.

Nietzsche never completed this musical metaphysics because he came to see that it rested on an untenable bifurcation of the world.

This insight was bound up with his rejection of Schopenhauer and Wagner. While music continued to play an important role in his thought, he increasingly began to subject his own metaphysical interpretation of music to a trenchant critique. As a result, music receded in importance during the middle period of his thought and was replaced by critical philosophy and psychology. In his later thought, however, a new idea of music begins to emerge, in which music is conjoined with philosophy in Nietzsche's *gaya scienza*. Music is no longer understood as the thing-in-itself but as the preeminent form of the will to power, more powerful finally than even philosophy. Philosophy allows man to understand the fundamental chaos of existence, but only music enables him to transfigure it into something higher.

What *is* for Nietzsche in his later thought is becoming. Traditional philosophy attempts to eliminate becoming by subordinating it to concepts. Becoming, however, eludes all concepts, slides out from under and away from them. Categorical thinking thus cannot master becoming. Indeed, it can only recognize becoming as a kind of negation, as not-being, as an apparent world in contrast to the real world that it sets up in concepts. Nietzsche's philosophy exposes the lies of traditional philosophy and reveals the chaos of existence, but it cannot transfigure this chaotic becoming. Music, however, can.

Music in the most general sense for Nietzsche is melody, the rhythmic development of harmony *(Harmoniefolge)*, from consonance to dissonance and back to consonance (*DW,* KGW III 2:49; cf. *NL,* KGW VIII 3:34). Rhythm shapes time by demarcating temporal periods. It achieves this goal not by the alternation of strong and weak stress—this is a modern misunderstanding—but by the alternation of long and short notes, or periods.[61] Rhythm breaks up the undifferentiated flux of becoming into regular intervals. It creates and controls time and sets the tempo of life.

Rhythm thus exercises an immense power over human beings. In ancient times, according to Nietzsche, men believed that rhythm was a magical power that could be employed to control even the gods, by fostering orgiastic states of excitement that satiated the demons who possessed human beings (*FW,* KGW V 2:115–18; *JGB,* KGW VI 2:92). Music was also the principal form of habituation and training. It aimed not at evoking passions but at constraining and organizing them, and its goal was not *pathos* but *ethos,* that is, the formation of character.[62] Nietzsche suggests that it achieves this goal by shaping the various rhythms of life, including the rhythms of the bodily organs (*RU*, KGW II 3:322). It thus trains men at a subrational level to march or dance in step with the prevailing melody. Rhythm is the discipline that creates the well-tempered human being. In its classical form, music thus seeks to order becoming rather than timidly surrender to it or vainly seek to eliminate it.

The melodic goal of the rhythmic determination of time is the transformation of dissonance into consonance, of contradictions into harmony. This goal is predicated on the notion that the chaos of becoming is essentially opposition or difference. The weak will is unable to master these differences. The world appears to it as a contradiction or antinomy, a tragedy that can be redeemed only by an act of grace. It thus falls into nihilistic despair, and seeks either passively to negate itself or actively to negate the world. The powerful will, by contrast, transfigures the chaos and contradiction of existence into a new harmony (*PTZG*, KGW III 2:316, 319, 324; cf. *NL*, KGW III 3:63).

Following both ancient and modern musical theorists, Nietzsche was convinced that the various musical modes exercise a particular force upon the passions, turning the listener in one direction or another. By nature, human beings are rent by multiple, contradictory passions. Music orders these passions to create a way of life in which all of the passions are directed to a single end. Music achieves this by establishing a rank order that harmonizes the cacophony of the passions into a beautiful melody. Such a melody is achieved by a musical modulation that brings each of the different passions from its prevailing mode into the tonic. The rhythmic transformation of the passions under the hegemony of a particular passion thus creates a harmonic whole. The will as music thus transfigures itself into a whole.

Music is consequently not the play of difference for Nietzsche but the source of unity and identity. This identity, however, is a harmonic and not a logical identity.[63] The world-harmony is "the unity of the manifold and the harmony of conflicting dispositions. If contradiction is an element in everything, then harmony is in everything too" (*NL*, GA 10:119). Music preserves differences but harmonizes them with one another. Dissonance itself is redeemed as a subordinate moment of a larger musical whole (*GT*, KGW III 1, 40, 148). Harmony for Nietzsche thus replaces the principle of noncontradiction, and melody (understood as *Harmoniefolge*) replaces the principle of sufficient reason. The whole that Nietzsche presents is governed not by the laws of reason but by aesthetic laws.

The claim that Nietzsche's thought is dialectical is thus mistaken.[64] It is true that he, like Fichte and Hegel, continually juxta-poses opposites, but his understanding of opposition is different from theirs in crucial respects. Opposition for Nietzsche is musical, not dialectical, and his musical logic seeks not the synthesis of contradic-tions but the transfiguration of dissonance into a higher harmony, into a beauty of such magnitude that one wants the contradiction and the dissonance again and again, because they are integral to the exu-berant fertility of the primordial creative force that one at least for a brief, ecstatic moment *is*.

Not all music, however, establishes such an identity. Romantic music in particular fails to do so. It is subjectivistic and emphasizes the value of symbols and the effect of music on the emotions, the psy-che, and the subconscious.[65] It thus does not organize the passions but surrenders to them. Wagnerian music, in Nietzsche's view, is typ-ical. Wagner perceived the chaotic character of actuality but he was unable to transfigure it musically. He thus presented only the vague hope of redemption from this chaos. In his art, the part dominates the whole, the phrase dominates the melody, the moment dominates time, *pathos* dominates *ethos*, and *esprit* dominates sense (*NL,* KGW VIII 3:286).[66] Life is contradiction, tragedy. As a result, it is not har-mony but dissonance that is the center of his musical compositions, expressing the pain of contradiction and the unfulfillable longing for reconciliation. As a result, his music achieves no harmonic resolution through melody, for Wagnerian melody is always incomplete and therefore infinite, a succession of tones pointing toward a reconcilia-tion that can never be attained.

In his early thought, Nietzsche admired Wagner's use of disso-nance and especially its intimations of the infinite (*GT,* KGW III 1:148; *W,* KGW VI 3:18). During this period Nietzsche saw Wagner as the musical equivalent of Heracleitus (*UB,* KGW IV 1:66). In his later thought, he recognized the illusory character of this infinite and the defective character of a music that remains at the level of disso-nance. Infinite melody, in Nietzsche's view, is not melody at all. It does not regularize and harmonize becoming. Real melody is the expression of a powerful will that produces a unified whole. Wagner's infinite melody is eternally incomplete and thus a reflection of Wag-ner's decadence, of a weakness of will that is unable to establish order and leads to "paralysis, arduousness, torpidity or hostility and chaos"(*W,* KGW VI 3:21; cf. *NcW,* KGW VI 3:419–21). Wagner thus did not create a new musical form; his music is only formlessness (*NL,* KGW VIII 1:88).[67] It is "the decay of melody," and his so-called "'dramatic music' . . . is simply bad music" (*NL,* KGW VIII 2:188). In fact, Wagner is not even really musical; he is an actor whose music is driven by a melodramatic impulse that reveals the chaos of Wagner's own soul and the decadence of the German people (*N,* KGW VI 3:26–31; *NcW,* KGW VI 3:416–18; *NL,* KGW VIII 3:293). Wagner's music in Nietzsche's terms thus "makes sick" (*NcW,* KGW VI 3:417; *W,* KGW VI 3:15). It is ultimately only a surrender to the chaos of becoming.

The music that Nietzsche seeks to develop as part of his *gaya scienza* masters chaos with melodies that progress from dissonance to harmony.[68] Such an effort, in Nietzsche's opinion, characterized Greek music as well as the music of Monteverdi, Handel, Haydn, and Mozart among others (*NL,* KGW II 2:31; VIII 1:245). This kind of music aims at producing a beautiful whole in which "opposites are tamed . . . without tension . . . violence is no longer needed . . . everything follows, obeys, so easily and so pleasantly" (*NL,* KGW VIII 1:266). It lets "a harmony sound forth from every conflict," bestowing "upon things their own power and self-redemption" (*NL,* KGW VIII 1:293; 2:223). It does not seek to evoke passions and longings that cannot be stilled but to create perfection as a resolution of contradictions, of conflicting passions and desires (*FW,* KGW V 2:298–300).

Such music is not simply tragic. It recognizes the tragic moment in existence but subordinates the tragic contradictions within a larger harmonic whole. Nietzsche thus prefers Bizet's *Carmen* to Wagner's *Tristan and Isolde* not because it is more profound but because it is healthier, because it turns tragedy into something beautiful and complete rather than something that can only point to an infinite beyond (*W,* KGW VI 3:7–10). True music in this sense is Dionysian, the moment of the will to power that affirms and unifies existence, that is able to affirm existence because it can unify it, because it can harmonize all of its contradictions.

Such music does not strive for truth but for beauty and perfection. Nietzsche thus praises classical Italian opera, which Wagner saw as ludicrous and superficial (*WS,* KGW IV 3:26). He similarly prefers Offenbach to Wagner because his music still knows how to dance, whereas Wagner teaches music to swim (*NcW,* KGW VI 3:419–20). Offenbach's music may be superficial but only because it recognizes the profundity in superficiality. In this respect, it has a great deal in common with Nietzsche's own *gaya scienza.*[69] Nietzsche describes this kind of art in the last paragraph of *Nietzsche contra Wagner:*

Oh, those Greeks! They knew how to live. What is required for that is to stop courageously at the surface, the fold, the skin, to adore appearance, to believe in forms, tones, words, in the whole Olympus of appearance. Those Greeks were superficial—*out of profundity*. And is not this precisely what we are again coming back to, we daredevils of the spirit who have climbed the highest and most dangerous peak of present thought and looked down from there? Are we not, precisely in this respect, Greeks? Adorers of forms, of tones, of words? And therefore—*artists?* (KGW VI 3:437)

Nietzsche believed that few of his contemporaries were able to reach such heights. At best, they climbed only small hills and produced brief moments of perfection. His music and the music of those great geniuses-to-come aims at something more, the grand style, in order "to become master of the chaos one is; to compel one's chaos to become form: to become logical, simple, unambiguous, mathematics, *law*" (*NL,* KGW VIII 3:39). The grand style does not consist in evoking beautiful feelings but in expressing the tension of the will, in the certainty with which chaos obeys the artistic command, and in the necessity that the artist's hand lays in the sequence of forms (*NL,* KGW VIII 3:298). It is the triumph of harmony over dissonance, of the beautiful rhythm of the dance over infinite melody, and of musical form over dramatic structure. It does not merely create a place of rest and relaxation; it commands and imposes its will on the world. This art is not mimetic but creative—it does not describe the world as it is but determines the world as it will be, as this will wills it to be. It establishes a rhythm and a vision of harmony that shape succeeding generations. It thus commands obedience to its own way of seeing and being. In the strict sense of the term, it thus lies, constructing boundaries and limits where there are no boundaries and limits, creating a rhythmic and harmonic whole where there is only chaos. This lie, however, preserves man, for it shuts out the unbearable fact of chaos. "Truth is ugly," Nietzsche argues; "We possess art lest we *perish of the truth*" (*NL,* KGW VIII 3:296; cf. *NL,* KGW VIII 2:435). It also is the means by which man is overcome. This lie thus creates a new nobility and a new order of rank.

The creation of this aesthetic whole, however, is always the work of an individual musical genius or philosopher who creates the whole according to his own commanding passion. The whole that he creates is thus always only one possible whole. Moreover, this whole is constructed by harmonizing contradictions and not by destroying them. The musical reconciliation he achieves is thus neither permanent nor complete. The world in which the musical philosopher lives and works is not a universe but a cosmos, a beautiful but variegated jewel that sparkles differently when seen from different perspectives. It is a music box that eternally repeats its tune, but it plays a tune that may never be called a melody because it is not and cannot truly be a whole (*FW*, KGW V 2:146). The whole is rather a series of "wholes," a series of songs sung by the disciples of Dionysus and thus governed by his indomitable but fundamentally capricious will. Each of these songs harmonizes and unifies the whole but each represents only a particular perspective on the whole. None is able to completely dominate or exhaust it.

The greatest of these songs is the song of the eternal recurrence, the song that Zarathustra calls "the Yes and Amen song" (KGW VI 1:283). This song, however, is not definitive or absolute. It is only the greatest lie, the supreme moment of the will to power in which it unifies itself as a whole. This whole, however, is not the whole itself; it is still partial and finite. The doctrine of the eternal recurrence reconciles the most profound contradictions, but this reconciliation is at heart a harmonization that leaves the opposites and the tension between these opposites intact. It is thus at best a momentary balancing of forces, each of which continues to strive to overcome and devour the others.

While Nietzsche strives to bring about the transformation of contemporary culture, he knows he cannot achieve this alone. His principal goal is thus to create the human beings capable of bringing about such a transformation. These are the children and heirs that he longs for. Nietzsche believes that the nihilistic catastrophe that is looming on the horizon will bring forth such musical philosophers, and that their art will give birth to a new order of rank and a new Dionysian age.[70] In place of Fichte's scholars and Hegel's bureaucrats, artist-philosophers, or as Nietzsche occasionally refers to them, artist-tyrants, will rule, geniuses who will reshape the world under the inspiration of Dionysian music (*NL*, KGW VIII 1:85–87).

The world defined by Dionysian music is not a world of eternal peace such as Kant imagined nor even Hegel's world of limited conflict. It is to its very core a world in opposition to itself, a world of constant and universal war in which every being seeks to conquer and subdue every other being (*EH*, KGW VI 3:310–11). Nietzsche, however, does not end with this pessimistic, Schopenhauerian vision. While war may be unending, it is not a device to destroy all human happiness. It is rather a glorious game played by a child, a game in which there is no resentment and no desire for revenge, a game played simply for the love of play. It is the eternal recurrence of the same. For Nietzsche, there is thus no evil genius whose goal is to deceive and destroy us, but a cosmic genius beyond both good and evil who crushes us for his sport. We may be destroyed by this god, but through his musical disciple we can appreciate and ultimately will our own destruction, for we glory in the inexhaustible strength and fertility of this genius, indeed through this genius we *are* at least for a moment this inexhaustible strength and fertility.[71] Nietzsche thus adopts a more affirmative stance than Turgenev or Schopenhauer. His musical genius teaches us to will and affirm our own destruction as part of our affirmation of life itself. Where Bazarov sighs "It is enough!" Zarathustra sings "Once more!"

Nietzsche's elevation of the musical genius seems to undermine the role of Dionysus, for the musical philosopher seems to become the god who is repeatedly torn to pieces and repeatedly reconstituted, to become Dionysus.[72] Lou Salomé had already argued in 1894 that "the possibility of finding a substitute for the lost God in the various forms of self-deification is the history of his [Nietzsche's] spirit, of his works, of his sickness."[73] Müller-Lauter agrees: "Nietzsche's thinking in its execution makes the claim to prepare the dissolution of human god formation through the apotheosis of man."[74] Nietzsche's position in this respect is strikingly similar to the Prometheanism of the Russian nihilists.

Nietzsche, however, is never willing simply to proclaim that man is god or that the divine is a human creation. He argues that the overman comes into being when man ceases to flow out into a god, but he also suggests that the overman is the product of Dionysus's attempt to make man stronger, more evil, more profound, and more beautiful (*FW*, KGW V 2:7; *JGB* KGW VI 2:249; *NL*, KGW VII 3:200, 203, 419–20; VIII 1:74, 180). This overman is the heir of all history and enjoys the happiness of a god full of power and love, but he is capable of such heights only because he is a moment of the procreative will to power that wills its own eternal recurrence (*FW*, KGW V 2:244–45). The existence of the overman thus depends on the death of the Christian God and the return of Dionysus. Man can become god only as a moment of the will to power understood as primordial music which wills its own deification and reconciliation as Dionysus or the eternal recurrence of the same.

THE ROMANTIC ORIGINS OF THE DIONYSIAN

Nietzsche's Dionysus is his ultimate answer to the nihilism of Christianity. But is this Dionysus in fact the true alternative to the Christian tradition? A full answer to this question is beyond the scope of this work, but in what follows, I will try to show that it is indebted in decisive ways to the Christian tradition as it manifests itself in Romanticism and German idealism.

It has often been asserted that Nietzsche is a Romantic, but this claim is rendered problematic by the fact that Nietzsche himself is so critical of Romanticism.[75] In his view, Romanticism and German idealism are the last remnants of Christian morality. That Nietzsche criticized Romanticism, however, does not prove that he was not a Romantic or that he was not deeply influenced by Romanticism. The Romanticism that Nietzsche knew and criticized was late Romanticism, and he apparently knew it primarily in its French and German forms.[76] Indeed, Wagner was his principal example. By contrast, he apparently knew little of the early Romanticism, with which he has the greatest affinity. Moreover, what he did know of these Romantics he often knew only at second hand, for example, from Goethe, whose own relationship to Romanticism was so ambivalent. Regardless of his knowledge of Romanticism, however, Nietzsche either does not understand or wants to conceal the ways in which his thought is indebted to early Romanticism. This is particularly true of his concept of the Dionysian.

The concept of the Dionysian first appeared in the eighteenth century in the work of Heinse, Hamann, and Herder.[77] Drawing on these works, Winckelmann gave the concept an aesthetic definition, setting up Apollo and Dionysus as types of ideal beauty in his *History of Ancient Art*, a work Nietzsche knew well. The concept was important for the early German Romantics. Fichte's student Friedrich Schlegel, for example, proclaimed Dionysus the god of immortal joy, wonderful fullness, and liberation.[78] Nietzsche probably did not know this work, but he was deeply influenced by the work of Schlegel's brother, August Wilhelm Schlegel, whose use of the concept was derivative from that of his brother.[79] Two other Fichte students, Novalis and Hölderlin, drawing on the mystery of bread and wine, identified Dionysus with Christ.[80] This identification was decisive for Romanticism and helped to legitimate Dionysus as the god of universal reconciliation.

The Romantics saw Dionysus as the apogee of Greek culture,

while the defenders of classicism regarded the Dionysian as a sickness. The principal defenders of the Romantic position were Georg Creuzer, who placed Greek, Egyptian, and Indian mysteries under the sway of Dionysus in his *Symbolism and Mythology of Ancient Nations,* and Joseph Görres, who described the mythical origin of the world as the epiphany of Dionysus. The foremost defender of the classical position was Johann Voss, who directed his *Antisymbolism* against Creuzer. Goethe followed this debate and it helped shape his notion of the antithesis of Romanticism and classicism, which had such a strong influence on Nietzsche.[81] Nietzsche borrowed Creuzer's work from the library during the latter stages of work on *The Birth,* but he was probably already well acquainted with this debate through his friend Johann Bachofen, who had asserted in his *Tomb Symbolism of the Ancients* that the principle of the inner unity in all cosmic life was passed over to Dionysus in the secret Orphic religion and that Dionysus united in himself a whole host of deities. Nietzsche also mentions Christian Lobeck's *Aglaophamus,* the Romantic response to Voss, in order to dismiss its account of the Dionysian as "contemptible babble" (*GD,* KGW VI 3:152–53).

The first philosopher to employ the term seriously was Schelling in his *Philosophy of Mythology.* He was probably acquainted with the concept through his brothers-in-law, the Schlegels. His account of Dionysus as the intoxicating power of poetic genius, and of Apollo as the reactive power of form that negates Dionysus, is astonishingly similar to Nietzsche's, but there is no evidence that Nietzsche read this work.[82] Like Bachofen, however, Schelling was heavily dependent on Creuzer. This Romantic vision of the Dionysian was silently adopted by Karl Müller in his *Handbook of the Archaeology of Art,* Ludwig Preller in his *Greek Mythology,* and Friedrich Welcker in his *Myths of the Greek Gods.* Nietzsche consulted the last two works while writing *The Birth.*

Despite his dependence on the Romantics, Nietzsche sees his concept of the Dionysian as anti-Romantic.[83] He apparently came to this conclusion because like Heine he rejected the Romantic identification of Dionysus and Christ.[84] In his *Gods in Exile,* Heine parodied the Romantic attempt to identify Dionysus and Christ, setting them in opposition to one another and portraying Dionysus as Mephistophelian, a seductive and immoral god.[85] The synthesis of Dionysus and the Crucified that many Romantics had accepted was thus transposed into an antithesis. This antithesis was popularized by Robert Hamerling in his best selling *Ahasuerus in Rome.* We know

Nietzsche read other works by Hamerling, and he may have read this one as well.

The initial source of Nietzsche's fascination with the Dionysian was probably Bonaventura Genelli's Romantic watercolor of Dionysus among the Muses which Nietzsche saw and discussed with the Wagners at Tribschen. Genelli derived the idea for his watercolor from the *Sturm und Drang* poet Maler Müller, who was an outspoken advocate of the demonic titanism so important to the early Romantics. Genelli was much taken with Müller's attribution of this wild and drunken freedom to Bacchus and sought to portray it in his watercolor.[86] For Nietzsche, this watercolor allegorized the transition from the barbarism that preceded the springtime of Homer, and Genelli's archaic Dionysus and Apollo are in this sense prototypes for Nietzsche.[87] This initial inspiration apparently led Nietzsche to the earlier sources on Dionysus.

Even this short discussion of the earlier history of the Dionysian reveals Nietzsche's great debt to the early German Romantics who had been inspired by Fichte. The extent of this debt becomes even clearer when we examine Creuzer's *Symbolism and Mythology*, which was central to the earlier understanding of the Dionysian. Creuzer, like Hegel and Schelling, worked within the framework of a Fichtean philosophy of absolute subjectivity.[88] Indeed, in his view, all religion is the progressive revelation of this absolute. The world is only the alienated self of the absolute, the not-I that has been created by the absolute I, to use Fichtean terminology, and the process by which this being reveals itself to man is also the process by which it comes back to itself and reconstitutes its lost unity. The history of religion in Creuzer's view is thus the history of the reconciliation of the absolute with itself.

Greek religion, for Creuzer, is one stage in the continuing revelation of the divine that began in ancient India. This oriental revelation came to the Greeks through the Egyptians and Orphic cults such as the Pythagoreans. At its center, Creuzer argues, was a god of gods whom the Indians called Vishnu, the Egyptians Osiris, and the Greeks Dionysus.[89] He was nature personified. Creuzer's account is at odds with the Greek view of Dionysus as the youngest of the gods, but he argues that Dionysus was seen as the youngest only because he arrived later in Greece than the other gods. In the original oriental revelation and in the mystery religion of the Greeks, he was recognized as original and supreme. He was able to attain this status, however, only by fighting a pitched battle against Apollo, whose light-worship had already long been established in Greece. The history of Greek religion is the history of Dionysus's conquest and subordination of Apollo.[90] Dionysus was thus recognized as the god who stands at the beginning of the world and is involved in its creation, as the overflowing power of nature, the one living being who creates the world out of his own abundance.[91] The other gods are mere moments of Dionysus, masks of this one true reality.[92] They and all individual beings are only the self-alienation of this primordial unity. Human beings are themselves thus moments of the godhead, of Dionysus, and consequently long to be reunited with him in the primordial unity.[93]

Dionysus, like Osiris, is thus the god of dispersion and reconciliation, who is repeatedly torn to pieces and repeatedly reborn.[94] His mysteries are a celebration of his return and reconstitution. Such a reconciliation, however, entails the negation of all individuality. The age of Dionysus, according to Creuzer, is thus the age of Shiva, the destroyer, who returns everything to primordial fire or becoming.[95]

Dionysian religion, however, cannot satisfy man's spiritual longing for reconciliation. Creuzer, like the idealists, believes that true reconciliation requires an act of the highest freedom in which that which is externalized by god out of his own being is again able to be in god. Reconciliation thus can never be brought about through nature, which always contains an element of necessity at odds with freedom and subjectivity. This great goal to which all religion aspires is finally achieved only by Christianity.[96] Dionysus must be repeatedly sacrificed and reborn to redeem the suffering of his worshipers because he is the deification of nature and is constrained by the cycles of nature. Christ, by contrast, represents true freedom because he rises above nature. His self-sacrifice is unique, made once and for all time. He thus promises his worshipers a redemption that frees them from the cycles of nature, from time, and from all suffering.

Like Hegel and Goethe, whom he admires, Creuzer thus subordinates the demonic to the divine. All of the earlier gods and Dionysus in particular are conceived as failed attempts to reconstitute the primordial unity and bring man into union with primordial being. Viewed from a divine perspective, these religions are the absolute's failed efforts to reconstitute the identity that was shattered by the creation of the world. For Creuzer, as for Fichte, the principle force in human life is thus longing, but in contrast to Fichte and more in the spirit of Hegel and Schelling, he believes that this longing does eventually find satisfaction in and through Christianity.

Even from this brief account, we can begin to see the many ways in which Nietzsche was indebted to the Romantic notion of Dionysus. Many of the principal features of Nietzsche's Dionysus are already present in Creuzer. In fact, Nietzsche and Creuzer really differ in only two crucial respects. First, Creuzer explicitly rejects the aesthetic reading of Dionysus that is so important to Nietzsche.[97] He thus barely mentions the connection of Dionysus to tragedy. Second, Nietzsche rejects Creuzer's vision of Dionysus as an imperfect approximation of the Christian God. Both of these differences are related. The Christian God in Nietzsche's view is the denial of tragedy, the flight from the contradictions of this world into a rational beyond. To see Dionysus as an imperfect version of the Christian God is thus possible only if one accepts the existence of the ideal or transcendent world that Christianity proclaims as reality. If such a world is only a fable, then Dionysus cannot be merely an imperfect Christian God. Indeed, the Christian God then appears as an imperfect form of Dionysus. Nietzsche suggests as much in a late note: "Let us remove supreme goodness from the concept of God: it is unworthy of a god. Let us also remove supreme wisdom: it is the vanity of philosophers that is to be blamed for this mad notion of a God as a monster of wisdom: he had to be as like them as possible. No! God the *supreme power*—that suffices! Everything follows from it, 'the world' follows from it!" (*NL,* KGW VIII 2:173; cf. 2:7, 201).

With the death of the Christian God, Dionysus in Nietzsche's view thus steps forth in his own right as the god of nature and of the cycles of nature, of birth, and death, and rebirth, as the god of tragedy and the god of comedy, in short as the god of life.

Nietzsche goes beyond Creuzer in important ways, drawing upon the anti-Romantic critique of Heine and others to transform the Romantic identification of Dionysus and Christ into an antithesis. The antithesis between Dionysus and Christ that Nietzsche constructs, however, conceals the underlying similarities between the two that are apparent in Creuzer and that Nietzsche silently adopts. Moreover, even those elements that Nietzsche believes crucially distinguish Dionysus from the Christian God are themselves ultimately derivative from this God understood in nominalist fashion as a God of will. Nietzsche, however, apparently did not recognize the formative role that this Christian God played in shaping his notion of the Dionysian because he did not understand the idealist origins of either the concept of the Dionysian or the notion of will that he imagines to be essential to the Dionysian. He believed, as we have seen, that his notion of the Dionysian and the will to power were novel and revolutionary. A closer examination of the genesis of this idea in German idealism, however, calls this claim into question as well.

NIETZSCHE'S DEBT TO SPECULATIVE IDEALISM

The question of Nietzsche's debt to speculative idealism has for the most part been reduced to the question of his debt to Hegel. This is hardly surprising, since twentieth-century scholarship has repeatedly portrayed Hegel as the culmination and completion of post-Kantian idealism. As we saw in chapters 3 and 4, however, such an account is an oversimplification that conceals the profound differences between post-Kantian idealists and especially between Fichte and Hegel. It was not Hegel but Fichte who redirected the Kantian revolution into a radical philosophy of will. Hegel, by contrast, tried to restrain the revolutionary voluntarism of Fichte by establishing a new synthesis of reason and will. As we saw in chapters 4–6, this attempt foundered because Hegel's speculative synthesis failed to convince his successors that the rational was actual and the actual rational. The general tendency to reduce all of speculative idealism to Hegel has thus concealed the debt of many of the anti-Hegelian thinkers of the nineteenth century to earlier idealists and to Fichte in particular. We have seen how the early German Romantics, the Left Hegelians, the Russian nihilists, and Schopenhauer operated within the unperceived horizon of the Fichtean philosophy of will. A similar argument can be made for Nietzsche as well.

Nietzsche was deeply indebted to the thought of German idealism in general and Fichte in particular. Nietzsche, however, never acknowledges this debt and may very well have been unaware of it. Neither Hegel nor Fichte were widely read in the 1860s and 1870s. Windelband remarked in 1878, for example, that the race who had read Hegel's *Phenomenology* was dying out. Nietzsche himself actually knew surprisingly little of the philosophic tradition. He read a number of the works of ancient philosophy and worked extensively on Diogenes Laertius's compendium of philosophic lives in the course of his philological studies, but his knowledge of medieval and modern philosophy was not extensive. He knew Schopenhauer, and had read some of Kant's *Critique of Judgment,* some of Montaigne, Spinoza, Voltaire, Rousseau, and Emerson, and a smattering of Hegel, Strauss, and Feuerbach.[98] The rest of his knowledge of this tradition he derived mainly from Schopenhauer, the neo-Kantian

Kuno Fischer, and the materialist Friedrich Lange. He read Hegel for a few weeks before he discovered Schopenhauer, but apparently never returned to his thought. His further knowledge of Hegel and the other German idealists was largely derived from the Left Hegelians and Schopenhauer and he generally accepts their distortions.[99] Nietzsche thus probably did not understand how his critique and transformation of Schopenhauer led him back to a Fichtean philosophy of will.[100] Whether Nietzsche understood his debt to this tradition, however, is not decisive. What really matters is that he is indebted to this tradition, for as we have seen, it is precisely this strain of modern thought that lies at the core of nihilism.

The problem that Nietzsche sets at the center of his thought is the death of God. He was certainly not the first to recognize this problem. Jacobi and Hegel, among others, were already aware of it. In their minds, it was intimately connected to the contradictions of modern thought that found their foremost expression in Kant's antinomies. It was these antinomies, in fact, that seemed to a whole generation of thinkers to open up an unbridgeable gap between God and man. If God was inaccessible to human reason, and divine will could have no effect upon the phenomenal world, then God was superfluous and, for all intents and purposes, dead.

Kant believed he had solved the problem of the antinomies with his transcendental idealism. To many of his immediate successors, however, he only bifurcated consciousness and rendered it contradictory. The antinomies and Kant's proposed solution to them seemed to split the world in two. Speculative idealism sought to resolve this problem by reunifying the world. Fichte believed this could be achieved by demonstrating that the phenomenal world is not independent, as Kant had asserted, but is in reality the product of an absolute will. For Hegel, reconciliation is achieved by spelling out the dialectical rationality that arises from the *necessity* of the contradiction at the heart of the antinomies.

Nietzsche too sees the antinomies as the decisive turning point in European thinking, but he sees them not as a tremendous problem but as a great opportunity—the long tyranny of reason is coming to an end and a radically new creation may soon be possible. He thus does not want to restore and perfect the lost unity of reason, but to raise humanity to new and glorious heights on the wings of his musical philosophy. Following Schopenhauer, he sees idealism as a reversion to the illusions of a Platonized Christianity: "Fichte, Schelling, Hegel, Feuerbach, Strauss.—all stink of theologians and church fathers" (*NL,* GA 13:14). While he too seeks reconciliation, it is an aesthetic reconciliation that aims not at eliminating contradictions but at harmonizing and ennobling them.

He rejects the Hegelian conclusion that what is rational is actual and what is actual is rational: "In contrast to Hegel's attempt to bring reason into the notion of development, I see logic itself as a kind of unreason and accident" (*NL,* KGW 2:251). In his view, there is no final reconciliation. The Dionysian is a contradictory unity that repeatedly reconstitutes and repeatedly shatters itself. It is the will to power that constantly seeks to overcome itself, to exceed itself, to encompass more and more of existence, but that in its very success turns against itself and destroys itself. The Dionysian unity of the will to power is thus a fractured unity and it provides the foundation for a tragic, not a rational, age. Hegel's optimistic logic, in Nietzsche's view, is incompatible with such tragic wisdom and thus cannot provide the foundation for the culture Nietzsche hopes to establish.[101] Nietzsche's rejection of Hegel thus parallels that of the Left Hegelians, and like them he thereby returns, in a way he almost certainly does not understand, to Fichte.[102]

There are many similarities between Nietzsche and Fichte. Perhaps the most obvious is that both place the will at the center of their account of the world. This fact, however, is often discounted because of the widespread assumption that Nietzsche and Fichte operate within radically different frameworks. Fichte's thought, according to this view, is a philosophy of consciousness, while Nietzsche's thinking begins and ends with the pre- or subconscious world of passions, instincts, and affects.[103] The meaning and function of the will within their respective philosophies is thus held to be radically different. Such an assumption, however, is mistaken. They are in fact much closer to one another than is generally assumed.

In his early thought Nietzsche often employs the conceptual framework of German idealism.[104] His description of Dionysus as an absolute subject in *The Birth* is typical and indicative of his debt to Fichte. Dionysus for Nietzsche is the "world genius," the "primordial artist of the world," who at the most fundamental level posits himself as an absolute I through the Dionysian poet (*GT,* KGW III 1:40, 43). In conceptual language reminiscent of Fichte and Hegel, Nietzsche characterizes him as the "one truly existent subject" who is "both subject and object" (*GT,* KGW III 1:43). His earlier discussion of Dionysus is thus shaped by the categories of German idealism. Dionysus is the absolute subject or absolute I whose essence is will, who is the source of the distinction between subject and object as well as the basis for their reconciliation, and who is both the whole and all individual beings. It may be that Nietzsche relies here more on Creuzer and the Romantics than on Hegel or Fichte, but as we have seen, this Romantic notion of the Dionysian is itself deeply indebted to Fichte, Schelling, and Hegel. German idealism in this way sets the framework for Nietzsche's project.

It is true that during his middle period, Nietzsche distances himself from the subjectivistic framework of this artists' metaphysics and turns to an investigation of the ways in which such subjectivity itself is guided and misguided by subconscious passions and drives. Even this psychological investigation, however, remains within the wider Fichtean orbit. As we saw in chapter 3, Fichte is not simply a philosopher of consciousness. His analysis of the decisive role of practical reason is in fact an analysis of what goes on *behind* consciousness. In his view, we come to understand the absolute will in the most profound sense not as knowing beings but as feeling beings. Nietzsche's investigation of the feelings or passions is clearly more concrete and materialistic than Fichte's, but it follows the same path. Fichte was one of the first to turn to this preconscious level and to identify it with the will. His thought is thus one of the important but most concealed sources of the psychological approach that later thinkers such as Nietzsche employed more openly and to greater effect. Nietzsche recognized that his concept of the will was indebted to Schopenhauer, but he rightly felt that he had turned Schopenhauer's notion of will on its head. In his hands, Schopenhauer's resignation became absolute affirmation. He apparently did not understand, however, the way in which his reversal of Schopenhauer was a reversal of Schopenhauer's reversal of Fichte that brought him full circle back to Fichte. Nietzsche in this respect simply accepted Schopenhauer's claim that he had originated this philosophy of will.

Nietzsche's debt to Fichte becomes more pronounced in his late thought. His turn toward a more metaphysical interpretation of the will after *The Gay Science* makes the connection to Fichte even more apparent. For both Fichte and Nietzsche, the will is a complex phenomenon. As the absolute I, the Fichtean will is dispersed into the multiplicity of human beings (the empirical I) and individual natural entities (the not-I) and constantly attempts to reestablish its lost unity. It pursues this goal through individual human beings, who experience this impulse as a longing for reconciliation that drives them to overturn all obstacles to union with the absolute, to eliminate all otherness, and to construct ever grander concepts, images, and forms in an attempt to encompass the infinite. The will for Fichte in this sense is thetic, that is, it establishes or sets itself in opposition to the other, that is, as the antithesis of the empirical I and the not-I. As such, conflict and the struggle for dominance is essential, and it is through this struggle that the will is able to obliterate the otherness of nature and encompass it within the expanding sphere of the self. For Nietzsche, the Dionysian will to power is constantly dispersed into centers of power that strive to master and subordinate one another. This struggle, however, is also the subliminal striving of the will to reconstitute its lost unity, to reconstitute Dionysus. Like Fichte's will, the will to power is thetic, or, to use Nietzsche's own terminology, poetic. "The world," Nietzsche asserts, "is a self-generating work of art" (*NL*, KGW VIII 1:117). It too sets or establishes itself and the forms of its existence in opposition to others. As the will to power, however, Dionysus works through all things to reconstitute himself by conquering and subordinating all beings within an ever more encompassing structure of power.

In his later thought, it is not so much the I or the subject that comes to the fore but nature understood as the will to power. In this respect, Nietzsche moves away from his subjectivistic Fichtean beginning in the direction of Schelling's philosophy of nature, which identifies will with primal being. Schelling's movement toward a vision of nature as the absolute, however, did not seek to eliminate subjectivity. It was rather an attempt to discern the absolute I in and through the not-I rather than the empirical I, that is, in and through the natural world rather than the self. It was still an effort to see all beings as the manifestation of the absolute will. Thus, for Schelling nature as a whole took on the character of a self or a god. Despite his differences with Fichte, his thought remains within the orbit of absolute subjectivity.

Nietzsche, like Fichte, Schelling, and Hegel, conceives of all human and all natural beings as projections or emanations of the absolute will. Like them, he also assumes that the relationships between these beings are governed by the oppositions within this will and the will's primordial impulse toward self-reconciliation, although he typically understands this reconciliation more as self-conquest than as joyful reunion. During his middle period, he places more weight on the individual wills and their efforts to project a whole, than on the will's efforts to reconstitute itself through the individual wills; but with his formulation of the notion of the will to power and the eternal recurrence, he returns to a more unified notion. Finally, Nietzsche's return to Dionysus in the last years of his creative life is at least a partial indication that he too continues to conceive of this will not merely as universal substance but also as a kind of self or subject. Indeed, in Nietzsche's later thought, this idealist vision of the absolute is conjoined with the Romantic notion of Dionysus as the god of gods who creates the world out of himself and constantly reunites it in himself. As we have seen, however, it was just this Romantic vision of Dionysus that was so deeply indebted to Fichte.

While there are many similarities between Nietzsche and Fichte, and Nietzsche and the German idealism in general, Nietzsche's voluntarism is ultimately more radical than any of his idealist predecessors, including Fichte. This is especially apparent in their contrasting views of teleology.[105] Fichte, for example, sets a specific goal for human striving in the complete reconciliation of the empirical I and the absolute I, which is to be achieved by the elimination of the not-I or natural world. While Fichte admits that this goal can never be attained, he believes that it should direct human striving. His thought is thus at least implicitly teleological. Nietzsche, by contrast, is convinced that we cannot know such a final goal because such a goal does not exist. For Fichte, the absolute establishes itself once and for all time; for Nietzsche this "absolute," as Dionysus or the will to power or primordial music, must constantly reestablish itself and does so in ever changing forms.

Nietzsche recognized that such an uncompromisingly antiteleological doctrine reduces everything to the antagonistic chaos of pure becoming. He thus reinstituted an attenuated teleological element with his doctrine of the eternal recurrence. Insofar as the eternal recurrence defines an ontology, Nietzsche steps back from the complete rejection of the essential relationship between unity and being. Understood in even the most orthodox metaphysical sense, however, the eternal recurrence is little more than a great circle around becoming. It may posit a whole, but it determines no specific content or order within that whole. Thus, in contrast to Fichte's absolute I, the eternal recurrence does not define a specific order or purpose and consequently cannot impose a moral duty or obligation. What happens, happens; and it happens over and over again for all time. The appropriate stance toward existence is thus either resignation or affirmation, the rejection of existence or *amor fati*. Schopenhauer chose the former; Nietzsche, for reasons we have discussed, the latter. He believed it to be the highest Dionysian stance toward life (*NL,* KGW VIII 3:285).

Nietzsche's antiteleological stance follows from his assertion of the aesthetic character of existence. His fundamental principle is a cosmic artist. Being for him is power *(dynamis)* or energy *(energeia)* because it is the product of *poiēsis.*[106] As a self-generating work of art, nature is an artistic will that constantly but unsuccessfully attempts to represent its own infinity in finite forms.[107] While this conception of the absolute will as a maker rather than a knower, or as a poet rather than a philosopher, is strongly reminiscent of German idealism, it actually moves beyond even the most radical forms of idealism in its assertion of this will's power and scope. Here Nietzsche is closer to Schopenhauer and the Romantics. For Nietzsche as for Schopenhauer, the will can do anything. By contrast, even Fichte, who granted the absolute a broader scope than any of his contemporaries, believed that the self-production of the absolute was in large measure limited by its own previous determinations. It created the world out of itself by a self-negation and was constrained in its further creation by the structure of the world it had created. It acted not by obliterating the world and creating it anew but by modifying the world it had already established. All change, according to idealism, is thus the result of determinate rather than absolute negation and consequently follows a dialectical path. Nietzsche, by contrast, imagines that the Dionysian will is radically free and is not bound by its past actions. Change is the result not of determinate negation but of absolute negation. The will levels the ground completely to open a space for the spontaneous generation of a radically new possibility. For Nietzsche, nihilism is such a leveling and it thus heralds a new dawn. Nietzsche's path in this respect parallels that of Bazarov, Bakunin, and Nechaev.

Nietzsche, however, is even more radical than his Russian predecessors. His turn away from logic and dialectic to music propels him beyond them. While he adopts the general goal of reconciliation that characterized German idealism and its nineteenth-century progeny, he cannot specify any particular form of reconciliation as superior to any other. There is not one goal or one path to this goal, because the end is not the true but the beautiful and there are many forms of beauty and many different ways of constructing the beautiful.[108] In the words of Zarathustra, "There are yet many houses to be built" (KGW VI 1:145). There are many different melodies that can harmonize contradictions. While the will constantly strives for a musical reconciliation, it strives in many different directions. While it is guided by the intrinsic order of music, it pursues only momentary fancies and not final purposes. Because it has no real goal, it also has no real work. In its cosmic activity, it is play, a "world-game" (*GT,* KGW III 1:149; cf. *PTZG,* KGW III 2:322). Through art and the artistic genius, man can participate in this game not merely as a piece on the board but as a player, and can take pleasure in the game even when he and his fellow pieces are annihilated.

This element in Nietzsche's thought has played a central role in the postmodern enterprise. For Deleuze and others, it is this element that most distinguishes Nietzsche from the whole philosophic tradition that finds its last refuge in Hegelian dialectic.[109] It is also a central element in their efforts to construct a postmodern way of thinking that is liberated from the confining conceptual net of traditional philosophic thought. Although the notion of will as capricious activity is clearly at odds with the teleology of German idealism, we cannot therefore conclude that it is a radically new idea. In fact, the vision of such a capricious transrational will, as we have seen, was intrinsic to the nominalist notion of God. He was the transrational creator of the world, beyond all teleology, and beyond all good and evil. His creation too was a kind of divine play, a play of indifference. Nietzsche's rejection of teleology thus may lead him away from modern philosophy, but only because this rejection rests upon premodern premises. Even in his most radical incarnation as the world-game or pure music, Dionysus remains within the horizon of the philosophy of will that had its origins in the omnipotent God of nominalism.

The philosophic debate that has raged around Nietzsche's work in recent years turns on the question of the relationship of his thought to modernity and the principle element of modern thought, subjectivity. Heidegger, as we have seen, tried to argue that Nietzsche remains entwined in metaphysics, while postmodernist thinkers have drawn heavily upon Nietzsche in their efforts to obliterate the subject. Nietzsche's Dionysus, however, is both modern and postmodern, both Cartesian and post-Cartesian.[110] Dionysus begins with but also passes beyond the realm of subjectivity that Descartes established as the home of modern man. The postmodern element in Nietzsche's thought, however, is in many respects unknowingly premodern, drawing upon the nominalist notion of will. Dionysus in this sense is not a new God who rises up to replace the old God who has died, but that old God, who appears under a new mask. Dionysus, for Nietzsche, was the solution to nihilism, which he saw as the final form of Christianity. We have seen that Nietzsche was mistaken about the origins of nihilism and we see here that he was equally mistaken about its solution, for his Dionysus is not the great antagonist of the Christian God but only his most recent incarnation.[111]

Epilogue

At the end of modernity among the twilit ruins of the citadel of reason, the victor in the great battle for control of the Cartesian fortress sits atop a pile of rubble, crowned with the leaves of the vine, singing the song of primal unity and primal contradiction, looking with steely eyes toward the horizon and dreaming of new conquests. He bears a surprising resemblance to the omnipotent God of Christianity, his supposed enemy and opponent. Like that God, he is beyond reason, beyond nature, and beyond good and evil. He calls into question all that is stable and certain. He is a god of terror and of joy. He is everything's creator, everything's destroyer, and everything's redeemer.

Modernity was a response to the breakdown of the scholastic synthesis of reason and revelation and the assertion of a new idea of God in late medieval Christianity. This new nominalist God was a terrifying, transrational, transnatural God of will, an omnipotent God whose absolute power reduced nature to a chaos of radically individual and unconnected beings. This idea of God in combination with the Black Death and the papal schism brought the medieval world to an end and left man afloat in an infinite and incomprehensible universe with no guarantee of happiness in this world or the next.

Descartes constructed his bastion of reason to shield man from this god and to establish a certain and secure citadel from which to undertake the conquest of the natural world. He was able to accomplish this, however, only by attributing to man the same infinite will that had proven so problematic in God. In this way, will was established as the foundation of modern reason. This notion of will, which remained implicit in Descartes' thought, became increasingly explicit in continental thought from Fichte to Nietzsche. The history of nihilism is the history of the development of this notion of will. The crucial step in this process was Fichte's idea of an absolute I or absolute will that manifests itself in the opposition of the I and the not-I

255

and that constantly strives for reconciliation with itself by attempting to eliminate the not-I.

It was this idea of an absolute will that gave birth to the idea of nihilism, for if the I is everything, then, as Jacobi pointed out, God is nothing. Nihilism, as it was originally understood, was thus not the result of the degeneration of man and his concomitant inability to sustain a God. It was rather the consequence of the assertion of an absolute human will that renders God superfluous and thus for all intents and purposes dead. For Fichte himself, however, the absolute I cannot be equated with the human will or even with the will of humanity as a whole. Indeed, in his later thought Fichte actually calls this absolute I "God."

The transformation of this notion of the absolute I into an absolute human will was the work of Fichte's students, the early German Romantics, who depicted the striving to attain such an absolute will in their demonic heros. While both Goethe and Hegel had serious misgivings about this demonic titanism and attempted to constrain it, they were also attracted to it. Ironically, it was through their efforts to constrain this Fichtean will that it became a world-historical force, first as Left Hegelianism and then as Russian nihilism.

Fichte also exercised a decisive influence on Schopenhauer's notion of the will to life. In contrast to Fichte, Schopenhauer saw the striving that was essential to the will not as a noble moral task but as an illusion meant to draw man into a purposeless existence that was nothing other than the criminal war of all against all. The solution to the problems that bedeviled human life was thus resignation. This Schopenhauerian notion of the will in turn informed Nietzsche's notion of the Dionysian will to power. Nietzsche rejected Schopenhauer's pessimistic reading of the will and argued that the will in its strength was able to affirm even the most abysmal possibilities. Nietzsche's reversal of Schopenhauer, however, is only a reversal of Schopenhauer's reversal of Fichte, and Nietzsche in this way unknowingly returns to a Fichtean position. This is the basis for his notion of the Dionysian. Nietzsche, however, moves beyond Fichte in decoupling this Dionysian will from even dialectical reason and tying it to music. In this respect, however, he returns full circle to the notion of the omnipotent will with which we began. Nietzsche's purported solution to nihilism is thus intimately bound up with the notion of will that lies at the heart of nihilism.

The history of modern thought has thus been the ever more explicit revelation of the hidden foundation of modern reason in will.

From another perspective, however, this is the history of the recon-
quest of the bastion of reason by the omnipotent God behind the
mask of human will. At the end of modernity, we are thus brought
face to face with this dark God that modernity was constructed to
constrain. The possibility of coming to terms with modernity or pass-
ing beyond it depends upon our capacity to face this question.

List of Abbreviations

DESCARTES

AT   *Oeuvres de Descartes,* ed. Charles Adam and Paul Tannery, 13 vols. (Paris: Vrin, 1957–68)

CSM   *The Philosophical Writings of Descartes,* trans. John Cottingham, Robert Stoothoff, and Dugald Murdoch, 2 vols. (Cambridge: Cambridge University Press, 1985)

FICHTE

BG   *Die Bestimmung eines Gelehrten*

NR   *Grundlage des Naturrechts*

RDN   *Reden an die deutsche Nation*

SK   *Science of Knowledge*

SS   *Das System der Sittenlehre*

SW   *Johann Gottlieb Fichte's sämmtliche Werke,* ed. I. H. Fichte, 8 vols. (Berlin: Veit, 1845–46)

WL   *Grundlage der gesamten Wissenschaftslehre*

GUTZKOW

N   *Die Nihilisten* (1853), in *Gutzkows Werke,* ed. Reinhold Genfel, 12 vols. (Berlin: Bong, 1910), 5:181–274.

KANT

KrV   *Kritik der reinen Vernunft*

NIETZSCHE

AC   *Der AntiChrist*

BA   *Historische-Kritische-Gesamtausgabe,* 5 vols. (Munich: Beck, 1934–49)

DW   *Die dionysische Weltanschauung*

EH   *Ecce Homo*

FW   *Der Fröhliche Wissenschaft*

GA   *Werke: Grossoktavausgabe,* 2nd ed., 19 vols. (Leipzig: Kroner, 1901–13)

GD	*Götzen-Dämmerung*
GM	*Zur Genealogie der Moral*
GS	*Der Griechische Staat*
GT	*Die Geburt der Tragödie*
HW	*Homers Wettkampf*
JGB	*Jenseits von Gut und Böse*
KGB	*Nietzsche Briefwechsel: Kritische Gesamtausgabe,* ed. G. Colli and M. Montinari, 18 vols. in 3 parts and one supplement (Berlin: de Gruyter, 1975–84)
KGW	*Werke: Kritische Gesamtausgabe,* ed. Giorgio Colli and Mazzino Montinari (Berlin: de Gruyter, 1967–).
M	*Morgenröthe*
MusA	*Gesammelte Werke,* 23 vols. (Munich: Musarion, 1920–29)
NcW	*Nietzsche contra Wagner*
NL	*Nachlass*
PTZG	*Die Philosophie im tragischen Zeitalter der Griechen*
RU	*Rythmische Untersuchungen*
UB	*Unzeitgemässe Betrachtungen*
W	*Der Fall Wagner*
WS	*Der Wanderer und sein Schatten*
Z	*Also Sprach Zarathustra*

SCHOPENHAUER

HN	*Der handschriftliche Nachlass,* ed. A. Hübscher, 5 vols. (Frankfurt am Main: Kramer, 1966–75; reprint ed. 1985)
WWR	*The World as Will and Representation,* trans. E. F. J. Payne, 2 vols. (New York: Dover, 1966)
WWV	*Die Welt als Wille und Vorstellung,* in *Werke in fünf Bänden,* ed. Ludger Lutkehaus, 5 vols. (Berlin: Haym, 1851; reprint ed. Zürich: Haffman, 1988)

TURGENEV

FAS	*Fathers and Sons, The Author on the Novel, Contemporary Reactions, Essays in Criticism,* ed. and trans. Ralph E. Matlaw (New York: Norton, 1966)

Notes

INTRODUCTION

1. All references to Nietzsche's works list title, edition, and relevant division, volume, and page numbers. See List of Abbreviations.

2. On this point, see my "History and Temporality in the Thought of Heidegger," *Revue Internationale de Philosophie* 43 (1989): 33–51.

3. Hans Blumenberg, *The Legitimacy of the Modern Age,* trans. Robert W. Wallace (Cambridge: M.I.T. Press, 1983).

4. Bernard Yack, *The Longing for Total Revolution: Philosophic Sources of Social Discontent from Rousseau to Marx and Nietzsche* (Princeton, NJ: Princeton University Press, 1986).

CHAPTER ONE

1. All references to Descartes' works list title, edition, volume, and page numbers. See List of Abbreviations. I have occasionally modified the English translation in keeping with my reading of the French or Latin.

2. See Hiram Caton, *The Origin of Subjectivity: An Essay on Descartes* (New Haven: Yale University Press, 1973), 40, 63, 65.

3. See Descartes to Mersenne, March 1637; and to Vatuer, 22 February 1638, AT, 1:363, 365, 560–61.

4. This reading has been developed in different ways by such scholars as Louis Laird, Charles Adam, Etienne Gilson, Lucien Laberthonnière, Jean Laport, Hiram Caton, Richard Kennington, and Stanley Rosen.

5. This position has been defended by Alfred Espinas, Alexander Koyré, Henri Gouhier, and Jean-Luc Marion, among others.

6. Descartes to Mersenne, 14 August 1634, 22 June 1637, and 11 October 1638, AT, 1:305, 392; 2:380.

7. The account is actually an idealization of his life experience. See Harry Frankfurt, *Demons, Dreamers, and Madmen: The Defense of Reason in Descartes' Meditations* (Indianapolis: Bobbs-Merrill, 1970), 5.

8. Frankfort, *Demons,* 9.

9. See ibid., 40.

10. Even if we regard dreams as forms of *divine deception,* as the Stoics held, they are not sufficient to engender truly radical doubt because they cannot bring us to doubt the laws of mathematics. Leo Groarke, "Descartes'

First Meditation: Something Old, Something New, Something Borrowed," *Journal of the History of Philosophy* 22, no. 3 (July 1984): 287.

11. Frankfurt, *Demons*, 74.

12. See Karlo Oedingen, "Der genius malignus et summe potens et callidus bei Descartes," *Kant-Studien* 50 (1958–59): 178–87. Relying on the fact that God is not mentioned in the sentence in which our knowledge of mathematical truths is called into question, some scholars have argued that Descartes suggests only that God may have distorted nature and thus made Cartesian science impossible, but that God has not distorted human beings in such a way that they are incapable of grasping mathematical truths. This argument, however, overlooks the sentence earlier in the paragraph where Descartes refers to a God who has created him "such as I am" and the sentence following the passage quoted above in which he clearly points to the fact that God may have created him in such a way that he could not err. Even if God does not call mathematical truth into question in the First Meditation, he certainly does in the Third. Descartes notes there that he might doubt mathematical truths for no other reason than that "some God could have given me a nature such that I was deceived even in matters which seemed most evident." AT, 7:36; CSM, 2:25.

13. Richard Popkin argues that while Descartes begins from the Academic skepticism of Montaigne and Charron, the notion of a divine deceiver leads him to a new and deeper skeptical doubt. *The History of Skepticism from Erasmus to Spinoza* (Berkeley: University of California Press, 1979), 178–79.

14. Pascal, *Pensées*, ed. H. F. Stewart (New York: Pantheon, 1950), 147–53, 434; Hume, *Enquiry Concerning Human Understanding* (London: Oxford University Press, 1975), 150.

15. See, for example, O. K. Bouwsma's "Descartes' Evil Genius," in *Meta-Meditations: Studies in Descartes,* ed. Alexander Sesonske and Noel Fleming (Belmont, CA: Wadsworth, 1965).

16. Gérard Simon has argued that Descartes had to reject this position, which he discerned in Copernicus's view that the world was created by the most perfect of artists and in Kepler's notion that God himself could not distort the laws of mathematics, because it was a danger not merely to religion but to physics. "Les vérités éternelles de Descartes, évidences ontologiques," *Studia Cartesiana* 2 (1981): 133.

17. For a defense of this position, see Caton, *The Origin of Subjectivity;* Richard Kennington, "The 'Teaching of Nature' in Descartes' Soul Doctrine," *Review of Metaphysics* 26 (September 1972): 104; and Walter Soffer, *From Science to Subjectivity: An Interpretation of Descartes' Meditations* (New York: Greenwood, 1987), 19–40.

18. There has been considerable debate about the relationship of this so-called demon-doubt to the doubt evoked by the deceiver God and the atheist-doubt just mentioned. See Caton, *Origin of Subjectivity,* 119. Following Kenny and Röd, Caton identifies the evil genius with the deceiver God. Antony Kenny, *Descartes: A Study in His Philosophy* (New York: Random

House, 1968); Wolfgang Röd, *Descartes: Die innere Genesis des cartesianischen Systems* (Basel: Reinhardt, 1964). Caton argues persuasively that Descartes uses the phrase *genius malignus* for *deus deceptor* to avoid the charge of blasphemy. *Origins of Subjectivity,* 120. Richard Kennington has presented the strongest argument for separating the two, based on the fact that Descartes never describes the *genius malignus* as omnipotent but only as very powerful. "The Finitude of Descartes' Evil Genius," *Journal of the History of Ideas* 32 (1971): 441–46. See also his exchange with Caton in the *Journal of the History of Ideas* 34 (1973): 639–44. This distinction is rendered problematic, however, by Descartes' reference to this question at the beginning of the Second Meditation. While the French translation refers to "some God or some other power" the more authoritative Latin original refers to "a God, or whatever I may call him." AT, 7:24; CSM, 2:16.

19. See Frankfurt, *Demons,* 91–112.

20. Amos Funkenstein, *Theology and the Scientific Imagination from the Middle Ages to the Seventeenth Century* (Princeton: Princeton University Press, 1986), 128.

21. Joseph Michael Incandela, "Aquinas's Lost Legacy: God's Practical Knowledge and Situated Human Freedom" (Ph.D. dissertation, Princeton University, 1986), 82–83.

22. Edward Grant, "The Effect of the Condemnation of 1277," in *The Cambridge History of Later Medieval Philosophy,* ed. Norman Kretzmann et al. (London: Cambridge University Press, 1982), 537–39.

23. The term 'nominalist' was apparently first used in the twelfth century to describe a particular stance on universals, but fell into disuse around 1270 and did not reappear until the fifteenth century when it was employed as another name for the *via moderna,* the new philosophical method that departed from the *via antiqua* of Aristotle and the Aristotelian scholastics. William Courtenay, "Nominalism and Late Medieval Religion," in *The Pursuit of Holiness in Late Medieval and Renaissance Religion,* ed. Charles Trinkaus and Heiko Oberman (Leiden: Brill, 1974), 52–53.

24. On analogy in Aquinas, see Hampus Byttbens, *The Analogy between God and the World: An Investigation of Its Background and Interpretation of Its Use by Thomas of Aquino* (Uppsala: Almqvist & Wiksells, 1952).

25. Peter Damiani defended this radical position that God was not bound by the law of contradiction in the eleventh century, but this view was repudiated by all other medieval philosophers, including Scotus and Ockham. See Marilyn McCord Adams, *William Ockham,* 2 vols. (Notre Dame: University of Notre Dame Press), 2:1153.

26. Jurgen Miethke, *Ockhams Weg zur Sozialphilosophie* (Berlin: de Gruyter, 1969), 141–42; Erich Hochstetter, "Nominalismus?" *Franciscan Studies* 9 (1949): 374–75.

27. Albert S. *Th.* I m II tr. 19 qu. 77, *Opera omnia,* ed. A. Borgnet (Paris, 1890–99); *III Sent.* d. 20 b, a. 2; Thomas S. *Th.* I qu. 25 a. 5 ad 1. See also Ernst Borchert, "Der Einfluss des Nominalismus auf die Christologie der

Spätscholastik nach dem Traktat de Communicatione Idiomatum des Nicolaus Oresme," *Beiträge zur Geschichte der Philosophie und Theologie des Mittelalters* 35, no. 4/5 (1940): 50–54.

28. Bonaventure, *Opera Omnia,* ed. Collegium Sti. Bonaventurae, 10 vols. (Quarcchi and Florence: Collegii S. Bonaventure, 1882–1902), 5:216a.

29. See Adams, *Ockham,* 2:1180; and Georg Freiherr von Hertling, "Descartes' Beziehung zur Scholastik," Kgl. Bayerische Akad. d. Wissenschaften in München, *Sitzungsber d. philos.-histor. Klasse* (1897): 14–15.

30. *Opera omnia,* ed. K. Balic (Rome: Typis Polyglottis Vaticanis, 1950–), 6:364–68.

31. While there are many important differences among nominalist thinkers, they are all united at least on the centrality of divine freedom and omnipotence. See Courtenay, "Nominalism"; and the responses of Charles Davis, "Ockham and the Zeitgeist"; and Paul Kristeller, "The Validity of the Term: 'Nominalism," in *The Pursuit of Holiness,* ed. Trinkaus and Oberman, 26–66; as well as Heiko Oberman, "Some Notes on the Theology of Nominalism with Attention to Its Relation to the Renaissance," *Harvard Theological Review* 53 (1960): 47–76.

32. Henning Graf Reventlow, *The Authority of the Bible and the Rise of the Modern World* (Philadelphia: Fortress, 1985), 35.

33. Adams, *Ockham,* 2:1201.

34. Ibid. 1257.

35. Léon Baudry, Philotheus Boehner, Jürgen Miethke, and Marilyn McCord Adams have played an important roll in reshaping our understanding of Ockham.

36. Ockham *I Sent.* d. 43 qu. 2F, *Opera philosophica et theologica,* ed. Stephen Brown (New York: St. Bonaventure Press, 1967). See A. B. Wolter, "Ockham and the Textbooks: On the Origin of Possibility," *Franziskanische Studien* 32 (1950): 70–92; Miethke, *Ockhams Weg,* 139–40; William of Ockham, *Philosophical Writings,* ed. and trans. Philotheus Boehner (London: Thomas Nelson & Sons, 1957), xix; and Blumenberg, *Legitimacy,* 161–62.

37. William of Ockham, *Predestination, God's Foreknowledge, and Future Contingents,* ed. and trans. Marilyn McCord Adams and Norman Kretzmann, 2nd ed. (Indianapolis: Hackett, 1983), 13.

38. Ockham *I Sent* d. 42 qu. A-F; Scotus *Rep. Par.* I d. 17 qu. I n. 7. See also Miethke, *Ockhams Weg,* 157; Blumenberg, *Legitimacy,* 189; Boehner, ed., *Philosophical Writings,* xix.

39. *I Sent.* d. 4 qu. U.H. (ad 2 m).

40. Blumenberg, *Legitimacy,* 174–77.

41. See Martin Tweedale, "Scotus and Ockham on the Infinity of the Most Eminent Being," *Franciscan Studies* 23 (1963): 257–67.

42. Ockham *I Sent.* d. 35 qu. 2 C; and *II Sent.* qu. 4–5 D-E (*II-IV Sent.* in *Opera plurima,* Lyon, 1494–96). See also Etienne Gilson, *A Gilson Reader,* ed. Anton C. Pegis (Garden City, NY: Hanover House, 1957), 134.

43. Adams, *Ockham,* 2:1050.

44. Funkenstein points out that this principle of annihilation is used to

determine the reality of any thing: "Every absolute thing, distinct in subject and place from another absolute thing, can exist by divine power even while [any] other absolute thing is destroyed." *Theology*, 135. This principle, consistently applied, eliminates all universals. For Ockham, in Funkenstein's view, only those things are truly things that can be conceived *toto mundo destructo*. Ibid. See also André Goddu, *The Physics of William of Ockham* (Leiden and Cologne: Brill, 1984).

45. *I Sent.* d. 2 qu. 6 F.

46. See Jean Largeault, *Enquête sur le nominalisme* (Paris and Louvain: Beatrice-Nauwelaerts, 1971), 154.

47. Adams, *Ockham*, 2:1036–56.

48. *II Sent.* qu. 14–15 D; qu. 17 Q; qu. 18 E, F; qu. 22 D; qu. 24 Q; *IV Sent.* qu. 3 N, qu. 8–9 O. Blumenberg points out that this principle does not follow from the fact that God is economical but from the fact that man is finite. *Legitimacy*, 154. Hence its fuller form reads: "No plurality should be assumed unless it can be proved by reason, or by experience, or by some infallible authority." *Ord.* I, d. 30, qu. 1.

49. *II Sent.* qu. 14–15 Z.

50. See Miethke, *Ockhams Weg*, 192.

51. *Sent.* Prol. qu. 1, KK. See David W. Clark, "Ockham on Human and Divine Freedom," *Franciscan Studies* 38 (1978): 130.

52. Ockham at times considers the possibility of natural signification but does not develop this idea more fully. Stephen Tornay, *The Nominalism of William of Ockham* (Chicago: University of Chicago Libraries, 1936), 260, 266.

53. On Ockham's concept of knowledge, see Miethke, *Ockhams Weg*, 245–99; Philotheus Boehner, "The Notitia Intuitiva of Non-Existents According to William of Ockham," *Traditio* 1 (1943): 223–75; and Sebastian Day, *Intuitive Cognition: A Key to the Significance of the Later Scholastics* (St. Bonaventure, NY: Franciscan Institute, 1947).

54. *I Sent.* d. 30 qu. 1 E; *III Sent.* qu. 8 D.

55. Miethke, *Ockhams Weg*, 227, 275, 284; Blumenberg, *Legitimacy*, 164; Tweedale, "Scotus and Ockham," 265.

56. See Adams, *Ockham*, 2:795. Nature for Ockham is reduced to matter in motion that can be grasped only quantitatively in terms of its extension. *I Summ. Phys.* 14 (*Philosophia Naturalis Guilielmi Occham*, Rome, 1637). See Meyrick H. Carré, *Realists and Nominalists* (Oxford: Oxford University Press, 1946), 119; Tornay, *Nominalism of Ockham*, 36.

57. See Gilson, *Reader*, 138.

58. Carré, *Realists and Nominalists*, 121.

59. *Predestination*, esp. 11, 16, and 28. See also Adams, *Ockham*, 2:1149.

60. See Miethke, *Ockhams Weg*, 312–13.

61. *IV Sent.* q. 14 D (ad 5 um).

62. Adams, *Ockham*, 2:1257–1337.

63. *Contra Ben.* IV 1–15, *Opera politica*, ed. J. G. Sikes and H. S. Offler, 3 vols. (Manchester: University of Manchester, 1940–63); *Comp. Err.* c. 8,

Monarchia S. Romani Imperii, ed. M. Goldast (Frankfurt am Main, 1614); *Brev. II* 13, V 4, *Wilhelm von Ockham als politischer Denker und sein Breviloquium der principatu tyrannico,* ed. R. Scholz (Leipzig: Hiersemann, 1944). See Miethke, *Ockhams Weg,* 298.

64. Miethke, *Ockhams Weg,* 300.

65. On Ockham's political philosophy, see Arthur Stephen McGrade, *The Political Thought of William Ockham: Personal and Institutional Principles* (Cambridge: Cambridge University Press, 1974); and Miethke, *Ockhams Weg.*

66. David Clark, "Ockham on Human and Divine Freedom," *Franciscan Studies* 38 (1978): 160.

67. Adams, *Ockham,* 2:979–87.

68. Blumenberg, *Legitimacy,* 195, 197, 617.

69. *De causa Dei contra Pelagium* 1. 9. 190D.

70. See Funkenstein, *Theology,* 144–45; and Anneliese Maier, *Studien zur Naturphilosophie der Spätscholastik,* vol. 4, *Metaphysische Hintergründe der scholastischen Naturphilosophie,* 2nd ed. (Rome: Edizioni di Storia e Litteratura, 1952–68).

71. See Adams, *Ockham,* 2:1310.

72. See Funkenstein, *Theology;* Koyré, *From Closed World to Infinite Universe* (Baltimore: Johns Hopkins Press, 1957); and A. C. Crombie, *Robert Grossete and the Origins of Experimental Science* (Oxford: Oxford University Press, 1953).

73. See Funkenstein, *Theology,* 334; and Michael Oakeshott's introduction to Hobbes, *Leviathan* (Oxford: Blackwell, 1955), esp. xx.

74. See Ludger Meier, "Research That Has Been Made and Is Yet to Be Made on the Ockhamism of Martin Luther at Erfurt," *Archivum Franciscanum Historicum* 43 (1950): 56–67; Paul Vignaux, "Luther commentateur des Sentences," *Études de Philosophie Médiévale* 21 (1935); and Courtenay, "Nominalism," 58.

75. See Paul Vignaux, "On Luther and Ockham," *The Reformation in Medieval Perspective,* ed. Steven Ozment (Chicago: Quadrangle, 1971), 107–18.

76. *Institutes of the Christian Religion* 1, 16, 2.

77. Cited in Bernard C. Flynn, "Descartes and the Ontology of Subjectivity," *Man and World* 16 (1983): 5.

78. Etienne Gilson, *The Unity of Philosophical Experience* (New York: Scribner's Sons, 1941), 61–91; A. C. Pegis, "Concerning William of Ockham," *Traditio* 2 (1944): 465–80; and Robert Guelluy, *Philosophie et theologie chez Guillaume d'Ockham* (Louvain: 1947), 375–76. Adams has shown that Ockham himself was probably not a skeptic but that his thought gave rise to the skepticism of Nicholas of Autrecourt and others. *Ockham,* 1:552, 625–29.

79. Popkin, *Scepticism,* 18–66. On Montaigne's skepticism, see Hugo Friedrich, *Montaigne* (Bern: Francke, 1949), 161–79; and David Lewis Schaefer, *The Political Philosophy of Montaigne* (Ithaca: Cornell University

Press, 1990), 73–152. On Sanchez, see Joseph Moreau, "Sanchez, pré-cartésien," *Révue Philosophique de la France et de l' Étranger* 92 (1967): 264–70.

80. See Etienne Gilson, *La Liberté chez Descartes et la théologie* (Paris: Alcan, 1912), 6; Camille de Rochmonteix, *Un Collège de Jesuites aux XVIIe et XVIIIe siècles,* 4 vols. (Le Mans: Leguicheux, 1889), 4:2–3, 30; and Norman Wells, "Descartes and the Scholastics Briefly Revisited," *New Scholasticism* 35, no. 2 (1961): 172–90.

81. Rochmonteix believes he was, but Popkin indicates that this was unlikely. *Un Collège,* 30; *Scepticism,* 70–75, 173.

82. Hertling, "Scholastik," 18; Geneviève Rodis-Lewis, "Descartes aurait-il eu un professeur nominaliste?" *Archives de Philosophie* 34 (1971): 37–46.

83. See Andre de Muralt, "Époche—Malin Génine—Théologies de la toute-puissance divine," *Studia Philosophica* 26 (1966): 159, 172–91; Blumenberg, *Legitimacy,* 181–203; Jean Luc Marion, *Sur la théologie blanche de Descartes: Analogie, création des vérités éternelles et fondement* (Paris: Presses universitaires de France, 1981), 303–4, 330–40; and Funkenstein, *Theology and the Scientific Imagination,* 180, 185, 187.

84. Suarez, *Disputationes metaphysicae; De legibus* 2, 6, nr. 4. See also Hertling, "Scholastik," 15, 18, 342; Alexander Koyré, *Descartes und die Scholastik* (Bonn: Cohen, 1923), 17, 147; Gilson, *Liberté,* 13; *Études sur le rôle de la pensée médiévale dans la formation du système cartésien* (Paris: Vrin, 1930), 221; and *Index scholastico-Cartesien* (Paris: Alcan, 1913). Hertling, Koyré, and especially Gilson have demonstrated beyond the shadow of a doubt that Descartes was deeply indebted to scholastic thought, but in their desire to show that many of Descartes' ideas were reformulations of scholastic notions, they have neglected the important ways in which nominalism posed the central questions or aporiae that impelled his thinking.

85. Koyré, *Descartes und die Scholastik,* 81–82, 86, 94, 95. See also Jacob Klein, *Greek Mathematical Thought and the Origin of Algebra,* trans. Eva Brann (Cambridge: M.I.T. Press, 1968), 300–306; and Joaquin Iriarte Agrirrezabal, *Kartesischer oder Sanchezischer Zweifel* (Bottrop i.W.: Postberg, 1935).

86. Descartes was also almost certainly ignorant of Abu Hamid al-Ghazali. Ghazali rejected the neo-Platonism of al-Farabi and Avicenna, and like Descartes followed the path of doubt to its conclusion in a skeptical crisis engendered by the idea of an omnipotent God bound by neither logic nor arithmetic. See Leo Groarke, "Descartes' First Meditation," 288–92.

87. See Descartes to Gibieuf, 18 July 1629, AT, 1:16.

88. This conclusion, however, is not intended to apply to the moral law. Later letters, from the period after the publication of the *Meditations,* present a similar picture of God. In a letter to Mésland of 2 May 1644, he describes an omnipotence that goes beyond even that of the *Meditations:* "The power of God can have no limits. . . . God cannot have been determined to make it true that contradictions cannot be together, and consequently He could have

done the contrary." AT, 4:110. This astonishing declaration calls into question the efforts of all those who argue that Descartes never doubted the veracity of the principle of contradiction. In a letter to Arnauld of 29 July 1648, he reaffirms this position, declaring that it is not impossible for God to make a mountain without a valley or to make one plus two not equal three. AT, 5:223–24. He wrote Henri More in a letter of 5 February 1649 that God can do everything, God creates everything, God is free, and God is the freely creating cause of essence and existences, of the possible and the real, and of being and truth. AT, 5:275; cf. also his letter to Clersellier of 23 April 1649, AT, 5:377, 545. On this question, see Funkenstein, *Theology and the Scientific Imagination,* 117; Gilson, *Liberté,* 27; and Koyré, *Descartes und die Scholastik,* 26. Stephen Nadler argues that Descartes has an even more radical notion of divine omnipotence than the nominalists. "Scientific Certainty and the Creation of Eternal Truths: A Problem in Descartes," *Southern Journal of Philosophy* 25, no. 2 (1987): 175–91. See also *La création des vérités éternelles, Studia Cartesiana* 2 (1981).

CHAPTER 2

1. See Martin Heidegger, *Nietzsche,* 2 vols. (Pfullingen: Neske, 1961), 2:161–62.

2. Bernard Williams, *Descartes: The Project of Pure Enquiry* (Atlantic Highlands, NJ: Humanities Press, 1978), 28.

3. In his early thought, Descartes often uses the terms 'deduction,' 'demonstration,' and 'induction' interchangeably. On this point, see Nadler, "Scientific Certainty," 179; and Desmond Clark, *Descartes' Philosophy of Science* (University Park, PA: Pennsylvania State University Press, 1982), 65–70.

4. See Klein, *Greek Mathematical Thought,* 197–211, 293–309; and Dennis Sepper, "Descartes and the Eclipse of Imagination, 1618–1633," *Journal of the History of Philosophy* 27 (July 1989): 379–403.

5. See Stanley Rosen, "A Central Ambiguity in Descartes," in *Cartesian Essays: A Collection of Critical Studies,* ed. Bernd Magnus and James B. Wilbur (The Hague: Nijhoff, 1969), 24.

6. Memory in Descartes' view is not ultimately distinct from imagination. *Rules,* AT, 10:414; CSM, 1:41–42. He later distinguished corporeal and intellectual memory. See Descartes to Mersenne, 1 April 1640, 11 June 1640, 6 August 1640; to Huygens, 10 October 1642; and to Arnauld, June-July 1648; AT, 3:48, 84–85, 143, 580; 5:193. He regarded both as fallible and untrustworthy.

7. See also Descartes to Mersenne, May 1637; and to Reneri, April-May 1638; AT, 1:366; 2:36. Descartes gives a similar account which also includes memory as a fifth category in *The Description of the Human Body,* AT, 11:224.

8. See also Descartes to Regius, May 1646; AT, 3:372.

9. See Descartes to Mersenne, July 1641, AT, 3:395.

10. See Descartes to Gibieuf, 19 January 1642; and to More, August 1649; AT, 3:479; 5:402.

11. See Peter Schouls, *Descartes and the Enlightenment* (Edinburgh: Edinburgh University Press, 1989), esp. 35–50. Antony Kenny points out that while a number of scholastics had argued that the will could command assent and dissent, Descartes was the first to see judgment as an unmediated act of the will. "Descartes on the Will, in *Cartesian Studies,* ed. R. J. Butler (New York: Barnes & Noble, 1972), 4.

12. See David Rosenthal, "Will and the Theory of Judgment," in *Essays on Descartes' Meditations,* ed. Amélie Oksenberg Rorty (Berkeley: University of California Press, 1986), 429.

13. Sartre argues that while Descartes defends a radical notion of freedom, he is not radical enough because he ultimately attributes this freedom to God and not to man. Jean Paul Sartre, *Descartes* (Paris: Trois collines, 1946), 9–52. The argument presented here calls this conclusion into question and suggests that God is in fact redefined on the basis of a potentially absolute freedom discovered in man himself.

14. The most notable exception is Heinrich Scholz, who asserts that the suppressed major premise is not "Everything that thinks is," but "Whenever I think, I am." "Über das Cogito, Ergo Sum," *Kant-Studien* 36, no. 1/2 (1931): 126–47. There is no evidence, however, that Descartes ever conceived of this ingenious solution.

15. Jaako Hintikka was one of the first to make this argument in his important article, "Cogito, ergo sum: Inference or Performance," in *Meta-Meditations,* 50–76. Perhaps the best alternative interpretation is given by Weinberg, who argues that the *cogito* is a nonsyllogistic logical inference. *Ockham,* p. 91. He suggests that Descartes adopts the position of the Megaric-Stoic logicians popular among scholastics in the twelfth and fourteenth centuries that a conditional proposition is true provided that the antecedent is incompatible with the denial of its consequent. Weinberg relies here upon the notions of *conjunctio* and *connexio necessaria* that Descartes employs in the *Rules.* We have tried to show, however, that Descartes abandons these notions as insufficient in his later thought as a result of his confrontation with the problem of divine omnipotence. Even if one overlooks this, it is by no means clear that the denial of the *cogito* is *logically* incompatible with the denial of the *sum.* Descartes clearly asserts that this is something that the mind has to learn through experience.

16. Hintikka calls this act of the will "a performative utterance." "Inference or Performance," 60–61. Caton correctly points out that this act is not necessarily public and therefore not necessarily a performance. *Subjectivity,* 143.

17. Gerard Simon argues that this principle of negation is an ontological and not merely a logical principle. "Les vérités éternelles de Descartes," 126–129. Descartes himself argues that "nothing presupposes being, is comprehended in juxtaposition to it, but being is itself always thought by means of nothing." *Burman,* AT, 5:153.

18. See Heidegger, *Nietzsche,* 2:148–58.

19. In the *Principles* Descartes suggests that "it is a contradiction to suppose that what thinks does not at the very time when I am thinking it, exist." AT, 8A:7; CSM, 1:195. This is not, however, a contradiction in the traditional logical sense, that is, it does not assume A and not-A at the same time. Rather it assumes that A does B and that if B then A. This, however, can be known only through experience. More characteristic of Descartes is his assertion in the *Search* that his fundamental principle is more certain than the principle of noncontradiction and his suggestion in the *Replies* that the principle of noncontradiction is based upon *cogito ergo sum.* AT, 10:522; CSM, 2:416; AT, 7:140–41; CSM, 2:100. The *cogito ergo sum* thus plays the same role in Descartes' thought that the principle of noncontradiction plays in Aristotle's. Scholz, "Über das Cogito, Ergo Sum," 322.

20. Plato *Alcybiades I* 133B-C. The disputed authorship of this dialogue need not concern us here. See also Plato, *Theaetetus* 186D; and Aristotle, *Nichomachean Ethics* 1170a29–1170b3. See Weinberg, *Ockham, Descartes, and Hume,* 83–91.

21. *De anima* 432a2.

22. 1074b35–1075a4. On the connection of self-consciousness and the prime mover see Stanley Rosen, "*Sophrosyne* and *Selbstbewusstsein,*" *Review of Metaphysics* 26 (1973): 617–42.

23. *Enneads* 5.9.1–14.

24. See for example, Ockham, *Sent.* Prol. qu. 1, KK.

25. Blumenberg argues that on a fundamental level both Augustine and Descartes face the same problem, i.e., the problem of gnosticism. In his view, it is because Augustine fails to overcome gnosticism that a second overcoming by Descartes is necessary. *Legitimacy,* 127–36, 172–79. This conclusion, however, blurs the crucial differences between the problems that these two thinkers faced.

26. See Gerhard Kruger, who argues that in Descartes "self-consciousness constitutes itself in defiance of all omnipotence." "Die Herkunft des philosophischen Selbstbewusstseins," *Logos, Internationale Zeitschrift für Philosophie der Kultur* 22 (1933): 246.

27. 429a–429b.

28. *Enneads* 5.9.3.

29. See Hintikka, "Inference or Performance," 68.

30. It is this capacity that differentiates human sensation from sensation in the beasts. *Replies,* AT, 7:269–70; CSM, 2:187–88.

31. This misunderstanding of the Cartesian *cogito me cogitare* is characteristic of analytic philosophy and lies behind A. J. Ayer's famous objection that the conclusion from Descartes' "I think" is not "I exist," but only "there is thought now." *The Problems of Knowledge* (London: Macmillan, 1956), 45–54. This conclusion would be correct if the self-consciousness that characterized the *res cogitans* was just the thinking of thinking. As we shall see, however, it is not.

32. Descartes himself undertakes such an imaginative reconstruction and appropriation of the world. See *Discourse,* AT, 6:42–46; CSM, 1:131–34.

33. Funkenstein argues that Descartes and the seventeenth century generally developed an *ergetic* ideal that replaced the contemplative ideal of antiquity: God constructed nature and Descartes tries to reconstruct it in order to understand it. *Theology and the Scientific Imagination,* 191, 297. Funkenstein is essentially correct, but he undervalues the practical goal of Descartes' science and the consequent struggle with God for the mastery of the world.

34. See Flynn, "Descartes and the Ontology of Subjectivity," 13.

35. See Koyré, *Descartes und die Scholastik,* 43.

36. See also Koyré, *Descartes und die Scholastik,* 24, 29, 34–35.

37. Marc-Wogau, "Der Zweifel Descartes und das Cogito ergo sum," *Theoria* 20 (1954): 135. Ferdinand Alquié claims that the creation of eternal truths and divine omnipotence are "the foundation of Descartes' metaphysics"; Alquié, ed., *Descartes: Oeuvres Philosophiques,* 3 vols. (Paris: Garnier, 1963), 1:208. Descartes even seems to suggest on occasion that God might still change the "eternal truths." The French version of the *Meditations* characterizes God as immutable, but the more authoritative Latin version omits this characteristic. This calls into question Descartes' claim in his letter to Mersenne of 15 April 1630 that the eternal truths are unvarying. AT, 1:135–36.

38. Harry Frankfurt, "Descartes on the Creation of Eternal Truths," *Philosophical Review* 86, no. 1 (January 1977): 38.

39. On Aristotle's conception of causality, see Helene Weiss, *Kausalität und Zufall in der Philosophie des Aristotles* (Basel: Falken, 1942).

40. Blumenberg thus argues that nominalism creates a *deus absconditus,* who becomes irrelevant for modern science. *Legitimacy,* 184. While he is correct in a narrow sense, Blumenberg fails to recognize the importance of this God for the construction of the modern self, in large part because his analysis remains conditioned by his belief in a transcendental self. History in his view is a series of epochs in which the unchanging self confronts the same perennial problems within changing contexts. The argument presented here suggests that the origin of the modern notion of the self is a unique response to a particular metaphysical understanding of God and the world.

41. See Funkenstein, *Theology and the Scientific Imagination,* 74.

42. God in this sense is interpreted in terms of causality as the *causa sui.* Jean-Luc Marion has pointed out that such an interpretation of God was probably unknown before Descartes. "The Essential Incoherence of Descartes' Definition of Divinity," in *Essays on Descartes' Meditations,* 325–27. Even for Ockham, God is not an efficient cause but a free cause. Adams, *Ockham,* 2:1179. To say that God has no other cause than his own essence, according to Marion, is to interpret him as infinite power but at the same time to subject him to the dictate of reason that everything has a cause. Marion thus sees this proof of God as incompatible with Descartes' charac-

terization of him as infinite and incomprehensible. As we shall see, however, it is precisely God's infinity, understood in Descartes' sense, that makes him identical with the whole. To claim that he is a *causa sui* is thus to claim that causality itself is self-causing, that it is pure willing.

Leibniz recognized this conclusion quite clearly and was obviously distressed by it. He writes: "God or the perfect being of Descartes is not a God such as one imagines, and as one would wish, that is to say, just and wise, doing all things for the good of the creatures so far as possible, but rather something approaching the God of Spinoza, that is to say, the principle of things and a certain sovereign power called primitive, which puts all in action, and does all that can be done; which has no will nor understanding, since according to Descartes he does not have the good for the object of his will, nor the true for the object of his understanding." Letter to Malebranche [?], June 1679. Cited in A. Robinet, *Malebranche et Leibniz* (Paris: Vris, 1955), 114–20. See also Frankfurt, "Eternal Truths," 54.

43. See Descartes to Mésland, 2 May 1644; AT, 4:117.

44. See Stanley Rosen, *Nihilism: A Philosophical Essay* (New Haven: Yale University Press, 1969), 62–65.

45. The central term that Gibieuf uses to describe both man and God is 'amplitude,' which includes everything that falls under the name 'liberty' and 'will.' Francis Ferrier, "L'Amplitude chez Gibieuf," *Revue Internationale de Philosophie* 114 (1975): 475–95. Freedom, according to Gibieuf, "is situated in that which is not enclosed by any limit, but rests in an *infinite amplitude*." *De libertate Dei et creatura*, 370. This means that man participates in the infinite. "To be plenitudinous with liberty is also to be deified, and reciprocally to be deified, is to be plenitudinous with liberty." Ibid., 480–81. Creatures for Gibieuf are emanations of God and he tries to measure their freedom or amplitude in terms of their nearness to God. In this respect, he follows his mentor Bérulle, who believed that God manifests himself as an emanation, the formal cause for the essence of both the human soul and matter. Gibieuf's doctrine of liberty, however, undermines the notion of divine authority, for he is able to define God's commands only in terms of their universality. Ibid., 489. For Gibieuf, as for Arnauld, the will's rationality is defined in terms of its generality. On the immense importance of this redefinition of reason and will, see Patrick Riley's superb *The General Will before Rousseau* (Princeton: Princeton University Press, 1986).

46. Descartes to Mersenne, 25 December 1639, AT, 2:628; Gilson, *Liberté*, 25.

47. On this point see Koyré, *Descartes und die Scholastik*, 44; Gilson, *Liberté*, 26; Margaret Wilson, "Can I Be the Cause of My Idea of the World? (Descartes on the Infinite and the Indefinite)," in *Essays on Descartes' Meditations*, 350. Antony Kenny has presented perhaps the most compelling argument against this reading of Descartes' notion of an indifferent human will. In "Descartes on the Will" he argues that because we are unable to disbelieve clear and distinct truths while we think them, we are not indifferent and free in the same sense as God. Peter Schouls suggests that for Descartes

we are free to withhold our assent from clear and distinct ideas in order to demonstrate our freedom. *Descartes and the Enlightenment*, 90. More decisively, Georges Moyal has shown that according to Descartes' account, we are bound by clear and distinct ideas only if we choose to be rational and that we need not so choose. "The Unity of Descartes' Conception of Freedom," *International Studies in Philosophy* 19, no. 1 (1987): 46. Descartes' claim in the Fourth Meditation that we act ever more freely as we act less indifferently thus must be understood as provisional in the most important respects. AT, 7:58–59; CSM, 2:41. This is especially true for the natural sciences. In his account of the creation of the world in the *Discourse*, Descartes claims that there are a number of general truths that must hold in any possible world. AT, 6:40–60; CSM, 131–41. As a result, certain general truths about nature may be deducible. These deducible truths, however, do not in any case extend to the level of those matters that are of relevance for human life. The number of possible causal paths at this level is so vast that multitudinous experiments are needed to determine which ones God or nature actually employs. Because there are others, however, we are not constrained to follow nature in the strict sense of the term. Thus, when we have established a real *mathesis universalis* we will be able to pursue whichever paths we choose. With respect to the matters of human life, we will thus be essentially indifferent, no longer a servant to a divinely ordered nature, but its master. We will have become a god with respect to nature.

48. See Descartes to Elizabeth, 3 November 1645, AT, 4:332.

49. Descartes to Hyperaspistas, August 1641, AT, 3:432.

50. Koyré argues that for Descartes we are the source of error and have the capacity to overcome it, to possess the absolute perfection of God. *Descartes und die Scholastik*, 47, 52.

51. This secularization argument is generally identified with Karl Löwith. *Gott, Mensch und Welt in der Metaphysik von Descartes bis zu Nietzsche* (Göttingen: Vandenhoeck & Ruprecht, 1967), 24–40. While rejecting the conception of secularization as a superficial misunderstanding, Heidegger, too, notes the importance of Luther's notion of the certainty of salvation for Descartes. *Nietzsche*, 2:142, 145; Martin Heidegger, *Seminaire tenu par le Professeur Martin Heidegger sur las Differenzschrift de Hegel* (Paris: by Roger Munier, 1968), 8. Popkin places Descartes even closer to the Reformers. In his view, true knowledge for Descartes is acquired only through a continuous act of grace which maintains the innate ideas and by the natural light that compels us to accept as true what we are unable to doubt. *Scepticism*, 184, 189.

52. Oedingen, "Der Genius Malignus," 182; Frankfurt, *Demons*, 172.

53. I follow Marion's division here. See "Incoherence," 299.

54. Ibid., 297–338.

55. Koyré, *Descartes und die Scholastik*, 142.

56. See Jean-Luc Marion, "Is the Ontological Argument Ontological? The Argument According to Anselm and Its Metaphysical Interpretation According to Kant," *Journal of the History of Philosophy* 30, no. 2 (April 1992): 208–17.

57. Marion, "Incoherence," 325.

58. *Itinerarium* 3, 4.

59. Ibid., 5, 7. See also Koyré, *Descartes und die Scholastik,* 115–17. Descartes is able to present and compare God geometrically to his creatures because he has already defined God as a substance that is not merely analogically similar to all other beings but identical to them in every respect except quantity; God is infinite while they are finite. See Jean Marie Beyssade, "Création des verités éternelles et doubte metaphysique," *Studia Cartesiana* 2 (1981): 93; and Marion, "Incoherence," 303–7. This move is a clear departure from Descartes' scholastic predecessors. Marion sees it as a diminution of God's true divinity. He argues that the three arguments of the Fifth Meditation reduce to the point of suppression the caesura of the infinite and the finite: "This is a stupefying declaration: The idea of God is found to be on the same footing, at least in me, as the idea of the triangle; therefore God becomes an idea in the same manner as the simple natures." "Incoherence," 323.

60. Descartes to Clerselier, 1646, AT, 4:445–46.

61. Descartes to Hyperaspistas, August 1641, AT, 3:427.

62. Descartes to Chanut, 6 June 1647, AT, 5:51. Margaret Wilson has suggested that this infinite/indefinite distinction may be a ploy, since Descartes also characterizes the human will as infinite. "Can I Be the Cause," 349–50.

63. Beyssade argues that this means we can never have an adequate concept of God. "Création," 95. However, while divine incomprehensibility seems to follow from divine infinity, this may not be the case. God is characterized as incomprehensible because he cannot be conceived, that is, because he cannot be imagined. Descartes claims, however, that he can be understood. Ibid., 92–93. See also Wilson, "Can I Be the Cause," 358. Therefore, we can have a clear and distinct idea of God, indeed an idea that is more clear and distinct than any other idea even though we cannot imagine or represent God.

64. Descartes to Mersenne, 21 April 1641, AT, 3:360.

65. See also Koyré, *Descartes und die Scholastik,* 104, 112; Martial Gueroult, *Descartes selon l'ordre des raisons,* 2 vols. (Paris: Aubier, 1953), 1:245; Caton, *Subjectivity,* 130. Indeed, one might argue that doubt itself, which is the capacity of the will to extract itself from all determinations by calling them into question, already is divine or at least draws upon the infinite that Descartes identifies as the divine.

66. See Frankfurt, "Eternal Truths," 40.

67. As Soffer puts it: "Cartesian nature has become detheologized by means of a divine inscrutability as the personification of Cartesian mechanics." Soffer, *From Science to Subjectivity,* 155. See also Schouls, *Descartes and the Enlightenment,* 51, 60, 61.

68. See Funkenstein, *Theology and the Scientific Imagination,* 327.

69. See Michael Buckley, *At the Origins of Modern Atheism* (New Haven: Yale University Press, 1987), 97–98.

70. Annette Baier suggests that the real God for Descartes is the self-conscious meditator. "The Idea of the True God in Descartes," in *Essays on Descartes' Meditations,* 365. This conclusion, however, reads too much of Fichte and Hegel into Descartes. Descartes does not yet put man in God's place; he renders God irrelevant and opens up the way for man to become godlike. Margaret Wilson is closer to the mark: "Descartes *does* think his power of generating conceptions of the indefinite cannot be accounted for by his own nature, but requires the existence of something outside himself. The fact that he ascribes to himself an unlimited power of willing doesn't seem to affect his judgment." "Can I Be the Cause," 355. For whatever reason, Descartes is ultimately unwilling simply to dispense with God, although the predominant impulse in his own thought rests upon a notion of infinite human will that could be put in God's place.

71. Gottfried Wilhelm Freiherr von Leibniz, *Die Philosophische Schriften,* ed. C. J. Gerhard, 7 vols. (Berlin: Weidmann, 1875–90; reprint, Hildesheim: Olms, 1960), 4:428.

72. *Oeuvres complètes,* intro. Henri Gouhier, 22 vols. (Paris: Vrin, 1958–84), 16:100. On this point see Riley, *The General Will before Rousseau,* 57–62; Ferdinand Aliqué, *Cartesianisme de Malebranche* (Paris: Vrin, 1974), 226–33; and Geneviève Rodis-Lewis, "Polémiques sur la création des possibles et sur l'impossible dans l'école cartésienne," *Studia Cartesiana* 2 (1981): 105–23.

CHAPTER 3

1. Jean Paul, *Werke,* 6 vols. (Munich: Hanser, 1959), 2:268–71.

2. *Horn of Oberon: Jean Paul Richter's School for Aesthetics,* trans. Margaret Hale (Detroit: Wayne State University Press, 1973), 15. For a more extensive discussion of the development of nihilism within German Romanticism, see Werner Kohlschmidt, *Form und Innerlichkeit* (Bern: Francke, 1955); and Dieter Arendt, *Der 'poetische Nihilismus' in der Romantik: Studien zum Verhältnis von Dichtung und Wirklichkeit in der Frühromantik,* 2 vols. (Tübingen: Niemeyer, 1972).

3. *School for Aesthetics,* 15.

4. Ibid.

5. F. H. Jacobi, *Werke,* 3 vols. (Leipzig: Fleischer, 1812–25; reprint ed. Darmstadt: Wissenschaftliche Buchgesellschaft, 1968), 3:44. As Wolfgang Müller-Lauter has shown, we do not know whether Jacobi adopted the word from Jenisch or some earlier source. "Nihilismus als Konsequenz des Idealismus: F. H. Jacobis Kritik der Transzendentalphilosophie und ihre philosophiegeschichtliche Folgen," in *Denken im Schatten des Nihilismus,* ed. Alexander Schwann (Darmstadt: Wissenschaftliche Buchgesellschaft, 1975), 114. It is possible that Jacobi drew on an earlier French usage to tie Fichte to the radicals of the French Revolution. While there is no unequivocal evidence of such a usage, Louis-Sébastien Mercier lists the term in his *Néologie: ou Vocabulaire des mots nouveaux à renouveler, ou pris dans des acceptions nou-*

velles, 2 vols. (Paris: Moussard, 1801). The entry reads as follows: "NIHILIST OR NOTHINGIST *(RIENNISTE).* One who believes in nothing, who interests himself in nothing. A beautiful result of the bad philosophy which brought itself into the world in the great *Dictionnaire encyclopaédique!" Néologie,* 2:143. Jacobi may have been influenced by the similar term '*Nihilianismus.*' We know that he used Cramer's *Dictionary,* which lists the term as the name of a Christian heresy that implied that if God is man he is nothing. Another possible source is F. Nicolai, who charged Fichte in 1798 with "annihilation." This charge was leveled against Fichte by an anonymous author during the atheism controversy, and while Jacobi was not this author, he may have been influenced by this usage. Müller-Lauter, "Nihilismus als Konsequenz des Idealismus," 114–17. Without further evidence, it seems unlikely that we will be better able to determine the origin of Jacobi's use of the term. On this topic, also see Theobald Süss, "Der Nihilismus bei F. H. Jacobi," *Theologische Literaturzeitung* 76 (1951): 193–200; and Otto Pöggeler, "Hegel und die Anfänge der Nihilismus-Diskussion," in Dieter Arendt, ed., *Der Nihilismus als Phänomen der Geistesgeschichte in der wissenschaftlichen Diskussion unseres Jahrhunderts* (Darmstadt: Wissenschaftliche Buchgesellschaft, 1974), 307–49.

6. See Frederick C. Beiser, *The Fate of Reason: German Philosophy from Kant to Fichte* (Cambridge: Harvard University Press, 1987), 44–91.

7. Jacobi, *Werke,* 3:29.

8. Ibid., 36.

9. See Müller-Lauter, "Nihilismus als Konsequenz des Idealismus," 146.

10. Jacobi, *Werke,* 3:49.

11. (Stuttgart: Cotta, 1960), 232. See Jürgen Gebhardt, ed., *Die Revolution des Geistes* (Munich: List, 1968), 7–13.

12. Friedrich Hölderlin, *Gesammelte Werke,* ed. Wilhelm Böhm, 5 vols. (Jena: Diederichs, 1924), 5:96.

13. See Charles E. Vaughan, *Studies in the History of Political Philosophy before and after Rousseau,* ed. A. G. Little, 2 vols. (New York, Russell & Russell, 1960), 126; and Carl Trautwein, *Über Ferdinand Lassalle und sein Verhältnis zur Fichteschen Sozialphilosophie* (Jena: Fischer, 1913).

14. See Andreas Wildt, *Autonomie und Anerkennung: Hegels Moralitätskritik im Lichte seiner Fichte-Rezeption* (Stuttgart: Klett-Cotta, 1982); and Stanley Rosen, *The Limits of Analysis* (New York: Basic Books, 1980), 182.

15. Immanuel Kant to Garve, 26 September 1798. Immanuel Kant, *Gesammelte Schriften,* ed. Königlich Preussischen Akademie der Wissenschaften (Berlin: Reiman, 1900–), 12:257–58; cf. also 4:338, 341n; 10:252; 18:60–62. See also Hans Feist, *Der Antinomiegedanke bei Kant und seine Entwicklung in den vorkritischen Schriften* (Borna-Leipzig: Noske, 1932; dissertation, Berlin 1932), esp. 3–17.

16. See Richard Velkley, *Freedom and the End of Reason: On the Moral Foundation of Kant's Critical Philosophy* (Chicago: University of Chicago Press, 1989).

17. G. F. W. Hegel, *Werke in 20 Bänden,* ed. Eva Moldenhauer and Karl Markus Michel, 20 vols. (Frankfurt am Main: Suhrkamp, 1970–71), 20:359.

18. See Beiser, *Fate of Reason,* 266–84; and Dieter Henrich, "Fichtes ursprüngliche Einsicht," in *Subjektivität und Metaphysik* (Frankfurt am Main: Klostermann, 1966), 224.

19. This search for a systematic solution to the problems of Kantianism was not the only development of Kantian thought. Schiller and others followed an aesthetic path that was also of profound importance for later thought. For a fuller discussion of this path, see Yack, *The Longing for Total Revolution,* 133–84.

20. Charles Taylor has described the larger context of this attempt to come to terms with the "self-unfolding subject" in his *Hegel* (Cambridge: Cambridge University Press, 1975), 3–51.

21. George Armstrong Kelly, *Idealism, Politics, and History: Sources of Hegelian Thought* (Cambridge: Cambridge University Press, 1969), 193. See also Bernard Willms, *Die totale Freiheit: Fichtes politische Philosophie* (Cologne: Westdeutscher, 1967). Ernst Gelpcke rejects this view, arguing that the *Sturm und Drang* was the decisive influence upon Fichte: *Fichte und die Gedankenwelt des Sturm und Drang* (Leipzig: Meiner, 1928).

22. Willms, *Freiheit,* 16. On Fichte's personal disgust with the ancien régime, see Antony J. La Vopa, *Grace, Talent, and Merit* (Cambridge: Cambridge University Press, 1988), 356.

23. Fichte's works are cited by title, edition, volume, and page number. See List of Abbreviations.

24. See Hans Freyer, *Über Fichtes Machiavelli-Aufsatz* (Leipzig: Hirzel, 1936); Eduard Zeller, *Vorträge und Abhandlungen geschichtlichen Inhalts* (Leipzig: Fues, 1865), 142, 144; and Manfred Buhr, ed., *Wissen und Gewissen: Beiträge Zum 200. Geburtstag Johann Gottlieb Fichtes, 1762–1814* (Berlin: Academie, 1962), 158–60. On the relation of Fichte and Rousseau see Richard Fester, *Rousseau und die deutsche Geschichtsphilosophie* (Stuttgart: Göschen, 1890); Georg Gurwitsch, "Kant und Fichte als Rousseau-Interpreten," *Kantstudien* 27 (1922): 138; Franz Haymann, *Weltbürgertum und Vaterlandsliebe in der Staatslehre Rousseaus und Fichtes* (Berlin: Heise, 1924).

25. Willms, *Freiheit,* 18.

26. Ibid., 22, 26.

27. Roger Garaudy, *Gott ist Tot: Das System und die Methode Hegels* (Frankfurt am Main: Europäische Verlagsanstalt, 1965), 149.

28. See Daniel Breazeale, "Fichte's Aenesidemus Review and the Transformation of German Idealism," *Review of Metaphysics* 34 (March 1981): 545–68.

29. Fichte to J. J. Baggessen (?), 1795 (?), J. G. Fichte, *Briefwechsel,* ed. Hans Schutz, 2 vols. (Hildesheim: Olms, 1967), 1:449–50. See Zeller, *Vorträge,* 144; Wilhelm Metzger, *Gesellschaft, Recht und Staat in der Ethik des Deutschen Idealismus* (Heidelberg: Winter 1917), 154; Gelpcke, *Fichte,* 64, 159; and Willms, *Freiheit,* 59–60.

30. *Fichtes Freiheitslehre,* ed. Theodor Ballauf and Ignaz Klein (Dussel-dorf: Schwann, 1956), 9; Kelly, *Idealism,* 191. See also Wilhelm Metzger, *Gesellschaft, Recht und Staat,* 154; and Gelpcke, *Fichte,* 64, 149.

31. As Robert Pippin has pointed out, Fichte believed that Kant did not sufficiently investigate the subject and thus could not explain how the "I that thinks" or the apperceptive subject which is the necessary presupposition of experience is itself possible. *Hegel's Idealism: The Satisfactions of Self-Con-sciousness* (Cambridge: Cambridge University Press, 1989), 43.

32. See Henrich Steffens, *Was ich erlebte* (Breslau: Max, 1841), 161–62. In response to Fichte's claims, Kant argued that his three *Critiques* were already a fully grounded system and declared Fichte's system "totally unten-able." *J. G. Fichte im Gespräch: Berichte der Zeitgenossen,* ed. F. Fuchs, R. Lauth, and W. Schreche, 4 vols. (Stuttgart–Bad Cannstatt: Frommann-Holzboog, 1978), 2:217. Kant, however, apparently never read the *Science of Knowledge.* Moreover, in the "Transcendental Deduction," he claims that while such a system is possible, the *Critique of Pure Reason* is not such a sys-tem but rather a critique of reason. *KrV* A83/B109.

33. Reinhart Lauth, "J. G. Fichtes Gesamtidee der Philosophie," *Philosophisches Jahrbuch* 71, no. 2 (1964): 267.

34. While Fichte's contemporaries and most present-day scholars have assumed that Fichte's goal is a demonstration of the truth and meaning of his fundamental principles, this assumption is not uncontested. Alexis Philo-nenko, for example, has argued that Fichte's project is essentially critical and that he consequently attempts to demonstrate not the truth of his funda-mental principles but their insufficiency and falsity. *L'Oeuvre de Fichte* (Paris: Vrin, 1984). Such a reading suggests that the goal of Fichte's work is more epistemological than ontological. While this account helps to explain many of the apparent inconsistencies in Fichte's *Doctrine of Science,* it contradicts many of the claims Fichte makes in other works. It has consequently not won wide support. A notable exception is Luc Ferry, *Rights—The New Quarrel between the Ancients and the Moderns,* trans. Franklin Philip (Chicago: Uni-versity of Chicago Press, 1990), 77. Even if Philonenko is correct, the Fichte he portrays was not the Fichte the nineteenth century knew, and it is this lat-ter Fichte who was so important for the development of nihilism.

35. Pippin argues that Fichte draws on a real element in Kant's thought here. Kant defines "the mind's power of producing representations from itself" (*KrV,* A51/B75) as "the spontaneity of knowledge," and spontaneity is also the term he uses in describing the unconditioned causality of freedom (*KrV,* A533/B561). *Hegel's Idealism,* 45.

36. Fichte expanded this formulation in 1797 to "The I begins by abso-lutely positing its own existence as self-positing." SW, 1:528. See Henrich, "Einsicht," 202–3.

37. Ibid., 198. See also Fichte to Achelis, 1790. J. G. Fichte, *Gesamtaus-gabe der Bayerischen Akademie der Wissenschaften,* ed. Reinhard Lauth and Hans Jacob (Stuttgart–Bad Cannstatt: Frommann, 1964–), 3.1:193–94.

38. Karl Löwith points out that in contrast to Kant, Fichte sees man not

as a mere copula between God and the world but as the absolute, creative source of both God and the world. He thus concludes that for Fichte, God himself disappears in the moral world-order of the self-positing I. *Gott, Mensch und Welt,* 92, 95.

39. See Heidegger, *Nietzsche,* 2:163.

40. Goethe, *Faust,* 1236. Kelly, *Idealism,* 184.

41. Ballauf and Klein, ed., *Fichtes Freiheitslehre,* 37; Garaudy, *Gott ist Tod,* 150. For an interesting attempt to reinterpret this Fichtean claim in a Kantian manner see Pippin, *Hegel's Idealism,* 56.

42. Henrich, "Einsicht," 191.

43. Ibid., 194.

44. John Lachs, "Fichte's Idealism," *American Philosophical Quarterly* 9, no. 4 (October 1972): 313.

45. Ibid., 314.

46. Kelly, *Idealism,* 207.

47. *J. G. Fichtes Leben und literarischer Briefwechsel,* ed. I. H. Fichte, 2 vols. (Sulzbach: Seidel, 1830), 2:255. See also Kelly, *Idealism,* 184–85. Leszeck Kolakowski argues that Fichte's dialectic of self-canceling exteriorization is rooted in the whole history of neo-Platonic theogony and in all the doctrines that present God as coming into being through his own creative activity. In Fichte, however, the attributes of divine being are transferred to the human mind. *Main Currents of Marxism,* trans. P. S. Falla, 3 vols. (Oxford: Oxford University Press, 1978), 52. This theological moment of Fichte's thought is almost entirely neglected by scholars like Neuhouser and Luc Ferry who present Fichte as a proponent of individualism. Self-positing is treated not as an absolute activity in which individual human beings in some sense take part but as a merely mental operation by means of which individual human beings give themselves their own values. See Neuhouser, *Fichte's Theory of Subjectivity* (Cambridge: Cambridge University Press, 1990), 111, 122, 124.

48. *New Exposition of the Science of Knowledge,* trans. A. E. Kroeger (St. Louis, 1869), 124. See Kelly, *Idealism,* 184.

49. See Kelly, *Idealism,* 216.

50. Lachs, "Fichte's Idealism," 313.

51. *Werke,* 20:397. For Fichte, however, this principle can never be a true ground, since an ultimate reconciliation of the I and the not-I is impossible. On this point see Pippin, *Hegel's Idealism,* 57.

52. See Ballauf and Klein, eds., *Fichtes Freiheitslehre,* 25; and Julius Drechsler, *Fichtes Lehre vom Bild* (Stuttgart: Kohlhammer, 1955).

53. In light of this conclusion, it is clear why Fichte was unable to follow the aesthetic path that Schiller laid out and that was so important to many of their contemporaries and successors. Art at its best can produce only an approximation of the infinite. Goethe and others could content themselves with this approximation as the best human possibility. For Fichte, such a stance is an abdication of moral responsibility. As we shall see, it is this utopian dream of realizing the infinite in contrast to the neohumanist vision

of the perfected finite form that comes to constitute the essence of nihilism in the nineteenth and twentieth centuries.

54. See Kolakowski, *Main Currents,* 1:53.

55. See Hegel's early essay "Glauben und Wissen." *Werke,* 2:296.

56. Kelly calls this the ontological priority of the ideal. *Idealism,* 218.

57. See Lachs, "Fichte's Idealism," 313.

58. *Werke,* 20:407.

59. Ballauf and Klein, eds., *Fichtes Freiheitslehre,* 32.

60. See Lachs, "Fichte's Idealism," 312.

61. *Werke,* 20:407.

62. See Kolakowski, *Main Currents,* 1:53.

63. Willms, *Freiheit,* 110.

64. Ibid., 94.

65. This fact was apparent to many of Fichte's contemporaries. See, for example, Hegel, *Werke,* 2:474–80, 519–20; and Fredrich Julius Stahl, *Philosophie des Rechts nach geschishtl. Ansicht,* 2 vols. (Heidelberg: Mohr, 1830), 1:159, 165. Among contemporary scholars, see, for example, Willms, *Freiheit;* and G. A. Walz, *Die Staatsidee des Rationalismus und der Romantik und die Staatsphilosophie Fichtes* (Berlin: Rothschild, 1928), 596. Zwi Batscha and Manfred Buhr, by contrast, see more room for individual freedom in Fichte's state because of the autonomy of the society from the state. Batscha, *Gesellschaft und Staat in der politischen Philosophie Fichtes* (Frankfurt am Main: Europäische Verlagsanstalt, 1970); and Buhr, *Revolution und Philosophie: Die ursprüngliche Philosophie Johann Gottlieb Fichtes und die Französische Revolution* (Berlin: Deutscher Verlag der Wissenschaften, 1965).

66. See Metzger, *Gesellschaft, Recht und Staat,* 139; Walz, *Staatsidee,* 430; and Reinhard Strecker, *Die Anfänge von Fichtes Staatsphilosophie* (Leipzig: Weiner, 1916), 106, 173.

67. Fichte follows Kant in this transformation of the Lockean notion of property. See Susan Meld Shell, *The Rights of Reason: A Study of Kant's Philosophy and Politics* (Toronto: University of Toronto Press, 1980), 127–52.

68. See La Vopa, *Grace, Talent, and Merit,* 367.

69. Ibid., 365, 366.

70. La Vopa, *Grace, Talent, and Merit,* 371.

71. Willms, *Freiheit,* 135.

CHAPTER FOUR

1. This original text of the poem appears in John Grant, "The Art and Argument of 'The Tyger,'" *Texas Studies in Literature and Language* 2, no. 1 (Spring 1960): 38–39.

2. Morton Paley suggests that for Blake the age of innocence represented by the lamb comes to be through the terror of the tiger. Blake's poem, "The Little Girl Found," for example, ends with the discovery of the "sleeping child / Among tygers wild." Paley also suggests that the poem has a political message. The forests of the night are the unjust monarchical regimes of the old world, which along with the Newtonian mechanics of the stars men-

tioned in the fifth stanza have destroyed virtue and innocence. The tiger is the Terror of the French Revolution, understood as an incarnation of divine wrath, which sweeps this corrupt world away. "Tyger of Wrath," *PMLA* 81, no. 7 (1966): 540–51.

3. See Grant, "The Art and Argument of 'The Tyger,'" 40, 48, 49; Mark Schorer, *William Blake: The Politics of Vision* (New York: Holt, 1946), 250–51; and Martin Nurmi, "Blake's Revisions of *The Tyger*," *PMLA* 71 (1956): 669–85.

4. In his prophetic works, Blake assigns the hammer, anvil, furnace, and chain, that is, the tools of the tiger's creator, to Los, the eternal prophet and symbol of the imagination. Hazard Adams, *Blake and Yeats: The Contrary Vision* (Ithaca, NY: Cornell University Press, 1955), 238.

5. On Blake's demonic creator see Paul Cantor, *Creature and Creator: Myth-Making and English Romanticism* (Cambridge: Cambridge University Press, 1984), 29–54. Blake, like many Romantics, was deeply influenced by the theosophistic writings of Paracelsus and Jakob Böhme, who asserts that God manifests himself in two contrary principles: wrath and love, fire and light, Father and Son. As Paley points out, "These principles are not dualistically opposed: they are contraries in an unending dialectic whose synthesis is the Godhead." "Tyger of Wrath," 543. This view is especially evident in Blake's *Marriage of Heaven and Hell*, which many scholars have related to "The Tyger." See Grant, "The Art and Argument of 'The Tyger,'" 43–44. Blake himself asserted that "the Creator of the World must be a very Cruel Being." *The Complete Writings of William Blake,* ed. Geoffrey Keynes (London: Nonesuch, 1957), 617. Such remarks led Algernon Charles Swinburne to see the poem as a piece of Romantic satanism. *William Blake* (London: Hotten, 1868), 120.

6. The term 'Romanticism' was first coined by Fichte's student Friedrich Schlegel to distinguish a new expressivist style from the mimetic style that characterized eighteenth-century classicism. In the course of its development, however, Romanticism came to encompass such a variety of forms and authors that it became difficult to conceive of it as a unified movement. On the long-standing debate between scholars such as A. O. Lovejoy, who argue that the only principle of Romanticism is infinite diversity, and others such as René Wellek and M. H. Abrams, who accept Schlegel's original claim, see Marilyn Butler, *Romantics, Rebels, and Revolutionaries: English Literature and Its Background, 1760–1830* (Oxford: Oxford University Press, 1981), 2–9. While this chapter traces the development of Romantic nihilism, it does not claim that all Romanticism is nihilism.

7. *Manfred,* 1.1.12.

8. Some modern scholars have characterized this element in Romanticism as gnosticism. See Harold Bloom, *Poetry and Repression* (New Haven: Yale University Press, 1976); his *Agon: Toward a Theory of Revisionism* (New York: Oxford University Press, 1982), 3–90; and Cantor, *Creature and Creator.*

9. See Richard Hannah, *The Fichtean Dynamic of Novalis' Poetics* (Bern:

Lang, 1980); Geza von Molnar, *Novalis' "Fichte Studies": The Foundations of His Aesthetics* (The Hague: Mouton, 1970); and Stefan Summerer, *Wirkliche Sittlichkeit und äesthetische Illusion: Die Fichterezeption in den Fragmenten und Aufzeichnungen Fr. Schlegels und Hardenbergs* (Bonn: Bouvier, 1974).

10. M. H. Abrams points to this Romantic tendency to naturalize the supernatural and humanize the divine in his *Natural Supernaturalism: Tradition and Revolution in Romantic Literature* (New York: Norton, 1971).

11. *School for Aesthetics*, 15.

12. *William Lovell* (Stuttgart: Reclam, 1986). On Lovell as the first nihilist, see Bruno Hillebrand, "Literarische Aspekte des Nihilismus," *Nietzsche-Studien* 13 (1984): 91.

13. Hillebrand, "Literarische Aspekte," 95.

14. For a comprehensive discussion of *William Lovell*, see Arendt, *Der 'poetische Nihilismus,'* 2:330-84.

15. F. H. Jacobi, *Jacobis auserlesener Briefwechsel*, 2 vols. (Leipzig: Fleischer, 1825), 2:398.

16. On Frankenstein, see Cantor, *Creature and Creator*, 103–32.

17. Johann Peter Eckermann, *Gespräche mit Goethe in den letzten Jahren seines Lebens*, ed. H. H. Harben (Wiesbaden: Brockhaus, 1959), 253. Goethe was especially critical of the Romantics' titanism. On Goethe's relation to Romanticism see Karl Viëtor, *Goethe: The Thinker*, trans. Bayard Q. Morgan (Cambridge: Harvard University Press, 1949), 147–64.

18. Eric Heller, "Goethe and the Avoidance of Tragedy," in *The Disinherited Mind* (Cambridge: Bowes & Bowes, 1952), 29–49.

19. See John R. Williams, *Goethe's Faust* (London: Allen & Unwin, 1987), 47–62; and Rudiger Scholz, *Goethes 'Faust' in der wissenschaftlichen Interpretation von Schelling und Hegel bis heute: Ein einführender Forschungsbericht* (Rheinfelden: Schauble, 1983).

20. Johann Wolfgang von Goethe, *Werke*, 14 vols. (Hamburg: Wegner, 1950–60), 10:177. At various times Goethe described Napoleon, Karl August, Byron, Paganini, Fredrich II of Prussia, and Peter the Great of Russia as demonic natures. Ibid., 10:651.

21. Ibid., 12:299.

22. The force of which he is a part is almost certainly the spirit of the earth, who overawed Faust. Mephistopheles, however, is only a determinate moment of this infinite force.

23. *Werke*, 9:350–53. Goethe considers the mixture of darkness and light as the ground of the possibility of color and thus of experience in his *Farbenlehre*. See Hans Heinrich Schaeder, "Urform und Fortbildung des Manichäischen Systems," *Vorträge der Bibliotek Warburg, 1924–25* (Leipzig: Teubner, 1927), 65–157; and Dennis Sepper, *Goethe contra Newton: Polemics and the Project for a New Science of Color* (Cambridge: Cambridge University Press, 1988).

24. See Heller, "The Avoidance of Tragedy," 29–49.

25. A number of Romantic authors, including Kleist, Hölderlin, Novalis, and Schelling, map out a similar "great circle" route back to salvation. The

shattering of the paradisal unity into the conflict between the self and the external world is understood as a necessary departure that makes possible a higher reunion with alienated nature. Abrams, *Natural Supernaturalism*, 221–51. In contrast to Goethe, however, most of these Romantics believe that this goal is at best only an aesthetic possibility.

26. On this point, see my *Hegel, Heidegger, and the Ground of History* (Chicago: University of Chicago Press, 1984), 47-56, 96-115.

27. See Pöggeler, "Hegel und die Anfänge der Nihilismus-Diskussion," 307–49.

28. *Werke*, 6:24-25.

29. Ibid., 2:432-33.

30. Ibid., 12:533.

31. Ibid., 7:24.

32. Hegel, *Philosophie des Rechts: Die Vorlesung von 1819/20 in einer Nachschrift*, ed. Dieter Henrich (Frankfurt am Main: Suhrkamp, 1983), 51.

33. *Werke*, 7:464.

34. On this point, see my "War and Bourgeoisification in the Thought of Hegel," in *Understanding the Political Spirit*, ed. Catherine Zuckert (New Haven: Yale University Press, 1988), 153–79.

35. See Wolfgang Bartuschat, *Nietzsche: Selbstsein und Negativität; Zur Problematik einer Philosophie des sich selbst vollenden Willens* (Dissertation, Heidelberg, 1968), 181.

36. Williams, *Goethe's Faust*, 48.

37. Ibid., 49.

38. See Byron to Rogers, 4 April 1817; to Jeffrey, of 12 October 1817; and to Murray of 7 June 1820. *The Works of Lord Byron*, ed. Rowland Prothero, 13 vols. (New York: Scribner's Sons, 1900), 11:97, 174; 12:36–37. The differences were apparent to Goethe. See Goethe to Knebel, October 1817. *Goethes Werke*, ed. Gustav v. Loeper et al., 133 vols. (Weimar: Böhlaus, 1887–1912), 4.28:277–28.

39. Zamiruddin argues that the drama cannot end with an unraveling of Manfred's crimes because then, "he would have ceased to be a hero." "*Manfred*: Restudied as Drama," in *New Light on Byron*, ed. James Hogg (Salzburg: Universität Salzburg, 1978), 39.

40. On the importance of radical autonomy in *Manfred*, see Frederick Garber, *Self, Text, and Romantic Irony: The Example of Byron* (Princeton: Princeton University Press, 1988), 126–35.

41. Albert Camus, *The Rebel: An Essay on Man in Revolt* (New York: Knopf, 1956), 47–54.

42. "The self can go no further in the direction Manfred takes it than Manfred actually goes. At the dead end there is only himself, those closed-in walls and that bitter kingdom of the mind in which he is lord and subject and, he argues, his own destroyer." Garber, *Self, Text, and Romantic Irony*, 134.

43. *Werke*, 10:187.

44. See Hermann Lubbe, ed., *Die Hegelsche Rechte* (Stuttgart–Bad Cannstatt: Frommann, 1962).

45. See Karl Löwith, *Von Hegel zu Nietzsche: Der Revolutionäre Bruch im Denken des neunzehnten Jahrhunderts* (Zurich: Europa, 1941).

46. *Werke in sechs Bänden,* ed. H. M. Sass, 6 vols. (Frankfurt am Main: Suhrkamp, 1975), 5:32.

47. Ibid., 3:261.

48. Tom Rockmore has shown in great detail how truly important Fichte was for the Left Hegelians. *Fichte, Marx, and the German Philosophical Tradition* (Carbondale: Southern Illinois University Press, 1980).

49. See C. P. Magill, "Young Germany: A Revaluation," in *German Studies* (Oxford: Basil Blackwell, 1952), 108–19.

50. References to this work are cited by title and page number. See List of Abbreviations.

CHAPTER FIVE

1. *Werke,* 1:44–46.

2. James H. Billington, *The Icon and the Axe: An Interpretive History of Russian Culture* (New York: Knopf, 1966), 309–10. My discussion of the impact of German idealism on Russian thought in the prenihilist period draws on Billington.

3. Ibid., 316.

4. Franco Venturi, *Roots of Revolution: A History of the Populist and Socialist Movements in Nineteenth Century Russia,* trans. Francis Haskell, intro. Isaiah Berlin (Chicago: University of Chicago Press, 1960), 38.

5. Cited in Billington, *Icon,* 325. See Arthur Mendel, *Michael Bakunin: Roots of Apocalypse* (New York: Praeger, 1981), 84–112; and Aileen Kelly, *Mikhail Bakunin: A Study in the Psychology and Politics of Utopianism* (Oxford: Clarenden, 1982), 142–64.

6. Martin Katz, *Mikhail N. Katkov: A Personal Biography 1818–1887* (The Hague: Mouton, 1966), 31.

7. Cited in Venturi, *Roots,* 15.

8. References to Turgenev's work are cited by title and page number. See List of Abbreviations.

9. Alexander Herzen, *My Past and Thoughts: The Memoirs of Alexander Herzen,* trans. Constance Garnett (New York: Knopf, 1973), 642.

10. *Underground Russia* (New York: Scribner's, 1883), 4.

11. "Nihilism in Russia," *Fortnightly Review* (1 August 1868): 132.

12. See Mendel, *Bakunin,* 56–83, 134–36, 145.

13. Cited in Charles A. Moser, *Antinihilism in the Russian Novel of the 1860s* (The Hague: Mouton, 1964), 37.

14. Isaiah Berlin argues that for the activists it was only necessary to "strike the chains from the captive hero, and he will stretch himself to his full height and live in freedom and happiness ever after." Venturi, *Roots,* xvii.

15. Nikolai Valentinov (N. K. Volski), *The Early Years of Lenin,* trans. Rolf H. W. Theen (Ann Arbor: University of Michigan Press, 1969), 209–10.

16. Billington, *Icon,* 386.

17. In *Roots of Revolution,* Venturi characterizes the *Contemporary* group

as populists and Pisarev's group as nihilists on the basis of the latter's elitism and positivism. He also points to the willingness of Pisarev's group to accept the label of nihilists which the *Contemporary* group rejected. This distinction has had great influence in shaping the contemporary understanding of the character of the revolutionary movement in Russia. It is, however, arbitrary and unconvincing. The word 'populist' did not become current in Russian as the name for this movement or any part of it until the 1870s. At a much earlier date, members of both groups were described as nihilists by Katkov, Turgenev, Herzen, and others, and Peter Kropotkin still described the revolutionary movement as nihilism as late as 1897–98. Herzen, *My Past*, 642; Kropotkin, *Memoirs of a Revolutionist* (Montreal: Black Rose Books, 1989), 275–82. His opinion was echoed by many others. While this designation upset Chernyshevsky and Dobrolyubov, Pisarev accepted it. In this respect, he was perhaps more honest or more politically naive than Chernyshevsky and Dobrolyubov. The differences between the two groups were not that great. Even Venturi sees a convergence of both groups after 1862, but then wants to call both groups populist, reserving the name 'nihilist' for the Jacobin populists. Venturi, *Roots*, 325–26. Venturi thereby distorts and conceals the essentially nihilistic character of this radical movement.

18. Pisarev introduced Comte's thought to Russia in 1865. James H. Billington, "The Intelligentsia and the Religion of Humanity," *American Historical Review* 65, no. 4 (July 1960): 813.

19. Cited in Rogers, "Darwinism," 14.

20. Tony Cliff, *Lenin*, 4 vols. (London, Pluto, 1975), 1:11; Venturi, *Roots*, 285–94.

21. Katz, *Katkov*, 75.

22. Billington, *Icon*, 390.

23. Fedor Stepun, "The Russian Intelligentsia and Bolshevism," *Russian Review* 17, no. 4 (October 1958): 269.

24. *Bell*, no. 187 (15 July 1864): 1534.

25. David Lowe, *Turgenev's Fathers and Sons* (Ann Arbor: Ardis, 1983), 66.

26. Pugachev was the Cossack leader of the revolt against Catherine II.

27. Lowe, *Fathers and Sons*, 56. Helen Muchnec argues that "Bazarov is bigger than he shows himself to be. He is not fine because, but in spite of, his views and actions. His greatness is implicit; what he really is is a contradiction of what he represents himself to be. What is obvious in him is limited and unpleasant; what is hidden is big." *An Introduction to Russian Literature* (New York: Doubleday, 1947), 116.

28. Ivan Turgenev, *Literary Reminiscences and Autobiographical Fragments*, trans. David Magarshack (London: Faber, 1959), 173.

29. Edward Garnett, *Turgenev: A Study* (London: Collins, 1917), 121.

30. Venturi, *Roots*, 157; Moser, *Antinihilism*, 26.

31. Ralph E. Matlaw, "Turgenev's Novels and *Fathers and Sons*," in *FAS*, 274.

32. Turgenev, *Reminiscences*, 168.

33. Dmitri Pisarev, "Bazarov," in *FAS,* 196–97.

34. Ibid., 210.

35. Ibid., 217.

36. William C. Brumfield, "Bazarov and Rjazanov: The Romantic Archetype in Russian Nihilism," *Slavic and East European Journal* 21, no. 4 (Winter 1977), 495. Herzen believed Pisarev misconstrued Bazarov. Alexander Herzen, "Bazarov Once Again," in *FAS,* 232.

37. André Mazon, "L'élaboration d'un roman de Turgenev: *Terres vierges,*" *Revue des études slaves* 5 (1925): 87–88.

38. Cited in Brumfield, "Bazarov and Rjazanov," 499.

39. Ibid., 500.

40. Turgenev's most strident critic, M. A. Antonovich, pointed out that Turgenev portrayed his hero as a "demonic or Byronic character, something on the order of Hamlet." N. N. Strakhov, "Fathers and Sons," in *FAS,* 219.

41. Leonard Schapiro, *Turgenev: His Life and Times* (New York: Random House, 1978), 149.

42. Strakhov, "Fathers and Sons," 224.

43. Pisarev, "Bazarov," 199.

44. Ibid.

45. Strakhov, "Fathers and Sons," 224.

46. *FAS,* 187.

47. Bazarov's egoism is thus not a defect, as Rufus Mathewson and others have argued. *The Positive Hero,* 136. It is the source of his heroism, but it is a tragic heroism, doomed by its Promethean stance to succumb to the all-conquering Zeus, that is, to the irresistible force of nature.

48. Garnett, *Turgenev,* 120.

49. Lowe, *Turgenev's Fathers and Sons,* 72.

50. Strakhov, "Fathers and Sons," 229. See also Alexander Fischler, "The Garden Motif and the Structure of Turgenev's *Fathers and Sons,*" *Novel* 9 (1976): 245.

51. Lowe, *Turgenev's Fathers and Sons,* 80.

52. See Richard Freeborn, *Turgenev: The Novelist's Novelist* (Oxford: Oxford University Press, 1960), 121.

53. Charles Bachman, "Tragedy and Self-Deception," *Revue des Langues Vivantes/Tidschrift voor Levende Talen* 34 (1968): 275.

54. Matlaw, "Turgenev's Novels," 278.

55. Venturi, *Roots,* xxxi.

56. Nikolai Chernyshevsky, *What Is to Be Done?,* trans. N. Dole and S. S. Skidelsky (Ann Arbor: Ardis, 1986), 40, 70.

57. Ibid., 198.

58. Ibid., 306.

59. Ibid., 170–71.

60. Ibid., 375–77.

61. Ibid., 381, 387.

62. Ibid., xxxviii.

63. Ibid., 352.

64. Ibid., 313.

65. Ibid., 291.

66. See Peter Kropotkin, *Memoirs of a Revolutionist,* 280.

67. Venturi, *Roots,* 331–34.

68. Volodymyr Varlamov, "Bakunin and the Russian Jacobins and Blanquists," in *Rewriting Russian History: Soviet Interpretations of Russia's Past,* ed. Cyril E. Black, 2nd ed. (New York: Random House, 1962), 291.

69. Michael Bakounine, *God and the State,* trans. Benjamin Tucker (New York: Benj. R. Tucker, 1895), 15, 25.

70. Michael Bakunin, "Reaction in Germany," in *Michael Bakunin: Selected Writings,* trans. Steven Cox and Olive Stevens, ed. Arthur Lehning (New York: Grove, 1973), 58. Belinski saw in Bakunin's words the germ of a complete negation of laws and government. Venturi, *Roots,* 61. Venturi points out that Bakunin emphasized the negative, entirely destructive value which Blanqui assigned to revolutionary dictatorship. *Roots,* 62. Isaiah Berlin sees this sentiment as typical of the whole Jacobin strain of Russian radicals. *Roots,* xiii. Richard Saltman argues that this view is misguided because it does not see the positive side of Bakunin's program. *The Social and Political Thought of Michael Bakunin* (Westport, CT: Greenwood, 1983). Saltman claims that Bakunin draws upon Feuerbach, Hegel, and Lamarck to develop a notion of freedom that is not merely negative but positive, imbedded in the natural world and essentially interactive. Saltman, however, discounts too readily the effect of Fichte upon Bakunin and does not see the Fichtean character of Left Hegelianism or the Fichtean origin of the notion of mutual interaction.

71. Michael Bakunin, "Appeal to the Slavs," in George Woodcock, *Anarchism* (Cleveland: World, 1962), 171.

72. Venturi, *Roots,* 362.

73. Michael Prawdin (pseud. M. Charol), *The Unmentionable Nechaev: A Key to Bolshevism* (London: Allen & Unwin, 1961), 63.

74. Venturi, *Roots,* 365.

75. Prawdin, *Nechaev,* 74–75.

76. Moser, *Antinihilism,* 137–39.

77. Ibid., 154.

78. Venturi, *Roots,* 473.

79. Billington, *Icon,* 400.

80. Valentinov, *Early Years,* 49–57.

81. Ibid., 126.

82. Ibid., 219.

83. Ibid., 67, 77. Dietrich Geyer thinks that Valentinov exaggerates Chernyshevsky's influence on Lenin. *Lenin in der russischen Sozialdemokratie* (Cologne: Böhlau, 1962), 40.

84. Valentinov, *The Early Years,* 254.

85. Richard Pipes, "Russian Marxism and Its Populist Background: The Late Nineteenth Century," *Russian Review* 19, no. 4 (October 1960): 331.

86. Valentinov, *Early Years,* 206.

87. See Prawdin, *Nechaev.*

88. *The Russian Revolution, and Leninism or Marxism* (Ann Arbor: University of Michigan Press, 1961), 107.

89. Billington, *Icon,* 488. The discussion of Russian Prometheanism presented here follows Billington's account.

90. *The Meaning of the Creative Act,* trans. Donald A. Lowrie (New York: Harper & Brothers, 1955), 225, 245–46.

91. *The Fourth Way* (New York: Knopf, 1957), 97–104.

92. L. I. Schwarzmann (pseud. Leo Shestov), *All Things Are Possible,* trans. S. S. Koteliansky (New York: McBride, 1920), 241.

93. Cited in Billington, *Icon,* 490.

94. Camilla Gray, *The Great Experiment: Russian Art 1863–1922,* (New York: Abrams, 1970), 308.

95. Cited in A. Haskell, *Diaghileff: His Artistic and Private Life* (New York: Simon and Schuster, 1935), 137.

96. *Three Plays* (London: Routledge, 1923), 132.

97. *Confession* (London: Everett, 1910).

98. Ibid.

99. "On Literature, Revolution, and Entropy," trans. W. Vickery, *Partisan Review,* no. 3–4 (1961): 373.

100. Trotsky, *Literature and Revolution* (New York: Russell & Russell, 1957), 256.

101. Stalin, *Works,* 13 vols. (Moscow: Foreign Language Publishing House, 1955), 13:67–75.

CHAPTER SIX

1. See Ernst Bertram, *Nietzsche: Versuch einer Mythologie* (Berlin: Bondi, 1918); and Karl Justus Obenauer, *Friedrich Nietzsche: Der ekstatische Nihilist; Eine Studie zur Krise des religiosen Bewusstseins* (Jena: Diederichs, 1924).

2. See Bernd Magnus, "The Use and Abuse of *The Will to Power,*" in *Reading Nietzsche,* ed. Robert Solomon and Kathleen Higgins (Oxford: Oxford University Press, 1988), 218–35. Magnus reasonably argues that we should accept as authentic only ideas that appear in Nietzsche's published works. Nietzsche, however, often speaks in intentionally obscure fashion, and the *Nachlass* can sometimes help in untangling Nietzsche's thought. In what follows, I try to employ the *Nachlass* only to clarify or expand upon what Nietzsche presents in his published works, or to detail the development of ideas that do not necessarily appear in these works but that came to play an important role in the picture of Nietzsche that arose after his death.

3. *Nietzsche,* 1:467–68. On the deficiencies of Heidegger's account, see my "Heidegger's Nietzsche," *Political Theory* 15, no. 3 (August 1987): 424–35.

4. *Nietzsche: Philosopher, Psychologist, Antichrist,* 3rd ed. (New York: Random House, 1968), 129, 410–11. KGW VI 3:153.

5. On this interpretation of Nietzsche and its problems, see Gianni Vattimo, "Nietzsche and Contemporary Hermeneutics," in *Nietzsche as Affirmative Thinker*, ed. Yirmiyahu Yovel (Dordrecht: Nijhoff, 1986), 60–61.

6. *Nietzsche and Philosophy*, trans. Hugh Tomlinson (New York: Columbia University Press, 1983), 17, 195.

7. "Nietzsche and Metaphysical Language," in *The New Nietzsche*, ed. David Allison (Cambridge: MIT Press, 1985), 6–7. See also Jean-Michel Rey, "Commentary," in *Nietzsche's New Seas: Explorations in Philosophy, Aesthetics, and Politics*, ed. Michael Allen Gillespie and Tracy Strong (Chicago: University of Chicago Press, 1988): 75–96.

8. "Nomad Thought," in *The New Nietzsche*, 142–49.

9. "Active and Reactive," in *The New Nietzsche*, 89, 94.

10. On the inadequacies of Deleuze's reading of Nietzsche, see Daniel Breazeale, "The Hegel-Nietzsche Problem," *Nietzsche-Studien* 4 (1975): 146–64.

11. *Nietzsche: Einführung in das Verständnis seines Philosophierens* (Berlin: de Gruyter, 1936).

12. *Nietzsche: Seine Philosophie der Gegensätze und die Gegensätze seiner Philosophie* (Berlin: de Gruyter, 1971).

13. "Perspectivism and Interpretation," in *The New Nietzsche*, 190–91. See also Tracy B. Strong, *Friedrich Nietzsche and the Politics of Transfiguration*, expanded ed. (Berkeley: University of California Press, 1988), 294–318.

14. *Nietzsches Philosophie* (Stuttgart: Kohlhammer, 1960).

15. *Philosophie und Politik bei Nietzsche* (Berlin: de Gruyter, 1987), 393.

16. For an account that tries to steer a path between these extremes, see Strong, *Friedrich Nietzsche*, 108–85.

17. See also Hans Peter Balmer, *Freiheit statt Teleologie: Ein Grundgedanke von Nietzsche* (Freiburg: Alber, 1977), 43. There is a possibility that Nietzsche may have used the term 'nihilism' to characterize Buddhism as early as 1865. On this point, see Johann Figl, "Nietzsches frühe Begegnung mit dem Denken Indiens: Auf der Grundlage seines unveröffentlichten Kollegennachschrift aus Philosophiegeschichte (1865)," *Nietzsche-Studien* 18 (1989): 466. Even if this was the case, the concept apparently played no role in his thought during the intervening years and there is no evidence that he remembered it.

18. Elisabeth Kuhn has argued that Nietzsche's earlier concepts of pessimism, Nirvana, nothing, and not-being are substantially equivalent to this later notion of nihilism. *Friedrich Nietzsches Philosophie des europäischen Nihilismus* (Berlin: de Gruyter, 1992), 5–17. Her examination of Nietzsche's thought, however, focuses on the historical/philological question of nihilism and not its philosophic significance.

19. Ibid., 266; Ottman, *Philosophie und Politik*, 335, 338–39.

20. For Nietzsche's identification of nihilism with Russian nihilism, see *FW*, KGW V 2:264; *GM*, KGW VI 2:424; *NL*, KGW III 4:182; VIII 1:125. Elisabeth Kuhn has shown that Nietzsche's first references to nihilism derive

from the French translations of Turgenev's *Fathers and Sons* and *Virgin Soil,* and Prosper Mérimée's discussion of these novels in his "Lettre à M. Charpentier" and his "Lettre à l'éditeur," in *Oeuvre complètes,* ed. P. Trahard and H. Champion, 12 vols. (Paris, 1927–33), 9:cviii–cix, 11:548. "Nietzsches Quelle des Nihilismus-Begriffs," *Nietzsche-Studien* 13 (1984): 262–63. On Nietzsche's Russian sources, see Müller-Lauter, *Nietzsche,* 66–67; Mazzino Montinari, *Das Leben Friedrich Nietzsches in den Jahren 1875–1879. Chronik,* in KGW IV 4:27; Friedrich Chr. Würzbach, in MusA, 16:432; Ottman, *Philosophie und Politik,* 332–33; C. A. Miller, "Nietzsches 'Soteriopsychologie' im Spiegel von Dostojewskijs Auseinandersetzung mit dem europäischen Nihilismus," *Nietzsche-Studien* 7 (1978): 130–49; and "The Nihilist as Tempter-Redeemer: Dostoevski's 'Man-God' in Nietzsche's Notebooks," *Nietzsche-Studien* 4 (1975): 165–226; Kuhn, *Nietzsches Philosophie,* 21; and Curt Paul Janz, *Nietzsche: Biographie,* 3 vols. (Munich: Hanser, 1978), 1:677. Paul Bourget, who describes the nihilism of Turgenev and Flaubert, helped to shape Nietzsche's reception of the concept in important ways. *Essais de psychologie contemporaine,* 2 vols. (Paris: Lemerre, 1885), 1:16, 139, 144.

21. He was misled on this matter by Mérimée and Bourget. Kuhn, "Nietzsches Quelle des Nihilismus-Begriffs," 266, 269, 271; Bourget, *Essais,* 2:225, 239.

22. See also Nietzsche to Köselitz, 10 November 1887, KGB III 5:191–92; and Müller-Lauter, *Nietzsche,* 68.

23. Kuhn, *Nietzsches Philosophie,* 244.

24. The failure to distinguish the active nihilist from the Dionysian man leads to the mistaken conclusion that active nihilism for Nietzsche is a replacement for religion. See, for example, Leslie Thiele, *Friedrich Nietzsche and the Politics of the Soul: A Study of Heroic Individualism* (Princeton: Princeton University Press, 1990), 180.

25. Jean Granier sees in such remarks the creative power of negativity that characterizes the Dionysian man, and he thus rejects Deleuze's claim that Nietzsche is opposed to all negativity. Granier, *La Problème de la vérité dans la philosophie de Nietzsche* (Paris: Seuil, 1966), 48–50; Deleuze, *Nietzsche and Philosophy,* 198.

26. See Kuhn, *Nietzsches Philosophie,* 213–14. Contrary to commentators such as Alexander Nehamas, Nietzsche thus clearly advocates and values violence. *Nietzsche: Life as Literature* (Cambridge: Harvard University Press, 1985), 224–27. He remarks in a late note: "I am *glad* about the military development of Europe; also of the internal states of anarchy: the time of repose and Chinese ossification, which Galiani predicted for this century, is over. . . . The barbarian in each of us is affirmed; also the wild beast. Precisely for that reason philosophers have a future." *NL,* KGW VII 2:261. For a sound account of Nietzsche's thoughts about politics, see Bruce Detwiler, *Nietzsche and the Politics of Aristocratic Radicalism* (Chicago: University of Chicago Press, 1990); or Ottman, *Philosophie und Politik.*

27. Schopenhauer had already been characterized as a nihilist by J. W. Hanne, M. Müller, and Feuerbach well before Nietzsche was acquainted

with the concept. Müller-Lauter, "Nihilismus als Konsequenz des Idealismus," 161.

28. Building on Heidegger, Bartuschat tries to show that the Dionysian is merely a form of the will in order to show that Nietzsche was even in this instance a metaphysician. *Nietzsche*, 90.

29. From the publication of Georg Simmel's *Schopenhauer und Nietzsche* (Leipzig: Duncker & Humblot, 1907) until 1984, no major work focused on the relationship of Nietzsche and Schopenhauer. For a discussion of the reasons for this neglect, see Jörg Salaquarda, "Zur gegenseitigen Verdrängung von Schopenhauer und Nietzsche," *Schopenhauer Jahrbuch* 65 (1984): 13–30. In the last ten years, scholars have increasingly turned their attention to this crucial connection.

30. See Georges Goedert, "Nietzsche und Schopenhauer," *Nietzsche-Studien* 7 (1978): 9, 11.

31. *Nietzsche: Biographie*, 3 vols. (Munich: Hanser, 1978), 1:182.

32. See Nietzsche to Cosima Wagner, 19 December 1876, KGB II 5:21; and to Paul Deussen, August 1877, KGB II 5:265.

33. See Reinhard Margreiter, "Allverneinung und Allbejahung: Der Grund des Willens bei Schopenhauer und Nietzsche," *Schopenhauer Jahrbuch* 65 (1984): 103–18; and Goedert, "Nietzsche und Schopenhauer," 1–6.

34. See Alfred Bauemler, *Nietzsche der Philosoph und Politiker* (Leipzig: Reclam, 1931), 56; Heidegger, *Nietzsche*, 1:44; Fink, *Nietzsches Philosophie*, 27; Löwith, *Von Hegel zu Nietzsche*, 193.

35. Friedhelm Decher, "Nietzsche: Metaphysik in der 'Geburt der Tragödie' im Verhältnis zur Philosophie Schopenhauers," *Nietzsche-Studien* 14 (1985): 22; Ottman, *Philosophie und Politik*, 57.

36. On Schulze's thought, see Beiser, *The Fate of Reason*, 266–84.

37. Arthur Schopenhauer, *Gesammelte Briefe*, ed. A. Hübscher (Bonn: Bouvier, 1978), 654.

38. Rudiger Safranski, *Schopenhauer und die wilden Jahre der Philosophie: Eine Biographie* (Munich: Hanser, 1987), 213.

39. All references to Schopenhauer's *World as Will and Representation* are cited by volume and page number. See List of Abbreviations.

40. Safranski, *Schopenhauer*, 310.

41. Martial Gueroult, "Schopenhauer et Fichte," *Études Philosophique* 4 (1945): 81–82.

42. Schopenhauer's understanding of Indian religion was largely derived from the German Romantics. Safranski, *Schopenhauer*, 301. A second source for this notion of will may have been the German mystics of the fifteenth and sixteenth centuries, including Jakob Böhme and Johannes Tauler. Alexis Philonenko, "Schopenhauer Critique de Kant," *Revue Internationale de Philosophie* 42, no. 1 (1988): 63; Safranski, *Schopenhauer*, 203.

43. Arthur Schopenhauer, *Sämtliche Werke*, ed. A. Hübscher, 7 vols. (Wiesbaden: Brockhaus, 1948–61), 7:91.

44. Arthur Schopenhauer, *Sämtliche Werke*, ed. Wolfgang Freiherr von Löhneipen, 5 vols. (Leipzig: Insel, [n.d.]), 1:520.

45. Schopenhauer apparently does not recognize that if space and time are the conditions of plurality, they are also the conditions of unity. The will must thus be beyond both unity and plurality.

46. Safranski argues that this element in Schopenhauer's notion of the will is derived from Left Hegelian David F. Strauss's notion of "free activity, not directed to any purpose or need." Safranski, *Schopenhauer,* 333.

47. This absolute distinction of will and representation is problematic. As Gueroult points out, it is difficult to understand how the will can know itself when it is not a capacity for knowing and how the capacity for knowing can move and thus know if it is severed from the will. "Schopenhauer et Fichte," 116–18. Schopenhauer himself did not always consistently maintain this distinction. In his practical reflections, for example, he identified women with representation and men with will.

48. Iulii Isarvich Eichenwal, "A Note on Schopenhauer (1910)," trans. Nina J. Katz, in *Schopenhauer: New Essays in Honor of His Two Hundredth Birthday,* ed. Eric von der Luft (Lewiston: Edwin Mellen, 1988), 146.

49. Arthur Schopenhauer, *Gespräche,* ed. A. Hübscher (Stuttgart–Bad Cannstatt: Frommann, 1971), 131.

50. Eichenwal, "A Note," 146.

51. Arthur Schopenhauer, *Sämtliche Werke,* ed. Paul Deussen (Munich: Piper, 1911), 11:157.

52. See Rudolf Malter, "Erlösung durch Erkenntnis: Über die Bedingung der Möglichkeit der Schopenhauerschen Lehre von der Willensverneinung," in *Zeit der Ernte: Studien zum Stand der Schopenhauer-Forschung,* ed. Wolfgang Schirmacher (Stuttgart: Frommann-Holzboog, 1982), 41–44.

53. Walter Schulz, "Philosophie des Überganges: Grundtendenzen in Schopenhauers Ethik," in Schirmacher, ed., *Zeit der Ernte,* 37; Malter, "Erlösung durch Erkenntnis," 58.

54. Arthur Schopenhauer, *Parerga und Paralipomena: Kleine Philosophische Schriften,* in *Werke in fünf Bänden,* ed. Ludger Lutkehaus, 4:134. K. F. A. Schelling, ed., *Sämtliche Werke,* 14 vols. (Stuttgart: Cotta, 1856–61), 7:38.

55. "Schopenhauer et Fichte," 81–142.

56. Ibid., 85, 135–37, 139.

57. Ibid., 139–41. William Desmond sees a similar connection to speculative idealism, arguing that Schopenhauer's notion of the will is "Hegel's 'bad infinity' [i.e., Fichte] in aesthetic dress: desire without end becoming a vanishing infinite because it eventually proves to be an objectless restlessness. Nothing can satisfy it; no finite thing will ever satisfy it—hence anguish." "Schopenhauer, Art, and the Dark Origin," in *Schopenhauer,* ed. von der Luft, 115. See also Wolfgang Schirmacher, "Asketische Vernunft—Schopenhauer im Deutschen Idealismus," *Schopenhauer Jahrbuch* 65 (1984): 197–208; and Yasuo Kamata, *Der Junge Schopenhauer: Genese des Grundgedankens der Welt als Wille und Vorstellung* (Munich: Alber, 1988), 39.

58. Kamata, *Der Junge Schopenhauer,* 121.

59. Harald Schöndorf, *Der Leib im Denken Schopenhauers und Fichtes*

(Munich: Berchmans, 1982), 12, 105. This idea was not original to Fichte, for it is already present in the thought of the German pietists.

60. Gueroult, "Schopenhauer et Fichte," 126.

61. See Kamata, *Der Junge Schopenhauer,* 162, 164; and Gueroult, "Schopenhauer et Fichte," 105.

62. *Nietzsche,* 55.

63. Safranski, *Schopenhauer,* 104.

64. Eichenwal, "A Note," 145.

65. Heinz Heimsoeth calls this Schopenhauer's "Pandemonism." *Metaphysische Voraussetzungen und Antriebe in Nietzsches Immoralismus* (Mainz: Akademie, 1955), 53. Georges Goedert remarks that nature for Schopenhauer is not divine but "devilish." "Nietzsche und Schopenhauer," *Nietzsche-Studien* 7 (1978): 3.

66. Friedrich Nietzsche, *Werke in Drei Bänden,* ed. Karl Schlecta (Munich: Hanser, 1954), 3:148.

67. Nietzsche to Gersdorff, 7 April 1866. KGB I 2:121–22.

68. Nietzsche to Rohde, 3 April 1868. KGB I 2:265. He adds in the next sentence that instinct speaks to him like a *daimonion.*

69. *Werke,* 5:14.

70. Philippe Lacoue-Labarthe, "History and Mimesis," in *Looking after Nietzsche,* ed. Laurence A. Rickels (Albany: SUNY Press, 1990), 216–20.

71. Judith Shklar, *After Utopia: The Decline of Political Faith* (Princeton: Princeton University Press, 1957), 80–81.

72. Nietzsche to Rohde, 8 October 1868, KGB I 2:322.

73. See Curt Paul Janz, "Die Kompositionen Friedrich Nietzsches," *Nietzsche-Studien* 1 (1972): 172–84. Robert Rethy points out that the Schopenhauerian notion of music that Nietzsche was so attached to contradicts Schopenhauer's theory of art as to both its object and function. Nietzsche's critique and ultimate rejection of Schopenhauer's thought thus did not entail a rejection of Schopenhauer's understanding of the relationship of music and the will. "The Tragic Affirmation of the *Birth of Tragedy,*" *Nietzsche-Studien* 17 (1988): 15.

74. See his "Fragment of a Critique of Schopenhauerian Philosophy," MusA 1:392–401. Also see Claudia Crawford in *The Beginning of Nietzsche's Theory of Language* (Berlin: de Gruyter, 1988), 158–92.

75. Nietzsche finds Schopenhauer's claim to immediate knowledge of the "I will" to be as ludicrous as Descartes' claim to know the "I think." *JGB,* KGW VI 2:23. See Friedhelm Decher, *Wille zum Leben—Wille zur Macht: Eine Untersuchung zu Schopenhauer und Nietzsche* (Würzburg: Königshausen and Neumann, 1984), 54.

76. See Catherine Zuckert, "Nature, History, and the Self: Friedrich Nietzsche's Untimely Considerations," *Nietzsche-Studien* 5 (1976): 77.

CHAPTER 7

1. Nietzsche's insistence on the affirmation of the tragic character of existence is evident in his rejection of Goethe's conclusion to *Faust.* As Eric

Heller has pointed out, Nietzsche saw the appropriate end to *Faust* in Mephistopheles' great lament at the futility of all striving and not in the *chorus mysticus* of Faust's salvation: "To insist on the Mephistophelean prospect, and yet not to despair, and yet to glorify, indeed to transfigure existence—this is the goal of Nietzsche's desperate strategy. . . . to go to the very end of disillusionment . . . and *then* bring to life once more Goethe's vision of the glorious integrity of things." *The Importance of Nietzsche: Ten Essays* (Chicago: University of Chicago Press, 1988), 35–37. As Rethy points out, Nietzsche thus seeks to replace Schopenhauer's concept of tragedy as resignation with a concept of tragedy as affirmation. "The Tragic Affirmation," 4–5.

2. *Nietzsche,* 1:434. See also Hans Pfeil, *Von Christus zu Dionysos: Nietzsches religiöse Entwicklung* (Meisenheim am Glan: Hain, 1975), 143.

3. The exact relationship of Dionysus to the will in *The Birth* is never entirely clear. Rethy argues that while Dionysus seems to be more than a mere representation, he is in fact still only an affective representation of primordial pain, and thus only the last, faint shadow of the already shadowy metaphysical will of Schopenhauer. "Tragic Affirmation," 12–13. By contrast, Margot Fleischer suggests that Dionysus is the image produced by the primordial artist of the world that saves it from the primordial pain of contradiction by establishing the joyful play of seeming. He is thus the thing-in-itself. "Dionysos al Ding an Sich," *Nietzsche-Studien* 17 (1988): 80–83. In *The Birth,* Dionysus thus seems to be both an image of the will and the will itself. As we shall see, however, he is ultimately more primordial than will or representation.

4. The nature of this reconciliation is much debated. Many scholars argue that this reconciliation annihilates individuality. See Sarah Kofman, "Metaphor, Symbol, Metamorphosis," in *The New Nietzsche,* 205; Fink, *Nietzsches Philosophie,* 30; Valadier, "Dionysus versus the Crucified," 248; and Charles Senn Taylor, "Nietzsche's Schopenhauerianism," *Nietzsche-Studien* 17 (1988): 54. In *The Dionysian Worldview,* Nietzsche does argue that "in the self-forgetfulness of Dionysian conditions the individual with his limits and measure perished" (KGW III 2:58). This passage, however, was deleted in *The Birth.* Moreover, if the Dionysian is as fundamental as this interpretation suggests, then all individuality must also spring from Dionysus. More convincing is the claim that reconciliation means the elevation of the individual to the level of the primordial unity. Rethy, for example, argues that in his identification with the powers of *genesis,* the artist as an individual merges as "genius" with the primordial artist of the world in an act of artistic generation. "Tragic Affirmation," 3. See also Ingrid Barole, "Subjektivität als Abgrund: Bermerkung über Nietzsches Beziehung zu den Frühromantischen Kunsttheorien," *Nietzsche-Studien* 18 (1989): 173.

5. Valadier, "Dionysus versus the Crucified," 255. Nietzsche's interpretation of the Dionysian experience here is heavily influenced by the early Romantic notion that freedom and wisdom can be attained only by shattering the bonds of morality. His Dionysian hero thus shares many of the char-

acteristics of William Lovell, Manfred, Bazarov, and the other heros of Romanticism.

6. Blondel, "Nietzsche: Life as Metaphor," in *The New Nietzsche*, 162.

7. John Sallis, *Crossings: Nietzsche and the Space of Tragedy* (Chicago: University of Chicago Press, 1991), 58, 70, 71. The discussion of the ameliorating effect of the Apollinian that follows draws upon Sallis.

8. Fleischer, "Dionysos als Ding an Sich," 89. For a defense of the independence of Apollo, see I. N. Bulhof, *Apollos Wiederkehr: Eine Untersuchung der Rolle des Kreises in Nietzsches Denken über Geschichte und Zeit* (The Hague: Nijhoff, 1969), 57; and Paul de Man, *Allegories of Reading: Figural Language in Rousseau, Nietzsche, Rilke, and Proust* (New Haven: Yale University Press, 1979), 117–18.

9. See Rethy, "Tragic Affirmation," 7–12; Fink, *Nietzsches Philosophie*, 18; Martin Vogel, *Apollinisch und Dionysisch: Geschichte eines genialen Irrtums* (Regensburg: Bosse, 1966), 249; and Blondel, "Life as Metaphor," 173.

10. See Granier, "Nietzsche's Conception of Chaos," in *The New Nietzsche*, 137–41; Rethy, "Tragic Affirmation," 7–12; Charles Barrack, "Nietzsche's Dionysus and Apollo: Gods in Transition," *Nietzsche-Studien* 3 (1974): 115, 117; George Wells, "*The Birth of Tragedy*: Analysis and Assessment of Nietzsche's Essay," *Trivium* 3 (1968): 59; and Alfred v. Martin, *Nietzsche und Burckhardt: Zwei geistige Welten im Dialog* (Basel: Reinhardt, 1945), 196.

11. Rethy, "Tragic Affirmation," 43. This conclusion cannot help but remind us of Bazarov.

12. For an alternative account of the origin of the Dionysian will that discounts the importance of Schopenhauer, see Otto Most, *Zeitliches und Ewiges in der Philosophie Nietzsches und Schopenhauers*, ed. Hannes Böhringer (Frankfurt am Main: Klostermann, 1977), 103.

13. See Lacoue-Labarthe, "History and Mimesis," 221–24.

14. On Nietzsche's ambivalent relationship to Socrates, see Werner Dannhauser, *Nietzsche's View of Socrates* (Ithaca: Cornell University Press, 1974).

15. On Nietzsche's interpretation of Pauline Christianity, see Jörg Salaquarda, "Dionysus gegen den Gekruezigten: Nietzsches Verständnis des Apostels Paulus," *Zeitschrift für Religions- und Geistesgeschichte* 26, no. 2 (1974): 97–124.

16. Nietzsche sees Christianity through the distorting lens of Schopenhauer, Heine, and Wellhausen merely as a religion of pity and not as a way of life. See Goedert, "Nietzsche und Schopenhauer," 8; Wilhelm Schmidt-Biggeman, *Geschichte als absoluter Begriff: Der Lauf der neueren deutschen Philosophie* (Frankfurt a.M.: Suhrkamp, 1991), 47–51; and Julius Wellhausen's *Prolegomena zur Geschichte der Religion und Philosophie in Deutschland* (1834). He thus never comes to terms with either scholasticism or medieval Christianity.

17. See Manfred Riedel, "Die 'Wundersame Doppelnatur' der Philoso-

phie: Nietzsches Bestimmung der ursprünglich griechischen Denker-fahrung," *Nietzsche-Studien* 19 (1990): 10.

18. Janz, *Nietzsche*, 1:822–23.

19. Nietzsche describes this musical philosopher in a note of the period: "He is visual like the artist who works in forms, empathetic like the religious man, causal like the scientist: he wants to let all of the tones of the world echo in him and to set this entire sound into concepts." *NL*, KGW III 4:30. See also *PTZG*, KGW III 2:310–11. On Nietzsche's view of philosophy as half art and half science, see Jean-Noël Vuarnet, "Le Philosophe-artiste," in *Nietzsche Aujourd'hui*, 2 vols. (Paris: U.G.E., 1973), 1:337–70.

20. On the planned Empedocles drama, see Jürgen Söring, "Nietzsches Empedokles-Plan," *Nietzsche-Studien* 19 (1990): 176–211.

21. See Sallis, *Crossings*, 107; and Ottman, *Philosophie und Politik*, 53. Vuarnet points out that Heracleitus and Empedocles are connected by the sign of fire. "Le Philosophe-artiste," 1:339.

22. In his earlier lectures, Nietzsche linked Socrates to the Apollinian. On this basis, Fink concludes that Nietzsche understands Socrates as Apollinian, painting his grey on grey over the colorful world that Dionysus reveals. *Nietzsches Philosophie*, 29. This connection, however, is suppressed in *The Birth*. Jerry Clegg thus suggests that Socrates does not replace Apollo, but constitutes a third force. "Nietzsche's Gods in *The Birth of Tragedy*," *Journal of the History of Philosophy* 10, no. 4 (October 1972): 438.

23. Söring, "Nietzsches Empedokles-Plan," 190.

24. He focused his efforts on Shakespeare, whom he described as the musical Socrates who brought Greek tragedy to fulfillment. *NL*, KGW III 3:201, 326, 332, 334. See also Sallis, *Crossings*, 139.

25. Detwiler, *Aristocratic Radicalism*, 183.

26. See Barrack, "Nietzsche's Dionysus and Apollo," 125. In this period, art takes on a new critical role. As de Man argues, "Art is no longer associated with the Dionysian immediacy of music but is now openly Socratic in its deconstructive function." *Allegories*, 113. De Man, however, does not see how this Socratic role of art is combined with the earlier vision of a Dionysian art in Nietzsche's later thought.

27. See Nietzsche to Overbeck, 2 July 1885, KGB III 3:62. Eckhard Heftrich argues that even his later preface to *The Birth*, "Attempt at a Self-Critique," criticizes the style of the work only in an effort to justify its substance. "Die Geburt der Tragödie: Eine Präfiguration von Nietzsches Philosophie?" *Nietzsche-Studien* 18 (1989): 107. On the continued importance of the Dionysian, see Vogel, *Apollinisch und Dionysisch* 194; Georg Siegmund, "Kosmischer Rausch—als neue Religion?" in *Stimmen der Zeit* 134 (1938): 283; Richard Oehler, *Friedrich Nietzsche und die Vorsokratiker* (Leipzig: Durr'schen Buchhandlung, 1904), 24; and Barole, "Subjektivität als Abgrund," 171–72.

28. Detwiler, *Aristocratic Radicalism*, 154. Wolfram Groddeck suggests that the artists' metaphysics reappears in the 1886 prefaces to his older

works. "'Die Geburt der Tragödie' in 'Ecce Homo,'" *Nietzsche-Studien* 13 (1984): 330.

29. Fink, *Nietzsches Philosophie*, 52–60, 552.

30. *Aristocratic Radicalism*, 167. See also Peter Sloterdijk, *Thinker on Stage: Nietzsche's Materialism*, trans. J. O. Daniel (Minneapolis: University of Minnesota Press, 1989), 61, 63.

31. See Fink, "Nietzsche's Experience of World," 203–10.

32. For an alternative account that connects Dionysus to life and Apollo to the will to power, see Bulhof, *Apollos Wiederkehr*, 98. Bulhof's analysis is flawed by her failure to recognize that the Apollinian is ultimately a moment of the Dionysian. She also does not understand how Apollo is displaced by Socrates in Nietzsche's later thought. On this point, see Barrack, "Nietzsche's Dionysus and Apollo," 118–24; and Rosen, *Limits of Analysis* (New York: Basic, 1980), 215.

33. On the connection of Zarathustra to Dionysus, see *EH, KGW* VI 3:333–47. Laurence Lampert has shown in great detail the hidden role of Dionysus in *Thus Spoke Zarathustra*. See his *Nietzsche's Teaching: An Interpretation of Thus Spoke Zarathustra* (New Haven: Yale University Press, 1986). See also Pierre Trotignon, "Circulus vitiosus, deus-circulus, vitiosus deus," *Revue Philosophique* 96 (1971): 306.

34. "Dionysos als Ding an sich," 89–90. Paul Valadier argues in a similar vein that "even if Dionysus does recede, he doesn't entirely disappear, his presence becomes more subtle and concealed. The apparent withdrawal of the 'god' with light feet only makes his discrete visits more significant . . . [This] discrete presence of Dionysus after *The Birth of Tragedy* is tantamount to a sort of purification or 'demythification.'. . . [Nietzsche] did not repudiate Dionysianism. . . . Stripped of his mythic garb, he is still a god who announced the vision and the doctrine of the eternal recurrence." "Dionysus versus the Crucified," in *The New Nietzsche*, 256.

35. See Heidegger, *Nietzsche*, 1:11–79; and Bartuschat, *Nietzsche*.

36. See, for example, Michael Haar, "Nietzsche and Metaphysical Language," in *The New Nietzsche*, 10; and Müller-Lauter, *Nietzsche*, 29.

37. Klossowski, "Nietzsche's Experience of the Eternal Return," in *The New Nietzsche*, 119. James Leigh similarly claims that there is no will that desires power but only power that wills. "Deleuze, Nietzsche, and the Eternal Return," *Philosophy Today* 22 (1978): 17.

38. Bernard Pautrat, *Version du soleil: Figures et système de Nietzsche* (Paris: Seuil, 1971), 163–67; Jacques Derrida, "Interpreting Signatures (Nietzsche/Heidegger): Two Questions," in *Looking after Nietzsche*, 15.

39. Eugen Biser correctly points out that Nietzsche's atheism is not absolute but merely a weapon he employs in his struggle against Christianity. "Nietzsche und Heine: Kritik des christlichen Gottesbegriffs," in *Nietzsche as Affirmative Thinker*, ed. Yirmiyahu Yovel (Dordrecht: Nijhoff, 1986), 206. Nietzsche's religiosity has been thoughtfully analyzed by Most in his *Zeitliches und Ewiges*, 99–160.

40. He describes, however, only four. The thousand and first goal, according to Zarathustra, is not the goal of a particular people but of humanity. This goal is the overman. This passage points to the supranational moment in Nietzsche's thought that ends in the formation of the new human being Nietzsche later called "the good European."

41. Valadier points out the decisive difference between the Pauline Savior on the Cross, whose death is unwanted and must thus be redeemed, and Nietzsche's Dionysus, who confronts death certain of the overfullness of life and his own re-creative power. "Dionysus versus the Crucified," 250. See also Heftrich, "Die Geburt der Tragödie," 113.

42. Already as a high-school student, Nietzsche had imagined such a god. *NL,* BA, 1:48, 3:129; *NL,* KGW VIII 1:217–18; and Balmer, *Freiheit statt Teleologie,* 41. See also *NL,* KGW VIII 2:173–74; 3:283; 323–24.

43. Friedrich Nietzsche, *Die Unschuld des Werdens,* ed. Alfred Baeumler, 2 vols. (Stuttgart: Kröner, 1956), 2:337. See *AC,* KGW VI 3:181; *NL,* KGW VII 3:414–16.

44. Sloterdijk argues that Nietzsche had already conceived Socrates in *The Birth* as a manifestation of Dionysus, who appears incognito in the audience in the guise of a philosophic fool, making fun of the Apollinian heros. Dionysus in this sense prevails in the *modus* of his withdrawal and awakens in his own right only in the epochal ruptures of thought. *Thinker on Stage,* 53–60. There is, however, little evidence for such an interpretation of Socrates in Nietzsche's early work.

45. On Nietzsche's admiration for the Socrates of the *Symposium,* see *NL,* KGW III 3:138.

46. Walter Kaufmann draws attention to this connection in his translation of *Beyond Good and Evil* (New York: Random House, 1966), 234.

47. See Sloterdijk, *Thinker on Stage,* 54–57.

48. Nietzsche points out that Dionysus has two faces, one laughing and joyful, the other filled with an ecstatic sadness. *NL,* MusA 5:121. In his later additions to *The Gay Science,* Nietzsche suggests that his *incipit tragodia,* which originally ended the work and pointed toward *Zarathustra,* should perhaps be read as *incipit parodia.* KGW V 2:14.

49. Erich Podach, *Friedrich Nietzsches Werke des Zusammenbruchs* (Heidelberg: Kampmann, 1961), 236; *JGB,* KGW VI 2:43.

50. Söring, "Nietzsche's Empedokles-Plan," 204–5.

51. "The comic," Nietzsche remarks in *The Birth,* is "the artistic discharge of the disgust with the absurd." KGW III 1:53. See also ibid., 10; and Sallis, *Crossings,* 109.

52. Dancing already appears in *Zarathustra* as a quasi-divine activity but it is treated as explicitly divine only in Nietzsche's later thought. Nietzsche remarks in a late note that "light feet belong to the concept 'god,' beyond all reason and philistinism, beyond good and evil. . . . Zarathustra says he would only believe in a god who could dance but Zarathustra is only an old atheist, he says he would believe but he really would not." *NL,* KGW VIII 3:321.

53. He also calls it "an attempt to philosophize in a divine way" and, reduplicating the subtitle of *Beyond Good and Evil*, "a prelude to a philosophy of the future." *NL, KGW* VII 3:214, 275.

54. See Sarah Kofman, "Baubô: Theological Perversion and Fetishism," in *Nietzsche's New Seas*, 175–202. Nietzsche was aware that Dionysus was often characterized as hermaphroditic in Greek sources from his reading of Friedrich Creuzer's *Symbolik und Mythologie der alten Völker, besonders der Griechen*, 3rd ed., 4 vols. (Leipzig: Leske, 1836), 4:80.

55. He writes in *The Case of Wagner*, "Has it been noticed that music liberates the spirit? gives wings to thought? that one becomes more a philosopher the more one becomes a musician?" *KGW* VI 3:8.

56. Janz has demonstrated that Nietzsche's concern for music and composition was fundamental. "Die Kompositionen Friedrich Nietzsches," 185. Nietzsche remarked in a letter to Hermann Levi of 20 October 1887 that "there was perhaps never a philosopher who was a musician to the degree that I am." *KGB* III 5:172. He was an accomplished pianist and an enthusiastic but ineffective composer. This love of music shaped his philosophical enterprise in many ways. Not only did many of his works deal with musical subjects and the meaning of music for contemporary culture, but, as Janz has pointed out, his own works themselves have "a musical-theoretical foundation, a musical architecture." *Nietzsche*, 2:215. Also see Most, *Zeitliches und Ewiges*, 104–5.

57. Pautrat conflates Nietzsche and Schopenhauer when he argues that for Nietzsche music is the becoming sensible of the will, its most adequate appearance. *Versions du soleil*, 60. Kofman more correctly points out that it is only when the various arts are taken in respective hierarchies subordinated to music and seen as a totality that we can say that art symbolizes Dionysus. "Metaphor, Symbol, Metamorphosis," in *The New Nietzsche*, 203–5. See also Rethy, "Tragic Affirmation," 8–10.

58. Both Pautrat and Kofman argue that Nietzsche's claim that music is primordial is finally merely metaphorical. *Versions du soleil*, 62; "Metaphor, Symbol, Metamorphosis," 202. They thus fail to recognize how truly radical Nietzsche is. For him, the world is not something in itself but the mimesis of music and thus of Dionysus. See *NL, KGW* III 3:1; 4:37.

59. Failure to recognize the central importance of music for Nietzsche has led some postmodernist interpreters of Nietzsche to conclude that he rejects all logic in favor of genealogy. See Haar, "Nietzsche and Metaphysical Language," 17. Pautrat argues more persuasively that music for Nietzsche is true philosophy. Nietzsche in his view replaces the logocentrism of traditional philosophy with melocentrism. *Versions du soleil*, 71. He is critical of Nietzsche, however, because his thought remains melo*centric*, that is, because Nietzsche accepts the idea of a center and does not reject the idea of dominance. Nietzsche thus does not present us with a real alternative to traditional philosophy. *Versions du Soleil*, 72. Hamacher and a number of other scholars disagree, suggesting that Nietzsche's turn to music does not aim at establishing a new hierarchy but at decentering all orders. Werner Hamacher,

"The Promise of Interpretation: Reflections on the Hermeneutical Imperative in Kant and Nietzsche," in *Looking after Nietzsche*, 41. In view of Nietzsche's understanding of the close connection of music and mathematics, which we will discuss below, such a reading is implausible. *NL*, KGW III 2:66. In fact, music for Nietzsche is an even more powerful assertion of dominance and rank order than Pautrat suggests.

60. Nietzsche knew of this connection through Creuzer, *Symbolik und Mythologie*, 4:37.

61. Nietzsche to Fuchs, Winter 1884–85, in *Selected Letters of Friedrich Nietzsche*, ed. and trans. Christopher Middelton (Chicago: University of Chicago Press, 1969), 232–35; Nietzsche to Fuchs, August 1888, KGB III 5:399–403. On this point, see Nietzsche's early lectures on Greek rhythmics and metrics. KGW II 3:101–338. M. S. Silk and J. P. Stern argue that Nietzsche is wrong to believe that Greek music involved any kind of harmony or counterpoint comparable to modern music. *Nietzsche on Tragedy* (Cambridge: Cambridge University Press, 1981), 134.

62. Nietzsche to Fuchs, August 1888, KGB III 5:399–403.

63. Cf. Klaus-Detlef Bruse, "Die Griechische Trägodie als 'Gesamtkunstwerk'—Anmerkungen zu den Musikästhetischen Reflexionen des frühen Nietzsche," *Nietzsche-Studien* 13 (1984): 156–76.

64. See Granier, *Le Problème de la vérité*, 47; or Angèle Kremer-Marietti, "Hegel et Nietzsche," in *La Révue des Lettres Modernes* 76–77 (1962–63): 22.

65. Curt Paul Janz, "The Form-Content Problem in Friedrich Nietzsche's Conception of Music," in *Nietzsche's New Seas*, 105.

66. Nietzsche to Fuchs, Winter 1884–85, *Selected Letters*, 233.

67. Janz, "The Form-Content Problem," 109.

68. For a discussion of the way in which Nietzsche seeks to achieve this end in his own works, see my "Nietzsche's Musical Politics," in *Nietzsche's New Seas*, 117–49.

69. Nietzsche ties Offenbach to Petronius and thus to Menippean satire, which was the model for Nietzsche's *gaya scienza*. *NL*, KGW VIII 3:404, 431.

70. On the thousand-year Dionysian empire that Nietzsche foresees, see Kuhn, *Nietzsches Philosophie*, 237.

71. See Taylor, "Nietzsche's Schopenhauerianism," 54.

72. Detwiler, *Aristocratic Radicalism*, 162–63.

73. *Friedrich Nietzsche in seinem Werken* (Vienna: Konegan, 1894), 38–39. See also Sander L. Gilman, ed., *Begegnung mit Nietzsche*, 2nd ed. (Bonn: Bouvier, 1987), 423; and Most, *Zeitliches und Ewiges*, 144.

74. *Nietzsche*, 151.

75. For the characterization of Nietzsche as a Romantic, see Bertram, *Nietzsche: Versuch einer Mythologie*; Karl Joel, *Nietzsche und die Romantik* (Leipzig: Diederichs, 1905); Thomas Mann, *Last Essays* (Knopf, 1959); and Shklar, *After Utopia*, 36, 51–53, 61–64, 80–85.

76. See Barole, "Subjektivität als Abgrund," 158–81.

77. On the history of the Dionysian, see Max L. Baeumer, "Nietzsche and the Tradition of the Dionysian," in *Studies in Nietzsche and the Classical Tradition*, 165–89; and "Die romantische Epiphanie des Dionysos," *Monatshefte* 57 (1965): 225–36; Vogel, *Apollinisch und Dionysisch;* and Joachim Rosteutscher, *Die Wiederkunft des Dionysos: Der naturmystische Irrationalismus in Deutschland* (Bern: Francke, 1947). The following discussion draws on these sources.

78. *Sämtliche Werke*, 15 vols. (Vienna: Klang, 1846), 4:22–23.

79. Ernst Behler, "Sokrates und die Griechische Tragödie: Nietzsche und die Brüder Schlegel über den Ursprung der Moderne," *Nietzsche-Studien* 18 (1989): 141–42; Albert Hinrichs, "Euripides at Second hand: Nietzsche's Use of A. W. Schlegel," *Greek, Roman, and Byzantine Studies* 27 (1986): 376–85.

80. Hölderlin's friend Hegel described the Dionysian as an incomplete form of Christian spirituality. *Werke*, 17:137, 152.

81. Baeumer, "The Tradition," 181.

82. Vogel, *Apollinisch und Dionysisch*, 97.

83. Nietzsche argues that "it is ultimately a matter of strength: this entire Romantic art could be redirected by an overrich artist of great willpower completely into the anti-Romantic or—to use my formulation—into the Dionysian." *NL, GA*, 14:162.

84. On the importance of Heine for Nietzsche, see E. M. Butler, *Heinrich Heine: A Biography* (London: Hogarth, 1956), 232–33; Hannah Spencer, "Heine and Nietzsche," *Heine Jahrbuch* 11 (1972): 150–52; A. I. Sandor, *The Exile of the Gods: Interpretation of a Theme, a Theory, and a Technique in the Work of Heinrich Heine* (The Hague: Mouton, 1967), esp. 13–42; and Linda Duncan, "Heine and Nietzsche," *Nietzsche-Studien* 19 (1990): 336–45.

85. Baeumer, "The Tradition," 166, 173–76.

86. Vogel, *Apollinisch und Dionysisch*, 134–37.

87. Siegfried Mandel, "Genelli and Wagner: Midwives to Nietzsche's *The Birth of Tragedy*," *Nietzsche-Studien* 19 (1990): 221–23.

88. See Creuzer, *Symbolik und Mythologie*, 1:x, xv.

89. Ibid., 4:22, 30, 37, 88, 138, 405, 456–95, 497.

90. Ibid., 4:32–36.

91. Ibid., 4:25–26, 138.

92. Ibid., 4:88.

93. Ibid., 4:117, 408.

94. Ibid., 4:116–17.

95. Ibid., 4:88. Drawing on this connection of Dionysus and the universal fire, Creuzer argues that Heracleitus articulates an Orphic or Dionysian doctrine.

96. Ibid., 4:409.

97. Ibid., 1:x.

98. On this point see Janz, *Nietzsche;* and Hamacher, "The Promise of Interpretation," 29.

99. See Kuhn, *Nietzsches Philosophie*, 106; and Löwith, *Von Hegel zu Nietzsche*.

100. Nietzsche's debt to Fichte has rarely been recognized. Notable exceptions are Bartuschat, *Nietzsche*, 31–49; and Rosen, *Limits of Analysis*, 175–215.

101. See Granier, *La Problème de la vérité*, 44.

102. See Kuhn, *Nietzsches Philosophie*, 108–9.

103. Cf. ibid., 113.

104. In *Ecce Homo*, Nietzsche admits that *The Birth* "smells offensively Hegelian." KGW VI 3:308. Groddeck argues that in this way Nietzsche links the beginning of tragic wisdom, the *incipit tragodia* that later found its most stunning form in *Zarathustra*, to the completion of Hegelianism. "'Die Geburt der Tragödie' in 'Ecce Homo,'" 325–31.

105. See Bartuschat, *Nietzsche*, 50, 182.

106. Lacoue-Labarthe, "History and Mimesis," 217–18.

107. See Müller-Lauter, *Nietzsche*, 188.

108. See Friedrich Kaulbach, "Kant and Nietzsche im Zeichen der Kopernikanischen Wendung: Ein Beitrag zum Problem der Modernität," *Zeitschrift für Philosophische Forschung* 41, no. 3 (July–September 1987), 353.

109. Deleuze, *Nietzsche and Philosophy*, 17, 195.

110. See Fred Dallmayr, "Farewell to Metaphysics: *Nietzsche*," in his *Critical Encounters: Between Philosophy and Politics* (Notre Dame, University of Notre Dame Press, 1987).

111. See Pautrat, *Versions du soleil*, 73; and Jean-Luc Nancy, "Nietzsche's Thesis on Teleology," in *Looking after Nietzsche*, 62–63.

Index

Abelard, Peter 13–15
Abrams, M. H. 281–83
Achelis, Thomas 278
Adams, Hazard 281
Adams, Marilyn McCord 263–66, 271
Aeschylus 208
Agrirrezabal, Joaquin Iriarte 267
Albertus Magnus 14
Alexander II, Czar 138
Altenstein, Baron von 121
amor fati 222, 251
Andreas of Newcastle 29, 276
Annenkov, P. V. 153
Anselm 14, 29, 58, 59, 273
antinihilism 152, 164, 181, 284, 285
antinomy 116, 186, 235; for Kant xv, xviii, 69, 70, 72, 73
antithesis 82, 148, 242, 245, 250
Antonovich, M. A. 286
Apollinian 232, 295, 297, 298; contrasted with the Dionysian 205–9, 227; unification with the Dionysian 214, 228
Aquinas, Thomas: and Aristotle 13; his argument for the existence of God 25, 263; importance for Descartes 28; and Ockham 21, 23; and scholasticism 14, 53, 58; and Suarez 27, 29
Archilochus 207, 208
Arendt, Dieter 275, 276, 282, 304
Ariadne 231
Aristotelianism viii, 13, 14
Aristotle 27, 263, 270, 271; and Aquinas 13; and scholasticism 18, 21, 24, 25, 28, 43, 53; his notion of self-consciousness 47, 49, 50; and Trotsky 172

Arnauld 3, 268, 272
Asclepias 228
Augustine 270; and certainty 19; and divine illumination 37; and faith as an answer to skepticism 27, 42; and omnipotence 12; and self-consciousness 47–49
Augustinianism 12, 48
Avenarius 164
Avicenna 13, 17, 267
Ayer, A. J. 270

Bachman, Charles 286
Bachofen, Johann 242
Bacon, Francis 26, 72, 97; and Descartes 2, 9, 32, 34
Baeumler, Alfred 298, 301
Baggessen, J. J. 277
Baier, Annette 275
Bakunin, Mikhail 143, 168, 252, 284, 287; and Bazarov 149; importance of Fichte for 68, 141; influence of Hegel on 137; and Nechaev 160–64; importance for Nietzsche 178
Ballauf, Theodor 278–80
Balmer, Hans Peter 289, 298
Barole, Ingrid 294, 296, 300
Bartuschat, Wolfgang 196, 283, 291, 297, 302
Batscha, Zwi 280
Baubo 231
Baudry, Leon 264
Bauer, Bruno 129
Bazarov 145–56, 285; and Nietzsche 252; as compared to Rakhmetov 158–60; and Romanticism xix, 216; as Promethean 162, 163, 166, 169, 173; as compared to Zarathustra 240

303